Global Popular Music

Bassim Hamadeh, CEO and Publisher
Mieka Portier, Senior Acquisitions Editor
Susan Christie, Developmental Editor
Alia Bales, Production Editor
Miguel Macias, Senior Graphic Designer
Alisa Munoz, Licensing Coordinator
Jennifer Redding, Interior Designer
Natalie Piccotti, Director of Marketing
Kassie Graves, Vice President of Editorial
Jamie Giganti, Director of Academic Publishing

Cover image copyright © 2017 iStockphoto LP/Kuptsovas87.

Printed in the United States of America.

ISBN: 978-1-5165-2586-7 (pbk) / 978-1-5165-2587-4 (br)

Global Popular Music

First Edition

Edited by Thomas Garcia

Contents

An Introduction
Global Popular Music
What *Is* Pop?

This anthology is a survey of popular music throughout the world, looking at specific countries and genres, examining how popular music throughout the world is connected. It considers some basic questions: to what music do people around the globe listen? What do they watch? How do they access music? Through the study of specific cultures and repertories, students will explore popular music in various cultural contexts in the United States, Europe, Asia, Africa, and Latin America. The goal is to give students a broad understanding of what exactly is meant by popular music, how it can be defined, and the differences and similarities among diverse popular music traditions.

This anthology is designed to:

- Foment understanding and appreciation of the historical evolution of musical style, genre, and performance in various cultural contexts;
- Encourage the recognition and understanding of political, sociological, and cultural forces on music throughout the globe;
- Foster an understanding of the evolution of popular music in various cultural contexts;
- Examine local, regional, and global forces on the development of music and popular culture.

By the end of this anthology, students will be able to:

- Evaluate the impact of political, sociological, and cultural forces on popular music and the arts;
- Analyze and understand political and social forces in contemporary and historical popular music;
- Discuss the complex relationship among race, ethnicity, and class in the development of culture;
- Describe how technology has shaped the performance, composition, and consumption of music.

What is Popular Music?

This book is dedicated to global popular music. This brings up several questions: What is popular? What is global? How can we define either? What are the connections? How does popular music differ from classical? From folk? What separates classical, folk, and popular music is in many ways hard to define, but one thing that distinguishes all three is transmission: how music goes from person to person, from place to place, from time to time.

Classical Music

Classical music in most music cultures has some specific characteristics not present in folk or popular music. In most cases, in the Americas, Europe, Japan, India, or any other place with a strong classical music tradition, classical music tends to be the music of the elite. This may be the economic, social, or intellectual elite, a population that is generally educated and cultured. Classical music transmission in Western music culture is traditionally by means of notation, but this is not the case in many other classical music traditions, most of which do not have music notation system. Indian classical music, for example, differs in the North and South, but in either case this music is transmitted orally, not by means of notation. There is no traditional notation system in Indian music, although the Western notation system is used by many today. However, it does not function particularly well, due to the differences in scale and tuning in India compared to Western music. There is a developed and rigorous training system for Indian classical music, but it is learned by rote from master to apprentice, and although there is a standard repertory in Southern India (Northern Indian classical music is improvised based on very strict rules), pieces are passed down orally and undoubtedly have been subjected to changes due to this means of transmission.

Another common element in classical music traditions is training, which is for the most part by means of a master-apprentice relationship. In the Western classical music system, the study of classical music often begins at a young age, taking lessons either in school or with a private teacher. Who in today's day and age doesn't know someone who takes or has taken private lessons, be it for piano, singing, clarinet or what have you? This is also the case in many non-Western classical music traditions. For example, Indian children often take lessons with a guru, a teacher specializing in singing or one of many Indian classical instruments, usually with lessons in a group setting, studying for years by means of oral instruction. The common thread in all classical music is this idea of instruction, establishing a separate musician class, separating performer and audience, a phenomenon not common in folk music traditions in which audience and performer are often the same group of people.

Folk Music

"Folk music is music that has been submitted to the process of oral transmission; it is the product of evolution and is dependent on the circumstances of *continuity*, *variation*, and *selection*" (Karpeles 1955, 6; italics added):

- *"Continuity*, which links the present with the past;
- *Variation*, which springs from the creative impulse of the individual or the group;
- *Selection* by the community, which determines the form in which folk music survives" (International Folk Music Council 1955, 23).

This definition leaves out the origin of folk music, which in Western music evolved from rudimentary beginnings uninfluenced by art or classical music. It is also "music which has originated with an individual composer [or composers] and has subsequently been absorbed into the unwritten, living tradition of a community" (International Folk Music Council 1955). When a tune passes into oral tradition, it becomes subject to the forces of evolution and conforms to the demands of continuity, variation, and selection.

Folk music is not static but always changing. Often folk music is of communal authorship, in which time is a factor. It is constantly altered through time by means of oral transmission in the great, cosmic game of telephone whereby one person says something which gets passed from person to person, changing as it is transmitted; in folk music, this telephone game is from person to person, community to community, through time and space. It changes by evolution, not revolution. Art music and folk music exist side by side, and there is often an interaction between the two; one has only to listen to the music of Aaron Copland or Bela Bartok to understand this connection. Folk music informs art music, and vice-versa.

Some scholars connect folk music to rural culture, and in many traditions, this seems to be the case. In much of Europe, for example, folk music is connected for the most part to rural areas, where it is passed down from generation to generation, with variations having to do with the particular villages; the village could have the same repertory with local changes or might have a completely different repertory or even style. In Norway, folk fiddling traditions, style, and repertory vary greatly from village to village, sometimes only a few miles apart. In West Virginia of the past, the music from one valley might differ greatly from that of the next valley. Historically, rural communities tended not to go very far from home; in the 19th and 20th centuries, this changed dramatically especially with immigration from Europe to the New World, taking with them their folk music, often informing popular music as formerly rural folk settled in cities. This is the case with many of the musical genres discussed in this anthology, which were taken from their place or origin to various places in the Americas, mixing with other immigrant and indigenous traditions to form the musical fusions that make up so much of global popular music today.

Popular Music

Popular music can be difficult to define. Some consider it "to be of lower value and complexity than art music," and it is "readily accessible to large numbers of musically uneducated listeners rather than to an elite" (Middleton 2001). The boundaries between pop, folk, and classical are often "hazy, with individual pieces or genres moving into or out of the category" (Middleton 2001, 129).

One means to determine if music is popular or not is through a scale of activity. In modern times, this can be measured through things like record or CD sales (or digital downloads) or sheet music sales. None of these criteria take into account qualitative factors but are by definition limited to quantitative factors. In this definition of "popular," socially diverse audiences are treated as one, and repeat hearings are not counted. But sales figures and airplay measure sales and airplay, not popularity. It is easy to link popularity with specific means of dissemination, especially in an era of mass media, in which there are shifts in the definition of popularity by location. It is also convenient to link popularity with social groups; does it appeal to a mass audience or a particular class or demographic? Is a particular kind of music for young audiences or perhaps for working class audiences? "Popular music has no permanent musical characteristics or social connections" (Middleton 2001, 129). So what is popular music?

There are no hard and fast rules as to what determines if a genre is popular music or something else. A piece might be characteristic of several different genres. Few pieces if any have every characteristic of any one genre. Robert Walser, in his book *Running with the Devil: Power, Gender and Madness in Heavy Metal Music*, states:

> Nowhere are the boundaries more fluid than in popular music. Just as it is impossible to point to a perfectly exemplary Haydn symphony, one that fulfills the "norm" in every respect, pieces within a popular genre rarely correspond slavishly to general criteria. Moreover, musicians are ceaselessly creating new fusions and extensions of popular genres. (Walser 1993, 27)

The performer plays little or no role in genre formation in classical music. That is the function of the composer. In popular music, the role of the performer is crucial in forming genre. Charles Hamm, in his article "Genre, Performance and Ideology in the Early Songs of Irving Berlin" makes this idea clear:

> In much popular music the performer shapes, reinforces, and even changes genre. In this repertory, genre is defined most importantly neither by formal structure nor by fixed elements of style such as melody and harmony, but by audience perception of the meaning of a song, shaped at the moment of performance. (Hamm 1994, 374)

Popular music is nothing new. There was popular music in all eras of music history, often defined by transmission, class, and the "snob" factor. In the 19th and 20th centuries popular music went through the process of industrialization in terms of production and dissemination. Instruments, heretofore the domain of the wealthy and educated, became more available and affordable with developments in technology and mass production, meaning that the working class could participate in making music much more easily. The means of transmission changed greatly with technology, allowing for new, faster, and cheaper means of getting music to the people. Developments such as recordings, radio, film, television and the Internet changed the way music spread and was enjoyed, leading to increasing availability of music to the masses, redefining the means by which "popular" could be judged.

Global Popular Music: the Anthology

Each chapter in this anthology is dedicated to a specific musical genre, all of which have become popular not just in their countries of origin but in many other parts of the world. Chapters begin with an introduction, setting the context for the culture and the genre which is the focus of the chapter. This is followed by a discussion of the development of the genre, in most cases fusing multiple ideas and traditions into a new music that has become popular far beyond its original borders. Each chapter has one or two readings selected to highlight a specific aspect of the musical genre or the culture from which it originated. These readings are followed by questions for thought about the culture and genre, with the goal of clarifying the points, ideas, and concepts presented in the chapter and the readings. Each chapter ends with an activity that includes examples of the music covered, allowing the students to hear the music presented in order to get a deeper understanding of the diverse points presented in the text.

The anthology explores popular music in a global context, looking for the trends, tendencies, and similarities that connect music today. Much of the book examines specific genres of music in the Americas, Europe, Africa, and Asia, examining the connections that these genres have with music elsewhere, all contributing to the world popular music scene, which has changed and intensified with the developments in communications and dissemination that new technologies made possible. All of the chapters save one deal with music of fusion: music that has taken characteristics and repertories from two or more musical traditions to form a new, hybrid local form that had not existed before. These fusions, for many genres, mix African and European musical ideas; others blend local ideas with European or American music. In most cases, issues of race, slavery, and the history of slavery, class, migration, and immigration inform the discussion, with music moving from place to place through time in a variety of ways, with a variety of results.

The first chapter of this anthology is an exploration of African-American music, beginning with the roots of American music and the influences of European and African music. The history of African-American music is linked to slavery and the slave trade, which is true of the music of much of the Americas, as will be covered in this anthology. American popular music resulted in a cross-pollination that is unique to the United States and that distinguishes American music from European and African music. The makeup of the population of the United States, having to do with colonial and African populations mixed with continuing immigration throughout the 18th and 19th centuries, created a music that is uniquely American. Other countries in the Americas had similar circumstances, but the differences in the European colonial forces, with differences in language and culture, and the differences in the numbers and origins of the slaves taken to different parts of the Americas, made for musical traditions with some similarities but many more differences. The chapter includes discussions of music of worship and music of play in the African-American community and goes on to discuss traditions connected in different ways to African-American culture: minstrelsy, ragtime and the blues.

The reading for this chapter is on the blues, the most important and influential African-American musical tradition, which influenced American and world music throughout the 20th century and beyond. The blues had a great impact on most American popular music forms, including jazz, bluegrass, rock and roll and others. The blues, and subsequent American popular music, had a great impact on popular music globally; many of the genres covered in this anthology owe a great debt to American music of African roots. It, therefore, is the first musical tradition examined.

The next chapter is dedicated to Brazilian music, focusing on the country's most important musical genre, samba, and Brazil's most important cultural event, Carnaval. As is the case with American popular music, Brazilian music has its roots in Europe and Africa. What distinguishes the development of this music from American music are the differences in European colonial powers—England and Portugal—and the differences in the origins and numbers of Africans forced into slavery—Brazil imported more than ten times as many slaves as the United States/British North America—as well as the differences in the ways slaves were treated.

Samba developed in Brazil among slave populations principally in the Northeast of the country, and like the blues, went from black culture to the mainstream. Samba and Afro-Brazilian religious traditions are connected, and patterns of migration after emancipation led to its moving from rural Brazil to the major cities in the Southeast. In cities such as Rio de Janeiro, the samba became the most important genre and came to be the dominant music in Carnaval, eventually becoming the musical genre used in all aspects of Carnaval, most notably in the most important Carnaval tradition, samba school competitions. Samba took on influences from other musical traditions in the Americas, and one of the readings is dedicated to samba-reggae, one of many such musical hybrids. The other covers the history of Samba School competitions from its roots in black communities in Rio de Janeiro to the cultural powerhouse that it is today.

The Brazil discussion is followed by a chapter on tango, the national dance of Argentina that has been embraced in many parts of the world to the point that it is a truly global genre. The discussion begins with the birth of tango in Buenos Aires, again representing a mixture of African and European musical traditions. It began in the poor neighborhoods of the Argentine capital, moving into the mainstream by the end of the 19th century. Tango developed and evolved, adding words in the early 20th century as the *tango-canción* and moving out of dance clubs to the stage and the concert hall by the middle of the century with nuevo tango.

Tango was an international dance from early in its history, introduced to Europe by the beginning of the 20th century, eventually embraced in countries in the Americas, Europe, and Asia. The readings for this chapter focus on tango as a global phenomenon; the first one is about tango in Finland, the country in which the dance is most popular after Argentina and a country which frowns upon public displays of affection and touching. The other reading is about the globalization of tango, tracing how it became important globally historically.

The tango discussion is followed by a chapter dedicated to Mexican music in Mexico and elsewhere. Many musical traditions that came together to make up Mexican music, including Spanish, indigenous, African and Northern European, blending into genres that have local, regional, national and transnational implications today. Much of Mexico's music developed from similar sources, leading to regional genres in what can be referred to as the *son* complex. The focus of the chapter is on two genres that are important on both sides of the Rio Grande, mariachi and música norteña.

Mariachi is probably the most recognized Mexican genre, popular on both sides of the border. It developed from the *son jalisciense*, from the Western state of Jalisco, and was a rural music that featured strings and harp for much of its history. Modern mariachi, which is more an urban music, includes the use of trumpets and *guitarrón*, a large acoustic bass guitar. Mariachi is popular throughout Mexico and the American Southwest, and can be found throughout the United States. Música norteña, as the name implies, comes from northern Mexico but is equally popular in the Southwest of the United States. It features the accordion as part of its sound. Both genres are often heard in Mexican restaurants in throughout the United States as part of the ambiance. The reading for this chapter discusses music of a "nation between nations," using música norteña as a model for the transnational nature of Mexican music.

Continuing with music in Latin America, the next chapter is dedicated to salsa and the many musical traditions that came together to form this very popular music. As is the case for much of the music covered in this anthology, salsa represents a fusion of many musical traditions, including Spanish, Northern European, indigenous and African. Among its roots are Cuban music, including the Afro-Cuban religion *Santería*. The various genres that came together to form salsa have unifying elements, most notably the *clave* pattern, a recurring rhythm from African roots that is common in many Latin American genres.

Salsa is one of several Latin American genres that have been popular in the United States in the 20th and 21st centuries, coming to the country in various stages of assimilation. Salsa got its start in the Latino communities of New York and Miami and spread in popularity throughout the country. Its popularity today is worldwide, and one can find salsa clubs and hear salsa music throughout the Americas, Europe, and Asia. The reading for this chapter places salsa in a global context. Salsa's roots are in Cuba and Puerto Rico, but it has become a pan-Latin genre, embraced throughout the world.

Concluding the discussions on music in the Western Hemisphere, the next chapter is dedicated to music in the Caribbean, focusing on Jamaica and Trinidad and Tobago. The popular music of both of these countries developed in the 20th century, once again blending African, European, and indigenous musical traditions to form music unique to the Caribbean but with similarities between the music of these two countries. Jamaican popular music today has its roots in the 1940s, with a genre known as mento, which is often confused for Trinidadian calypso. Mento is the first Jamaican genre to incorporate the skank rhythm, which has strong emphasis on the offbeat and is a feature of all the popular music genres that followed: ska, rock steady and reggae, which is probably Jamaica's most recognized musical export, exerting a great influence on the music of the United States, Brazil, much of Europe, and Asia. Also included in this chapter is calypso, the first Trinidadian genre with a global reach, and the more recent genre that developed from it, soca, or soul calypso.

One of the readings for this chapter looks at reggae, arguing that it is the most important and influential Caribbean musical genre. The author contends that reggae came to dominate Latin music because of Jamaica's booming tourist industry and Cuba's isolation following the Communist revolution of the late 1950s. The other article examines aspects of the unity and diversity of Caribbean culture and music. It explores the African connections to music throughout the Caribbean, regardless of language and the colonial powers that settled each country, presenting the Caribbean, its music, and its culture as coming from an "island continent."

With the next chapter this anthology turns from music in the Americas, which owes much to its legacy of African music, to the music of Africa itself, focusing on two of the many genres originating on the continent, both of which fused elements of African and European music. The first genre covered is highlife, a West African genre with roots in Ghana and Nigeria that was one of the earliest successful fusions of African, European, and New World music in Africa. It first appeared in the 1920s as Ghanaian and Nigerian musicians started incorporating foreign influences from genres such as the foxtrot. The reading about highlife in this chapter explores the history and development of the genre. Included in the discussion are the genres and ensembles that merged to form highlife, as well as the most important musicians in the history of the genre, including the great E.T. Mensah.

The other musical tradition discussed in this chapter is the South African a cappella choir tradition that fuses Christian hymnody and other European ideas with the music of the Zulu choral tradition of *mbube*. This music has been around since the 1920s and evolved into its current form known as *isicathamiya*, which can be translated as "tip-toe guys" or "walking softly." The most famous group in this tradition, Ladysmith Black Mambazo, has been around since the 1960s, and like many groups in this tradition, got its start in the migrant mineworker communities of South Africa. In 1986, the group collaborated with Paul Simon on his album *Graceland*, which helped give Ladysmith Black Mambazo international recognition. The other reading for this chapter takes a close look at the making of this album and the political context of this collaboration, which took place before the end of Apartheid, and explores how musical traditions and ideas were blended in the process of making the album.

Indian music is the topic of the next chapter, which features Bollywood music and bhangra, two musical traditions than mix Indian classical and popular music with American genres such as rock and roll. Bollywood takes its name from Hollywood, reflective of the importance of the Indian film industry, which produces more films than the American film industry. An overwhelming majority of Indian films are musicals, and the music from these movies, known as *filmi*, is one of the most important popular music traditions in India. The first reading in this chapter covers the history of Indian classical music, its influence on film music, and the importance of film and *filmi* in Indian culture at home and abroad.

The other genre discussed in this chapter is bhangra, which also fuses Indian and Western music. The original version of bhangra, which developed in the state of Punjab in the North of India, was a celebratory music used frequently at festivals and weddings. Modern bhangra developed in the 1970s and was first popular in the Punjabi community in England. The other reading for this chapter places bhangra in the mix of the globalization of music, beginning with a discussion of imperialism and its impact on music. The reading contends that bhangra demonstrates how local cultures not only encounter global imperialism but can appropriate it for reinventing themselves.

In recent years, no music has been more global in its impact than K-pop, the topic of the next chapter, a modern form of South Korean popular music that developed in the 1990s and has spread throughout the world. As is true for all of the music discussed in this anthology, K-pop fuses local musical ideas with foreign musical influences, in this case American and European popular music including electronic dance music, disco, the blues and rock and roll. K-pop is audio and visual in performance, which is common in the post-MTV world. Performers, both soloist and bands, usually go through an extensive and expensive training process in order to have a chance at fame and fortune, building massive debt to the entertainment companies that provide this training and represent the potential recording stars.

Although K-pop is most popular in Asia, in recent years it has garnered a huge following around the world, relying heavily on social media such as Facebook and Twitter. The reading for this chapter focuses on the history and development of K-pop, touching on the recruitment and training of K-pop musicians, as well as the finances and popularity of the genre. K-pop has positioned itself to appeal to worldwide audiences; it has the potential to be a global force in the music industry for some time.

The next chapter is a departure from the pattern of this anthology. It focuses on the English progressive rock band Radiohead. Unlike the other chapters, which deal with local musical genres that blend ideas and traditions from other parts of the world, this chapter deals with a band that changed the world. Finding itself without a recording contract and with a studio and the technology necessary to record, produce, and disseminate music independently, the group posted its music on its website for free, telling fans to pay what they want. The results were extraordinary: the group made more money from the pay-what-you-want model than it had for any of its previous albums. The reading for this chapter discusses the band's importance and the impact it had on popular culture. The author compares Radiohead to a British band from the previous generation, Pink Floyd, itself an innovative band that used technology in new and exciting ways. Both bands pushed the technology of the time to the edge and set the model for other bands for years to come.

The final chapter in this anthology is about the globalization of hip-hop culture and rap music. This American music has been borrowed, adopted, and adapted by diverse music cultures throughout the world, at first in its original form and later modified to local tastes, languages, politics, and culture. The focus is on hip-hop in Europe as a model for the ways in which this phenomenon became an important part of global music culture, found throughout the Americas, Europe, Asia, and Africa.

Hip-hop in Europe is strongest in several countries among immigrant people who make up much of the lower classes. In France and Germany, for instance, which have had a great deal of immigration from the Middle East and Africa, as well as from other countries in Europe, hip-hop culture is dominated by people of Arab, African, and Turkish origins. Language is the most important part of rap, and in Europe the use of language is in some ways similar to American rap, often borrowing English or using literal translations of English. European rap tends to reproduce many of the themes of American rap, including politics, oppression of minorities, and the hardship of everyday life in the marginal neighborhoods where so many immigrants reside.

The discussion turns to hip-hop in France, which has a long history of American cultural influence, particularly after the Great War and World War II. French rap artists borrowed heavily from the American models, including attitude, dress, bling, break dancing, and tagging, or graffiti. The focus of French rap has been on social criticism, including topics such as xenophobia and discrimination. The reading for this chapter examines hip-hop and rap in this global context, focusing on Continental Europe, England, and the United States. It traces the history and development of hip-hop from its roots in New York City's rough neighborhoods, spreading throughout the country and eventually the world.

Conclusion

By examining specific countries, musical traditions, and genres, this anthology examines the state of global popular music at local, regional, and global levels. What connects the music discussed is the fusion of diverse musical elements that moved from place to place with the migration and immigration of peoples, with changes in communications and technologies, and with the cultural mélange that these changes brought. Global popular music is about borrowing from one's own culture, adopting ideas and concepts from other cultures, and adapting these influences into a new and vibrant musical culture. These changes have taken place around the world, blending old and new, familiar and foreign, traditional and progressive. Your adventure with these popular musical traditions, and your understanding of the way these musical traditions developed and evolved, begins.

References

Hamm, Charles. "Genre, Performance and Ideology in the Early Songs of Irving Berlin." *Popular Music* 13, no. 2 (May 1994): 143–150.

International Folk Music Council. "Resolutions." *Journal of the International Folk Music Council* 7 (1955): 23. http://www.jstor.org/stable/834530.

Karpeles, Maud. "Definition of Folk Music." *Journal of the International Folk Music Council* 7 (1955): 6–7. http://www.jstor.org/stable/834518.

Middleton, Richard. "Popular Music." *The New Grove Dictionary of Music and Musicians.* Edited by Stanley Sadie and and J. Tyrrel. London: Macmillan, 2001. xx: 128-153.

Walser, Robert. *Running with the Devil: Power, Gender and Madness in Heavy Metal Music.* Middletown, CT: Wesleyan University Press, 1993.

CHAPTER ONE

African-American Music:
Blues, Blood, and a Backbeat

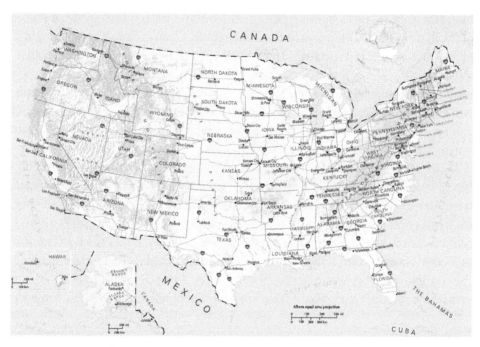

FIGURE 1.1 *Map of the United States*

Introduction

The question posed in the article for this chapter is, simply, where did the blues come from? In other words, what are the roots of the blues? The blues, and all of American music, comes from many sources, and the roots of the blues have to do with the ways in which Africans, most of whom came as slaves, came to the United States, the first arriving in 1619, and how their music developed, evolved, and mixed with music from other sources. The uniqueness of the blues as an American art form has to do with the ways that African and Colonial music and culture came

1

together, combined, and formed the hybrid that is African-American music. Many musical traditions came out of this hybridity, including music of worship, music of work, minstrelsy, ragtime and the blues.

African-American Music

The roots of African-American music are international and come from three distinct musical traditions: art music from Europe, folk music from the British Isles, and West African music traditions. European art, or classical, music came to the New World with the European colonists from several parts of Europe. Among the most heard traditions were art song and opera arias. These songs, many originally in German, Italian and French, were often translated and simplified for the middle and lower classes. Most popular songs published in the United States before the Civil War were based on European classical music.

Another source of music in early America was folk music from the British Isles. The large numbers of immigrants from England, Scotland, and Ireland brought with them a variety of popular music traditions, including fiddle tunes, songs, and ballads that rapidly became part of the American repertory. These folk songs were different than the urban popular music heard in places like New York and Boston and were mostly heard in rural settings, where large numbers of these British immigrants found themselves. Many traditions in American music are drawn from this folk music, most importantly minstrelsy, which we will see was an important part of the development of popular music in the United States during the 19th century.

Many of the important roots of American popular music come from African sources. Slaves came to United States directly and indirectly from Africa. Those that came directly from Africa came from places such as the Gold Coast (what is now Nigeria, the Ivory Coast, etc.), from the Congo area, and from farther south in what is now the area around Angola, bringing with them many aspects of their music cultures. Other musical traditions came to North America indirectly from the Caribbean, with slaves who then made up part of the triangle trade between the Caribbean, North America, and England. Because slaves came from multiple regions of Africa, many different musical traditions came with them.

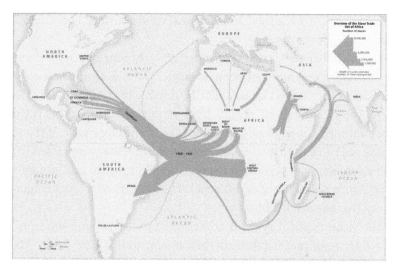

FIGURE 1.2 *Slave routes and numbers taken from Africa*

The result of these different sources of the popular music was a musical cross-pollination that is unique to the United States and distinguishes American popular music from African and European traditions. The one aspect of this combined music was *backbeat*, the rhythmic feature that is a distinguishing characteristic for American popular music styles since the turn of the 20th century. Popular music throughout the Americas can be said to have a similar cross-pollination, but what distinguishes all of the music traditions in the Americas is the different ways in which colonial and enslaved cultures interacted. American music, as a result of these different sources, is a hybrid that joins characteristics from different African and European sources. This does not mean that European musical traditions were abandoned, and indeed European classical and folk music remained vibrant throughout the colonial period and in the early independent American states.

Although slavery was common to most parts of the Americas, treatment of slaves was not the same. Unlike countries with larger slave populations, such as Brazil and Cuba, in North America, Africans were not able to keep their musical traditions intact. Family groups and language groups were often separated in this country, which was not so in other colonies. To put these differences in perspective, the number of slaves taken to colonial North America was somewhere in the order of half a million; the number of slaves taken to the West Indies was around four million; and in Brazil, the number was something more than five million. These differences reflect, among other forces and factors, the fact that Brazil and the West Indies were much closer to Africa, and, therefore, it was much more economical to transport large numbers of slaves to these places. This resulted in a different colonial-African cultural interaction, which, in turn, resulted in unique musical practices throughout the Americas. Despite this suppression of African cultural practices that took place in North America, African musical values surfaced in American popular music primarily through rhythm.

The African musical heritage is an important part of American popular music. Indeed, African rhythm permeates American popular music, and the steady increase of the influence of African musical values is remarkable. The result is that African-American musical roots dominate American popular music. Truly remarkable is that this is the first time in history that a minority population has shaped the dominant music of the society. This is all the more remarkable in that so much African culture was suppressed in the United States: African slaves were not permitted to practice their musical traditions on American plantations, and African-Americans of different backgrounds and mother languages created their own distinctive musical traditions.

Many West African musical systems contributed to the unique sound of American popular music in terms of vocal timbre, rhythm, and melodic shape. Many African music languages are tonal, meaning that the same syllable may have different meanings depending on pitch and inflection, which results in spoken languages that often approaching song. West African vocal music is very similar in many ways to African American blues in its basic sound. The melodic shape for both the blues and African music is commonly from high to low, and in both there is rhythmic freedom of delivery. Scales and pitch choice in the blues and West African song both often feature *melismas*, long, florid melodic fragments.

African music also contributed to American music in terms of instruments. Percussion instruments of all shapes and sizes came to the Americas with African slaves. Drums are perhaps the most important, and there are many different types and techniques. Cowbells and other instruments, such as shakers and scratchers, also came from Africa. The African approach to instrumental style also had a profound impact on American popular music in two ways. One is the distinctive sound that many African American performers achieve on various instruments. The other is through experimentation with alternative sounds and instruments, such as the washtub bass, the knife and plate, spoons, and even scratching in hip-hop. One of the most important African American instruments is an adaptation of West African guitar-like instruments, such as the *banjar*, a gourd guitar adapted to what we now call the banjo.

FIGURE 1.3 *The Old Plantation: African-American Slaves playing banjo and percussion*

Music of Work

Call and response, a practice in which one person sings a musical phrase which is answered by other singers, is present in other African-American musical traditions, including the music of work. African-derived work songs were widely reported among black slaves in the West Indies in the 18th century and in North America in the 19th century (Titon 2009, 157). They were probably present throughout colonial times as well. Although there is little documentary evidence to this, the use of work songs was widespread in Africa and in Europe, continuing well-established work-song traditions. A typical and well-known African-American work song is "Rosie," typically sung by prison chain gangs throughout the South.

These songs have many of the same characteristics of other African-American genres, most importantly the blues: they feature call and response, have similar singing styles, have similar rhythms, and use similar melodic ideas, including blue scales and blue notes, and include improvisation.

FIGURE 1.4 *African-American Chain Gang*

Music of Worship

A part of the African-American musical tradition that had a great impact on subsequent genres, and continues to influence popular music, is music of worship. One of the most unique aspects of this musical tradition is call and response, a performance practice common

in many West African musical traditions that found its way into many popular practices as well. An interesting type of call and response is called lining out, a practice in which the song leader starts and the congregation follows immediately. It was standard procedure in colonial America, not only in African-American worship, but in other worship practices as well. This makes sense considering the population of most churches was illiterate, and this was a way to learn the music with no training. African-American church music also shares singing style, vocal quality, and melodic ornamentation with secular traditions such as the blues.

FIGURE 1.5 *African American Church Service*

The Minstrel Show

One of the most important 19th century popular musical traditions was the minstrel show, which had its roots in medieval European culture. The American version of minstrelsy was a new and uniquely American genre, an American entertainment and recognized as so. It was popular and home grown and featured many folk elements, humor, and a lack of pretension. The European models were still important, but America minstrelsy was an American style, by Americans, and for an American market. The American minstrel show appeared at a time in which there was a political shift from the eastern, wealthy aristocracy to a more populist sentiment, best reflected in the presidency of Andrew Jackson. The minstrel show of the 1840s and 50s reflected this political change. Minstrel shows were informal, humorous, vigorous, and not stuffy, which was very much not aristocratic. At the same time, it was crude, cool, and a vicious portrayal of African-American culture, most apparent in the fact that most performers in the early shows were white and performed in blackface. This blackface reflected Jacksonian values; it was the best and worst of American populism.

Blackface as an impersonation of African Americans had been around for a long time when the first minstrel shows appeared in 1840s. These shows often featured a stereotypical city slicker and a country bumpkin, known respectively as Zip Coon and Jim Crow. The first minstrel show was in 1843 in New York, featuring a group that call themselves *the Virginia Minstrels*, all of whom where northerners and white.

FIGURE 1.6 *The Virginia Minstrels, 1843*

These minstrels performed in blackface in a parody or caricature of black performers. None of these performers had ever been to the South and quite probably knew very few if any black performers. This did not stop their caricature of African Americans and African-American culture.

The American blackface minstrel show was very popular and represented four firsts in American music:

1. It was the first American genre marketed to the masses, meant to entertain rather than uplift or educate.
2. It was in vernacular speech and music (if inaccurate) and often featured a parody of upper classes as well as African Americans.

FIGURE 1.7 *Primrose and West's Big Minstrels, a blackface minstrel troupe*

3. It was a synthesis of European popular and folk music that led to an entirely new style.
4. It was the first instance of a pattern of periodic invigoration of mainstream popular music through energetic, danceable music.

Ragtime

Ragtime began as an obscure dance style in the Mississippi Valley and was one of the first genres based on real African-American music to greatly impact the musical mainstream. Its roots, however, were similar to other genres found throughout the Americas, which combined European and African dance traditions. Ragtime is a genre that has parallels throughout the new world. Many European dances were popular throughout the Americas. One of the most important was the polka, which came to the New World in the 1840s with a large immigrant population from Germany and Eastern Europe. These Eastern Europeans immigrated to many parts of the New World, including many parts of the United States, Mexico, Central and South America. The polka, which featured European harmony, melody, and instruments, would blend with African drums and rhythms, varying throughout the Americas, depending on slave and former slave populations and colonial influences. The resultant hybrids are the most important dance genres in the Americas:

- Tango (Argentina)
- Plena and Bomba (Puerto Rico)
- Ragtime (United States)
- Rumba (Cuba)
- Beguine (Martinique)
- Maxixe and Choro (Brazil)

All of these dances appeared at approximately the same time, roughly the 1860s or 1870s, and share similar characteristics; they were originally part of black culture that moved gradually into the mainstream. The differences in these dances reflect the differences in language and culture in different places throughout the Americas.

Ragtime began as a style of playing all sorts of European music with an African-American rhythmic feel, thus modifying preexisting material. The style of playing was so popular that in the early 20th century, any syncopated instrumental music was called ragtime. It developed in the Midwest and the Mississippi Valley and often was heard on paddle-wheeled steamers going up and down the river. It was also commonly heard in houses of ill repute; it was considered in polite circles to be scandalous. Over time, it became a more mainstream genre and found its way into dance halls and home parlors throughout the country.

Most early performers could not read music and played only by ear; they were expected to demonstrate a developed technique. Over time, ragtime came to feature syncopated melodies with an on-the-beat accompaniment. It was perfectly suited to the polka, and ragtime and the other dances listed above modified the polka to local tastes. Most ragtime pieces feature the polka's harmonic structure and two-beat rhythm, often called two-steps. Other dances, such as the waltz, also became part of the ragtime tradition, which was originally only for piano, but later evolved into a band genre as well. Ragtime was rhythmically complex and highly syncopated, features that came directly from black influence. Most early performers, not surprisingly, were black. It features repetitive sections, and often was in an open form, meaning it ended in a different key and different melody than the opening of the piece.

Ragtime was all the rage by the turn of the 20th century, by which time it could be heard throughout the country. This led to the introduction of ragtime sheet music, often in simplified form, so that amateur musicians not well versed in the tradition, anywhere in the country, could play ragtime. This new sheet music, even though it was simplified, introduced complex rhythms to the mainstream. Ragtime was also one of the first genres to be available for the player piano, and many performances by early ragtime pioneers such as Scott Joplin were preserved by this technology.

FIGURE 1.8 *Maple Leaf Rag by Scott Joplin*

Ragtime songs also became popular in the early part of the century. They tended to be less rhythmically complex than instrumental ragtime and were sung by both African-American and white performers. Many became so popular that they were often interpolated, or substituted, into Broadway shows. Although ragtime was originally part of Midwest and Mississippi Valley saloon culture and featured a great deal of interaction between performers and the audience, as it evolved, it became more appropriate in other venues and became popular throughout the country.

The Blues

The most important and influential African-American musical tradition which influenced American and world music throughout the 20th century and beyond is the blues. Defining the blues can be tricky. It is different and separate from jazz, not a subset. The blues is "a feeling … as well as a specific musical form" (Titon 2009, 165), although jazz musicians often play the blues, and it influenced much jazz. Jazz musicians applied their technique to the blues, but the blues did not lose its identity. The blues are more than just a significant part of black music culture, but rather have become firmly embedded in the musical culture of the United States and the world.

What are the blues? Many characteristics can be found in most blues songs:

- The blues are a specific form: 12 bars with a basic three-chord progression;
- They feature a three- or four-line stanza of poetry;
- There is much rhythmic crossing between the vocal part and the accompaniment, resulting in both polyrhythm and polymeter;
- There is often an element of call and response between the vocal and instrumental parts;
- The blues features a great deal of improvisation, both poetically and musically;
- The blues use scales beyond the diatonic scale, often referred to as blues scales, and performers often sing slightly out of tune as ornamentation to the melodic line, known as blue notes;
- The blues feature an element of swing in which the beat is not symmetrically divided, resulting in a lilting feeling.

The blues first appeared around the turn of the 20th century, and early blues are connected to minstrelsy because many of the early blues musicians were minstrels. An example is Ma Rainey, a famous minstrel who toured the southern United States. Another early performer was Bessie Smith, who was one of the first to record the blues as well.

FIGURE 1.9 *Blues singer Bessie Smith*

The blues had a great impact on other American musical forms, including jazz, bluegrass, rock and roll and others. By the 1950s the blues had become old fashioned in the African-American community, and outside the blues strongholds such as the Mississippi Delta, Chicago, and St. Louis, it was somewhat marginalized. The blues enjoyed a strong revival in the 1960s, when it was embraced by many of the great mainstream African-American performers such as Ray Charles, B.B. King (Blues Boy King), James Brown, Aretha Franklin, John Lee Hooker and many others. It remains one of the most important musical genres in the United States and the world.

The blues and the genres that developed from the blues are the most important and recognizable aspects of American popular music. The blues, rock and roll, jazz, ragtime, rap and other musical genres that continue the legacy of African-American music have had great influence on popular music throughout the world. As will be seen in this anthology, these genres have driven the development of popular music on a global scale, and there are many musical traditions throughout the world that are strongly connected to this uniquely American music. This has resulted in a rich, vibrant global music scene, much of which owes a debt to African-American music.

Reading

The reading for this chapter, "The Roots of the Blues: 1916–1919," discusses the early blues, covering in depth how the blues came to be and including the African music traits that makes the unique genre that is the blues. The author touches on other African-American music, including details about each genre and how it contributed to the development of American music, both at home and on the world stage. The blues resulted from the social, economic, and racial makeup of the South after the Civil War and Reconstruction, and an understanding of these social conditions helps bring the development of the blues into focus.

THE ROOTS OF THE BLUES: 1619–1919

Dick Weissman

This chapter will introduce us to the blues in various ways. First, we will trace the history of the blues, from their African American roots through various nineteenth-century African American musical styles, including worksongs, spirituals, and popular "minstrel" songs. We will then examine the social conditions at the time of the birth of the blues, and how these conditions influenced the new musical form. We will take a look at some early outgrowths from blues, including ragtime and the beginnings of jazz. We will then briefly examine the typical structure of a blues song. Finally, for those interested in playing blues music, we will give some basic pointers about how to learn to perform them.

HISTORY AND ORIGINS OF THE BLUES

Where did the blues come from? When did they start, and where did they first appear? The blues are an African American form, so it is natural to seek the answers to these questions in the history of how Africans came to the United States, and what music they brought with them.

TIMELINE: 1619–1919

1619	First slaves brought to United States
1781	United States defeated British, became an independent nation
1803	Through Louisiana Purchase from France, United States, doubled its size, acquired Louisiana and extended western frontiers all the way to Rocky Mountains
1808	Congress legislated an end to the slave trade
1847	United States defeated Mexico, acquired area from Texas through California
1861	Civil War began
1863	Lincoln freed the slaves with the Emancipation Proclamation
1865	Civil War ended; Reconstruction began
1867	*Slave Songs of the United States* published
1877	Reconstruction ended when federal troops withdrawn from South
1890–1910	Various racist laws passed restricting African Americans from voting, and from eating or traveling with whites. Number of lynchings increased.
1899	Scott Joplin's "Maple Leaf Rag" published
1902	First recording of black music issued by Victor Records: "Camp Meeting Shouts"
1903	W.C. Handy saw bluesman playing guitar with a knife at Mississippi train station
1909	Founding of the NAACP (National Association for the Advancement of Colored People)
1910	The *Journal of American Folklore* published extensive article by Howard Odum that included numerous blues texts collected in Georgia, 1906–1908
1912	First sheet music publication of blues songs
1914	World War I began
1917	United States entered the war
	First jazz recording by white Original Dixieland Jazz Band
1919	Race riots took place in Chicago, Charleston, S.C., East St. Louis, Houston, and in many other major U.S. cities

Most Africans came to the United States as slaves. The first slaves were brought here in 1619, and the slave trade lasted until 1809, with the illegal importation of slaves continuing up until the Civil War. It is generally acknowledged that most of the slaves imported into the United States came from West Africa, although many different tribes and languages were represented. Although there are no absolutely reliable estimates of how many slaves were brought in illegally, one estimate puts the number at 54,000. However, the precise number of Africans removed from their homes is a matter of some controversy and conjecture. We know that for every slave who reached the United States many died in the inhuman and overcrowded conditions aboard the slave ships. Some committed suicide, throwing themselves overboard rather than accepting life as slaves.

Some of the ship captains actually compelled the slaves to sing and dance on the slave ships—believing that the exercise from dancing would help keep them healthy during the dangerous trip—and we have reports that some of these songs appeared to be laments about the exile of the slaves. Slaves were not allowed to bring instruments from Africa, so the music on board the ships was entirely vocal music. The slaves were brought up on deck, and although they were kept in chains in order to avoid any form of protest or revolt, they were encouraged to dance. At times, they were even whipped if they did not dance. It is presumed that *some* musical instruments came over with their owners, but we do not know exactly what these instruments were. We do know that the playing of drums, certainly common in virtually every African tribe, was discouraged by the slave owners. There are reports of slaves playing the fiddle or the banjo in various eighteenth-century journals, and paintings that show slaves playing banjos. Cecilia Conway, in her book *African Banjo Echoes in Appalachia*, lists 12 references to black banjoists prior to 1800, and another 21 references printed by 1856. Dena Epstein, in her book *Sinful Tunes and Spirituals: Black Folk Music to the Civil War*, reports references to slaves playing the fiddle as early as the 1690s, and references to slave banjoists date back to 1754 and 1774. She also writes that simple flutes like quills and pipes were used, and that by the eighteenth-century black fiddlers were a normal part of the musical scene on the plantation. Obviously, the slave musicians also entertained their own people when not performing for the whites.

In his book *Savannah Syncopators*, Paul Oliver mentions that Robert Winans examined the slave narratives collected by the Work Progress Administration (WPA) during the 1930s. Winans found 295 references by ex-slaves to fiddle players, 106 to banjo players, 30 to the playing of the quills (or panpipes), and only 8 to drums. There are also numerous references to slaves playing musical instruments in the form of written advertisements seeking the return of escaped slaves, or in flyers where masters were attempting to sell slaves, which listed their musical talents as a sort of bonus to enhance the salability of the slave. Other instruments reported are the bones, the jawbone of an ass scraped with a wire or brush, tambourine, and the thumb piano (*mbira*).

The banjo itself seems to be a descendant of an instrument from Senegal called the *halam*, which like the five-string banjo has one string that runs about three quarters of the way up the neck of the instrument. In both instruments, the highest and lowest strings are adjacent to one another, and the African playing technique of using the fingernails of the right index and middle fingers and the thumb parallel early American banjo styles.

Some slave owners encouraged the slaves to play music, sing, or dance, feeling that it was a harmless diversion that could amuse the master and mistress. A happy slave was less apt to consider rebellion, might tend to work harder, and might have a better feeling about his or her life. On the other hand, the master could not really control the content of the slave's songs. If the songs were sung in any sort of African dialect, dangerous information could be spread. Even without the use of the African language, lyrics could carry coded messages with different meanings for the slave and the plantation owner. A well-known blues song underscores this duality, stating, "when I'm laughing, I'm laughing just to keep from crying."

Dancing might represent an even clearer danger to the master class, because dance is intrinsically sensuous and potentially erotic. The planter class was ambivalent about black eroticism, seeing it as a sort of devilish temptation not only to the slaves but also to their owners. Such eroticism might lead to potentially "immoral" behavior.

As slavery developed, it became increasingly centered in the southern states. For the most part, the north did not have large farms or need a labor force to work these farms. There was also a certain amount of early antislavery sentiment in the north from groups such as the Quakers in Philadelphia, who regarded slavery as evil.

AFRICAN MUSICAL TRAITS IN AFRICAN AMERICAN MUSIC

Various authors have delineated African musical traits that they feel are traceable in the music of black Americans. These traits include:

- *Flatting of the third and seventh notes of the scale, and sometimes the fifth as well.* (In the key of C these notes would be E, B, and G, respectively.)
- *A metronome sense.* Metronome sense is a clear delineation of where the beats of a measure are located.
- *Music is functional, rather than designed to be "beautiful."* Worksongs were used while people were working; other forms of music might be used for dancing, for religious purposes, or for personal expression.
- *Call-and-response singing.* Call-and-response singing occurs when one person sings a part, and multiple voices answer. In his book *Origins of the Popular Style*, Peter Van Der Merwe points out that dialogue can be another form of call and response, as when a guitar answers a vocal phrase in a blues song.
- *Special vocal techniques.* These include *melisma* (the use of several notes in singing a single syllable) and specialized vocal techniques, such as falsetto or growling.
- *Musical instruments.* A number of African musical instruments were played by African Americans. These include the banjo, bones, mouth-bow, quills, tambourine, and diddley bow, a one-string instrument mounted on a board. Many of the early blues guitarists used the diddley bow as their first instrument, often in their childhood.
- *Use of handclapping.* There were numerous reports of the slaves "patting juba," using handclaps as part of a dance or song.

Whatever parallels we find in African music and the blues, we need to keep in mind that we do not have any recorded examples of African music or blues from the late nineteenth century, the time when scholars believe the blues first evolved. We should also note that the savannah—the part of Africa that spawned musical instruments that were similar to the ones slaves played in America—was an Arabic culture, whose use of vocal shakes and vibrato is found in African American music. Arabic music also featured the lengthening of individual notes, a quality that puzzled some early white (and classically trained black) musicians when they first heard blues singers, because they could not understand the structure of the music. In other words, Africa does not contain a single musical style, or culture, and African influences are more complex than many scholars have acknowledged.

One of the confusing aspects of attempting to trace African elements in African American music is that the importation of slaves was continuous from 1619 until 1807. The slaves came from various tribes and linguistic groups, and there were differences in the music among the various tribal groups. Not only do we have to factor in all of the different tribes and languages that originally came here, but as new groups of slaves appeared, they in turn would be bringing in whatever influences they had been subject to at the time of their capture. These new arrivals interacted with second-and third-generation slaves, who to some extent were already integrated into American musical practices, or had developed their own fusions of African and American music. Since this is a 250-year period, and we know virtually nothing about African music at any point in the process, it is virtually impossible to make any definitive connections between "original" African music and the new African American forms that developed. Given these circumstances, scholarship necessarily turns into speculation.

AFRICAN AMERICAN SPIRITUALS

The first music performed by African Americans that gained recognition on the larger American musical scene was the so-called African American spiritual. Many slave owners encouraged blacks to attend church, and the imagery of freedom from bondage on earth, "escaping" to a promised land, must have resonated with the slaves' own situation of oppression. Plus, singing hymns would have been acceptable to the white masters, whereas secular songs and dances might have been seen as more threatening.

The first black minister given a license to preach was George Leile Kiokee, who set up an African Baptist Church in Savannah in 1780. In 1801, a free black man named Richard Allen published the first hymnbook for blacks, and established his own church. Allen used quite a few of the Isaac Watts hymns, and he also added lines and phrases to existing white hymns.

The first example of the music of black Americans in print appeared in 1867 in the book *Slave Songs of the United States*. Almost all the songs are hymns or religious songs, with a small representation of secular songs; so it reinforced the notion that African American music centered on the spiritual. The authors refer to improvisation of texts, and "shouting," or dramatic emotive singing taking place in a circle or ring. This book's 102 songs were collected from 1861 to 1864 primarily by the book's authors—William Francis Allen, Charles Pickard Ware, and Lucy McKim Garrison—who were working in an educational program on the Port Royal Islands, off the coast of South Carolina. Allen, Ware, and Garrison found no musical instruments among the singers they knew, and remark that it was difficult to get freedmen to sing the older songs, attributing this fact to the ex-slaves repudiating the "undignified" aspects of their past lives.

Black religious songs were referred to as "Negro spirituals." Spirituals were songs with religious themes, often looking toward a better life in heaven after the singer's time on earth was over. However, the songs also sometimes contained double meanings, known as *coded messages*. The songs could have one meaning to the singers and a black audience, and an entirely different one to any white listeners. The messages could involve analogies between biblical oppression and the plight of the slaves, or could even offer directions for help in escaping from the plantation, as in the song *Follow the Drinking Gourd.*

Spirituals are generally regarded as folk songs that evolved through the process of oral transmission—songs that were passed on from one person to another and then changed either deliberately or accidentally. The spirituals were sung by groups of people, rather than individuals, and generally utilized the call-and-response pattern in which a singer would sing a line or a verse, and then the group would chime in with a response to that line, or would wait until the chorus of the song.

The first successful "serious" African American performing group was the Fisk Jubilee Singers, who performed highly arranged versions of spirituals in harmonized settings. Formed in the 1870s at Fisk University in Nashville to raise money for the all-black college, the group toured in the United States and eventually Europe, and made some early recordings of their "concert" versions of spirituals. They influenced countless other groups, and again helped solidify the notion that the spiritual was the "highest" form of African American music. Twenty-five of their songs were published in souvenir programs that were sold when the group performed, and in 1872, an entire volume of their repertoire appeared. This book went through many editions, and was very influential in spreading spirituals to a broader audience.

The Fisk singers were so successful in their fund-raising efforts that a number of other schools, such as the Hampton Institute and Tuskegee Choir, attempted similar touring and fund-raising efforts. Other groups not connected with schools also began to compete with the Fisk groups, including some bogus groups that attempted to use the "Jubilee Singers" name without permission. The performances by these groups leaned toward formal arrangements, often with piano accompaniment.

The history of the spiritual, then, involves European sources—early hymnbooks—that were reworked by African American musicians to form a new musical style. This interplay between black and white is typical of much of the history of American popular music. Nonetheless, throughout the twentieth century, there was an extended controversy as to whether white hymns came from black spirituals, or vice versa. The proponents for the white origins of spirituals were in effect arguing that African Americans lacked the superior inventiveness of their white compatriots. Black scholars took the opposite view, presenting a view of slaves as relentlessly creative human beings, endowed with more musical talent than their white contemporaries.

George Pullen Jackson, the foremost advocate for the white origin of spirituals, related the tunes of several hundred African American spirituals to tunes found in the British Isles. He also found parallels in the use of the flatted third and seventh notes of the scale that are usually attributed to African Americans. However, Jackson did not spend much time analyzing the texts, nor did he factor in the improvisational aspects of musical performances. Melodies in folk tradition are not stagnant, but change from one performance to another. Not surprisingly some black scholars claimed earlier origins of the black songs. These scholars pointed out that the first publication of the songs did not necessarily prove an earlier origin than songs that might have been sung without ever having been published. The truth probably lies somewhere in between. Dena Epstein sees the development of spirituals as an exchange of songs during the early-nineteenth-century camp meetings that both whites and blacks attended.

A number of black composer-arrangers, such as John W. Work, J. Rosamond Johnson, his brother James Weldon Johnson, and Nathaniel Dett, expanded on the work of the Jubilee Singers, and made formal musical arrangements of traditional spirituals. During the twentieth century virtually all black concert or opera singers performed spirituals. Some of the famous performers were Roland Hayes, Paul Robeson, and Marian Anderson.

When the Czech composer Antonin Dvořák visited the United States in 1893, he enthusiastically endorsed the work of the Jubilee Singers, and wrote a symphony, known as *The New World Symphony,* that incorporated melodies that were obviously derived from the spirituals. This work became influential and popular, spreading the influence of the spirituals in yet another arena.

Blues and spirituals share some common musical features, particularly the use of the blues scale. However, there are some fundamental differences between them. One is that spirituals usually referred to a better land awaiting the singers after death, while blues focused on the singer's more immediate or practical needs, especially romantic ones. The blues also gloried in using bawdy images and double entendres, which were not acceptable in spirituals. To put it in another way, the blues were about the here and now, the spirituals were about the afterlife. Blues are generally performed by vocal soloists, whereas the spirituals almost always involved groups of singers.

The two musical forms came together by the 1920s in the form of *holy blues*—songs that utilized blues instruments and musical style, but had religious texts.

EARLY BLACK SECULAR MUSIC

Various travelers, historians, and journalists of the eighteenth and nineteenth centuries make reference to the singing or playing of slaves. In addition to spirituals, they note several different forms of secular songs, including work songs, hollers, and ring shouts. Unfortunately, it was not until the late 1890s that folklorists started to collect folk music in the United States, and it was not until the 1920s that we had recordings of this music. This was also the period when blues, ragtime, and jazz were all developing. Consequently, it is difficult for us to know what the hollers sounded like in their "pure" state, when they were relatively uninfluenced by other musical styles.

One primary difference between the work songs, hollers, and ring shouts and later musical styles was that these songs were sung without any accompanying instruments. It is a safe assumption that more African traits can be found in unaccompanied music. We do have a number of recorded examples of work songs, and some of hollers, but they date from a much later time, and the work songs were mostly recorded in prisons. Writing in 1925, Dorothy Scarborough pointed out that work songs were sometimes performed by a group of people working together, but also might be sung by individuals in cases where slaves were working as a group, but separated from one another.

THE MINSTREL SHOW

Beginning in the early nineteenth century, black secular music came to the attention of many Americans through the vehicle of the *minstrel show*. Scholars date the earliest example of white performers using blackface to the late 1820s. By that time a half-dozen performers toured the nation, performing songs and dances between the acts of plays. Two of the most famous of these performers were Thomas Dartmouth "Daddy" Rice and George Washington Dixon. Author Robert C. Toll, in his book *Blacking Up: The Minstrel Show in Nineteenth-Century America*, reports two of the tunes performed as *Zip Coon* (later known as *Turkey in the Straw*) and *Jump Jim Crow*. The two stereotypical characters of the minstrel show are represented in these two songs: Zip Coon was the well dressed city dweller who knew all the latest trends; Jim Crow was his rural brother, the country bumpkin who stayed home on the farm. In addition to dressing up as plantation black men by using burnt cork on their faces, white performers also sang in African American dialects. Some of the songs of the minstrels, such as "*The Boatman's Dance*, passed into folk tradition, and were still being performed 100 years later.

Complete minstrel shows began during the 1830s, and featured skits, dances, and singing. They were, in effect, mini-theatrical performances that presented blackface comedy and song. There were actors, singers, and instrumentalists, especially banjo and fiddle players. Often the shows made fun of African American's use of language, by presenting it as either pompous or foolish. The show's master of ceremonies was known as The Interlocutor, and typically Tambo and Bones, two comic characters named for the musical instruments that they played—the tambourine and bones—made fun of him. Although slaves were generally portrayed as lazy, shiftless, fun-loving, and irresponsible, occasional minstrel productions depicted them in more human terms.

The first popular minstrel troupe was the Virginia Minstrels, formed in New York City in 1843 by four individuals who had achieved some fame as solo blackface performers: Billy Whitlock, Dan Emmett, Frank Brower, and Dick Pelham. E.P. Christy and his Christy Minstrels were among the most successful of the rapidly developing competitors of the Virginians. The music of these performers had a strong Irish-English tinge, blended with African American styles that many of the artists had heard from performers in the south, and sought to imitate. The banjoists often consciously imitated the work of black musicians, who themselves had been influenced by white dance music, as well as their own musical traditions. The later performing groups were larger, and often featured multiple musicians, two fiddlers and two banjoists, for example, instead of one. One of the most important composers who worked in the minstrel idiom, although not exclusively so, was Stephen Collins Foster, who wrote a number of songs that are still heard today, including *Oh! Susannah* and *Old Folks At Home* (popularly known as *Swanee River*). Foster was not a performer, but is often regarded as America's first professional songwriter; one of his first and best customers was E.P. Christy, who took author credit for some of Foster's first hits. Most of Foster's songs were highly sentimental, and depicted the slave as yearning for his master and the old plantation.

Minstrel songs varied in their attitudes toward slavery. In addition to depicting "the old plantation," some of the songs protested, or at least mentioned, that slavery often led to the breakup of families, as the master sold off a husband without a wife, or vice versa. Several scholars have pointed out that the very fact that there was so much interest in African Americans music and lifestyles was a step forward in the ultimate acceptance of African Americans into American life.

Minstrel shows were popular both in the cities and in the rural areas. Some of the companies had runs as long as 10 years in such cities as Boston, New York, and Philadelphia. However, in the early days of the minstrel show, black performers were rare. William Henry Lane, known as "Master Juba," was one of the few black performers in the early minstrel days. He was considered a magnificent dancer, and was victorious over John Diamond, his white rival, in dancing contests. By the end of the Civil War, many of the touring companies were black, although they were usually owned by white entrepreneurs. A number of jazz performers got their start playing in touring minstrel shows, including W.C. Handy, Ma Rainey, and Bessie Smith. Black minstrel groups drew black audiences, as well as the usual white curiosity-seekers.

By the turn of the twentieth century, minstrel shows were no longer popular in the northern cities, and were replaced by vaudeville shows. Performers such as Al Jolson and Eddie Cantor continued to perform in blackface, however, through the 1920s. The burnt cork tradition continued in rural communities up until World War II.

Early folklorists assumed that the negative imaging of the minstrel shows contributed to the abandonment of the banjo by black musicians. This seemed to be borne out by the fact that, prior to the mid-1970s, the Library of Congress collection of thousands of recorded songs and instrumental pieces included less than a dozen recordings of black old-time banjo players. However, extensive field research by Bruce Bastin, Cecilia Conway, and Tommy Thompson in the mid-1970s turned up far more black musicians who played the five-string banjo. Their picking styles were somewhat similar to those of white players in the Southern Appalachian mountains. This has raised some intriguing but unanswered questions about the relationship between white and black music, and who originated what styles.

THE EARLY BLUES
SOCIAL CONDITIONS AT THE BIRTH OF THE BLUES: 1870s–1900

After the Civil War, social conditions in the south appeared to change radically for the freedmen. The period 1865–1880 represented a period of hope for southern blacks. There was a general optimism among African Americans, who felt that they were "free at last, free at last." Slavery was abolished, some ex-slaves were able to buy land, and they voted in local and national elections. African Americans were elected to state offices and to the U.S. House of Representatives, and there were even a few elected to the U.S. Senate. Northern troops occupied the south, and missionaries established schools.

However, northern troops withdrew from the south in 1877, and conditions quickly deteriorated. Freedoms were curtailed, and many blacks were barred from voting—either outright or through the imposition of restrictive "poll taxes" or fees charged to exercise the right to vote. The sharecropping system, in which whites owned the land and black workers were forced to pay rent for its use, became common. The blacks also often had to purchase seed and other supplies from the landowners, often at inflated prices, so that most—if not all—of their harvest went to re-paying loans and rent. The system was in effect similar to slavery, and some of the sharecroppers were perpetually in debt to the landowners. To aggravate matters, the northerners largely lost interest in the freedmen, and various political deals were made that removed any federal control over the racist practices prevalent in the south.

It is possible to make the case that it was the very nature and extent of repression that led to the dynamic emergence of new musical forms. In *Bleaching Our Roots: Race and Culture in American Popular Music*, performer-scholar Dave Lippman makes the interesting point that the slave owners, attempts to repress African music necessarily led to the development of new and unique musical forms by the slaves. We can hypothesize that the repressive period of 1890–1920 similarly led southern African Americans to create new musical forms.

THE BLUES: 1890–1920

Unfortunately, we do not have much in the way of printed texts to show us how and when the blues evolved. No one was very interested in secular black music in the late nineteenth century, and of course there were no tape recorders available. What blues scholars have written about really stems largely from the recordings and recollections of the older generation of black blues artists, none of whom recorded before 1920.

However, there is one key source for studying the early blues. Howard Odum collected music in Georgia and Mississippi in 1905–1908 and published his work, initially in *The Journal of American Folklore*, and some 20 years later in two books of songs, coauthored by Guy Johnson. Odum published the first blues, and much of what we have said about the form of early blues comes from his researches. Unfortunately, his books do not specify which songs were collected in which states. Alan Lomax calls Mississippi "the land where the blues began," but we have no absolute evidence that this is literally true. We do know that the ways in which the blues developed vary in different regions […].

Odum classifies early blues musicians into three categories:

- The *songster* was a musician who performed blues, but also had a repertoire of many other songs, such as spirituals, work songs, and ballads.
- The *musicianer* was an instrumentalist.
- The *music physicianer* was a musician who traveled, and wrote and played his own songs.

It is possible that the songsters were the bridge between earlier black music forms and the blues. When one remembers that such musicians played for both black and white audiences, and would be attempting to please both groups, this seems even more plausible. The traveling music physicianers would then serve to spread the music far and wide, at least to the black populations in various parts of the country. The distinction between these various musicians has been over-drawn, in the sense that many musicians performed blues, other secular songs, and even religious tunes, and some musicians, such as Lonnie Johnson, sometimes recorded as vocalists, sometimes as an instrumental soloists, and sometimes as accompanists for other vocalists.

Another key early source for our knowledge of the blues comes from musician-composer W.C. Handy. In his autobiography (published many years later), Handy recalls seeing a black musician sitting by a railroad station in 1903, playing guitar with a knife in his left hand and singing *I'm goin' where the Southern cross the Yellow Dog*. Handy found that this song referred to a railroad junction in Morehead, Mississippi. There are other reports of the blues sung during the 1890s in the memoirs of various black musicians. Some blues singers have claimed that the song *Joe Turner* was the first blues song, and the others that developed were variations on it. Turner was a penal officer who transported convicts in Tennessee between 1892 and 1896, certainly the correct time period for the beginnings of the blues.

Handy was a trained musician who realized that the blues could bring him income and popularity. Not long after his first experience of hearing the blues, Handy's band was play-ing a dance in Cleveland, Mississippi, and saw a guitar, mandolin, and string bass trio play during the intermission of their show. The audience rewarded the trio's efforts with "a rain of silver dollars," causing Handy to immediately realize the financial potential of the folk blues. Because Handy was a bandleader, he needed to formalize the structure of the blues, and to write the blues down in sheet music form. Handy's *Memphis Blues* was published in in 1912, and his *St. Louis Blues* appeared in 1914. Handy used the AAB lyric form, and his songs were usually 12-bar blues (we will discuss the structure of a blues song shortly). The first blues vocal to be recorded was Handy's *Memphis Blues*, but, ironically, it was recorded by white musician Morton Harvey.

Handy's success inspired countless others to write "blues" songs, and this repertoire became known in the 1910s and 1920s as the "classic blues." Unlike their folk forebears, classic blues were composed blues songs, generally with a definite musical structure and a story line, and they were sung by female singers, many of whom were experienced performers, used to singing in front of theater audiences. This was very different from the style of folk blues, which were performed before small, informal audiences, or at dances. [...]

SUBJECT MATTER

The blues that Howard Odum found in Georgia and Mississippi before 1910, like the blues that are sung today, were largely about romantic situations between men and women. Some of the songs contained boastful lyrics about the sexual prowess of the singer, some were self-pitying lyr-ics about unfaithful women, or double-dealing friends. Some are simply celebrations of sexuality, others of the virtues or difficulties associated with drinking. Another common subject was travel, and often the railroad was mentioned either as a way to escape the often oppressive small-town life, or simply to enjoy a change of scenery. Many blues refer to specific towns or states of the singer's acquaintance. In an unfriendly world, jail was inevitably a possibility, and jail, judges, and prison guards make their way into early blues lyrics. Odum acknowledged that he was unable to print some blues lyrics on the basis of their immorality, the use of "unacceptable" sexual references. The same held true of some later collectors. Consequently, we will never know how many bawdy songs simply never appeared in print.

Various scholars have argued that the blues are a form of protest music, with the singer complaining about his lot in life. Others deny that protest is a significant aspect of blues style. Even in Odum's work we find complaints about jailers, bosses, and work. It is also important to remember that all of the early collectors were white. Many of the singers may have not trusted these scholars enough to sing songs that complained about their lives, or protested specific occurrences. We will return to this subject when we discuss Lawrence Gellert's collections of protest songs from the 1920s and 1930s.

Sometimes early blues lyrics did not tell a single coherent story, but rather used a number of unconnected images of what was floating through the singer's mind at the time of the performance. Sometimes this included combining verses from other songs, and transforming them into "new" creations. There were certainly a number of well-known blues verses that surfaced in various songs. After blues started to appear on records during the 1920s, the pirating of verses from various songs became a common procedure. Sometimes entire songs were "borrowed," with only the most minor changes, such as the singer changing the caliber of a gun or the name of the female protagonist in a song. This is partially due to the fact that record executives demanded that singers "write" their own material, hoping to benefit from ownership of their copyrights; many singers were not talented writers, and so took to reworking older songs in an attempt to pass them off as their own.

Although the slow blues definitely had a plaintive quality, faster tempo blues made good dance or party music. At times a sad lyric was combined with an up-tempo melody, or a faster tempo could mask the feelings of sadness in a thoughtful lyric. The blues had room for a wide range of emotions.

RAGTIME AND EARLY JAZZ

The beginnings of ragtime and jazz virtually paralleled the development of the blues form. In ragtime, unlike the blues, the piano was the main instrument. The early ragtime pianists were barroom players, who did not necessarily read music. Ingredients of ragtime began to appear in the pop songs of the 1890s. Known as "coon songs," these songs enjoyed enormous success and, as one might expect, treated African Americans in a derogatory fashion. They were essentially a repetition of the images that minstrels had painted of African Americans. Ironically, some of the composers of these songs were themselves black.

Instrumental ragtime developed during the 1890s, primarily in St. Louis and Sedalia, Missouri, but also in New Orleans. Eileen Southern, in her pioneering book *The Music of Black Americans*, also mentions piano players in such cities as Mobile, Alabama, Louisville, Kentucky, Memphis, Chicago, Philadelphia, and New York. As instrumental ragtime developed, it became very complex, containing as many as four different musical parts to a song. Composer-performers such as Scott Joplin or James Scott were sophisticated, trained musicians, who thought of themselves as serious composers. The first recorded ragtime pieces appeared in 1912 in two piano rolls recorded by the legendary black piano virtuoso Blind Boone; Joplin made some rolls well after his playing career was over 3 years later.

Ragtime piano was a sophisticated musical style, with the right hand playing syncopated or offbeat figures while the left hand kept the rhythm steady. Not only were such pieces as Joplin's work divided into different sections, there were often key changes from one section to the next. Gilbert Chase, in his book *America's Music*, suggests that the right-hand piano syncopations were derived from black banjo styles played on the five-string banjo. In these styles of banjo playing, the thumb played the fifth string of the banjo, sometimes playing that string off the beat.

Although ragtime was sometimes played on the banjo, the primary impact of ragtime on the blues was in the Piedmont guitar styles of the Carolinas and Georgia. As we will see in the next two chapters, these styles required a more sophisticated harmonic approach to the guitar than that of the folk blues players. The most advanced players, such as Blind Blake, wrote guitar instrumentals, rather than just using the guitar to accompany songs.

Most scholars agree that New Orleans was the central place where jazz developed, although there were black brass bands in various parts of the country in the middle of the nineteenth century. New Orleans had a particularly rich tradition of brass bands, dating from the 1870s. Sometime toward the end of the century, these musicians started to modify ragtime, and "swing the beat." The legendary cornetist Buddy Bolden was probably among the first of these early jazzmen. By the turn of the century such African American musicians as trumpet players Freddie Keppard and Bunk Johnson started to play downtown with the Creole musicians, and New Orleans jazz was born. However, by 1915, many African Americans moved out of the south, and in 1917, the U.S. Navy closed down the Storyville district. Storyville had been the entertainment center of New Orleans, complete with bordellos that employed many musicians. The next developments in jazz took place in Chicago.

Jazz utilized some of the harmonic devices of ragtime, but kept the spirit of the blues. The brass instruments moaned, growled, and bent notes to simulate blues growls and trills. The typical New Orleans combos had trumpet, trombone, and clarinet, and the rhythm section had a tuba instead of a string bass, a banjo, and a small drum set. In a good number of early jazz arrangements, the music was not written down, but was improvised, with beginnings and endings of songs worked out. The solos were entirely improvised.

Many of the early jazzmen played on records by the classic blues singers in the 1920s, although usually with small combos using only a handful of musicians. Oddly the first jazz recordings were made by a white group, The Original Dixieland Jazz Band, in 1917.

BLUES STRUCTURE

When we discussed W.C. Handy and his composition, we mentioned the lyric structure (AAB) and the form "12-bar blues." Students of the blues are familiar with these terms, but for others they may be slightly mystifying. Here is a brief explanation.

If we look at the way blues are performed by a contemporary artist, such as B.B. King, it is easy enough to analyze the musical and lyrical structure of one of his songs. Almost invariably the songs will be in 4/4 time, which means that there are four quarter notes in each measure of music. The verses will contain twelve bars of music, and the chord structure will usually consist of three basic chords, built on the first, fourth, and fifth notes of the scale. In the key of C, these chords will be C, F, and G7, with the C going to a C7 and the F chord moving to an F7. The lyrics will be in AAB form, which means that the first line of the song will be repeated, with the third line acting as a sort of answer to the previous (repeated) lines. The end of lines one and two typically rhymes with the end of line 3. An example, with the chords written in, is:

```
C                                                    C7
It's Monday morning, and I don't want to work no more,

F                          F7              C   C7
Yeah it's Monday morning, ain't gonna work no more,

G7                         F              C  F  C  G7
Wish I was in Texas, with the sun shining on my door.
```

Notice that there is a short chord sequence at the end of the verse. This is called a *turnaround*, and it leads back to the next verse, which will start with the C chord.

This is all very well, except that when we start to look at the origins of the blues, and how they developed, we find a number of disconcerting things. First, the earlier folk blues did not always contain twelve bars. They might have eleven, or thirteen, sixteen, or even twelve-and-a-half bars. It is quite possible that the twelve-bar form developed when musicians started to play together, or when a singer was accompanied by a guitarist or pianist. As soon as two or more musicians play together, they need to have some agreement about the length of musical phrases in order to stay together. Or perhaps Handy, being a "professional" musician, simply "evened out" a form that in the folk tradition was much more flexible. Blues did not always use three chords, either. Some of the Mississippi blues really consisted of a single chord, slightly modified to go with the melody of a particular song.

The lyrics were equally irregular. Howard Odum, working in 1906–1908, found that there were songs that consisted of a single repeated line, with no additional lyrics. Other lyrics patterns consist of a verse that has an opening line, with the second line repeated, instead of the first line as shown in the example above. This form can be indicated as an ABB form. An example is:

> Ain't no more cotton, cause the boll weevil ate it all,
>
> Gonna leave this town, goin' away before the fall,
>
> You know baby, I won't be here next fall.

Notice that in both lyrics the repeated lines are not identical. They are almost conversational, as though the singer is thinking about the lyrics as he sings.

The forms that blues songs can take are seemingly endless, and sometimes vary within a single song. I have an out-of-print recording by Hally Wood where she sings a song called *The Worried Blues*. The first verse goes like this:

> I've got the worried blues,
>
> I've got the worried blues,
>
> I've got the worried blues, oh my Lord;
>
> I've got the worried blues,
>
> I'm going where I've never been before.

I suppose we could call this form AAAAB. But, later in the song she sings

> I'm going where those orange blossoms bloom,
>
> I'm going where I never been before,
>
> I'm going where those orange blossoms bloom, oh my Lord;
>
> I'm going where those orange blossoms bloom,
>
> I'm going where I've never been before.

We might call this form ABAAB. The point is that the blues singer created the form around the lyrics of the song, rather than tailoring the lyrics of the song to fit a preconceived model.

At the turn of the twentieth century, there were ballads that had many elements of blues songs, but did not follow these lyric structures. For example, in the song *Frankie and Albert*—a version of the song *Frankie and Johnny* sung by Mississippi John Hurt and Leadbelly, among others—there is a recurrent last line ("he was her man, he was doin' her wrong"). In Furry Lewis's version of the ballad *Casey Jones*—which he calls *Kassie Jones*—he repeats the last (fourth line) of each verse. This form of song, with a repeated last line, is known as a "refrain," and is common in Anglo-American balladry as well.

Just as the blues make use of repetition in the construction of their lyrics, the same patterns also can be found in spirituals, and in traditional English ballads. For example, here is a verse of the sixteenth-century ballad *Pretty Polly*, a song that has been collected in numerous versions in the southern Appalachian mountains:

> I courted pretty Polly, all the livelong night,
>
> I courted pretty Polly, all the livelong night,
>
> I left her next morning, before it was light.

The spiritual *Lonesome Valley* has been collected from both white and black singers. It uses a different pattern of repeated phrases:

> You've got to walk that lonesome valley,
>
> You've got to walk it by yourself,
>
> Ain't nobody here, going to walk it for you,
>
> You've got to walk that lonesome valley by yourself.

In this instance, the lyric is not a word-for-word repetition. The second line is slightly different from the first line, and the fourth line combines elements from the first and second lines.

LEARNING TO PLAY OR SING THE BLUES

Before we proceed with the history of the blues, it might be useful for the interested reader to get a glimpse of how to learn to play or sing the blues. The earliest blues singers developed their knowledge of the music as a sort of communal experience, in the same way that communities in such diverse places as Bulgaria and West Africa have nurtured and developed their musical traditions. The Carolinas nurtured and developed the Piedmont blues, while in Texas and Mississippi relevant but different musical styles emerged. Further refinements that scholars ponder over include the differences between the delta Mississippi blues style that developed in the Clarksdale area, and the somewhat different and less intense Mississippi school that emerged around Bentonia, north of the city of Jackson.

One hundred and ten years later these local communities where music could be learned directly from older master performers no longer really exist. So how does the reader, black, white, or otherwise, learn how to play or sing the blues? The most typical path that people follow is to immerse themselves in the musical style through listening to CDs, watching videos, and buying instructional books and tapes. Fortunately, these resources are readily available in most cities, and if you do not live in a relatively large urban area they are available through mail order or internet purchases. In the appendix of this book is a large list of resources that can help. But let us discuss the way that these resources can be utilized most efficiently.

From the author's point of view, the most useful way to learn about a musical style, blues or otherwise, is to have as much direct contact as possible with a person or people for whom that style is natural. In other words, your best bet is to be around blues singers, players, and bands. The reason that this sort of immersion is the most successful way of learning about the blues is that not only will it show you the specific musical ways that, for example, a guitar is played, but it will also give you some feeling for the more subtle aspects of the music. In addition, you will begin to develop enough of an ear to understand what distinguishes one particular player from another. Mance Lipscomb and John Hurt had a similar feel in their playing, but they do not sound alike. Muddy Waters developed out of the Clarksdale tradition that spawned Robert Johnson, Son House, and Charley Patton, but Muddy really did not sound anything like these other blues artists. Each had certain distinguishing traits, whether right-hand picking styles, the use of musical dynamics or different guitar tunings, or vocal styles that could involve falsetto (a sort of fake high tenor) singing, grunts, doubling what the guitar was playing, and so on.

It is more convenient to learn from instructional videos, CDs, and books than to seek out artists who actually play and sing the blues. The problem with learning from these valuable resources is that they are tools, not substitutes for trial-and-error musical experiences. The same thing applies to taking guitar, piano, or vocal lessons. Blues is an improvisational genre of music, and although students often must go through a process of imitating a specific musician, this ultimately can be counterproductive to developing individual approaches to the music. So, the author recommends singing and playing along with records only up to a point. There should come a time when you put other people's styles away, and you make the choice to try it your own way.

Whether or not you will turn out to be a musical innovator is impossible to predict, but there is a great deal of joy to be experienced in playing your own songs, your own instrumental solos, or even your own musical arrangements of old standards.

SUMMARY

The blues began around 1890, possibly in Mississippi. The musical aspects of the blues utilized a number of African traits, and lyrics of the early blues were written in a stream-of-consciousness manner. Rather than telling a specific story, they reflected the moods and memories of the singer. The earliest blues were probably unaccompanied, but the instrument of choice quickly became the guitar. Blues drew on a variety of black popular styles, including spirituals, hollers, and worksongs, and European elements borrowed from ballads, dance tunes, and religious songs. Trained black musicians began to formalize the structure of the blues after 1910, and many of their more structured and pop-oriented songs were sung by women professional performers. Jazz and ragtime developed in a parallel stream to the blues, and these musical styles influenced one another.

BIBLIOGRAPHY

The Blues and Africa

Oliver, Paul. (2001) *Savannah syncopators; African retentions in blues*. Reprint of 1970 book, with a new afterword in *Yonder Come the Blues*.

The Minstrel Period

Toll, Robert C. (1974) *Blacking Up: the Minstrel Show in Nineteenth Century America*. New York, Oxford University Press.

Social and Musical Background of the Blues

Allen, William Francis, Charles Pickard Ware, Lucy McKim Garrison. (1867) *Slave Songs of the United States*. New York, Peter Smith, 1951 reprint.

Conway, Cecilia. (1995) *African Banjo Echoes in Appalachia: A Study of Folk Traditions*. Knoxville, TN, University of Tennessee Press.

Epstein, Dena J. (1977) *Sinful Tunes and Spirituals*. Urbana, IL, University of Illinois Press.

Odum, Howard W. and Guy B. Johnson. (1926) *The Negro and His Songs*. Chapel Hill, NC, University of North Carolina Press.

Scarborough, Dorothy. (1925) *On the Trail of Negro Folk-Songs*. Cambridge, Harvard University Press.

Southern, Eileen. (1971) *The Music of Black Americans: A History*. New York, W.W. Norton.

Van Der Merwe Peter. (1989) *Origins of the Popular Style: The Antecedents of Twentieth-Century Popular Music*. New York, Oxford University Press.

Biographies and Autobiographies

Handy, William Christopher. (1941) *Father of the Blues*. New York, The Macmillan Company.

Questions for thought

- Where did the blues first appear?
- How did the blues and other African-American musical forms develop from African musical origins?
- What are the characteristics that distinguish a blues song from any other?
- Can you think of music from any other genre (rock, jazz, etc.) that has characteristics from the blues?
- What were the political and social forces that sparked the formation and the spreading of the blues from the South to the rest of the country?
- How did African-American music influence popular music in the United States and worldwide?

Activity:

Search for Delta blues and Chicago blues in YouTube. How many recordings were you able to find for each type of blues? Compare recordings by two different artists from each type of the blues. What characteristics can you identify that are common to all of these recordings? How do they differ?

References

Titon, Jeff Todd. "North America/Black America." In *Worlds of Music: An Introduction to the Music of the World's Peoples*, 5th ed., edited by Jeff Todd Titon, 145–204. Belmont, CA: Schirmer Cengage Learning, 2009.

Figure Credits

CHAPTER TWO

Brazil: Samba, Samba-Reggae, and Carnaval

FIGURE 2.1 *Map of Brazil*

Introduction

When talking about Brazilian music, or for that matter music of any country, continent, or geographic area, the implication is that the music represents a homogeneous mass. Nothing could be further from the truth. Music in Brazil is as diverse as its people and it geography. This diversity in music is reflective of the diversity of Brazil's people, a large majority of whom can trace their roots back to Africa. However, Brazilians come from all over the globe, including Portugal, the rest of Europe, the Middle East, Asia, and elsewhere. The United States is often thought of as a melting pot. In many ways it is more like a salad, where individual parts maintain their identity, together forming the whole. In the United States, ethnicities often maintain their roots as part of their identity: Italian-American, Irish-American, Japanese-American, etc. In Brazil, this notion of a hyphenated identity does not exist with the populations forming a national identity that recognizes its roots but does not linger in its connections to those roots; they are Brazilian. That said, there are regional differences that are reflected in the music, which differs from the Northeast to the Southeast to the Amazon and to the South. This chapter focuses on one of the most important manifestations of Brazilian identity, the samba, the roots of which are in Africa, but it is engrained as the national music of Brazil. It has blended with other global musical forces such as reggae, but samba still stands as Brazil's most important musical genre.

Samba and Afro-Brazilian Culture

Samba came to Brazil from Africa in the slave trade. Brazil was a very large colony, and Portugal was a very small country with a relatively small population. In order to exploit Brazil to its fullest, Portugal had to find a large, stable labor force. After a failed attempt to enslave the indigenous populations (they had a tendency to flee into the jungle), Portugal started importing large numbers of slaves to Brazil from Africa.

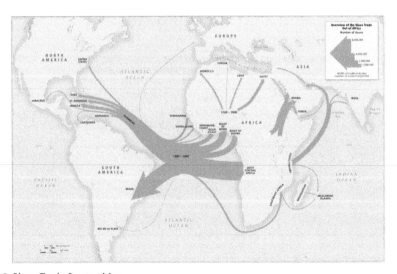

FIGURE 2.2 *Slave Trade Routes Map*

FIGURE 2.3 *Candomblé ceremony*

Slavery and the slave trade were different in Brazil than in the United States. The most obvious difference is in numbers. Brazil is a very large country; it is actually larger than the continental United States (Brazil, 3.288 million square miles, the United States without Alaska, 3.119 million square miles), and Portugal is roughly the size of Indiana. In order to exploit Brazil, Portugal imported between 3.5 and 6 million slaves from Africa (as compared to the United States, which imported less than half a million). In order to maintain order in the large population, family and language groups were kept together, which was not the case in the United States. There was a slave hierarchy to help maintain order. The slave trade and slavery also lasted one more generation than in the USA, and, as a result of all of these factors, slaves in Brazil were able to maintain much more of their cultural and religious practices, including the Afro-Brazilian religion known as *Candomblé*.

Candomblé is a mix of different religious traditions, most importantly from the Yorubá people of what is now Nigeria and Benin. It has parallels in the New World: in Cuba and Puerto Rico, the practice is known as *Santeria*, and in Haiti it is known as *Voudou* or *Voundun*. In all of these traditions, dance is an important part of the liturgy. Visually, Candomblé is a blend of Catholic and African traditions, the practice often disguised as Catholicism in order to avoid scrutiny of slave owners. Samba was the secular part of the Candomblé dance tradition.

Although the samba was strongly influenced by the Yorubá people, a current theory is that it may also have roots in Angola and that samba came from a dance called *semba*, meaning the "touching of bellies," a dance still practiced in Angola. Samba in Brazil traditionally has this touching, known as *umbigada* (umbilical), as part of the dance, lending credence to this argument. Considering the number of slaves taken from all over Africa to Brazil, a blending of traditions makes sense.

A majority of the slaves taken from Africa were taken to the Northeast state of Bahia, where both Candomblé and samba developed. With the emancipation of slaves in 1888, many former slaves headed to the southeast cities of Rio de Janeiro and São Paulo. They took with them the samba, which in Bahia was known as the *samba de roda*, or circle samba, because of the dance practice of a person dancing in the middle of a circle and then passing the dance to another participant. When the samba arrived in Rio de Janeiro, it came to be called the *samba do morro*, or hill samba, reflecting the steep hills where former slaves built their homes in places known as *favelas*, or slums. These favelas are where the most important Carnaval tradition developed: the escolas de samba, or samba schools, which embraced the samba as the dance used in the competition parades.

Reading #1: Samba-Reggae

Samba is undoubtedly Brazil's most important musical genre and an important cultural marker: it represents the fusion of African and European, of sacred and secular. It is not stagnant, however. Samba has been undergoing change from its development in Brazil, from the samba de roda in the Northeast of Brazil, to the samba do morro in Rio de Janeiro to the genre of Carnaval. Samba has also embraced influences from other genres. A common thread in music throughout the New World is the blending of genres from different places.

Nowhere is this more the case than Brazil, where musicians have embraced musical influences from many parts of the Americas. Samba has not remained stagnant but rather has been subject to constant change, refinement, and fusion with other genres, both Brazilian and from elsewhere. The blues, rock and roll, jazz and other genres from the United States have fused with Brazilian genres, leading to hybrids such as samba-rock and Brazilian jazz. Jamaican music has also had a great influence on Brazilian music, especially in the northeastern state of Bahia. One of the readings for this chapter, "Reggae and Samba-Reggae in Bahia: A Case of Long-Distance Belonging," looks at how reggae, arguably Jamaica's most important musical genre, has impacted the music of Bahia, leading to the fusion of samba and reggae, or samba-reggae.

> Eu ando aqui! Pela Babi!
> Eles me chamam de brasileiro
> Porém eu me sinto um estrangeiro
>
> [I walk around here, Babylon
> They call me Brazilian
> But I feel like a foreigner]
> —*Edson Gomes, 1990*

REGGAE AND *SAMBA-REGGAE* IN BAHIA

A Case of Long-Distance Belonging

Antonio J. V. dos Santos Godi

It should be noted at the outset that I don't intend to set the capitalist Babylon on fire, because the present moment is one of crisis and the contemporary flames affect our notions of time and space, and this cannot be solely attributed to the agents of reggae. At any rate, the Bahian reggae band Morrão Fumegante [Smoking Weed] set fire to the already hot Salvador summer of 1998 with its album *Fogo na Babilônia* [Fire in Babylon]. Despite these musical flames, the Bahian capital remains as it has always been. Reggae arrived, remained, and became Bahian.

It is not difficult to understand the globalizing surge of reggae and its localized manifestations in the Bahian capital. One might consider the emergence of reggae as another end-of-the-century novelty. Reggae is a cultural expression of a localized disorder, of a chaos with its own temporal and territorial context, even though this locality is not limited to Jamaica, its place of origin. Reggae is a product of the international recording industry and, as such, is reproduced beyond the boundaries of Jamaica, reflecting different notions of place as it develops in other nations and continents. Despite its cohabitation with reggae, the city of Salvador is not Jamaica, much less the Jamaica of the 1930s, which created Rastafarianism, or the Jamaica of the 1960s and 1970s, which gave birth to reggae.

One must bear in mind, however, that the markedly electronic and mediated contemporary moment can make long distances seem short. Jamaica can appear to be here and the mythified Ethiopia can be anywhere where the Rasta-reggae presence is found. As David Harvey suggests, new technologies of transportation and communication have created a compression of time and space.[1] Jamaica and Ethiopia remain where they have always been and the roots of reggae and Rasta remain geographically secure. However, these aesthetics and beliefs have had ramifications throughout the world as a pop-music style.

Between the 1960s and the 1970s, reggae and its embryonic forms, ska and rock steady, took root in diverse and distant locations. The British culture industry provided the first point of departure for these musical styles since Jamaica was an English colony until 1962. On the other hand, the electronic atmosphere that characterizes contemporary culture obeys neither national-geographic nor social-generational patterns.

Not coincidentally, the emergent expressions of electric pop of the 1970s and the 1980s, represented by the irreverence of punk rock, would find a curious complicity with the Jamaican musical aesthetic, most specifically with ska.[2] Both explicitly expressed a refusal of the established order and called for the destruction of the system. Reggae artists, in particular, announced the apocalyptic destruction of the capitalist "Babylon" and supported the return of blacks to a mythic Africa.

Punk rock and ska-reggae shared a certain social identity, the former being the electric expression of rebellious London youth and the second the musical expression of black immigrants from Jamaica.[3] That is to say, both were social presences marked by exclusion and lack of legitimate power. Despite this similarity, punk and ska-reggae evidence differences beyond the color of their practitioners. Punk spoke in a vocabulary of violent destruction and sadomasochism, while reggae spoke of peace and love. Despite such philosophical differences, these British and Jamaican musical expressions would find similarities in the critical character of their lyrics.

How does one explain the insinuating presence of Rasta-reggae expression today, and what are the cultural roots that justify its existence? How is this phenomenon, marked by the crossing of different traditions with contemporary sociocultural implications, articulated in the construction of this movement? Which cultural variables suggest a feeling of long-distance belonging? How do we explain the affinities between the Rasta-reggae culture in Jamaica and the aesthetic behavior of the *blocos afro* of the contemporary Bahian Carnival?

REGGAE: TRADITION, YOUTH, AND ELECTRONIC ETHNICITY

The mythical and theoretical narratives that attempt to explain the emergence of Rastafarianism underscore the prophetic discourse of Marcus Garvey: "Look to Africa, where a black king will be crowned, because the day of liberation will come next."[4] One could interpret as coincidence or prophecy the fact that, three years later, in 1930, a black king was indeed crowned in Ethiopia. Ras Tafari Makonnen would be referred to from then on as Haile Selassie, the "King of Kings" and the "Lion of the Tribe of Judah." According to some, Haile Selassie was the direct descendant of King Salomon and the Queen of Sheba, two important figures in Judeo-Christian history. However, Garvey's apparent prophecy was neither a coincidence nor a premonition, but rather the perception of a black militant profoundly in step with his time and with the ideas of an Ethiopianism that mythically constructed Africa as the cradle of Christianity.

By the middle of the 1970s, Jamaica already had close to 75,000 Rastas.[5] More recent data suggest that the Rastas represent 10 percent of the population of the island, constituting a group of about 250,000.[6] The biblical stories that justified and legitimated African slavery in the Americas would be reinterpreted by Jamaican Rastas so as to emphasize instead the liberation of black people, thought to be the manifestation of Jah, their supreme God. Reading the Old Testament in some unusual ways, the Rastas refused to cut the hair on their heads or bodies, leading to the creation of dreadlocks as one of their most important symbols of identity. Likewise, they refused to eat meat, in particular pork, adopting instead a diet based on fruits, vegetables, and grains. The Rastas are also known for their rejection of the laws and social behavior of "Babylon," opting instead for a radically alternative outlaw lifestyle.

Besides being based on the Africanized traditions of Christianity in Jamaica, the behavioral aesthetic of Rasta-reggae would assimilate elements of international youth culture of the era, especially electric pop music. Another characteristic of young people of that generation was the adoption of a free, adventurous lifestyle based on the love of nature and the rejection of moralizing hypocrisy and the unbridled consumerism of the capitalist world. The most seminal representation of youth culture during this time, the hippies, had a profound, worldwide influence, and shared many similarities with the Rasta-reggae movement. Music associated with social rebellion and spiritual revival was essential to both movements.

The youth of the 1960s and 1970s had attained a certain cultural autonomy that would substantially influence youth cultures in the following decades. The electronic dissemination of the behavioral aesthetic of rock was a determining factor in the cultural revolution of this period.[7] Likewise, the appearance of reggae in Jamaica and of *samba-reggae* in Bahia were phenomena engendered by irreverent, black youth cultures, contextualized in new social experiences for which music would be the most fundamental reference.

Livio Sansone, concerned with understanding the local and the global in relation to Brazilian funk, underscores the idea of cultural globalization and emphasizes the importance of youth culture. For the Italian anthropologist, "homogenization" and "massification" are not useful concepts in understanding the peripheral expressions of a globalized youth culture. Far from the old ethnocentric pretensions, the relationship between the local and the global engenders the construction of contextualized expressions.[8] Jamaican reggae and Bahian *samba-reggae* represent local reconstructions of originary representations of "Anglo-Saxon" youth cultures that have music as their crucial expression. I agree in part with Sansone, although to see these local presences as peripheral manifestations of a centralizing, determinant, and global "Anglo-Saxon" culture presents a flagrant paradox. The music that influenced both the development of reggae and the *blocos afro* [Afro-Bahian Carnival groups] was produced by African Americans. However, as blacks living in a world of racial inequality, these aesthetic agents maintained a certain feeling of transnational belonging, making it difficult to label their cultural expressions "Anglo-Saxon."

In the global context, in which the music of the African diaspora represents a crucial reference, there exists neither center nor periphery, but rather a space without borders. We are in a virtual dimension, characterized by a cultural environment without a determined space that adopts multiple global positions as sites of belonging and references of identity. Reggae might "originate" simultaneously in Jamaica and Brazil, as well as anywhere else in the world where electronic pop music is disseminated.

In its electronic and cultural aspects, globalization is an incontestable fact. However, with regard to geographic mobility and social contact among individuals across distant borders, the situation is different. The local press has noted various cases in which Brazilians have been violently denied entrance to other countries, even though they had appropriate legal documentation and proof of personal financial requirements. This suggests that, while long-distance electronic and cultural contact is easily exercised, people often have a difficult time crossing geographical borders.

John Naisbitt, a defender of free economy between nations and, consequently, a supporter of local privatization, suggests that the more globalized the economy, the more power acquired by its minor protagonists—nations, businesses, and individuals.[9] Certainly the Brazilian individuals who suffer disrespect in the airports of other nations would disagree with Naisbitfs ideas regarding the democratization of tourism. On the other hand, these same people could hardly disagree with him when he affirms that technological innovations allow people to "visit" any part of the world in the comfort of their own homes.

One should keep in mind, however, that not everybody possesses a home with the comfort that modern technology offers. The number of disenfranchised people in the world continues to rise. Contemporary globalization reflects the old contours of political and economic order with an increase in social inequalities on a local and international scale. This deserves careful attention.

Brazilian ethnomusicologist Jorge José de Carvalho notes that intellectuals from other countries have critiqued globalization as the dissemination of capitalist imperialism, while Brazilian studies, focused on culture and communication, have overlooked issues of power and domination which are at the core of end-of-the-century international relations.[10]

On the other hand, the presence of reggae introduces mythic notions of a type of social globalization, expressed in the idea of "Babylon," which represents a predatory capitalist imperialism. The many seemingly disconnected stories of reggae suggest a chaotic multiplicity of time and space, combining past history with contemporary experience. Discussions about contemporary cultural globalization and the phenomena of long-distance contacts and identifications can be discerned in reggae, where questions related to power and domination are considered in a new dimension characterized by the relationship between local and global connections.

LONG-DISTANCE BELONGING

Despite a lack of materials in Portuguese about Rasta-reggae culture, one notes in Brazil a remarkable growth of aficionados and followers of this behavioral and aesthetic complex. In greater Salvador, the appropriation of Rasta-reggae culture is notable in the suggestive presence of the many individuals who proudly wear dreadlocks, or in the production and consumption of reggae music. One might go so far as to say that the presence in Salvador of Ubaldo Uharú, Geraldo Cristal, Dionorina, Gilsan, Jorge de Angélica, Edson Gomes, and Sine Calmon, just to note a few of our most important reggae performers, is revealing proof of a sociocultural singularity that has been constituted at long distance. This might lead us to believe that the notion of belonging at the end of the century does not adhere to the same patterns of concepts such as "social identity" and "cultural identity," which have been essential to sociological and anthropological theory in the last few decades. Increasingly, feelings of belonging have been redimensionalized.

The formation of an electronic cultural market created by radio, television, the recording industry, and, most recently, information networks is essential to understand the complexity of contemporary society. The popularity of reggae would not have been possible without shortwave and AM radio transmissions from the southern United States, which were received in Jamaica in the 1960s and 1970s. During this time, distinct locations all over the planet were influenced by African-American popular music, leading to new ethnic and cultural expressions in various areas.

We might say that the utilization of African-American music and contemporary communication technologies led to the development of Jamaican reggae and the subsequent emergence of the Bahian *blocos afro*. Antonio Risério suggests that the musical movement of African-Americans was "the great catalyst" in the creation of the Carnival aesthetic introduced by the first *bloco afro*, Ilê Aiyê, in 1974. In this period there was a weekly television show with the Jackson Five, and the influence of this soul group on the contemporary behaviors of the black youth of Bahia was intense. In addition to this group, origin of the polemic megastar Michael Jackson, Risério emphasizes the presence of James Brown, who profoundly affected the "engineering" of popular culture in Salvador.[11] From there on, record and radio markets became determinant factors in the creation of long-distance cultural identifications.

The construction of an Afrocentric aesthetic in the Carnival of Salvador was one of the major cultural developments in recent Bahian history, and music was the fundamental expression of this phenomenon. Initially, this presence gained visibility and audibility in the localized dimension of the Carnival masses, and thereafter began its conquest of the mass media. From the outset, the local phenomenon of the *blocos afro* was related to Afro-diasporic musical forms with global projection. Though African-American music influenced the general elaboration of these entities, it would not determine the form of local musical expressions. Subsequently, traditional samba was filtered through contemporary and globalized musical motifs. *Samba-reggae* would come to represent a determining example of the mix between the local roots of samba and an already global reggae.[12]

The establishment of *samba-reggae* as the rhythm that generated a new musical movement in Bahia in the mid-1980s reveals the force of reggae in the new aesthetics and behaviors seen in the most predominantly black city in Brazil. The *bloco afro* Olodum and its former musical director, Neguinho do Samba, were the principal protagonists in the recent success of *samba-reggae*. However, other *blocos afro* were dedicated to the aesthetic of reggae, during the period before the construction of this hybrid Afro-Bahian musical form.

Malê Debalê and Muzenza are two *blocos afro* that provide early examples of an intense Bahian affinity for Jamaican reggae. Malê Debalê appeared in 1979, as the local cult of reggae, especially of Bob Marley, was beginning to emerge. The group pioneered the incorporation of reggae with its song "Coração Rastafari" [Rastafari heart] (1982), written by Djalma Luz and recorded by Lazzo Matumbi, another reggae artist in Salvador. Muzenza received attention for being the first to adopt a Jamaican behavioral aesthetic as a central theme. The group would later become known as Muzenza do Reggae.

The long-distance affinities between the *blocos afro* and Jamaican reggae can be explained by the fact that both movements arose from very similar political, cultural, and historical conditions. Both represented movements of young, dispossessed blacks fighting against social injustice. During this time cultural production became increasingly more global by means of multinational recording industries. It was not coincidental that both reggae and *bloco afro* aesthetics were cultivated with reference to a very specific conception of Africa. Africa was constructed by both groups as a mythic locus that provided a feeling of origin, dispersion, and symbolic reunion. The notion of black diaspora reflects strong associations with the development of new ideas of time and space within the electronic cultural market in which music plays a central role.[13] Ultimately, what was far away would appear close and points of reference of identity could be revisited by historic and geographic memory.

DEATH IN THE TRAJECTORY OF BELONGING

Death does not always signal the end. The passing of Robert Nesta Marley on May 11, 1981, led to the definitive incorporation of this date into the calendar of events of the black movement in Bahia. The month of May in Salvador ceased to be solely a time to commemorate the abolition of slavery (May 13,1888) and became the month of tributes to Bob Marley. Images of the musical hero would adorn the T-shirts of thousands of youths, including whites, blacks, and *mestiços*.

If May 13 represented a historical-ideological construction based on the official decrees of the past, May 11 would come to represent the invention of a recent tradition made possible by a mass-mediated and globalized cultural context that was determined primarily by black music.

The introduction of reggae in Bahia did not exactly coincide with the death of Bob Marley, even though the event brought greater attention to the reggae style. The event contributed decisively to the aesthetic re-elaboration of Muzenza, which was founded as a dissident group of Olodum in 1981. This phenomenon would lead to the creation of other *blocos afro* with reggae influences. In the Carnivals of 1997 and 1998, for instance, several reggae-influenced groups appeared, including the Amantes do Reggae, Ska Reggae, and Resistência Ativa.

Jamaican reggae led to the appearance of a new musical style in Bahia, *samba-reggae*, and a new Carnival subcategory. It should be noted that the Carnival scene had already been the primary site for the social and aesthetic innovation that revitalized the city each year. The 1970s saw the opening of reggae bars, beginning in the Maciel-Pelourinho neighborhood and spreading throughout the area. During the 1980s, reggae would be progressively disseminated in Salvador by means of extremely popular radio programs dedicated exclusively to the reggae genre. How was the insertion of reggae in Bahia processed, and what were the historical conditions that led to this new form of cultural belonging?

One of the first manifestations of Jamaican music in Brazil occurred in 1968 when reggae singer-songwriter Jimmy Cliff performed at the International Festival of Song in Rio de Janeiro. The festival was cosponsored and aired by TV Globo, an important national television network, which provided Cliff exposure to the Brazilian public. Reggae music was later introduced by Caetano Veloso and Gilberto Gil, who had first heard the new Jamaican music while exiled in London between 1969 and 1972.

Initially, reggae in Bahia was regarded as a marginal cultural movement, appearing in the working-class black neighborhoods. At this point, reggae was still rarely played on the radio, and scarcely available in record stores. In spite of this, reggae appeared in the bars and brothels of the historic downtown, Maciel-Pelourinho. Likewise, the music composed and performed by the *blocos afro* had yet to penetrate the radio or recording markets, despite its widespread performance by informal percussion groups during leisure time.

Spanish-Caribbean rhythms, referred to generically in Salvador as "merengue," were also widely heard in the brothels and at the weekend house parties of Maciel-Pelourinho. The long-distance connection between Bahia and the Caribbean existed before the recorded presence of reggae, and Maciel-Pelourinho, the emblematic territory of the Filhos de Gandhi and Olodum, was an important neighborhood in terms of racial and ethnic re-elaboration.

In the late 1970s, Pelourinho also came to be the subcultural territory of Salvador for artists and black militants. The first reggae bar opened in 1978, the same year as the creation of the Unified Black Movement (MNU), and of the establishment of the *festa da benção* [blessing party], which occurs every Tuesday evening in Maciel-Pelourinho.[14] The late 1970s and early 1980s was a period of profound changes in the ethnic and aesthetic image of the city. Afro-diasporic music, with its attendant cultural styles and political discourses, would play a determining role in this crucial process of local transformation.

In 1979, amidst the political opening of the military dictatorship and the founding of the *bloco afro* Olodum, Gilberto Gil would release a version of Bob Marley's "No Woman, No Cry," under the title "Não chore mais." The song would become an anthem of the struggle to end military rule in Brazil. From then on, reggae in Brazil would be sung in clear Portuguese and would progressively move from certain tribal territories to the dimension of electronic mass mediation throughout the nation.

On March 18, 1980, Bob Marley, the avatar of the Rasta-reggae style, visited Brazil, establishing important contact with local artists. On May 26, 1980, Gilberto Gil and Jimmy Cliff played a concert in Salvador that inaugurated a successful tour through the principal Brazilian cities. About 50,000 people came to see them at the main soccer stadium in the Bahian capital. In the same year, Peter Tosh came to Brazil to participate in the Second International Festival of Jazz in São Paulo, and was featured on an extremely popular soap opera. These local events led to the dissemination of reggae in Brazil, inspiring a growing sense of identity and long-distance belonging in Bahia.

RASTA-REGGAE AND ELECTRONIC MEDIA

Reggae is a contemporary behavioral and aesthetic invention. Despite its connections with mento, calypso, and other Carribean musics, it is also the direct descendant of rock music, soul, and rhythm and blues. These musical forms emerged with new electronic media markets connected to radio, television, and recording industries. Marshall McLuhan sees the invention of radio as a "tribalizing drum." For radio has a cloak of invisibility that is manifested intimately from person to person, striking remote and forgotten chords.[15] The recent success of Bahian music is a perfect example of the "magical power" of the radio to broadcast hot information and encourage the acceptance of new musical and behavioral languages.

The cooperation between Rádio Itapoan FM and the pioneering WR recording studio in Salvador led to the popularity of *samba-reggae* and so-called *axé music* in the late 1980s. Until that time, local radio rarely aired reggae, despite popular acceptance. Several FM stations currently have weekly reggae shows, which reflects changes in public taste and radio programming. The story of reggae and the radio market of Salvador has as its principal protagonist DJ Ray Company. Ray was a passionate fan of Jamaican music and collaborated on the "Roots Program," which aired in 1979 on Rádio Cruzeiro. He contributed to the pioneering program "Rock, Reggae, and Blues," on Rádio Piatã FM, in 1982 and 1983.[16]

In 1986, Ray Company organized two programs for Rádio Itaparica FM, "Mama Africa" and "Reggae Specials," the latter devoted entirely to reggae. Besides presenting an extensive and rare repertoire of music, "Reggae Specials" featured interviews with artists and devotees of reggae music. Lino de Almeida, a member of the black movement, would regularly visit the show, stimulating provocative discussions around the issue of ethnicity and its link to the Rasta-reggae movement.

FIGURE 2.4 *Dressed in the Carnival attire of* bloco afro *Ilê Aiyê, Gilberto Gil (right) welcomes Jimmy Cliff to Bahia at the international airport of Salvador, 1980. Archive of A* tarde.

It should also be noted that 1988 marked the commemoration of the centennial of the abolition of slavery in Brazil, an event that would focus media attention on black culture. In the 1980s, while *samba-reggae* was in its formative stage, a particular type of roots reggae with a local inflection was also being constructed in Salvador. Initially, this musical style would be reconstructed by means of local versions in which the deep pulsations of the bass guitar would be replaced by a pop-rock attack, as in Gilberto Gils cover of Bob Marley's "No Woman, No Cry." However, Bahian performers would soon achieve success in the recording and radio markets with specifically local elaborations of roots reggae.

The local social and spatial context of the *blocos afro*, the reggae bars, and the Rasta groups, interfaced with the chaotic and infinite universe of the masses, was transformed by radio and recording markets in Salvador. In addition to the radio programs, Bahian reggae would enter the mainstream recording market in 1988 with the release of albums by the Banda Terceiro Mundo [Third World Band] and Edson Gomes, who would gain considerable attention in Bahia and the northeast of Brazil in the 1990s. More recently, Sine Calmon's album Fogo *na Babilônia* would achieve formidable success between 1997 and 1998. In 1998, the radio-push song of this album, "Nayambing Blues," was a huge hit during Carnival, the principal thermometer of Bahian music. During ten years of Bahian reggae production, only a few bands were commercially successful in the recording market. This may reflect a certain mistrust among black youth in relation to local media.

In 1998 the city of Salvador had approximately ten FM radio stations, and a third of these stations had weekly reggae programs. Itaparica FM and Salvador FM still kick off the weekend with reggae shows, and Rádio Cidade has a Saturday program called "Cidade reggae" [Reggae city]. The fact that the reggae programs all air during the weekend is telling. In fact, the term "reggae" is currently used by Bahians to mean "party." This leads us to conclude that reggae was culturally assimilated in Salvador not only as a musical genre, but also as a lifestyle marked by pleasure. Beyond these theoretical elaborations, Jamaica is not here, but reggae is here, persisting as a local presence.

NOTES

1. David Harvey, *A condição pós-moderna: uma perspectiva sobre as origens da mudança cultural* (São Paulo: Loyola, 1989).
2. Roberto Muggiati, *Da utopia á incerteza (1967-1984)*, vol. 2 (São Paulo: Brasiliense, 1985), 80.
3. See Steven Connor, *Cultura pós-moderna: introdução às teorias do contemporâneo* (São Paulo: Loyola, 1992); and Dick Hebdige, *Cut 'n' Mix: Culture, Identity and Caribbean Music* (London: Routledge, 1987).
4. Quoted by Stephen Davis and Peter Simon, *Reggae, música e cultura da Jamaica* (Coimbra: Centelha, 1983), 62.
5. Davis and Simon, 59.
6. Otávio Rodrigues, "Os rastas," fascicule of *Revista Pianeta*, n/d., 7.
7. Eric J. Hobsbawm, *Era dos extremos: o breve século XX (1914–1991)* (São Paulo: Companhia das Letras, 1995), 318.
8. Livio Sansone, "Funk baiano: uma versão locai de um fenômeno global?" in *Ritmos em trânsito: sócio-antropologia da música baiana,* ed. Sansone and Jocélio Teles dos Santos (São Paulo: Dynamis Editorial; Salvador: Programa A Cor da Bahia e Projeto S A.M.B A, 1997), 137; cited below by editors.
9. John Naisbitt, *Paradoxo global: quanto maior a economia mundial, mais poderosos são os seus protagonistas menores: nações, empresas e indivíduos* (Rio de Janeiro: Campus, 1994), 137.
10. Jorge José de Carvalho, "Imperialismo cultural hoje: uma questão silenciada," in *Revista USP* 32 (1996–1997), 68.
11. Antonio Risério, *Carnaval ijexá: notas sobre afoxés e blocos do novo carnaval afrobaiano* (Salvador: Corrupio, 1981), 20–28.
12. Antonio J. V. dos Santos Godi, "Música afro-carnavalesca: das multidões para o sucesso das massas elétricas," in Sansone and Santos, eds. 73–96.
13. Paul Gilroy, *The Black Atlantic: Modernity and Double Consciousness* (London: Verso, 1993).
14. Osmundo de Araújo Pinho, "The songs of freedom: notas etnográficas sobre cultura negra global e práticas contraculturais locais," in Sansone and Santos, eds., 182–184.
15. Marshall McLuhan, *Understanding Media: The Extensions of Man* (New York: New American Library, 1964), 339.
16. Antonio J. V. dos Santos Godi, "Reggae na Bahia: história de uma presença recente," in *Folha do Reggae* 3 (1997).

Carnaval

Carnaval is Brazil's most important cultural event, celebrated throughout the world's largest, officially Catholic country. There are many parts of the celebration of Carnaval, including street celebrations, grand balls, and competitions of Carnaval *escolas de samba*, or samba schools, that take place throughout the country. The most important of these competitions is the samba school competition in Rio de Janeiro.

Carnaval takes place in February or March each year. It usually starts on a Friday and ends on the Tuesday before Ash Wednesday, which is forty days before Easter. This Tuesday is known in Brazil as *Terça-Feira Gorda* and in New Orleans as *Mardi Gras*, both of which translate as "Fat Tuesday." It is followed by Ash Wednesday, which is the beginning of Lent, a season of abstinence and frugality as well as fasting; Carnaval is the exact opposite. On Fat Tuesday, there are balls and dances throughout Brazil. In Rio, the Sunday and Monday before are the days of the samba schools special group, the most elite of the samba associations' divisions. On Friday and Saturday, the lesser divisions compete; samba schools can move up and down in the divisions, depending on each year's performance (much like the Premier League in soccer in England, in which unsuccessful teams can move down a division, and successful teams can move up). There are many elements judged in these competitions, the most important of which is the samba, a dance with roots can be traced directly to Africa.

Samba Schools and Other Carnaval Traditions

FIGURE 2.5 *Vila Isabel Samba School during Carnaval procession, 2006*

Carnaval came to the New World with Catholicism, but the tradition of Carnaval predates Christianity. There is some debate as to whether its origins are Greek or Roman; was it a celebration of Dionysius or Bacchus? In Roman times, there was a spring festival that included a temporary subversion of civil order, including wine, song, costumes and masked dancers, traditions that continue to modern-day Europe and the Americas. In France and Italy, traditions include a variety of events, with the Carnival of Venice remaining one of the most popular events for tourists today. The Portuguese brought their Carnaval traditions to Brazil, but they lacked the finesse of the French and Italian varieties.

In Brazil, a number of Carnaval activities remain popular today. One is the *entrudo*, a street tradition that includes general mayhem, spraying people with water guns, and other "fun" activities. Although it is past its peak popularity, remnants of this tradition remain today. On the opposite end of the Carnaval spectrum are the *Grande Sociedades,* the Great Societies, upper-class activities that included street parades, floats, and elaborate costume balls. The middle classes did not want to be left out, and they developed several street traditions, the most important of which are the *blocos*, the most important of which is *Cordão de Bola Preta*.

FIGURE 2.6 *Cordão de Bola Preta in 2008*

Blocos started much like the name in English implies, block parties. There were many blocos throughout the city of Rio de Janeiro where residents would celebrate Carnaval with dancing, costumes, and general revelry. In recent years, blocos have become much more popular and have grown in number; today, in Rio, there are over 400 blocos, to a large extent due to skyrocketing costs associated with other traditions such as samba schools. The Cordão de Bola Preta is a Carnaval celebration that has taken place on the Saturday of Carnaval since the early 20th century (in 2018 it turned 100!). It takes place in downtown Rio de Janeiro and has grown in number to more than two million participants. Cordão, or rope, refers to a dance procession much like a conga line in the United States. Participants dance through the streets, following the leader in a massive celebration of all things Carnaval.

The lower classes developed a tradition in the favelas and other lower-class neighborhoods called the *rancho*, which was similar to the bloco. These street celebrations evolved so that they included a theme for costumes and a theme samba, a master of ceremonies and a flag bearer, and a unified choreography that coordinated with the themes. Eventually, in the 1920s, these ranchos started competing, with several newspapers sponsoring multiple competitions. Over time, these competitions grew in popularity and size, with the number and size of the groups growing from a few dozen to several hundred. By the 1930s, these competitions were the most popular of the Carnaval celebrations and came to dominate

FIGURE 2.7 *Grande Rio Samba School, 2008*

the others. These groups organized into societies that would meet and rehearse throughout the year; they came to be known as samba schools.

By the 1950s, samba schools organized into distinct divisions according to their size and their quality in competitions. Much like the Premier League in soccer, these samba schools could move up or down in divisions depending on their success, or lack thereof. These samba schools diminished in number but grew in size to several thousand in each school, all processing through a boulevard in Rio's downtown. By the 1980s, it became apparent that the numbers were so large, and the angles and lighting were so difficult for television, that the city of Rio de Janeiro built a stadium dedicated to Carnaval competitions, the *Sambódromo*. The city justified the expense and effort by building multi-purpose structures in this stadium, functioning as a school during the year with seating above for the samba school competitions. It quickly became apparent that these structures were not well suited for school buildings, so that idea was quickly abandoned. Smaller copies of this stadium were built in other Brazilian cities that also developed samba schools and competitions, but the Rio competition remains the most popular event in Brazil, broadcast throughout the country and beyond.

FIGURE 2.8 *Sambódromo during Carnaval*

With the construction of the Sambódromo, samba school competitions increased in popularity and exposure due to live broadcast on national television, and as a consequence, grew in size. A school in the top division today can have as many as 5,000 participants, of whom approximately 500 are in the percussion section. As they grew, a new revenue stream developed: Carnaval tourism that includes participation in samba schools, both for Brazilians and foreigners; it is possible to buy a spot in a samba school online. The issue for the samba schools was the fact that these tourists did not know the dance or the lyrics of the samba. The solution was to develop commercial costume groups, or wings, within each school that would not be counted in the judging; participants in these wings would get no training, only general instructions as to choreography, and often are shuttled in from major tourist hotels. A consequence of this income stream is price inflation, pricing many residents of the traditional neighborhoods associated with these schools, for the most part poor and people of color, out of samba schools. These residents are participating less and less in samba schools, and tourists from Brazil and elsewhere are becoming more and more the norm in samba school competitions, in effect bleaching Carnaval from its Afro-Brazilian roots. As a result, other forms of celebration such as blocos are growing in popularity. Today, millions of people participate in the hundreds of blocos, many formed very recently, starting their celebrations weeks before the official start of Carnaval.

Carnaval is undoubtedly the most important cultural event in Rio de Janeiro and Brazil in general. The music and dance traditions of Carnaval come from Afro-Brazilian culture, specifically samba. Embedded in Carnaval traditions are issues of class and race, religious and secular celebrations. While the samba school traditions are still the most recognizable part of Carnaval, these schools are increasingly populated by people not of color, and the traditional participants have moved to other celebratory traditions because of the increasing costs of samba schools.

Reading #2

The other reading for this chapter, "From Popular Culture to Microenterprise: The History of Brazilian Samba Schools," explores the history of Carnaval and samba schools in Rio de Janeiro, from the first, prototypical samba schools of the 1920s that developed in Rio's slums to the modern era and their expansion into mainstream culture. The author discusses the political, economic, and cultural forces that drove the change from a popular cultural phenomenon to a microenterprise and tourist attraction, dependent on outside influences and financing to survive. These conditions have continued and intensified in recent years.

FROM POPULAR CULTURE TO MICROENTERPRISE: THE HISTORY OF BRAZILIAN SAMBA SCHOOLS

Alison Raphael

Rio de Janeiro's annual Carnival is touted by the country's national tourism agency as the "greatest popular festival in the world." Indeed, the vibrant and colorful all-night parade features an endless stream of luxuriously costumed dancers and singers, rich and poor alike, moving to the rhythm of the samba—considered to be Brazil's major contribution to the world of popular music. In Brazil the samba and the Samba Schools (the organized groups that parade on Carnival night) are widely viewed as examples of *cultura popular*, or popular culture: both have their origins among the city's poor, Black population and, today, participation by the popular masses remains high.

Many in Rio argue, however, that the Carnival has lost its authenticity, its spontaneity—its popular flavor. At the center of the argument are the Samba Schools, which have undergone important changes since the first school was founded in 1928. This article describes how the Samba Schools have been used as a convenient vehicle through which the larger society has coopted and undermined a genuine manifestation of popular culture. This article is extracted from doctoral research undertaken in the mid-1970s, which examines this theme as well as the impact of the Samba Schools on race relations in Rio.[1] Here, a description of the origins of the samba and its importance to the Afro-Brazilian community is followed by an explanation of how the Samba Schools emerged and were transformed over the years. Relying on primary and secondary sources as well as oral interviews with longtime Samba School members, this article attempts to describe the destruction of a genuine manifestation of popular culture.

THE ORIGIN OF THE URBAN SAMBA

The urban samba originally emerged from the slums of turn-of-the-century Rio de Janeiro. Its beginnings lay in the rhythmic drumbeats that traditionally accompanied African religious

Alison Raphael, "From Popular Culture to Microenterprise: This History of Brazilian Samba Schools," Latin American Music Review / Revista de Música Latinoamericana, vol. 11, no. 1, pp. 73-83. Copyright © 1990 by University of Texas Press. Reprinted with permission.

ceremonies brought to Brazil by African slaves. The African Dictionary of Umbanda terminology defines the Sudanese word *san-ba* as meaning "to pray." In Rio, one of the urban centers where Afro-Brazilians congregated in large numbers following emancipation in 1888, elderly Black religious leaders recently arrived from rural areas met frequently with younger, more streetwise mulattos in the homes of female community and religious leaders. A number of the earliest composers of samba are reported to have been *paes de santo*, or leaders of Afro-Brazilian religious cults. Over a period of some twenty years, the result of this interchange was a softening of the persistent drumbeat (*batuque*) of African religious ceremonies and an improvisation of lyrics to accompany it, which evolved into the samba as it is known today.

The samba became the chief social mobilizer within Rio's Afro-Brazilian community; to be invited to a samba in 1928 was roughly equivalent to being invited to an all-night party in the 1980s. One prominent samba dancer described to an interviewer in the 1970s what samba meant to the Afro-Brazilian community five decades earlier: "The samba was our family, our Sunday stroll, our movies, our lover. It was all we really knew of happiness there on the *morro* [hillside slum]."[2]

This was an era during which racism was widely prevalent in Brazilian society. Only recently freed from slavery, Blacks were still viewed by most Brazilians of Portuguese descent as inferior; most were uneducated and lived in precarious conditions. Afro-Brazilian religions were seen as akin to witchcraft and sorcery and were feared by the larger white society; the samba, with its possible origins in Afro-Brazilian religious celebrations, was not distinguished as a separate musical form for many years. From the turn of the century until the late 1920s the samba—as a musical phenomenon—was largely ignored by white Brazilians. Newspapers from the era show that rather than appreciate Afro-Brazilian music, whites in Rio instead called upon the police to deal harshly with Brazil's musical slum-dwellers. One contemporary letter to the editor proclaimed: "From Thursday to Friday, From Saturday to Sunday, all night long, these peoples' *batuque*, their screaming and the songs of these detestable revelers disturbs the sleep of their neighbors."[3] At Carnival time, Blacks who danced and sang on the streets or in public plazas were frequently attacked by the police. The city was attempting to develop into a European-style capital, and the prevalent ideology was that Blacks and mixed-race persons constituted a plague on the city's—and the nation's—future.[4]

During the course of the 1920s, although these attitudes prevailed, some members of the larger society developed an appreciation of the samba. The appearance of the radio and the record player during these years played an important role in this process; popular singers began seeking new material and began to buy—and sometimes steal—songs written by composers from Rio's slums. In an interview with a Brazilian journalist, a composer and founder of one of Brazil's top Samba Schools recalled how this process took place. His description is indicative of the perception of samba as a noncommercial, community phenomenon within the Afro-Brazilian population.

> Clovis came to tell me that Mario Reis [a then-popular white singer] wanted to buy one of my sambas. I told Clovis that I wasn't selling anything, that Mario Reis must be crazy. Buy a samba? For what? And Clovis said, "Ah,

sell, because he's going to make a record," and so forth. Although I wasn't planning to sell anything, Clovis insisted, so I went down to meet Mario Reis.

I got there, sang the samba Mario Reis wanted to hear, and he asked me how much I wanted for it. I said I didn't know much about prices. Then I whispered to Clovis, "I'm going to ask him for fifty *contos.*" Clovis replied, "You're crazy, ask him for five hundred and he will give it to you." But I didn't believe him. "Wait a minute, that man isn't crazy enough to give me five hundred *contos* for a samba!" So, I asked for three hundred. And he gave it to me.[5]

During this period, the samba had been evolving from its original hot drumbeat to a softer, more lyrical rhythm appropriate for the creation of love songs and other commercially viable lyrics. As the samba gained popularity in the late 1920s, a group of Black and mulatto Carnivalgoers and samba composers created the first Samba School and entered their parade in the Carnival competition in 1928. As legend has it, they called themselves a "Samba School" because their headquarters was located across the dirt lane from the neighborhood primary school and because they were proud to proclaim that they were the teachers of samba.

Until then, Rio's poor Black population had been largely excluded from the Carnival. The parade was dominated by clubs representing the city's white elite, known as the Grandes Sociedades, or High Society Clubs, whose specialty was political satire. The more established working-class neighborhoods in Rio, inhabited mostly by mulattos and Blacks, paraded on Carnival day in the form of "Ranchos," a tradition from Brazil's northeast, with costumes, musical instruments, and an overall theme. Both groups received a government subsidy to help finance their parades.

Blacks from the hillside slums and the outlying "suburbs" were not included in the formal Carnival. Instead, they joined together spontaneously in what were called *blocos de sujos*, or "ragamuffin bands," and went to the streets to sing and dance in an informal and disorganized fashion. The *blocos* had no fixed membership and little or no leadership; they were simply groups of friends from different neighborhoods who got together at Carnival time to sing and dance the samba. They dressed, sang, and danced as they pleased and traditionally visited other neighborhoods, asking for money from local merchants and passersby. Sometimes *blocos* from different neighborhoods clashed—usually over women, according to most informants. The *blocos* were often attacked by Rio's police. Following the formation of the first Samba School, numerous *blocos* converted their groups to Samba Schools, with an eye toward increasing their legitimacy and averting police repression.

The spirit among the newly forming schools in the late 1920s and early 1930s was one of friendship and mutual assistance. The leaders from the better-developed schools visited other *blocos* to help them organize and grow. These representatives of other neighborhoods were highly respected and their help was welcomed: the spirit was one of cooperation rather than competition.[6] The groups continued the longstanding *bloco* tradition of parading in each other's neighborhoods and serenading local crowds. One elderly *sambista* involved in the formation of what is today one of Rio's top Samba Schools (Portela) provided the following description of an early Samba School, originally called Vai Como Pode, or Come as You Can.

We had no intention of forming a Samba School. Nobody had given it a thought. I was only sixteen or seventeen. We used to live at my friend Paulo's parents' house. After a while, we had to move because we were disturbing Paulo's family with our noise. Se we decided to get ourselves a place.

But we weren't planning a Samba School. It was just to be a Center where we could spend time, play dominos, talk, relax. We were looking for a social environment, because social interaction is necessary to develop the mind.

Well, from there it kept growing. First Paulo wrote a samba, then me, and then Caetano wrote one. It began growing and pretty soon it was no longer just us three, but we were the leaders. It kept going, going, going, getting bigger and developing. Then, in 1932, we had to form a directorate. Caetano was the secretary, because he was the only one who knew how to do that sort of work. Paulo organized the group, and I was the treasurer. We had been called "Vai Como Pode," but the secretary of the auxiliary guard didn't think that was a good name and suggested we use the name of the street where we were located. So we took the name Portela. Many times I used to pay the rent on our little shack instead of paying rent on my own room.[7]

The regulations to which the informant, Rufino dos Reis, refers were imposed by the mayor appointed by Getulio Vargas to govern Rio when he took power in 1930. His appointee, Pedro Ernesto, sensed that there was much to be gained by authorizing the Samba Schools to parade. He offered the schools—and thus Rio's Black population—legitimacy and modest subsidies in return for their adherence to certain regulations. One of the new rules was that each school had to obtain a parade permit, which would be issued when the group registered with the police and provided the names of its officers and an "acceptable" name for the school. More important in the long run, however, was the ruling that each school must center its Carnival parade around an important event or figure of Brazilian history. These regulations reflected very well the trademarks of the Vargas regime: nationalism, corporatism, and populism. In any case, from the beginning of the 1930s the focus of the Afro-Brazilian Carnival celebration shifted from local neighborhoods to the spot downtown designated by the government for the Samba School parade/competition.

Ernesto's move represented the first government attempt to reach out to Rio's Black population, and the latter responded enthusiastically. A spirit of cooperation and mutual assistance pervaded in the early years of the Samba Schools. Paulo da Portela, the leader of Portela Samba School, was quoted in a 1933 newspaper article as saying: "It's not just a question of winning [the Carnival parade] but of the growth of the Escolas de Samba." The leadership and membership were entirely indigenous, coming from each individual neighborhood. Members gave from their own near-empty pockets to meet the schools' needs, and artisans gave freely of their skills to build the schools' floats. Female school members sewed costumes, men made their own instruments, the children caught the cats whose skins covered the homemade drums used in the rhythm section. Rehearsals for the Carnival parade were held in the dirt lanes of the *favelas;* when headquarters were built, local carpenters provided the labor.

Three other elderly *sambistas* and early members of Vai Como Pode described to me their memories of the early days:

> I've lost many a night's sleep because of this club. I've sweated, struggled, and cried for Vai Como Pode. We sometimes worked all night practicing and preparing for Carnival. We never had any money. Everybody worked for free and even paid dues. We worked all night and then at dawn, someone would make a snack, some coffee, a sandwich—and we would go straight to work. We were all factory workers—the directors, the members, everybody.
>
> Let me tell you what Carnival meant to me. It was our own thing. People made the greatest sacrifices—they even went hungry—in order to parade on Carnival day. They hocked their most precious possessions to buy their costumes and instruments. People wept when they couldn't parade, Once when my boss wouldn't give me the day off to parade, I quit my job! People really quit their jobs!

Recalling the early years of Portela's Carnival participation, the third informant noted:

> Everything was agreed on. Everybody understood each other. There was always harmony, understanding. We practiced in the rain and in the burning sun. Our costumes sometimes fell apart in the rain. Our headquarters was a humble little shack. But things were better then. People were more united, more united.

Another elderly sambista observed:

> Now the *blocos* are organized. In the past, they weren't. People just put on their straw hats and their sandals and did whatever they wanted. The *blocos* were great. We played, we had fun. I don't think they have as much fun now as we used to have.

OUTSIDE INFLUENCES

During the thirty to forty years intervening between these interviews and the emergence of the early Samba Schools, a number of trends converged to change the schools' fundamental nature and create the disharmony suggested by the last informant cited. The regulations imposed during the Vargas years as the price for acceptance into society were an important first step in the transformation that would change the schools from informal, community-led recreational organizations into small businesses controlled largely by outsiders. Other exogenous influences were the decision by Brazil's government to move the capital to Brasilia, thereby making Rio's economy increasingly dependent on tourism, and the growing effects of North American cultural and political influence in Brazil.

By offering the Samba Schools financial subsidies in exchange for their participation in the Carnival under certain conditions, the government brought the schools down from their hillside origins to the city's main avenues. There, their parades were judged by the city's elites, in accordance with standards that had nothing to do with the samba, its origins, its essentially Afro-Brazilian flavor, or the popular culture it represented. As the prizes became larger, the competition became more intense, undermining the spirit of cooperation that had prevailed during the formative years.

The pressure to win the Carnival parade—and thus the financial prize—meant that the schools began to orient their presentations to meet the criteria of the judges. One year in the 1950s, when it was suggested that audience applause should be the decisive factor in determining the winner of the Carnival parade, the Samba Schools threatened not to participate. They felt that judges more versed in cultural matters should decide the issue. Here was a telling statement of the extent to which the schools had abandoned their original roots and purpose.

In order to meet the criteria of the Carnival judges, the schools had to devote more and more resources to producing a "worthy" parade. One Carnival columnist commented in 1954 that the Samba School floats were making venerable historical figures into "dangling monsters" due to artistic ineptitude.

> Either the Samba Schools do not have artists capable of executing these works with finesse, or they don't have the funds to undertake artwork compatible with the grandeur of the spectacle as a whole.[8]

Elaborate floats and costumes and large rhythm sections with high-quality instruments raised the price of presenting the Samba School parade. In 1930, Portela had paraded with a ten to fifteen-man band, using mostly homemade instruments. By 1960 the size of the rhythm section had reached nearly two hundred, and new, manufactured instruments were being purchased each year. Within a year or so of the criticism of their floats, several Samba Schools began contracting with professional artists to make their "spectacles" conform more closely with the aesthetic standards of Rio's middle and upper class. Practices such as luring top dancers from other schools with offers of large cash amounts became common, as did payola to disk jockeys for promoting a particular samba theme song. One composer for a major Samba School told me frankly in 1977:

> The truth is that this is a war. Whoever has the best soldiers wins. None of the composers here is playing around. We are all here to win. That is where the conflict enters. The lucky ones with a friend at a radio station and a little money to spend . . . well, you know. . . .

Singers, dancers, and musicians belonging to a winning Samba School were more liable to be invited to make private appearances in clubs and private parties throughout Rio, thus stimulating further the desire of school members to win the Carnival prize. At a time when inflation was a major problem in Brazil, Samba School members were eager to profit personally from the popularity of their school. At the same time, artists, actors and actresses, and other members of the white middle class sought to associate themselves with the schools in the role of *destaque*, or superstar, appearing alone in luxurious costumes in the midst of the larger parade.

SAMBA AS A TOURIST ATTRACTION

Another important event influencing the evolution of the Samba Schools was the decision by Brazilian President Juscelino Kubitschek to move the capital from Rio de Janeiro to the newly constructed city of Brasilia. When the move took place in 1960, Rio was deprived of a great deal of its raison d'etre and its potential sources of revenues. City officials soon decided that Rio's tourism potential was great, and the Carnival was a natural attraction. Thus they began to exert more pressure on the Samba Schools to present a spectacle of luxury and beauty. They also began providing larger subsidies to the schools and offering higher prizes to the winners, thereby further fueling the growing spirit of competition.

New regulations were imposed to regulate the timing of each Samba School's parade, so that foreign tourists would not have to experience lengthy gaps between presentations. Samba School leaders had to become virtual efficiency experts, calculating how many people could parade down the avenue at a given rhythm in a given period of time. By the 1970s, some neighborhood members were being denied the right to parade on the basis that the school's group would be too big, thereby risking a penalty by the judges and jeopardizing the chance of winning first place.

As the requirements for presenting the Samba School parade grew more and more expensive during the 1960s and 1970s, the schools sought new ways to generate revenues. The larger, more established schools began to charge admission to their weekend "rehearsals," selling beer at inflated prices, and renting tables and chairs to those who could afford them. Taking this development one step further, some of the more enterprising schools began renting space in halls located in Rio's middle-class neighborhoods, while others built relatively luxurious new headquarters to attract wealthy samba "consumers." While some schools took out bank loans at high rates of interest to build these new facilities, others came under the control of gambling kingpins who financed their growth. As the Samba Schools became more and more entangled in the financial life of Rio de Janeiro, they looked less and less to their members for leadership and support. Increasingly, their focus turned away from the local neighborhoods and toward the city's white middle class for ideas and financial resources.

By the 1960s, acceptance of the Samba Schools had consolidated and interest in the schools became intense during the three months prior to Carnival. Middle-class intellectuals, in particular, looked to the Samba Schools as an authentic expression of national, popular culture and championed the samba in opposition to U.S. rock music, which was rapidly penetrating the Brazilian market. Members of the middle class began to parade with the schools, others assumed leadership positions. By the end of the 1960s, several of the schools had outsiders deciding on their Carnival theme, arranging the choreography of their parade, designing their floats, and dancing in key positions on Carnival night. Choreographers, designers, and others received large sums for their efforts. For the original members of the schools, however, simply finding the cash to pay for a costume had become an uphill struggle. In 1975, one school member who worked as a taxicab driver remarked to me: "Carnival is rough this year, really rough. In my section, the hats alone cost eight hundred cruzeiros." This was the equivalent of about eighty dollars at the time—or several months' salary for a worker earning the minimum wage.

Two white middle-class Brazilians who had become closely involved in the Samba Schools published a study in 1969 analyzing some of the issues that were emerging with regard to the schools. They attributed many of the schools' problems to the large-scale invasion by the middle class. Key problems, they wrote, were:

1. The break with authenticity and spontaneity in the Schools, the imposition of artificial forms based on exaggerated luxury. The groups are humble and poor, in contrast to the sophisticated exhibitions of wealth [by the middle class].
2. The exaltation of the individual over the group. The thirst to be seen in public has turned many Schools into showplaces for personal promotion. [The bad example catches on] and we find *sambistas* refusing to parade unless they receive the spotlight. The old and traditional solidarity is giving way to individualism.[9]

While these comments and an increasing number of critical articles in the Brazilian press stimulated the debate over the Samba Schools, they failed to halt the trends in question.

It is not difficult for the outside observer to imagine why the Samba School milieu is less agreeable, less fun for its low-income Black members than it was in the early days—prior to the schools' acceptance into Carnival and the pressures that this process has brought to bear. Yet interviews with the elderly *sambistas* revealed that only a few are conscious of the reasons for their disenchantment. One *sambista* whom I asked why things had changed so much responded: "That's what I'd like to know!"

On the one hand, the Samba School members whom I interviewed were unanimously enthusiastic about the involvement of outsiders in the schools, expressing the notion that it was a mark of prestige for the school. On the other, many were distressed at the way commercialization has affected them personally. A composer observed:

For a composer, samba is an inspiration—it is created walking from one block to the next. I don't *make* sambas—they're born! It's not supposed to be something that you are told to do. Now, they give you a theme and say 'Write a samba about this.' So, we fall into an obligation to produce, and we lose our spontaneity.

A female dancer told me:

I used to parade as a *destaque* (superstar) with a special costume and all that. I always made my own costume, Now I have to work and there's no time or money to make my costume. I just parade in one of the ordinary sections.

During my interviews with the elderly *sambistas*, few of them connected the commercialization of the Carnival and the Samba Schools with their own complaints. However, when I suggested that changing values and goals within the schools might be the cause of much of the negative trends, one informant agreed:

> There used to be more perfection when the school was smaller. Last year we paraded with more than four thousand people, everyone disconnected. It's gotten too big. But then there's the other side—the commercial aspect. They need to have those big headlines "X School Brings Five Thousand People to the Streets!" in order to take care of the financial element.

One of the most telling interviews was with an elderly woman involved in one of Rio's most beloved Samba Schools, Mangueira—named for the particularly poor favela where the schools' members live—since its inception and married to one of its founders and top composers. Speaking of the school's structure, she told me, with evident pride:

> We have a Legal Department, a Cultural Department, Social, Financial, and so forth. The majority are not from here on the *morro*. We have doctors and lawyers from Copacabana, Tijuca, and other places. They have helped the school very much, because . . . [pause] . . . the poor guy from here on the *morro* doesn't have . . . [pause] . . . can't direct a Samba School anymore because of the progress, you know? So we need capable people to help us out. When it began, the Carnival was such that any old person could be president of a Samba School. Even if he didn't know how to read, it didn't matter. But now, the school has to have culture.

Ironically, the neighborhood groups that once personified Brazilian popular culture had, by the mid-1970s, become entirely dependent on exogenous forces for their "culture." Early on, the state had begun to dictate the themes of the Samba Schools' parades and appointed judges unfamiliar with the origins and function of the samba to pronounce judgement on the schools' efforts. Later, using prize monies as a carrot, the state began to exercise decisive influence over the size of the parades and the types of costumes and floats used by the schools. By offering large prizes the state also stimulated competition among the schools and contributed to an inflationary spiral. In order to meet the demands of the state, the schools began paying outsiders to play key roles in the creation of their parades—functions that had previously been carried out gratis by school members. Finally, the schools had accepted the large-scale participation of white, middle-class outsiders in their Carnival parades. Instead of representing a spontaneous, indigenous, and authentic form of popular culture, the Samba Schools, by the late 1970s, had become profit-seeking microenterprises rendering services by contract to the city's tourism agency.

NOTES

1. Alison Raphael, "Samba and Social Control: Popular Culture and 'Racial Democracy' in Rio de Janeiro" (unpublished dissertation, Columbia University, 1980).
2. O Globo (Rio), interview with samba dancer Neide, April 1, 1978, p. 35.
3. *O Dia* (Rio), Jan. 1, 1922, p. 6.
4. Thomas E. Skidmore, *Black into White: Race and Nationality in Brazilian Thought* (New York: Oxford University Press, 1974).

5. Interview with Angenor de Oliveira (Cartola), in Sergio Cabral, *As Escolas de Samba: O Que, Quem, Como, Quando, e Porque* (Rio de Janeiro: Editora Fontana Ltda., 1974), p. 48.
6. Cabral, *As Escolas*, p. 44.
7. Author's interview with Rufino dos Reis, Rio, 1975.
8. *O Globo* (Rio), 1954, cited in Cabral, *As Escolas*, p. 125.
9. Amaury Jorio and Hiram Araujo, *Escolas de Samba em Desfile*, (Rio de Janeiro: Poligráfica Editora Ltda., 1969), p. 295.

Questions for thought:

- How are samba and reggae similar? How are they different?
- How has the hybridity of samba-reggae expressed itself musically and culturally?
- Trace the history of Carnaval celebrations in the black communities of Rio. What were the original celebrations that evolved into the samba schools?
- How have samba schools changed from their roots in the slums of Rio in the 1920s to today?
- How have these changes impacted on the communities from which samba schools developed?
- What was the reaction of Brazilian intellectuals to U.S. rock's penetration in the Brazilian market?
- What was the economic and cultural impact of government sponsorship of samba schools from the 1930s onward?

Activity:

Search for Carnaval in Rio on YouTube for the most recent year (e.g., Carnaval in Rio 2018), which will probably yield samba school processions in the Sambódromo. What are your impressions of the Sambódromo? Compare several of the videos in terms of music, costumes, floats, and choreography. Can you identify trends and patterns in the presentations? How are they similar? How are they different? Then, search Cordão de Bola Preta for the most recent year. How are these videos different from the samba school competitions? Are there elements in common?

Figure Credits

Fig 2-1: Source: https://commons.wikimedia.org/wiki/File:Brazil_sm05_tr.png.

Fig 2-2: Copyright © Flickr (CC by 2.0) at https://www.flickr.com/photos/45803876@N00/31911547722/in/photostream/.

Fig 2-3: Source: https://commons.wikimedia.org/wiki/File:Obaluaye_no_Opanij%C3%A9_Orossi.JPG.

Fig 2-8: Source: https://commons.wikimedia.org/wiki/File:Samba_school_parades_2004.jpg.

CHAPTER THREE

Argentina: It Takes
Two to Tango

FIGURE 3.1 *Map of Argentina*

Introduction

Tango is the national dance of Argentina. Its importance, however, goes far beyond the dancehalls of Buenos Aires and has been embraced in many parts of the world to the point that it can be viewed as a truly global genre. It can be heard and seen regularly in places as diverse as Helsinki, Tokyo, and Istanbul, and many, many other places. It evolved in its home country, beginning in the 1870s as a dance in the poor parts of the Argentine capital, moving more mainstream in the upper- and middle-class salons by the turn of the 20th century, developing into a song genre in the 1930s, and is now a global genre in many ways different from its Latin origin.

The Birth of Tango

As was stated in Chapter 2, many European dances were popular throughout the Americas during the 19th century. One of the most important was the polka, which came to the new world in the 1840s with a large immigrant population from Germany and Eastern Europe. These Eastern Europeans immigrated to many parts of the New World, including Argentina. The polka, which featured European harmony, melody, and instruments, formed a hybrid with African dance traditions, drums, and rhythms, varying throughout the Americas depending

FIGURE 3.2 *Tango dancers in Palermo, Argentina in 1890*

on slave and former-slave populations and colonial influences. The resultant hybrids are the most important dance genres in the Americas:

- Tango (Argentina)
- Plena and Bomba (Puerto Rico)
- Ragtime (United States)
- Rumba (Cuba)
- Beguine (Martinique)
- Maxixe and Choro (Brazil)

All of these dances appeared at approximately the same time in the 1870s and share similar characteristics. They were originally part of black culture that moved gradually into the mainstream. The differences in these dances reflect the differences in language and culture in different places throughout the Americas.

The number of African slaves taken to Argentina was much smaller than those taken to Brazil, and many who arrived in Buenos Aires were sent on to other Spanish colonial cities such as Valparaiso and Lima. Most of the slaves taken to Argentina were Bantu speakers from the Congo area, with some slaves coming from the Cape Verdes islands. Many of the black men were forced to fight in wars against Brazil and native populations, many of whom died in these conflicts. This disproportionate representation in the armed forces meant that there were many more Afro-Argentine women than men, leading to a great deal of miscegenation.

Argentina was a sparsely populated country until the late 19th century. Afro-Argentines mostly lived in marginal areas around Buenos Aires by the end of the 1800s. There were relatively few African slaves in Argentina, especially men, and there was a great demand for labor, leading to a surge in European immigration from Spain, Poland, England, Italy and later Germany, and rapid growth for the country and the capital. The population of Buenos Aires in 1869 was 180,000, but by 1914 it had grown to over a million and a half. This growing population brought many musical and dance traditions, and by the 1860s and 1870s dances such as the polka, waltz, mazurka, and habanera were commonly heard.

The etymology of the name tango is a source of dispute. One theory is that the name has African roots, although from which language is unclear, meaning a gathering place for dance. Another theory holds that it is a case of onomatopoeia, the word representing the sound of drums used in the early forms of the dance. Yet another theory holds that the word is from the Latin *tanguere* or the Portuguese *tanger,* meaning to touch (as in tangent).

Tango first appeared in the Slaughterhouse district of *Mataderos* on the outskirts of Buenos Aires.

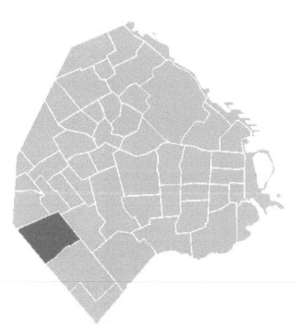

This was a rough neighborhood with a large Afro-Argentine population, and African-derived dances were popular. One such dance was the milonga, which mixed with the polka to form the tango. Some scholars suggest that this early tango was originally a solo dance for Afro-Argentine women, commonly danced in brothels and bars in lower-class neighborhood such as Matadores. From there, it started for find its way to middle- and upper-class neighborhoods, and eventually to Europe as Argentinians and Europeans took it with them on their travels known as the *Grand Tour.* By the early 1900s it was danced in Montmarte, the Bohemian neighborhood of Paris, and by 1912 it was all the rage in Paris and other European cities. There were tango teas, tango train excursions, and there were colors associated with tango (interestingly, orange was one of them).

FIGURE 3.3 *The Matadores neighborhood of Buenos Aires*

Tango was going through its first phase of globalization. It was an international phenomenon, popular in many European capitals. By 1913 it could be found in New York

City, and through the 1920s and 30s it spread throughout the world. By 1922, it was so popular in England that a set of rules for the "English" tango was published. All of this popularity did much to legitimize tango, and in Argentina it was more accepted by the middle and upper classes. Back in Buenos Aires, it became part of the musical and cultural mainstream, and huge numbers of sheet music publications and recordings were made; between 1902 and 1910, over a thousand recordings of tango were made in Buenos Aires.

As tango evolved, the musical forces became standardized in the ensemble known as the *orquesta típica*, a band commonly consisting of a string section of violins and sometimes viola and cello, a rhythm section of bass and piano, and occasionally instruments such as the guitar and flute. The core of the group is a type of button accordion called the *bandoneón*. This instrument takes its name from its German inventor, Heinrich Band (in Germany it is known as the Bandonion). The instrument is based on the concertina, a small button accordion. The Argentine version is a bit smaller than the German original, and the instrument is crucial to the sound of the tango ensemble.

FIGURE 3.4 *The bandoneón*

Tango-canción

By the early 20th century, tango was by far the dominant dance in Argentina. As happened with similar genres, a sung version of tango developed, known as *tango-canción*. The musician most associated with the development of the sung tango was Carlos Gardel (1887–1935), an immensely popular singer and composer. His songs were for the most part torch songs about love and loss, although his best-remembered tango-canción was "Por una Cabeza" ("By a Head"), which is about a racehorse losing a race by a head, and which is one of the most recognized tangos today, not least because it was featured in recent films including *True Lies, Scent of a Woman*, and *Schindler's List*. Gardel made several films, including a few in the United States, and unfortunately died in a plane crash in 1935. He is remembered today in Argentina as the most important tango composer before the 1950s.

FIGURE 3.5 *Carlos Gardel*

Nuevo Tango

By the 1950s, tango had lost some of its luster in Argentina. As a result, there was a movement to update Tango, spearheaded by Astor Piazzolla (1921–1992), who was famous as a bandoneón player who grew up in Buenos Aires and New York City, resulting in the *nuevo tango*. Piazzolla's desire to elevate tango to a more sophisticated art form took him to Paris, where he studied with the most respected composition teacher of the time, Nadia Boulanger (who had taught many noted composers, including Aaron Copland, Quincy Jones, Philip Glass, and many others). Boulanger urged him to continue with tango; he took his serious classical training and applied it to tango, resulting in nuevo tango, which he intended for concert performance and stage dancing, rather than the popular club setting of the traditional tango. He composed some of the most famous and popular tangos, such as "LiberTango," one of the most recorded of his works. He composed for many performing ensembles, including many *tangos simfonicos*, or symphonic tango. All told, he composed more than a thousand works.

FIGURE 3.6 *Astor Piazzolla in 1975, playing the bandoneón*

Piazzolla also changed the bandoneon's function in the orquesta típica. Traditionally, the instrument was in the background, an equal member of the ensemble, the musicians sitting in the group while playing melodic and accompaniment roles. Piazzolla would instead stand in front of the ensemble, using the bandoneon as the lead solo instrument for which he composed more complex, virtuoso parts. Other performers and composers followed suit, and the instrument remains the defining the sound of the nuevo tango.

Tango and Globalization

Tango had an international following early on in its history. As tango went around the world, it took on many local characteristics. Today, tango is an important musical and dance genre in many countries, and these adapted tangos that have little resemblance to the Argentine original. Nowhere is it more important than Finland, where tango was heard and danced as early as 1913. In traditional Finnish culture, public displays of affection are frowned upon; it is a culture in which touching of virtually any kind is inappropriate. Tango gives Finns a license to touch, to have physical contact, undoubtedly contributing to the immense popularity of this version of tango.

The Finnish tango is hugely popular, and there are hundreds of venues where tango is regularly danced in a country of five million people; the country is second only to Argentina in terms of tango venues. There are tangos events everywhere; it can be seen on the streets, in clubs, in dancehalls, and in community gyms. There are also dance competitions, as well as tango composition, singing, and performance competitions.

Reading #1

The first reading for this chapter, "Reinventing the Finnish Tango," gives a detailed account of the history and development of tango in Finland. It discusses the appeal of tango, an intimate dance, in a country in which public displays of affection are frowned upon and rare. The author includes in his narrative how tango developed both as a musical form and as a vehicle for Finnish composers, who have produced many uniquely Finnish tangos since the 1940s.

REINVENTING THE FINNISH TANGO

A century ago, Finland was one of the European countries to most passionately adopt the Argentine tango. Now a new generation is revitalizing the tradition.

Wif Stenger

Since the 1980s, the finnish tango scene has been dominated by a rather syrupy electronic pop version of the real thing—as epitomized by the annual Seinäjoki Tango Festival. One of the nation's biggest music events, it brings more than 100,000 Finns for a sweaty mass dancing and singing contest, cranked up by oceans of beer and blaring outdoor PA systems playing schmaltzy hits.

The dancing crowd and a jury together pick the Tango Monarch of the Year. The winner is guaranteed headlines in the tabloid press, a recording contract, radio airplay and steady gigs at dance halls in small towns around Finland and on passenger ferries to Tallinn and Stockholm.

In contrast, a new generation of younger city-dwellers is embracing and re-interpreting the more organic, elegant music of the golden age of Finnish tango, and even the Latin American original. With acoustic instruments and an energetic approach, they're breathing new life into the scene.

This year marks the 40th anniversary of the death of the greatest of all Finnish tango singers, Olavi Virta. In September, he was honored with a tribute concert at the World of Tango Festival in Tampere. Three young singers performed new takes on his classics, including Katwi Koivisto, a rather fierce-looking young woman with a pierced lip, minimal expression and dance moves, who delivered Virta in a deep, nearly gothic voice.

FIGURE 3.7 *Dancers at the 2012 World Tango Festival in Tampere*

She was followed onstage by one of the last few active stars from the golden era of Finnish tango, Markus Allan. Born into a Finnish Romany family in 1945, he began his career in the early 1960s with Virta as his mentor, also working closely with Finland's most legendary tango song-writer and composer, Toivo Kärki. In 1996, Allan gained an international cult following with his appearance in Aki Kaurismäki's film *Drifting Clouds,* going on to perform with the BBC Symphony Orchestra in London and at Carnegie Hall last winter. At 67, his voice is still tremendous and his stage manner charming.

Here, on one stage, was the past and future of Finnish tango.

Earlier in the day, the same red-brick building from 1901 hosted an old-fashioned *lavatanssi* or "stage dance" with two youthful bands, Tampere's own Sexteto Nautilus and Vallilan Tango, named after its scruffy home neighborhood in Helsinki.

Couples of wildly varying levels of skill, energy and passion whirled or shuffled around the room. Their approaches ranged from the giggly fumbles of beginners to the effortless together-ness of couples with a half-century of dance floor experience. The dancers revolved on the floor as the vocalists sang wistfully of fate, tears, dreams, sleepless nights and brief summers, their shortness a metaphor for the brevity of love and life itself.

Though the Finns do not seem outwardly passionate, with public displays of affection rare, the tango seems to be a natural outlet. Perhaps this style, with its tropical roots and melodramatic lyrics, gives this laconic people a way of tapping into passions that are usually kept under wraps.

FIGURE 3.8 *Dancers of a local dance association called Botafogo, based in the town of Seinäjoki.*

"Back in the 1950s, the tango was the only way to come into contact with the opposite sex in a way that was intimate but still proper and safe," Vallilan Tango accordionist Sakari Hyrkkö says afterwards with a grin. The local version of tango dancing is less overtly sensual than the Argentine original. The pair remains in contact but their bodies usually only touch above the belt. Their dance steps mirror each other and shoulders are held high.

"The feeling is similar but otherwise they're totally different," says the band's fiddler, Mari Koppinen. "The Argentinean version has more fire; it's more flowing and flexible." The four-beat per measure rhythm is the same in both tangos, but in the Finnish version the emphasis is on the first—as it is on the first syllable of Finnish words—while the Argentine original emphasizes both the first and the third.

And unlike most South American tangos, Finnish ones are nearly always slow and in minor keys. There's a darkness and melancholy that is also echoed in the nation's other beloved musical genre: heavy metal rock.

"People often repeat clichés about Slavic-Ugrian and Russian melancholy, but there's a bit of truth in them," says Simo Laihonen, drummer with Sexteto Nautilus. "A lot of those songs have Russian roots from the time before Finland became independent. But since then, it's grown into a form of its own in many ways here."

Indeed, tango dancing arrived in Finland in November 1913, four years before independence from Russia. A leading dance teacher performed two tango shows at a Helsinki movie theater and soon began teaching the dance. However the first tango songs translated into Finnish—and the first domestic original—were not recorded until 1929. And it did not blossom as an art form of its own until the 1940s.

Towards the end of World War II, Kärki "wisely . . . combined Russian romances and German marches into the Finnish tango," writes singer M.A. Numminen in his book about the tango.

"Back in the 1940s and 1950s, the best non-classical composers were writing tangos, like Kärki and Unto Mononen," Hyrkkö points out. "Nowadays the good composers just aren't writing tangos. So it seems that very few good new songs have come out in the past 10 years or so."

"The melodies in contemporary tangos aren't as good," agrees Koppinen. "They're quite simple and electronic. It's quite business-oriented, so they try to do them quite cheaply with as few people as possible, using synthesizers. But the results aren't as good as with real bands with lots of instruments."

Vallilan Tango, meanwhile, plays a fresh, rough-edged version of old dance music on acoustic instruments. They attract sell-out crowds, mostly in their 20s and 30s, for their annual May Day dance and end-of-summer Isle of Sheep festival in Helsinki.

And those crowds turn out to dance.

"People seem more interested in dancing these days," says Antti Alavuotunki, the band's co-founder and clarinetist. "There've been more really good dancers at our gigs in the past couple of years. I guess more people are taking lessons. When we first started in 2005, young people in Helsinki didn't really know how to dance to this kind of music. But we've helped to start a revival of interest in it."

So why the 1930s, 1940s and 1950s in particular?

"There's a certain romanticism surrounding that whole thing, those old bands, a traditional feeling and nostalgia," suggests Alavuotunki.

"This is the music I've been listening to all my life," says Koppinen simply. "My grandfather was a farmer who played accordion on the front lines during the war. Then he played it all the time at home. So it's in my genes.

I remember sitting next to him when I was a little girl, listening to him play tangos. For our parents and grandparents, it's part of their soul."

Last summer Vallilan Tango toured eastern Finland's lake district on a 1924 steamboat. The mainstream tango stars still relentlessly tour a circuit of dance halls in villages and provincial capitals around the country. These include Allan and a couple other active old-time stars such as Reijo Taipale, who recorded Mononen's iconic "Satumaa" ("Fairyland") half a century ago, and Eino Grön, 73, who winters in Florida and holds dual citizenship.

And while it is mostly a rural phenomenon, there's one regular tango dance spot in downtown Helsinki, Wanhan Kellari restaurant beneath the Old Student House. There are occasional dance events in nearby suburbs, including Pavi in Vantaa. This alcohol-free, smoke-free hall still stages dances between April and October, as it has since 1965.

One of the most bizarre moments in Finnish tango history came in 1974, when American avant-garde rocker Frank Zappa played an off-kilter version of "Satumaa" during a Helsinki concert that was later released as a live album (*You Can't Do That On Stage Anymore, Vol. 2*).

In that tradition, many Finnish rock, jazz and folk acts such as Alamaailman Vasarat, Nieminen & Litmanen, Mariska, and Lepistö & Lehti play their own versions of tangos—though they might be barely recognizable as such to aficionados in Seinäjoki or Buenos Aires.

FIGURE 3.9 *Wif Stenger is an American journalist who has lived in Finland on and off since childhood. He is an English news anchor with the Finnish Broadcasting Company (Yle).*

And indeed some Finnish musicians are seeking inspiration in faraway South America. These range from avant-garde accordionist Kimmo Pohjonen, who studied in Buenos Aires, to InTime Quintet, who play elegant versions of Astor Piazzolla's *tango nuevo* classics. Also strongly influenced by the propulsive tango nuevo style are Tanguedia Quintet and Otra Vez. The latter sometimes feature an Argentine singer, as does the female trio Las Chicas del Tango.

Taking such collaboration a step further is Aires de Finlandia, a pair of singer-songwriters from Helsinki and Buenos Aires who play Argentine arrangements of Finnish tangos such as "Täysikuu" ("Full Moon") and vice versa. Since 2004, they have released two albums—one in each country—with a third being completed in Buenos Aires this autumn for release next year.

And besides Koivisto, Vallilan Tango and Sexteto Nautilus, new acts pop up all the time to pay affectionate tribute to their grandparents' courtship music. For instance, last summer, a group of young men from Tampere and Turku knocked together an impromptu Virta tribute tour under the name August Saarinen & Vuolas Virta. As all these strands interweave, the future of the Finnish tango seems to be in good hands.

Another country in which touching is frowned upon and in which tango is very popular is Japan. It was first popular among the Japanese nobility as early as the 1920s, when it was brought to Japan by the Baron Megata. He opened a tango academy for the Japanese aristocracy. It grew in popularity in other parts of the social strata quickly, and by the 1950s there were over twenty tango orchestras

FIGURE 3.10 *A Tango event in Finland*

in the country. In 2000, Taro Hakashi, a well-known violinist, composed Japan's first worldwide tango hit, *Watashi*, which quickly was incorporated into the tango repertory around the world. In 2009, the husband-and-wife team of Hiroshi and Kyoko Yamao won *El Mundial*, the World Tango Championship in the tango salon category. Another Japanese dancer, Chizuko Kuwamoto, won the stage tango category with an Argentine partner in 2010. The Argentine Tango Dance Association of Japan sponsors many tango competitions and classes, and there are annual festivals as well.

Turkey is another country in which couples touching in public is not the norm and in which tango is growing in popularity. An indicator of this increasing popularity is the growing number of Tango festivals in the country. In 2004 there was one festival; by 2009 there were five. The numbers kept growing throughout the 2010s, reaching ten by 2013.

Reading #2

The other reading for this chapter, "Globalization and Tango," discusses tango as a global phenomenon historically and today. The authors highlight how tango became a global music in several interdependent ways, while remaining popular among the affluent in its native Argentina. They stress that this globalization took place in several stages and discuss tango today as a globalized genre at home, having lost its appeal among the poor of today's Buenos Aires and finding modern support from outsiders, especially tourists. They conclude with a picture of the contemporary tango and its presence in mass media, including films and recording, in the United States and elsewhere.

GLOBALIZATION AND THE TANGO

Chris Goertzen and María Susana Azzi

Over a century after its gestation in the slums of Buenos Aires and Montevideo, the tango has become a global music in several interdependent ways. It is global in the most literal sense of geographic reach, flourishing in Buenos Aires and Tokyo, in Saigon and Durban, in small towns in Scandinavia and in the U.S. It has attained and maintained such a reach through its distinctive and enduring musical profile and, more importantly, through several kinds of semantic flexibility. The tango bears strong yet mutable links to place and culture; it is variously but vividly perceived as belonging to the Río de la Plata culture of the Argentine and Uruguayan capitals, as the national music of Argentina, as more generically Latin, or just as pleasantly (or bizarrely) exotic, older dance music. It rewards the intense attention offered by aficionados in Buenos Aires, by a core of *tango kichigai* (tango fanatics) in Japan, and by serious devotees elsewhere, in addition to the passing notice of people exposed only to isolated dances in movies or at an ice-skating rink. For different populations, the tango is either a historical footnote, a healthful hobby, or a stunningly complex and all-consuming focus for emotional life.

The message of the tango is borne by dance and music elements that were rich and culturally diverse from the very beginning—one might have predicted the eventual global appeal of the tango from the global nature of its genesis and from pivotal moments in its early history. The

Chris Goertzen and María Susana Azzi, "Globalization and the Tango," Yearbook for Traditional Music, vol. 31, pp. 67-76. Copyright © 1999 by International Council for Traditional Music. Reprinted with permission rich and volatile cultural ferment of the late 19th-century slums of Buenos Aires and Montevideo brought together immigrants from Europe, especially Italians, and an ethnically mixed array of native Argentines looking for work in, for example, the meat industry and the growing export trade to Great Britain. The rhythmic underpinning of the tango is generally attributed to a black population of which few discernible traces remain; other elements are assigned to other Argentine ethnic and racial groups (see, e.g., Natale 1984 and Azzi 1991:76). Whether or not they are demonstrable, the tango's ethnically and racially inclusive roots help to justify the claim that, although always associated primarily with *porteños* (the name Buenos Aires' citizens give themselves), the tango is Argentina's national music.

The largely male underculture of turn-of-the-century Buenos Aires, reinforced by sympathetic upper-class men, first shaped the tango's wild, sensual choreography, many of its musical characteristics, some of its textual themes, and its linguistic texture. With the last term we refer to the peppering of lyrics with *lunfardo*, a lower-class dialect of Buenos Aires (see Gobello 1991). This first period, the *guardia vieja* (old guard), extended through the mid-1910s, when the tango first became internationally famous. (It is rare today to hear *guardia vieja* tangos or ensembles.) Most members of the Argentine upper class disdained the tango at first. But it was savored by rakes who sought out danger by rubbing shoulders with *compadritos* (stylish thugs with knives) in *arrabales* entertainment centers, rakes who would help transport the tango to Europe. In about 1910 the tango began a double journey: it shifted from tough slums to downtown cafés in Argentina, and at roughly the same time it became all the rage in Paris and then London. In Europe, it was the latest daring dance adopted by the new generation, and it provoked gratifying outrage from the European Catholic Church (including Pope Pius X) as well as from the Argentine diplomatic corps.

Although the dance was moving under its own power from slum to the center of Buenos Aires in the early 1910s, its conquering of Paris accelerated and amplified this shift. This process reflects what Slobin has termed "validation through visibility . . . when a higher profile causes a local or regional population to reconsider its own traditions, and the occasion for this moment is usually outside prompting" (1992:11). However, it was less the original constituency of the tango affected here than Buenos Aires' upper crust, which routinely validated its status through Parisian influence. Argentina, the most European country in South America, apes the state it would most like to resemble—France—through focusing national identity on its capital. Endorsement from abroad, especially from Paris, boosted upper-class domestic appreciation of the tango time after time; for example, it helped to legitimize Astor Piazzolla's innovations after World War II (that he studied with and was encouraged by Nadia Boulanger in 1954–55 certainly helped too). Foreign endorsement also fueled the revival based on staged dance that began with the 1983 Paris debut of the show *Tango Argentino*.

A second round of international popularizing of the tango followed its transformation in the late 1910s into the *tango-canción*, with more emphasis on newly serious texts that were more consistently sad. Around this time, Carlos Gardel, at first an urban singer of folklore genres conveyed to the city by rural migrants and itinerant folk singers (the *payadores*), transferred his attention to the tango, and through skilled showmanship and fine singing linked his name with the genre. This coupling of genre transformation with the appearance of a signature performer marks the beginning of the tango's *Epoca de Oro* (Golden Age), which lasted into the early 1950s. In Argentina, Gardel sang while wearing suave nightclub attire that advertised the tango as belonging to chic Buenos Aires and thus to European fashion. In Europe he adopted the complementary strategy of portraying the tango as generically Argentine, often donning the most distinctive national costume, although this costume was less characteristic of the metropolis home to the tango. He did wear gaucho garb in Argentina at a performance for the Prince of Wales (Collier 1986:86); in this case he was physically home, but the performance venue had become European.

While in Paris, Gardel probably visited El Garrón, a cabaret which was then Paris' strongest redoubt of tango music, and which Rudolph Valentino frequented (Collier 1986:81–82). We don't know if they met, but Gardel's and other tangueros' habit of wearing gaucho costumes when performing in Europe must in some way be behind Rudolph Valentino's quasi-gaucho dress in the 1921 silent film, *Four Horsemen of the Apocalypse*. Gardel's gaucho garb may have been glamorized, but Valentino's film costume—supplied by the studio and actually more Andalusian than Argentinian—established a near-imaginary stereotype. Featuring the tango in this widely distributed film, on the one hand, helped fuel the 1920s surge of the tango in industrialized nations of the north, and on the other, underlined the association of the reimagined gaucho with the tango, a link that, while ever more tenuous, was effective advertising among audiences with little knowledge of the dance.

The tango, as redefined in the cafés and tango-teas of Paris and London, didn't just go home triumphant, but stayed on in Europe and radiated out from there, for example, to Finland, where a modified tango became the central folk dance (Gronow 1973 and Isokangas 1994). Vernon and Irene Castle, dancers who spread several dance fads, carried the tango from Paris to New York and founded many Castle Tango Parlors. The Castles emphasized the relatively young, elegant side of the tango, minimized its sensuality, and seemed unacquainted with its sadness. Irene Castle stated that "when we danced there was nothing suggestive about it . . . If Vernon had ever looked into my eyes with smoldering passion during the tango, we would have both burst out laughing" (Castle 1980:86-87). Another observer of the time wrote,

> The much-misunderstood Tango becomes an evolution of the eigh-teenth-century Minuet. There is in it no strenuous clasping of partners, no hideous gyrations of the limbs, no abnormal twistings, no vicious angles . . . When the Tango degenerates into an acrobatic display or into salacious suggestion it is the fault of the dancers and not of the dance. The Castle Tango is courtly and artistic, and this is the only Tango taught by the Castle House instructors. (Marbury 1914:20)

This sanitized reinvention of the tango, appropriate in its new surroundings, constituted an early and powerful influence on how the dance would enter the ballroom repertoire, although Valentino would return the smoldering look to the U.S. tango, and the 1940s big band tango would also leave a mark. Today's standard English-language ballroom dance texts echo the time-hallowed misconception that the tango originated *on the pampas* among gauchos *ex-clusively* (e.g., Harris 1988:399; Ellfeldt and Morton 1974:48; Schild 1985:38). But it must be kept in mind that many outsiders would neither forget nor accept the serious passions of the Argentine tango.

THE TANGO TODAY: GLOBALIZATION AT HOME

Much of the modem support of the tango in its birthplace comes from outsiders, especially tourists, whose images of the tango must therefore be accommodated. The favorite music of today's poor in Buenos Aires is no longer the tango: while a fair number enjoy listening to or dancing tangos, their financial support of the genre is negligible. However, more affluent *porteños* still reserve a place in their hearts (and budgets) for the tango. The local government and the most informed fans support small but active formal organizations such as the Orquesta del Tango de Buenos Aires (the last of the tango big bands, with 25 performers), the Academia Nacional del Tango, and the Fundación Astor Piazzolla, plus a handful of clubs such as the Café Homero and the Club del Vino, which are outside the tourist mainstream in the northern neighborhood of Palermo Viejo. In contrast, two of the oldest neighborhoods near downtown, La Boca and San Telmo, have to some degree become "museums of themselves" (Kirshenblatt-Gimblett 1995:371). La Boca, a southern port *barrio* settled in the late nineteenth century by Genoese sailors and other poor immigrants, still contains a few tango bars. While tango festivals occasionally fill a much-touristed street called the Caminito, the link between neighborhood and dance is embodied principally in tourist *objets d'art*. The most common subject of these is the Caminito itself, but tango dancers finish a strong second.

Most of Buenos Aires' tango clubs now cluster in San Telmo, confirming their tourist orientation by their location. The Casablanca, among the most successful of these, is a favorite of guide books available in the United States, and aptly represents the majority of local tango clubs. An Andalusian (!) exterior leads to a room seating 380, with all chairs (and tables for drinks and ashtrays) facing the stage. A $35 cover (the Argentine currency is pegged to the dollar) includes drinks and a brochure, much of which is in both Spanish and English. As the show ends, one may buy a tape or CD of a similar performance. The brochure reproduces a statement of appreciation from Argentina's president and cites visits from dignitaries ranging from other Latin American leaders to tango aficionado Robert Duvall and to Eric Clapton. Shows such as those presented here are fast-paced Broadway-style revues including tango as dance, song, and concert music, often in addition to acts representing other Argentine traditional musics. Performances are virtuosic, but so short as to present the tango and other Argentine music in caricature, comfortably milking nostalgia.

A primary way that typical program brochures in such clubs assert the high quality of their performers is to note that most have toured Europe, Japan, and/or the Americas. This continued outside validation has a very practical function. The incomes of many skilled tango musicians and dancers are not limited to what native, insiders can pool together to savor variety and excellence in the tango. There are more performers with good incomes because they can ply their trade not just for those who appreciate them best, but also for somewhat—or much—less informed foreigners who visit, and for these and many other foreigners in their own countries. The main concert season in Argentina, as in Europe and the U.S., is the cooler half of the year; since Buenos Aires is in the southern hemisphere, and most foreign venues in the northern hemisphere, the top performers keep busy all year.

While live performance for visitors to Buenos Aires provides some financial support for the tango, sales of recordings are also important. Most of these consumers (both fans and souvenir-gatherers) are Latin American, though significant numbers of Japanese, Europeans, and North Americans buy tango recordings too. Latin American tourists relatively knowledgeable about the tango tend to purchase standard repertoire and performances that are not just old-fashioned, but old. Several factors contribute to this pattern of preference. These tourists seek authenticity when they buy tangos. Older tourists' perceptions of authenticity may be guided by more or less detailed memories of which tangos used to be performed in their homelands and which Argentine performers toured there. Buying a recording by a specific singer allows these tourists to display an intimacy with the genre. This informed nostalgia of fellow Latin Americans visiting Buenos Aires keeps a far wider array of tango recordings on downtown music stores' shelves (and thus available to *porteños*) than would be possible otherwise. In addition, the tango is taken quite seriously in some circles in Japan, despite language barriers (see Savigliano 1995:170-203), due to an asserted kinship between the tango and Japanese drama (Montes 1991); many Japanese believe in a special compatibility between the national psyches of Japan and Argentina. American and European visitors tend to know the least about the tango, and as a result concentrate on tapes and CDs whose very general appeal is made explicit in English titles such as *Buenos Aires by Night* (1993) and *Tangos for Export* (n.d.; "for export" may mean that all of the selections are instrumental, in line with general tango performance practice abroad, though occasional "for export" tapes contain some singing). The cover art of these recordings similarly retreats to a very general level, depicting a cabaret scene, Buenos Aires' central obelisk (which *tangueros* do indeed consider part of the tango landscape), or another prominent sight, whether or not it has much to do with the tango.

Until recently, it could have been said that the tango at home had experienced a relatively benign museumization through marketing. Among the Latin American tourist majority (including expatriate Argentine fans) who understand lyrics and know some tango history, many serve their educated nostalgia by buying recordings of specific performers from the past. The array of recordings needed by this population is also acceptable to less-informed Latin American visitors, to avid Japanese fans, and, when supplemented with very general compilations, to even the least informed tourists. The Argentine music industry, though normally eager to reap the benefits of changing fashions, has had little incentive to resist the museumization of the tango. Remastering old recordings is cheaper than producing new ones, expired copyrights are a bonus, and the 1930s-40s produced a rich enough legacy of good tango recordings to nearly saturate the market.

Taken together, the public and private institutions supporting the tango comprise much of the elite, formal side of Argentina's heritage industry, while heritage tourism constitutes the complementary but much larger populist arm. While these economic forces supporting and exploiting heritage contrast in both motives and means, the results they achieve are compatibly conservative for the tango. This is because the line between catering to nostalgia and searching for cultural authenticity is inevitably blurry. Both are value-added processes inventing images of the past, a time revised in the rosy memories of the nostalgic in ways that can be parallel to how that time is freshly imagined by heritage tourists.

Other less tangible but quite powerful factors impede significant change in the tango in Argentina. The first is bound up with the essential nature of the genre. The balance of meanings attached to any pop genre gradually tilts from novelty towards nostalgia, and from innovation towards authenticity, as its original fans age; surprises in text and music become less readily welcomed. From the beginning of the *Época de Oro*, the tango was explicitly nostalgic in most of its intertwined themes, and thus especially wedded to its own early days. Indeed, most *tangueros* are traditional in both habits and taste. The second factor is the issue of Gardel's celebrity. His urbane, poetic interpretations crystalized the identity of the tango song and, sixty-four years after his premature death in a plane crash, remain a sonic hagiography. It remains difficult for his successors to compete with him. The third factor is that the tango, as a national music, bears a certain unexpressed but weighty moral responsibility to remain respectable and easily recognizable, more important as a symbol than for day-to-day fun. Last is the tango's share in a worldwide phenomenon: the more music genres the mass media deliver to our doors, the smaller a fraction of our attention each of these genres can compel. We may have a long-term favorite genre or two, and may also keep up with current fashions. But beyond these few focuses, a clear and reliable profile will help keep smaller genres from falling out of the modest place they have on the radio, in stores, and in our homes and hearts.

However, despite the continued pressure of these forces, the tango is now undergoing a renaissance in Argentina. As the middle class refocuses attention on the tango, dance studios are proliferating and newspaper coverage of tango events increasing; a new television station devoted exclusively to the tango now supplements the all-tango radio station. These changes reflect an upswing in popularity of the jazz-influenced younger tango, particularly the music of Astor Piazzolla, who died in 1992. Piazzolla was himself a link between the tango at home and abroad; born in Mar del Plata, Argentina, he lived as a child in New York. He came to love the tango by listening to his father's collection of records by Carlos Gardel and Julio de Caro. Soon after his return to Argentina in 1937, he became active in the tango scene, first as a virtuoso on the *bandoneon* (the tango accordion), then as a composer. His striking compositions (he wrote over 3000), which were at first popular primarily with audiences for jazz and classical music, are now attracting crowds of fans among more traditional *tangueros*, a population that initially was not so welcoming (Azzi in Collier 1998:157-59).

THE TANGO IN SMALL-TOWN INDIANA

Of the authors of this article, Azzi lives in Buenos Aires, while Goertzen resides in Richmond, Indiana. This latter town's population of under forty thousand has no obvious special stake in the tango. But odd twists of fate bring compelling tango performances even to such locations. Just two weeks after performing at a gala White House dinner at which the Clintons feted

Argentina's President Menem, the Washington, D.C.-based ensemble Quintango brought virtuoso instrumental tangos by Gardel, Piazzolla, and others to Richmond's Earlham College. Why? A cousin of a member of the group works at that tiny school. The audience was packed with townsfolk, many of whom know the tango through ballroom dancing (there are a half-dozen dance studios within an easy drive), or through exhibition ice-skating at a rink just a half-hour's drive away. Others had gained or rekindled an enthusiasm for the tango after purchasing a recent widely distributed CD on which Yo-Yo Ma—a wonderful cellist with pop-star charisma and fame—passionately interprets works by Astor Piazzolla. Enthusiasm for the tango in art music circles is hardly new: some of the better-known art tangos are by Milhaud ("Tango des Fratellini," in *Boeuf sur la Toit*, 1919), Samuel Barber ("Hesitation Tango," from *Souvenirs*, 1952), Virgil Thomson (who composed several tangos), and Stravinsky (*Tango*, 1940, and the tango within *Histoire du Soldat*, 1918). Ma's CD, which garnered a 1999 Grammy (plus a second nomination) and sold over 600,000 copies, represents a fresh enthusiasm for the tango among prominent performers of art music. Just as at home, a reevaluation of Piazzolla's work is at the center of this new enthusiasm abroad: one can now buy CDs of his tangos as performed by Gidon Kremer (1996), Gary Burton (1998), the G-String Quartet (1996), and Daniel Barenboim (1996), among others.

However, the main exposure to the tango in towns like Richmond comes through the visual mass media, i.e., through watching TV or movies. Tangos appear on network television several times a week—while a given instance may caricature the genre as merely poignant, passionate, or silly, these impressions add up. The same holds true in movies, even blockbusters, in which the very same tango may be rendered as tender and evocative when danced by Al Pacino in *Scent of a Woman*, or as comic when strutted by Arnold Schwartzenegger in *True Lies*. A recent release, Carlos Saura's *Tango* (1998) will probably not be booked in any of Richmond's few (and cautious) movie theatres, but it will be available in video-rental outlets. No tango fan—or devotee of foreign films—could ignore reviews such as that by Maslin in *The New York Times*: "It's no slight to the lovers . . . that the kissing seen here is less torrid than the dancing . . . Eyes locked, bodies tensed, moves in perfect unison, [the dancers] need only display this dance's hypnotic blend of liquidity and fury, only revel in its dizzying complexity and split-second timing, to burn up the screen" (Feb. 12, 1999).

Tangos experienced outside of South America, as danced and seen in movies like these, usually lose their lyrics, or have new, lighter ones attached. Åhlén, a Swedish tango scholar, feels that this has resulted in a thorough and tragic impoverishment of the tango as it flourishes in Europe on the dance floor (1987). However, in films such as those mentioned above, the themes of tango texts may return, now transformed into visual symbols. Tango messages remain powerful and fresh today. Lyrics never contained many period-bound political references (in part, an oddly beneficial result of the history of censorship during the Perón era). It could be argued that the tango was born post-modern, i.e., that it resonates today in part because it predicted the essence of contemporary malaise.

MacCannell notes that "the progress of modernity (modernization) depends on its very sense of instability and inauthenticity. For modems, reality and authenticity are thought to be elsewhere: in other historical periods and other cultures, in purer, simpler life-styles" (1975:3). A concern for naturalness, nostalgia, and a search for authenticity are inevitable components of the "spirit of modernity—the grounds of its unifying consciousness" (ibid.). While tourists, in a literal sense, continue to provide much of the support of the tango and of many other repertoires taken to be characteristic of cultures attractive to travellers, many more of us are tourists in a broader sense, i.e., people who pursue authenticity in cultural materials we consider to be distant, different, and less tainted by the present. We buttress literal tourists' support of the tango in Argentina through buying tickets to exported tango events, by purchasing globally distributed tango products, and by visiting a substantial—and growing—number of Internet sites devoted to the tango and its stars.

Many genres that endure in the media age find their musical and lyric content changing less and less as time passes. Those that survive best will be those that are, like the tango, broadly based. Such genres need several audiences, differentiated by location or by socioeconomic levels or by generation. They find homes in niches immune to the cycles of fashion, and can be buoyed by symbolic associations with nation or race or ethnicity. To gain such a range of acceptance requires a balance between a durable semantic core and an apt potential for reinterpretation. When the perceived identity of a genre points more and more towards the past, it must do so in powerful and varied ways. Of course, the past is not just another country, but many. It can be mocked: an audience may feel more sophisticated because the past is so ludicrous. The frequent use of the tango to satirize passion among Latins or the middle-aged appears, for instance, in the recent movie *Addams Family Matters*. But most uses of the past paint it in a rosy light. Nostalgia, the search for authenticity, and, indeed, nationalism overlap as cultural processes. Both veteran *tangueros* and members of burgeoning new audiences associate the tango with a generalized earlier and better era, with the cultural setting of its origin, or with the time or place an individual first saw or danced a tango. At the same time, the semantic richness and varied audiences of this genre facilitate its transformation and renewal. The tango today is old, new, certainly vital, and undeniably global.

REFERENCES CITED

Addams Family Values
1994   Paramount film, dir. Barry Sonnenfeld.

Åhlén, Carl-Gunnar
1987   *Tangon i Europa: En Pyrrusseger? Studier kring mottagandet av tangon i Europa och genrens musikaliska omställningsprocess.* Stockholm: Proprius Förlag.

Azzi, María Susana
1991   *Antropología del Tango: Los Protagonistas.* Buenos Aires: Ediciones de Olavarría.

Barenboim, Daniel
1996   *Tangos Among Friends.* Teldec Classics International compact disc T2 13474.

Buenos Aires by Night: 20 Tangos Históricos de la Música Legendaria Argentina.
1993   EMI compact disc/cassette 7 89180 2.

Castle, Irene
1980 [1958]. *Castles in the Air.* New York: Da Capo Reprint.

Collier, Simon

1986 *The Life, Music and Times of Carlos Gardel*. Pittsburgh: University of Pittsburgh Press.

Collier, Simon, Artemis Cooper, María Susana Azzi, and Richard Martin

1995 *¡Tango!* London and New York: Thames and Hudson.

Ellfeldt, Lois and Virgil L. Morton

1974 *This is Ballroom Dance*. Palo Alto, CA: National Press Books.

Four Horsemen of the Apocalypse

1921 Metro film, dir. Rex Ingram.

Gobello, José

1991 *Nuevo Diccionario Lunfardo*. Buenos Aires: Ediciones Corregidor. Gronow, Pekka

1973 "Popular Music in Finland: A Preliminary Survey." *Ethnomusicology* 17(1):52-71.

G-String Quartet

1996 *G-String Quartet Plays Astor Piazzolla*. Koch Schwann compact disc SCH 364232.

Harris, Jane A., et al.

1988 [1950] *Dance a While: Handbook of Folk, Square, Contra and Social Dance*. 6th edition. New York: MacMillan.

Isokangas, Antti

1994 "Finnish Tango: Once a Fad, the Dance is Now a Tradition." *Billboard*, Feb. 12:1, 78.

Kirshenblatt-Gimblett, Barbara

1995 "Theorizing Heritage." *Ethnomusicology* 39(3):367-80.

Kremer, Gidon

1996 *Gidon Kremer: Homage a Piazzolla*. Nonesuch compact disc WEA 79407.

Ma, Yo-Yo

1997 *Yo-Yo Ma: Soul of the Tango: The Music of Astor Piazzolla*. Sony Classical compact disc SK 63122.

MacCannell, Dean

1975 *The Tourist: A New Theory of the Leisure Class*. New York: Schocken Books.

Marbury, Elizabeth

1914 "Introduction." *In Modern Dancing*, Irene and Vernon Castle. New York: Harper and Brothers.

Maslin, Janet

1999 "'Tango': With Sizzling Tangos, Who Needs a Plot?" *New York Times*, Feb. 12.

Montes, Jorge

1991 Notes to *Horacio Salgán; Ranko Fujisawa*. Music Hall compact disc MH 10-040-2.

Natale, Oscar

1984 *Buenos Aires, Negros y Tango*. Buenos Aires: Peña Lillo.

Savigliano, Marta E.

1995 *Tango and the Political Economy of Passion*. Boulder and San Francisco: Westview Press.

Scent of a Woman

1992 MCA Universal film, dir. Martin Brest.

Schild, Myrna Martin

1985 *Social Dance*. Dubuque: William C. Brown Co.

Slobin, Mark
1992   "Micromusics of the West: A Comparative Approach." *Ethnomusicology* 36(1): 1-88.
Strictly Ballroom
1993   Miramax film, dir. Baz Luhrmann.
The Tango Project
1982 Nonesuch compact disc D-79030.
Tango
1998   Sony Pictures Classics film, dir. Carlos Saura.
Tangos for Export
[n.d.] CBS compact disc/cassette 580.491.
True Lies
1994   Twentieth-Century Fox film, dir. James Cameron.

Tango Today

Tango remains one of the most popular and recognizable Latin dances, found throughout the world in a variety of styles and hybrids. There are dozens of tango festivals through-out the year worldwide, and the dance shows no signs of slipping in popularity. In 2009, tango was named to UNESCO's Representative List of the Intangible Cultural Heritage of Humanity, giving it protected cultural status and joining other traditions including Japanese kabuki and Indian vedic singing. In cities throughout the world one can hear and dance tango every day of the week. It has come a long way from the fringes of Argentina and remains vital and popular today.

Questions:

- How did the development of tango parallel the development of other dance genres in the Americas?
- In what part of Buenos Aires did tango first appear? Where did it go from there? How did changes in local population reflect changes in the dance and its place in society both in Argentina and elsewhere?
- Can you trace the globalization of tango from its roots in Argentina? How did tango first appear in Europe? How did it first appear in the rest of the world?
- What are the stages of tango globalization, and how does tango-canción figure in tango's global popularity?
- What are the musical and cultural differences between the Finnish tango and the Argentine original?
- Why do you think tango is so popular in Finland, Japan, and Turkey, countries that are culturally so different from Argentina, the original home of tango?

Activity:

Search YouTube for Argentine tango dance, Finnish tango dance, tango-canción and nuevo tango. Compare a few videos from each. What is your impression of these different versions of tango? How are these versions of tango similar in terms of music, choreography and performance style? How are they different?

Figure Credits

Fig. 3-1: Source: https://commons.wikimedia.org/wiki/File:Argentina-CIA_WFB_Map.png.

Fig. 3-2: Source: https://commons.wikimedia.org/wiki/File:Dancing_tango_palermo_1890.jpg.

Fig. 3-3: Copyright © wikipedia commons (CC by 3.0) at https://commons.wikimedia.org/wiki/File:Mataderos-Buenos_Aires_map.png.

Fig. 3-4: Copyright © Pavel Krok (CC by 2.5) at https://commons.wikimedia.org/wiki/File:Bandoneon.jpg.

Fig. 3-5: Source: https://commons.wikimedia.org/wiki/Carlos_Gardel#/media/File:Gardel.jpg.

Fig. 3-6: Source: https://avaxhome.unblocker.xyz/music/Astor_Piazzolla_in_conversation_and_in_concert_The_Next_Tango.html#.

Fig. 3-10: Source: https://commons.wikimedia.org/wiki/File:FinskTango.jpg.

CHAPTER FOUR

Mexico: Mariachi, Música Norteña, and Cross-Border Music

FIGURE 4.1 *A map of Mexico*

Introduction

The image that many Americans have of Mexican music is of a woman dancing around a hat, the "Mexican Hat Dance." Some may also remember Herb Alpert and the Tijuana Brass as Mexican music. Is that really the state of Mexican music? The answer is clearly no! There are many musical traditions that came together to make up Mexican classical, folk, and popular music, and there are local, regional, national and transnational implications in Mexican music today. The roots of Mexican music, as is the case in most of the Americas, come from Europe, Africa, and from indigenous populations, all mixing in unique ways depending on the colonial powers in specific places, the numbers and places of origins of African slaves, and the ways in which local populations were treated, exploited, and assimilated. Among the traditions that are important in Mexico today, and in Mexican populations in the United States and elsewhere, are music based on the Spanish and indigenous roots, such as *mariachi*, and music with Northern European roots, *música norteña*.

One aspect of Mexican music that is often overlooked is its African roots. African slaves were taken to Mexico since the Conquest, but the numbers were significantly less than in the rest of Latin America. Slaves never represented more than two percent of the population (as opposed to more than 30% in Brazil), but around 250,000 slaves were brought from Africa, most concentrated around Veracruz and Guerrero. Many Mexican genres have African influences. African rhythms mixed with European dances and instruments to form new hybrids throughout the New World; no dance was more influential than the polka, which blended with African and in some cases indigenous music and formed genres such as the tango in Argentina, the rumba in Cuba, ragtime in the United States, and música norteña in Mexico. All of these dances filled a similar cultural mix, often from marginal beginnings, and moved into the mainstream.

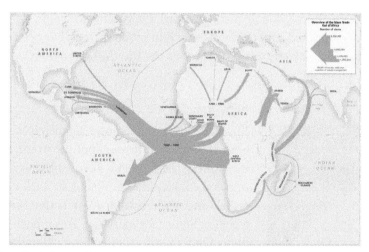

FIGURE 4.2 *Slave Trade Routes Map*

The Son Complex

Much of Mexico's music developed from the same sources, in varying degrees influenced by Spanish, African, and indigenous musical traditions. Several regional genres developed, many coming to be called the *son*, or sound in Spanish. The word means differing things in different regions, but, in all cases, it represents a folk genre that includes the use of string instruments, including members of the guitar and violin families and the harp. There are so many regional types that the entire repertory came to be known as the *son* complex, among the oldest repertory of traditional music in Mexico. There are some shared characteristics in most son traditions beyond the string instrumental ensemble, including a *zapateado*, or foot tapping, in the dance, an improvisatory singing structure, an alternation of double and triple meter (6/8 and 3/4), and a participatory nature.

Sones developed in different states throughout Mexico. One of the most well-known is the *son jarocho,* which developed in the state of Veracruz and remains popular in Mexican and Mexican-American communities. It is often played at fandangos, events similar to jam sessions involving singing, dancing, and playing. The most famous *son jarocho* is "La Bamba," made popular in the United States through a rock version by the Chicano musician Ritchie Valens (Richard Valenzuela). Traditionally, this version of the son is performed by a harp, the *requinto jarocho* (a small four-string guitar), a *jarana* (a five-string guitar), and sometimes the violin as well. The guitars are strummed percussively, playing tunes with simple harmonies.

The *son huasteco,* also known as the *son huapango,* is a version from the northeast of Mexico. Its ensemble traditionally consists of a *jarana huasteca* (a five-string rhythm guitar), the *quinta huapanguera* (an eight-string bass guitar) and a violin, and it is very popular at celebrations such as weddings. Another regional son that is popular on both sides of the border is the *son jalisciense,* from the state of Jalisco in the west of Mexico. Its ensemble is similar to the son jarocho but employs different string instruments: one or two violins, a *vihuela* (a small, six-course, double-strung guitar), the *guitarra de golpe,* a guitar which is struck as well as strummed, and the harp, which in modern times has been replaced by a *guitarrón,* a large acoustic bass guitar. This type of son was the basis of Mexico's best-known genre of music, mariachi.

Mariachi

FIGURE 4.3 *The Guitarrón*

Mariachi is one of the most recognized Mexican genres, both at home and throughout the world. The origin of the name of the genre has been subject to much speculation and conjecture. Many sources, including many CD jackets and travel brochures, state that the name comes from the French for marriage. This French connection is undoubtedly because of the French-installed government under the crown of Maximilian, Emperor of Mexico and the only monarch in the Second Mexican Empire. He was the brother of the Austrian emperor Franz Joseph I and was installed by Napoleon III of France, which had invaded Mexico in 1861. Maximilian ruled from 1864 to 1867, when his empire collapsed, and he was executed. All of that said, a connection of mariachi to anything French is a myth since it ignores the fact that the word predated the French invasion in literary references as early as 1852.

Mariachi developed from the son jalisciense, from the state of Jalisco in western Mexico, which traditionally was performed at social events on a wooden platform. The name mariachi perhaps comes from the indigenous name for the wood used to build the platform.

There are two types of mariachi, the traditional, or rural version, which uses strings and harp and goes back centuries and is very similar to the son jalisciense. The other type is the modern or urban mariachi, which uses the traditional ensemble with the addition of brass and the guitarrón. The modern version developed in the 1930s as mariachi became popular on radio. Around the same time, male performers started wearing the *traje de charro,* the traditional cowboy outfit of an embroidered waist jacket and pants with riding boots. This remains the standard clothing for male mariachi performers, and women often wear a variation of this outfit.

Before its popularity on radio, mariachi was a local, rural genre performed by semi-professional musicians, most of whom could not read music. With its modernization and popularity on radio and recordings, it came into the national and international spotlight, dramatically transforming the genre and the culture of Mexico. The group most responsible for this modernization was the *Mariachi Vargas de Tecalitlán*, a group founded by Gaspar Vargas in 1898. As was true with most mariachi, it originally was an all-string ensemble. Vargas moved his group to Mexico City, where

FIGURE 4.4 *Mariachi Vargas de Tecalitán*

the model changed to include brass; it was the toast of the town. The group was later led for fifty years by Rubén Fuentes, a trained musician who standardized arrangements of sones, which meant that all of the musicians in the group had to read music, thus becoming a truly professional ensemble. All of this coincided with the growth of radio (and later television) and recordings in Mexico. The group became the model of mariachi orchestration, with two trumpets, guitars, violins, harp, and guitarrón.

Mariachi remains an important and vibrant genre on both side of the U.S.-Mexican border. It grew in popularity and absorbed many aspects of Mexican musical history, embracing the polka and the waltz, similar to música norteña, and went north with the Mexican diaspora. There are many Mexican-American mariachi bands; it is so popular in Texas that many high schools have mariachi ensembles that compete in the all-state system. It has become a global genre as well and can be heard throughout the Americas, Europe, and Asia.

Música Norteña

As one might expect, the most important European country in terms of cultural and musical influence in Mexico was Spain. However, it was not the only European country with a strong cultural presence. In the 19th century, large numbers of Northern Europeans,

FIGURE 4.5 *The Mexican accordion*

including Germans and Czechs, immigrated to the New World. Many settled in the United States, in the rural Midwest, and in cities such as Chicago and Milwaukee, and many others settled in the Southern and Western United States. By the 1830s, large numbers of Germans and Czechs had established communities in Texas and Mexico in a wide swath that may be referred to as the German Belt, spanning both sides of the Rio Grande, which is a geographic and political border, not a cultural divide. As Texas became independent and later a part of the United States, these German communities found themselves in two countries but united by their musical and cultural roots. Many European dances—the polka, waltz, and mazurka, to name a few—became popular in northern Mexico and the southwest United States. The polka came to the New World in the 1840s and remains an important dance and musical tradition in Texas today. Over time, these northern Mexican polkas took on local flavors, evolving into what we now call música norteña.

FIGURE 4.6 *Los Tigres del Norte*

By the early 20th century, this music was popular throughout urban and rural northern Mexico and south Texas, along the Texas-Mexico border, and remains highly popular among Mexican immigrants in the USA. It has become the music of a "nation between nations." A distinguishing characteristic of música norteña is the use of German and Northern European instruments, most notably the accordion and the tuba. Although the accordion may be found in other Mexican genres, música norteña is accordion driven. The sound of the button accordion fused with the polka to form the basis of this music; both the instrument and the dance were creolized to local tastes.

Música norteña remains one of the most popular music genres in Mexico, but it is equally popular in the Mexican immigrant and Mexican-American populations in the USA. One of the most popular groups on both sides of the border is *Los Tigres del Norte*. Although originally from Rosa Morada, in the state of Sinaloa, Mexico, they have been based in San Jose, California since the late 1960s, and they reflected the bi-national nature of the genre and of música norteña in general. They helped make música norteña an international genre, modernizing the sound by infusing elements of rock and roll and other popular music genres, expanding into other dances such as the waltz, and embracing electronic and other effects. They have won many Latin Grammy Awards and have sold more than 30 million recordings.

Reading

The reading for this chapter, "Mexicanidad and Música Norteña in the 'Two Mexicos'" is about music in the "two Mexicos," one on each side of the border, using música norteña as a model. This music, also referred to as norteño, developed in Mexico and in Mexican communities in the United States. It has become one of the most popular genres in both communities and demonstrates the cultural, economic, and musical connections that bind Mexicans and Mexican-Americans. The author discusses the importance of this music in creating a "nation between nations" and music's role in maintaining these connections.

MEXICANIDAD AND MÚSICA NORTEÑA IN THE "TWO MEXICOS"

Catherine Ragland

THE CORRIDO AND NORTEÑA MUSIC
THE CORRIDO

Scholars in Chicano studies, Spanish literature, linguistics, and folklore in the United States and Mexico have produced ample research and writing on the corrido, but there is very little on norteña music, the popular music vehicle for the contemporary corrido. The traditional Mexican corrido is a topical narrative ballad sung, without a refrain, to a basic melody in waltz time (3/4); many contemporary corridos are played in a fast polka rhythm (2/4) more appropriate for a two-step type dance popular in northern Mexico and Texas. The corrido consists of eight-syllable lines organized in stanzas of four (quatrains) and maintains an *abcd* rhyme pattern, though this can vary at times. As a popular narrative song form, the corrido was the primary vehicle for the exploits of prerevolutionary and revolutionary bandit heroes from the mid-1800s to the early 1930s, and song topics range from stories about revolutionary heroes to U.S.-Mexico border conflict to illegal border crossing and drug smuggling. Since the early nineteenth century, the corrido has been associated with peasant and working-class communities of Mexico.

In an early study of the corrido, Armand Duvalier (1937) argues that the corrido descends from the Spanish *romance* (a classic poetic song form dating back to the 1500s, featuring octosyllabic lines alternating in pairs with rhymed assonance in the even lines). Vicente T. Mendoza (1954) agreed, attributing the corrido's features to the *decimal*, a Spanish poetic form consisting of one or more stanzas, each with ten octosyllabic lines. The origin of the corrido has since been a source of contention for scholars, particularly for the border scholar, folklorist, and Chicano Studies pioneer Américo Paredes (1958, 149–150), who challenged Mendoza and Duvalier by giving evidence of the rise of the romance corrido in New Spain during the mid-1700s and marking the appearance of the "true" corrido in the border region during the mid-1800s. Mendoza (1954, 1964) traces the corrido's profound connection to Mexican history and culture as it evolves from this period through to the height of its development in the 1930s [...]. However, all three scholars agree that the corrido ceased to be a true "epic" genre after the 1930s, since the songs could not be traced to specific persons, places, or events (Nicolopulos 1997). Paredes points out, moreover, that by this time the corrido had shed its "proletarian" audience and references as a result of commercialization of songs through the recording industry (on both sides of the border) and influence from the Mexican film industry (Paredes 1993, 136–138).

The majority of corrido recordings during the 1940s and 1950s were on independent labels located on both sides of the border, such as Ideal and Falcon in southern Texas and Orfeo in Monterrey, Nuevo León, Mexico. María Herrera-Sobek (1993) arranges many of these songs according to Paredes's research and collected recordings, ordering them chronologically and by popular themes. She identifies six primary themes of songs collected from 1848 to 1964, when the Bracero Program ended:

1. Cowboys and Outlaws
2. Working and Traveling on the Railroad
3. Revolution and Hard Times
4. Migrants and Renegades
5. Repatriation and Deportation
6. The Bracero Program

Herrera-Sobek (1993) identifies seven themes after 1964:

1. Songs of Protest
2. Border-Crossing Strategies
3. Racial Tensions
4. Poverty, Petroleum, and Amnesty
5. Love
6. Acculturation and Assimilation
7. Death

While there is no specific mention of mojado- or *narcotraficante*-themed songs, these protagonists (particularly the mojado) dominate nearly every genre except the first three (Cowboys and Outlaws, Working and Traveling on the Railroad, and Revolution and Hard Times), all of which were of the pre-1930s epic-heroic variety classified by Paredes. In fact, many of the songs listed under the remaining themes prior to 1964 are actually from before the 1930s, except for those associated with the Bracero Program, supporting Paredes's and Limón's assertions that the corrido went into decline (and decadence) after the 1930s. As Guillermo Hernández (1999) and James Nicolopulos (1997) have noted, however, a resurgence of corrido activity occurred in the late 1960s, with new compositions focusing on contemporary themes more closely linked to economic, social, and political developments among the Mexican immigrant laborer community in the United States.

The 1940s witnessed stylistic and compositional transformations of the corrido by composers and recording artists such as Los Alegres de Terán, Los Donneños, El Piporro, and Los Gorriones de Topo Chico, who responded to interest from Mexico City–based major labels; from both nationalistic and commercial motives, the labels sought out regional norteña artists with a potential for popularity throughout the country. These artists popularized the norteña ensemble along with newly composed *canción-corridos* that eliminated some of the traditional corrido characteristics, such as the opening address; the statement of location, year, and time; and the final farewell at the end of the song. While many of these recording artists were composing corridos with refrains and modifying corrido song form characteristics, they also introduced the norteña ensemble—featuring accordion, bajo sexto, and *tololoche* (traditionally handmade contrabass)—that would serve as the primary musical vehicle for the modern corrido, as well as rancheras (also known as *canciones rancheras* or *canciones típicas*; they are pastoral or "country" songs) and later the *canción romántica* and the Mexican *cumbia* (also called *tropical* or *colombiana* and based on the Afro-Colombian popular song and dance genre). Like the corrido, the ranchera is associated with rural life and culture and, since the 1920s, with working-class Mexicans on both sides of the border (Peña 1999a, 50–51). It is typically played in 2/4 time (derived from the polka) with the stress on the off-beats (two and four, in terms of eighth notes) for dancing. However, Paredes (1993, 139), along with later scholars such as José Limón (1992, 40–42) and María Herrera-Sobek (1993, 225–228), notes that contemporary norteña groups are still performing and commercially recording many pre-1930s epic corridos, thus preserving and perpetuating the song form.

While the canción-corrido maintained the corrido's strophic form and rhyme scheme, it added other popular song features such as refrains and instrumental interludes after stanzas. Early corridos had lasted twenty minutes or more, depending on the singer's elaborations on the storyline, but songs were shortened to the three minutes required by 45 rpm vinyl recordings. However, though the canción-corrido dominated recorded output after the 1940s, later corrido scholars, such as John Holmes McDowell (1972, 1981) and Herrera-Sobek (1990, 1993), focused on corridos written and composed in the traditional style that Duvalier (1937) and Mendoza (1964) had outlined. Some scholars, such as Limón (1992, 40–42), believed that continued research into "authentic" heroic and conflict corrido texts would remind the Mexican American community of the traditional heroic-epic songwriting and would serve as a historical and ideological expression of resistance, political and cultural autonomy, and the fight against commercialization.

Paredes dismissed these shorter canción-corridos as "movie corridos" (1958, 139–140) or "popular pseudo-corridos" (1958, 140; 1993, 138). Nevertheless, the late 1940s through the early 1950s proved to be an important period in the creation of a modern norteña music genre that would be instrumental in defining the intense demographic and cultural changes occurring in the region. Many popular artists, for example Los Alegres and Los Donneños, had experienced traveling and crossing the border as migrant workers, and their lyrics spoke of nostalgia, class and racial conflict, and the breakup of family life and love relationships. They recorded classic corridos from before the 1930s, composed their own border-crossing and conflict corridos in the traditional form, some of which are included in Herrera-Sobek's research (1979, 1993), and they wrote popular canción-corridos that drew on new and very personal feelings and experiences of the migrating community that had gone largely dismissed or unnoticed by scholars. Los Alegres and other norteña artists also competed with Texas-based groups such as those of Santiago Jiménez Sr., Narciso Martínez, and Lydia Mendoza, who were recording on regional labels and marketed to working-class Mexican American and new immigrant communities. Even after Mexico City– based labels moved away from recording and promoting regional popular music artists in the 1950s, Los Alegres and other border-based groups continued to record on independently owned Mexican and Mexican American labels located on both sides of the border. With a large part of the community traveling illegally during this time, partly because of the Bracero Program's end in 1964 and more ambiguous and complex immigration laws, the corrido resurfaced, incorporating features of the traditional corrido and the canción-corrido.

Two new corrido protagonists emerged: the narcotraficante and the mojado. Numerous corridos recorded in the 1960s and 1970s and still popular today feature either the narcotraficante or the mojado as a hero of the underclass. Hernández (1999) champions the narcotraficante and views him as a throwback to the heroic figures of resistance in both border conflict and revolutionary corrido narratives. While the fantastical narcotraficante in narcocorridos emerges as a powerful figure who overcomes North American domination, I contend that the mojado, as an outlaw, is also portrayed as heroic. He confronts authority, racism, displacement, and economic misfortune, emerging triumphant as a result of his bravery and self-sacrifice, two traits that were central to both heroic and conflict corridos in the border region.

In the majority of drug-trafficking and border-crossing corridos before the 1960s, the protagonist dies, goes to jail, or loses his family and money; these songs tend to deliver admonitions against such illegal activity (Nicolopulos 1997). However, a few scholars, such as Guillermo Hernández, James Nicolopulos, and Mark Cameron Edberg, have recognized the narcotraficante's role as a modern-day social bandit who rises from his poor and marginalized community to be a successful businessman of the drug trade by subverting authority, flirting with death, and knocking down social and political barriers. Mexican scholars, such as Luis Astorga (1996a, 1996b) and Juan Carlos Ramírez-Pimienta (2004, 1998), have likened corrupt Mexican politicians to narcotraficantes, both having the power and wealth to control and destroy the lives of individuals, one group legally and the other illegally. In these binational representations, the narcotraficante in today's corridos has superhuman qualities that allow him to subvert authority on both sides of the border; an admirable feat in the eyes of Mexican migrants, many of whom live in the United States illegally. The greater part of scholarly writing (e.g., Herrera-Sobek, Guillermo Hernández, Ramírez-Pimienta) and journalistic work (e.g., Quiñones, Wald) on corridos in recent years has focused on the narcocorrido as a means by which the underclass can vicariously transcend borders and subvert authority, both North American and Mexican.

Few of these scholars have discussed the mojado, who appears in many more modern corridos than the narcotraficante (and in some cases is also involved in drug smuggling) and might be viewed as the narcotraficante's alter ego. In Edberg's study (2004), the narcotraficante emerges as a vibrant persona who maintains distinct Mexican, or more specifically northern Mexican, cultural roots that are also transnational. Edberg asserts that the narcotraficante draws cultural meaning from the conditions of poverty created by U.S. domination and global capital, a long history of race and class-based border conflict, the Mexican tradition of individual power and agency (the strongest representation of this is among the Norteño people), and the "real" and "imagined" images of the lawless border region's brave and macho bandit hero, such as Pancho Villa and Heraclio Bernal (2004, 122–123). In the case of Villa, well-known throughout Mexico, his heroic status was also attributed to his fame as a border raider who went up against General John Pershing's forces and, by extension, North American encroachment (Paredes 1976, 39). However, the mojado, as the sociologist Glenn A. Martínez (1998) suggests, has also garnered meaning from similar circumstances by evading border control agents and resisting assimilation in the United States by maintaining long-distance connections to his region of origin, avoiding capture by authorities, and maintaining a strong work ethic and family ties. It is not surprising that a popular music genre and defiantly independent industry would be formed around a narrative ballad tradition that was initially shaped by powerful images of a community's fight to establish an identity and place in a conflicted border environment.

NORTEÑA MUSIC

While no scholarly publications exist about norteña music beyond those discussing its association with the corrido, it is sometimes mentioned in relation to the development of the regionally specific Texas-Mexican conjunto, a southern Texas variant of norteña with the same instrumentation that, beginning around the late 1940s, became specifically associated with Texas-Mexicans and later with more assimilated Chicanos throughout the Southwest. The folklorist and ethno-musicologist Manuel Peña's seminal research on conjunto music, which he describes as the working-class music of Mexican Americans of the Southwest, suggests that conjunto is a powerful expression of the modern working-class Tejano or Chicano experience, which contributed to its emergence as a highly stylized North American regional music phenomenon (1985). As this popular music became more assimilated, bilingual, and upwardly mobile, other more "Americanized" genres emerged from conjunto's core. *Orquesta tejana* evolved in the 1940s and 1950s in response to an expanding middle class of Texas-Mexicans. This genre merged North American popular styles such as rock and roll, Mexican folk song forms like rancheras and corridos, as well as popular Latin rhythms such as cumbia and salsa and elements of conjunto. This style is the predecessor to contemporary *música tejana*, or tejano, which evolved in the 1980s and 1990s (Peña 1999b).

Tejano spread throughout the Southwest and, owing to a prolific and active independent recording industry, gained some national recognition in the United States, alongside other popular pan-Latino styles, such as salsa and cumbia. While Peña's work broadened the interest in and subsequent reach of Mexican American and Chicano studies and contributed to North American popular music literature, it did so by moving the focus on Texas-Mexican border music and the Tejano community away from the border region and its nearby Mexican roots. Similarly, the local and global impact of norteña—which has a much larger audience; is more directly associated with nonassimilated, Spanish-speaking Mexican immigrants; and has a wider reach on both sides of the border than conjunto—has been largely ignored and there is little room for norteña in the North American popular music industry's marketing strategy for Hispanic and Latin American music. When some of norteña's most popular names, such as Ramón Ayala y Los Bravos del Norte, Los Tigres del Norte, and Los Tucanes del Norte, come up in the North American popular music market, they are often erroneously associated with the conjunto or tejano genres.

This confusion is understandable because tejano and conjunto are often presented to the public at large as the first truly "Chicano" or Mexican American music. Peña, for example, makes scant reference to norteña and its artists, simply referring to the genre as an "offshoot of música tejana" (1999a, 15). Tejano music is celebrated as the voice of a bilingual, middle-class Mexican American community whose members can trace their roots back to the early Spanish settlers in southern Texas or to families that immigrated from cities and towns in Mexican border states and crossed over just after the Mexican Revolution and before the Bracero Program was instituted. In contrast, norteña, with its focus on the narrative corrido or ranchera repertoire of songs, whose themes document the hardships of crossing the border, is associated with the displaced and marginalized.

Tejano and conjunto music are geared to a dancing public, and the lyrics deal with issues of love and celebrate Tejano/Chicano pride. The "folkloric" Texas-Mexican conjunto and the more modern *música tejana* hold a deeply powerful and symbolic role in the creation and strengthening of a distinct Texas-Mexican culture and identity, as Peña's writings clearly indicate (1985, 1999a, 1999b). While Mexican history and culture are invoked in these Texas-based traditions and are part of the reason conjunto still exists, they are imagined or "recreated" nostalgically. However, norteña, which has spawned a much larger transnational recording and touring industry, is the music of immigrants who are carving out a distinct Mexican diaspora community that celebrates Mexican culture, history, community relations, hard work, and resistance to assimilation.

WRITINGS ON THE CORRIDO AND NORTEÑA MUSIC

In recent years, the popular press on both sides of the border has weighed in, particularly on the subject of narcocorridos. The popular music journalist Sam Quiñones, a freelance writer based in Mexico since 1995 whose articles have appeared in such newspapers as the *Los Angeles Times,* the *Houston Chronicle,* and the *San Francisco Examiner,* has written frequently about the popularity of narcocorridos among Mexican laborers in rural villages and municipalities throughout Mexico. He also published a book, *True Tales from Another Mexico: The Lynch Mob, the Popsicle Kings, Chalino, and the Bronx* (2001), filled with stories about immigrant communities scraping out a living in a variety of creative and unthinkable ways—one of the few popular publications that takes a realistic look at the thoroughly modern and uniquely transnational Mexican diaspora. One of the most fascinating moments in Quiñones's book is the tragic real-life account of the narcocorrido composer—mojado, drug kingpin, and former prisoner—Chalino Sánchez, who almost single-handedly breathed new life into the norteña industry and the narcocorrido by writing songs that were more "realistic" and violent than those of Los Tigres and other norteña groups who came before him. Influenced by gangsta rap in Los Angeles, Sánchez brought a younger audience to the genre and, by living the life of many of his protagonists, he proved to be the ultimate "badass" by getting himself murdered in Sinaloa.

Elijah Wald is also a journalist turned book author, whose writings about narcocorridos and the genre's most popular group, Los Tigres del Norte, began to appear in the mainstream press just after the release of the group's influential recording *Jefe de Jefes* (Boss of Bosses) in 1997. In an article for the *Boston Globe,* Wald (1998) notes that mainstream North America has been out of touch with Mexican immigrant culture and its popular music, in particular the narcocorrido. He writes that Los Tigres are clever innovators of the narcocorrido tradition: They celebrate the ability of the marginalized Mexican immigrant laborer to subvert authority while calling the U.S. government to task for its role in rampant drug trafficking across the border. Wald's 2001 book, *Narcocorrido: A Journey into the Music of Drugs, Guns, and Guerrillas,* is a travelogue that chronicles his journey through Mexico in search of legendary composers of popular narcocorridos such as Andrés Contreras, Teodoro Bello, Enrique Franco, Julián Garza, and Gabriel Villanueva. Wald's approach resembles that of a cultural tourist who is fascinated by the "exotic" lawlessness of these modern-day social bandits. However, since he focuses his attention on musicians and composers as folk artists making a living as best they can, he tries to eschew any serious debates about celebrating this lifestyle or exoticizing "the other."

While many Mexican scholars and journalists treat norteña and its most popular artists, Los Tigres del Norte, as a symptom of neoliberal policies of the Mexican government or of migrants' increased exposure to North American pop culture and decadence, some still insist that the genre is uniquely Mexican and worthy of proper study. The poet and musicologist Mario Arturo Ramos published *Cien corridos: Alma de la canción mexicana* (2002), an anthology of one hundred corridos dating from 1810 to the present, which was well received by the academic community and in the popular press. The book was distributed to elementary and high schools across Mexico for nearly two years. When the legislators of several Mexican states discovered that the book contained four narcocorridos (some of which were actually mojado-themed corridos), they removed it from schools and libraries, and the government ordered the book's publisher, Editorial Océano, to cease production and distribution (García Hernández 2005).

Meanwhile, the popular book by the Spanish novelist Arturo Pérez-Reverte, *La reina del sur* (The queen of the South), which is based on one of the first narcocorridos (made famous in the 1970s by Los Tigres del Norte), continues to be available in Mexican bookstores and libraries throughout the country. It would seem that from an "official" standpoint, the narcocorrido as pulp fiction is acceptable and celebrated, but as a contemporary manifestation of the proletariat corrido tradition, it is unworthy of serious scholarly study. Finally, while the debate continues about the narcocorrido and mojado-themed songs, little can be found on the extraordinary impact of norteña music as the genre popular with immigrant laborers on both sides of the border. One book, Toño Carrizosa's *La onda grupera: Historia del movimiento grupero* (1997), makes a valiant attempt to examine the cumbia-laden popular music industry that exploded in the early 1980s in Monterrey and swept through the U.S.-based Mexican immigrant population through the early 1990s. While norteña music and the narcocorrido seemed to be on a hiatus during this period, cumbia (also, *onda grupera*) groups from Monterrey, dressed in glitzy western garb, like Los Bukis, Bronco, and Selena (from Texas) brought this popular genre to the attention of major international labels' Latin divisions, such as Discos Sony, WEA Latin, and Capitol EMI Latin. However, this trend was short-lived, and with the resurgence (again) of the narcocorrido—thanks in part to Chalino Sánchez and primarily California-based new groups like Los Tucanes de Tijuana (The Toucans of Tijuana)—norteña was back on top, with independent labels like Fonovisa (San José, California), Disa (Monterrey), and DLV (Monterrey) competing with these same major label players. For some scholars (Edberg and Ramírez-Pimienta in particular), norteña has been transformed and commodified by both the music industry and the drug trafficking industry as a highly marketable product with broad appeal, particularly among the marginalized, impoverished, and undocumented, bringing into question whether the narcocorrido is a true narrative of resistance.

MUSIC, MIGRATION, AND MEXICANIDAD

The impact of migration, particularly in the United States, has forced scholars to consider music, both traditional and popular, not as belonging to one place or another but as being associated with both here and there or, as the title of Los Tigres del Norte's song "Ni Aquí ni Allá" suggests, as belonging neither here nor there.[1] Music is no longer static and associated with a specific geographical site. The movement of people, along with new developments in technology, has spurred interest in issues of authenticity, tradition, and expanded networks for the performance and consumption of music. And while the music of migrating communities is being "reinvented" or "redefined" in new locales, it still allows community members to remain connected to a sense of history, culture, and identity (Hobsbawm 1983, 1–3). The long history and political and racial dynamics of the migration of Mexican laborers into the United States have profoundly influenced its society and culture. With over ten million Mexican Americans living legally in this country, it is no wonder that Mexican traditional and popular music and culture have significantly influenced North American society and culture (Arizpe 2004, 20–22). This culture is so visible in some regions such as the Southwest that mariachi music is taught in local schools and universities; new migration trends in the Midwest, Pacific Northwest, and Northeast are bringing mariachi schools and programs to these regions as well.

Researchers examining Mexican migration trends have noted the transnational and transcultural nature of migration over the past twenty-five years (e.g., Arizpe 2004; Massey, Durand, and Malone 2002; Smith 2000). Early migration, particularly from northern Mexican states to predominantly southwestern U.S. states, expanded an already Hispanicized and Mexicanized region. Many immigrants settled in this region, finding the linguistic, cultural, and social adjustments not so extreme, though they still experienced racism and discrimination. However, after 1973 and peaking in the mid-1990s, high unemployment rates and income inequality became the norm. Mexican immigrants could not find jobs in this region as easily as they had in the past, and they began fanning out across the United States (Durand, Massey, and Parrado 1999, 520). Before the Immigration Reform and Control Act (IRCA) was instituted in 1986, those who did travel for work outside the Southwest often stayed temporarily, returning to Mexico (many to border towns to work temporarily in *maquila* factories). The IRCA changed that pattern. The law offered amnesty to long-term undocumented workers at a time when Mexico was experiencing unusually severe inflation and unemployment, and many chose to remain in the United States. While the IRCA required undocumented immigrants to remain in the United States while their amnesty petitions were reviewed, the law's tighter control of the border, which included an increase in border patrol agents, encouraged new undocumented workers to remain in the United States rather than risk crossing back (1999, 521–524). Today, Mexicans make up almost 60 percent of the nation's undocumented population of over eleven million, and 80 to 85 percent of the migration from Mexico in recent years is undocumented (Passel 2005). The U.S. government has continued to fight migration at the border (and out of view of the North American public at large), but Mexican migration and its ensuing cultural impact have increased, becoming more visible in urban centers and rural towns throughout the United States.

Norteña music, with the corrido ballad song form at its core, is the popular music genre that initially traveled with migrant workers and, after the Bracero Program ended, with the undocumented traveler in particular. Though it is not unusual to encounter the occasional regional Mexican

1   *This title, like those of many songs and albums by Los Tigres del Norte and other popular norteña artists, uses the English-language form of capitalization. (According to Spanish-language rules for capitalization, only the first word and proper nouns are capitalized in titles.) As the norteña music industry became increasingly focused on the immigrant population in the United States, these titles, like the music itself, embodied the merging of Mexican and North American cultures. I have adopted this format throughout the book.*

son ensemble (string band) among immigrant communities, norteña is the modern popular music genre that became specifically associated with this community, the experience of migration, and the search for work. Thanks to pioneering artists like Los Alegres de Terán, El Piporro, Ramón Ayala y Los Bravos del Norte, and Los Tigres del Norte, the norteña ensemble sound was modernized and eventually tailored to the experiences and aesthetic tastes of this community. Similarly, the corrido was transformed from a heroic epic ballad to a topical narrative popular song form that expressed the ordeal of travel, displacement, cultural and racial conflict, and societal change. In large part as a result of the massive migration of this population, years of complex and ambiguous U.S. immigration policy, a volatile and increasingly criminalized border region, and escalating undocumented migration, norteña's audience grew. Movement is at the core of norteña's development. It was the migration of people that brought the corrido song tradition and the accordion and bajo sexto together. Travel to urban and rural locales farther north into the United States broadened this music's popularity, and the high mobility of its audience and performers meant that the industry evolved on both sides of the border, first in Texas, then Monterrey, and later in California.

The advent of cassette technology in the 1970s and 1980s brought another kind of mobility to the music, and, in cassette format, norteña began to travel back to Mexico, where it became associated with working-class populations throughout the country. Cassettes enabled individuals within this transnational migrant network to share the music with each other and with families and friends in Mexico. That cassettes were inexpensive to manufacture and duplicate not only made the music more accessible and readily available but also opened the industry to pirating, thus subverting the economic interests of major label control of popular music, as did the popularization and dissemination of Indian popular music in the 1970s and 1980s that Peter Manuel (1993) describes. Today, the music remains mobile, accessible, and exploitable thanks to technological advancements (e.g., CD and DVD duplication and the Internet) that have extended its popularity. Continued migration beyond the Southwest has secured markets for norteña throughout the Mexican diaspora (as well as among border-crossing migrants from Central America, Colombia, Ecuador, and Peru), situating the music as an important cultural agent in the creation of a "new Mexican global nation" (Arizpe 2004, 22).

The continued popularity of norteña music, a genre that is not viewed as purely "Mexican" by the mainstream Mexican music industry and that cannot cross over into the North American mainstream market, represents a new Mexican identity—or *mexicanidad*—shaped by the collective experience of travel and the constant flow of information, ideas, and culture. While mariachi ensembles—which feature songs from the Revolution, regional folk songs, and romantic ballads—are often promoted in the United States as the music of the Mexican "nation" by Mexican consular offices and cultural institutions, norteña has emerged as the voice of the present-day Mexican migrant experience. Because this experience has become so deeply rooted in the Mexican consciousness and in working-class society on both sides of the border, norteña has morphed from a regional genre of peasant laborers to a mass-produced popular music genre that speaks to the political, social, and cultural inequalities experienced by Mexican immigrant workers in the United States and their families and communities in Mexico.

Though song lyrics certainly document the hardship and alienation of this experience, they also remind immigrants of the importance of loyalty to one's family and country. In this case, mexicanidad is asserted through embracing a heritage that is indigenous as well as Mexican. Mexico's government and political elite have generally viewed border-crossing migrants and indigenous Mexicans as outcasts. Celebrating indigenous culture and identity was at the core of the emerging Mexican nationalistic movement of the 1930s and 1940s. Among Mexican immigrants today mexicanidad is represented through solidarity and connecting with communities across the diaspora and is based on pride of origin, both regional and national. Norteña's focus on the shared experiences of Mexican migrants in the United States combined with nostalgic references to the past embodies this postmodern sense of mexicanidad. In the popular corrido excerpted in Figure 1.1, "Soy Potosino" by the Texas-based norteña group Los Terribles del Norte, the border-crossing migrant clings, simultaneously, to his regional, indigenous, and Mexican national identity while affirming that he is "accustomed" (but not assimilated) to life in the United States. For its author and for many of his fellow migrant travelers, this song constructs an imagined community and nationality through both symbolic and experiential references to mexicanidad while it implies strong resistance to North American social domination and acculturation.

Soy Potosino	
Soy de tierras potosinas	I am from Potosino country*
y mi orgullo es ser de allá	and I am proud to be from there
Mis venas traen sangre azteca	I have Aztec blood in my veins
de mi tierra les quiero contar	I want to tell you about my country
Cien por ciento mexicano	One hundred percent Mexican
Mi sangre de indio no voy a negar	I will not deny my Indian blood
Soy de donde se da la tuna	I am from where you find the *tuna**
donde el águila bajó	where the eagle lands
Cuando mató a la serpiente	when he kills the serpent
y en la bandera quedó	and is pictured on our flag
Lo dicen los potosinos los compas	As good friends of Potosinos say
que bajan de otra región	who come from other regions
Tuve que dejar mi patria	I had to give up my country
con los gringos yo emigré	I had to emigrate to live with the gringos
Aunque estoy en tierra gringa	Even though I'm in gringo land
mis raíces yo no olvidaré	I will never forget my roots
Así hay como tanto hispano	Like so many Hispanic people
que llega a esta tierra	who come to this country
ya me acostumbré	now I am accustomed

FIGURE 4.7 *"Soy Potosino." Written by José G. Martínez in 2002. Recorded by Los Terribles del Norte in 2003. *Potosino country = San Luis Potosí; tuna = cactus pear.*

(From the CD La tercera es la vendida . . . eso! *[Freddie Records JMCD-1858]. Lyrics courtesy of Freddie Records/MARFRE Music.)*

The sociologist Robert Smith argues that tighter immigration laws and the inability to travel freely have prompted communities from which large groups of Mexican immigrants hail to maintain long-distance connections via grassroots organizations and through continuous involvement not only in family businesses and household decisions but also in local politics and community service (2003, 299–305). While immigrants are returning home less often, whether because of financial independence, growing family ties in the United States, or their undocumented status, they are participating in a more fluid and autonomous notion of a Mexican diasporic nation. Although it might seem that such limitations on physical travel would discourage commitment to Mexico, new technologies, an expanded number of Spanish-speaking Mexican enclaves throughout the United States, and the large percentage of undocumented travelers unable (or unwilling) to assimilate into Chicano or North American populations have reinforced these long-distance ties to Mexico. Traditionally, migration studies supported the notion that Mexican migrant populations maintained a "unidirectional shift," meaning that in spite of the fact that they often moved between communities on both sides of the border, they eventually focused their involvement in one. However, Roger Rouse (1991, 13–15) argues that advancements in communication technology and travel have allowed for a continued interest in remaining culturally, socially, and economically involved in more than one community or locale at the same time. Ironically, in my own observation, even though many undocumented immigrants cannot travel, many maintain businesses, relationships, and even residences in both locales (many living with the hope of returning one day). The Mexican government not only recognizes but also encourages a sense of dual nationality, in part because the country depends on remittances from this population. A recent example of this was legislation passed in March 2005, which gave immigrants the right to vote in Mexican elections from the United States (even if they have obtained U.S. citizenship). By reaching out to a population it had ignored for so many years, the Mexican government has signaled its recognition of the Mexican diaspora and the power this community holds financially, politically, and culturally. Mexican immigrants, in turn, have responded with a fervent revitalization of mexicanidad.

More than any other traditional, regional, or popular Mexican music genre, norteña embodies an immigrant notion of mexicanidad and, by extension, the new Mexican global nation. The genre's origins in the historically autonomous northernmost region of Mexico, its stylistic and popular evolution among migrating Mexicans who brought to it musical ideas and technological innovation from both sides of the border, and its initial commercial growth and marketing focus in the United States have positioned it as the voice of a nation of Mexican immigrants who are living in one locale and imagining themselves in another. In the corridos and rancheras of norteña music, the immigrant lives as an outcast (or outlaw if he or she is illegal) and can find a sense of belonging that is based on a shared understanding of history, migration, and values. Though this definition of norteña aligns it with the growth and dispersion of the immigrant community in the United States, norteña is also very widely disseminated and popular in Mexico. A long and highly politicized history of migration to the United States has profoundly and significantly affected Mexico, economically, socially, politically, and culturally (Smith 2003; Arizpe 2004). With one in every ten Mexicans migrating to the United States and with remittances and investments from immigrants totaling as much as $23.98 billion (Malkin 2008), Mexico has begun to embrace its diasporic population, recognizing the hybrid culture and nomadic lifestyle of that population, even though remittances have dropped in recent months because of the U.S. housing slump and economic crisis (Malkin 2008).

DEFINING A "MEXICAN" DIASPORA

According to Américo Paredes, "Every Mexican knows that there are in fact two Mexicos, just as he knows that there being two is not a purely metaphysical concept, although it has transcendental implications." There is the "real" Mexico, as he describes it, the territory physically occupied by a nation, and then there is the other Mexico, the one known to Mexicans as "México de afuera" (Mexico of the outside), made up of Mexicans living throughout the United States (Paredes 1993, 3). North American society's uneasiness with the social and cultural impact of "two Mexicos" is evidenced by moments in North American history when Mexicans have not been made to feel welcome, such as California's ill-conceived Proposition 187 in the mid-1990s and the U.S. government's aggressive stance on immigration, most recently after the "reforms" of 1996, which restricted or prohibited state and federal public services (such as health care) for certain immigrants, placed greater restrictions on immigration, and sought to strengthen policing of the border. Paredes's work focuses on the second of the two Mexicos, "México de afuera," which he asserts is made up of all persons of Mexican descent living in the United States (1993, 3). However, one cannot assume that all Mexicans in "México de afuera" are the same. In fact, to understand the role of norteña music as a means of understanding a complex and vast Mexican diaspora, one must distinguish the Tejano from the Chicano and the Mexican American from the Mexican national. There are also regional distinctions, within both the United States and Mexico, and divisions within the population that are based on such criteria as level of education, work experience (in a rural or urban context), and length of time away from the "first" Mexico. The popularity of norteña music has ebbed and flowed on the basis of the social and cultural dynamics of local and transnational distinctions that exist within Mexican communities. This study's documentation, research, and analysis of norteña music in both Mexicos examines these distinctions and the role they have played in the "coming together" and the transnational flow of the two Mexicos.

The once "regional" characteristics of norteña music and culture have been historicized, sensationalized, localized, and transformed by an expanding population of border-crossing Mexicans, particularly those labeled "illegal" (or mojado) who travel from all regions of the country. The most appealing character of norteña is the postmodern working-class "outlaw," who consistently eludes authority (both Mexican and North American) and bears no clear discernible attachment to either of the two Mexicos. This has long been the case with the Norteño people, who have been virtually self-ruling for decades and maintained an ambivalent (and somewhat distant) relationship with Mexico's administrative and nationalistic core amid what the historian David G. Gutiérrez describes as "the continuing social, cultural, and economic integration of the United States–Mexico border region" (1999, 509). Like the Norteño himself, traveling Mexican laborers from all regions of the country have grown accustomed to living and working in communities on both sides of the border. Perhaps it is more appropriate to look at norteña music and the working-class Mexican immigrant as together constituting both a blurring of boundaries that once defined "home" and "abroad" and a merging of cultures and identities.

The academic research and writings of James Clifford, Arjun Appadurai, Caren Kaplan, George Lipsitz, Homi Bhabha, and others have shown that migrant and "displaced" communities have had a profound impact on the culture, economics, and politics that have shaped the world and, in particular, North American society. Lipsitz has observed that Latin American immigrants (not unlike other diasporic communities) are perhaps more modernized and more accustomed than their countrymen who stayed behind (as well as many North Americans themselves) to the globalization of the United States. Because they were "created by the machinations of world capitalism over the centuries" and are thus "accustomed to code switching, syncretism, and hybridity," these communities may be better prepared for the more complex and sinuous notions of place, identity, and nationalism that are shaping the world today (1994, 31). This idea pertains especially to members of the Mexican immigrant population, who—from the social, cultural, and economic border-based conflicts between Norteño Mexicans and Anglo-American newcomers of the mid-nineteenth century to the current oppressive immigration laws and discrimination—have emerged resilient and ever more determined to seek a better life and economic freedom in the United States. Their experience in negotiating diverse social, political, and cultural landscapes has better equipped these immigrants to form transnational communal allegiances than to remain dependent on any one nation.

In the case of Mexico, this notion is best understood when considering the northernmost region and the borderlands, where a regional identity was formed partly in response to encroaching capitalism by an aggressive "foreign entity" and the oppressive authoritarianism of a distant nation. For more than a century, both real and imagined ideas and experiences of the U.S.-Mexico border have shaped a Mexican American history and imagination. These experiences created the foundation for defining a separate society and ideology, particularly in the Southwest. The historian Mario T. García (1996, 90) describes both the symbolic and the concrete effects the border has had on travelers and notes that each generation's interpretation of the border has profoundly shaped its political and cultural developments for years. The border figures prominently in the collective memory of what constitutes a "homeland" for many Mexicans and Mexican Americans, perhaps more so than Mexico itself. Conflicts within both Mexican and North American societies have contributed to the characteristics of a Mexican diaspora that can only be fully imagined by those who have crossed the border, regardless of which side they happen to be living on. Norteña music exists simultaneously as "border" music and as the music of immigrant Mexican laborers. It is a mechanism by which regional interpretations of the Mexican diaspora have been artistically and collectively expressed, particularly as divisions within the ethnic Mexican population itself have widened and become increasingly complex.

The reality of traveling for work has a long history in northern Mexico—from the Tlaxcalteca Indians who were brought to the area by Spanish colonizers from the Tlaxcala region of central Mexico in the seventeenth century to work in local mines to the Mexican cowboys who joined North American cattle drives in the 1800s to the Mexican laborers who now cross the U.S.-Mexico border for work on a daily basis. For these travelers, the experience of displacement and migration has merged with a global flow of ideologies, technology, and imagination that, through the years, has had a crucial role in shaping the shifting ideas of what constitutes Mexico and the United States. For the Mexican immigrant, norteña music, like the diaspora whose experiences it expresses, began in the border region, extended into the United States, and then extended into Mexico's interior. Because of its association with northern Mexico and border culture, norteña music and its social history have now become "slippery," to use Appadurai's term (1990, 44), as the genre's stylistic features and meaning have been affected by the fluidity of travel, the politicization of the border, and the localization of communities on both sides.

RACE, CLASS, AND IDENTITY IN THE MEXICAN DIASPORA

Issues of race, class, and identity have been tied to the development of popular music in the United States. Though popular music genres such as country, jazz, rhythm and blues, rock, hip hop, and rap evolved from a merging of African and European musical elements, they are also the result of marginalization and oppression. Prior to the civil rights movement, musicians and audiences were segregated, but as musical ideas and influences continued to flow back and forth, these once distanced and isolated communities came closer. While the coming together of cross-cultural musical ideas transcends the experience of discrimination and marginalization to some extent, our society is still grappling with racial, economic, and social inequalities in its musical and artistic life.

In the United States, race has been viewed in black and white terms; the issue has become much more complex as immigration continues from so many locales and racial mixing grows more common. The Mexican American or Chicano in this country has long been a racialized and marginalized minority. While many Mexican Americans came into this country through immigration, a large population in the Southwest suddenly found themselves in the United States after the Mexican American War ended in 1848 and the Treaty of Hidalgo ceded to the United States more than 525,000 square miles of former Mexican territory (Arizona, California, western Colorado, Nevada, New Mexico, Texas, and Utah). The agreement also established the U.S.-Mexican border at the Rio Grande and Gila rivers. Many Mexican residents in this new U.S. region were viewed as second-class citizens in the racial and class-based hierarchy imposed by Anglo-Americans. They were, as David G. Gutiérrez notes, "doubly marginalized as orphans of the Mexican nation and as outcasts within the newly expanded United States" (1999, 485).

Over the years, racial divisions between Mexicans and Anglo-Americans in the Southwest became more rigid and institutionalized, making it more difficult for Mexicans to integrate into North American society. Gutiérrez depicts a segregation and impoverishment that extended by the turn of the twentieth century throughout the Southwest in "run-down barrios and rural colonias," which he says also provided a safe haven for preserving traditional customs, language, and religious practices (1999, 488). The Mexican Revolution and the subsequent economic upheaval from 1910 to 1920 prompted the first large wave of Mexican migration into the United States, largely through illegal channels. During this time, rapid development in the Southwest produced jobs in mines, railroad construction, and farm labor (Gutiérrez 1999, 120–123).

Living in isolated communities and working in backbreaking jobs as migrant laborers, Mexicans experienced discrimination throughout the Southwest. In Texas, the Anglo-American population maintained a social policy of segregation and discrimination along with a cultural memory of the Alamo. Furthermore, native Spanish-speaking populations in this area (many of whom were descended from Spanish, rather than Mexican, settlers) campaigned to be accepted as "American" and lobbied to distance themselves from what they considered to be "lower-class" immigrants (Gutiérrez 1999, 129). Such attitudes set the stage for long-enduring class- and race-based divisions in Texas and the lower Rio Grande Valley, an agriculturally fertile area that borders Mexico. In this region and among the Mexican migrant workers who were forced to leave their villages and families for work "en el otro lado" (on the other side) the traditional border corrido and the accordion/bajo sexto–based norteña ensemble first came together. Manuel Peña describes this working-class norteña ensemble as a "proletarian expression" that would achieve cultural autonomy within the white hegemonic society that dominated the region's politics, society, and economy (1985, 145). As Paredes (1958, 1993) also suggests, the norteña ensemble, like the corrido, was a means by which this community could maintain control of its own forms of cultural and religious expression and thus exert power and resist total domination by the local society.

Peña's exhaustive work examined the evolution of the Texas-Mexican conjunto (as the norteña ensemble came to be known by Mexican-Americans in Texas) as the voice of a post–World War II emerging Mexican American (as well as Tejano and Chicano) middle class, which sought to assimilate but not to acculturate into North American society. The African American community's struggle for civil liberties in the 1950s and 1960s inspired many second- and third-generation Mexican Americans (many of whom now called themselves Chicanos and Chicanas) to embark on their own campaign for improvements in socioeconomic and educational conditions and to assert their rights as citizens of the United States (Gonzales 1999, 191). Peña (1985) notes that in this period Texas-Mexican conjunto declined as a popular music genre of the Mexican working class, being eclipsed by the more "sophisticated" orquesta tejana genre that replaced the accordion with brass instruments (and later keyboards) and the bajo sexto with electric guitar and bass.

Because, according to Peña, Texas-Mexican conjunto was a "counter-ideological response by Tejano (Texas-Mexican) workers to subordination under North American political, economic, and cultural hegemony" (1985, 110), it lost relevance as Chicanos and Tejanos achieved a higher social and economic status within North American society. By the mid-1960s, Texas-Mexican conjunto's evolution as a popular music genre ceased; it became "folk music" and was celebrated as a "symbol" of the Texas-Mexican's (and Chicano's) working-class past and struggle for recognition within the dominant Anglo-American culture. Outside interest in the music (for instance, by the Smithsonian Institution and independent audiophile record labels, such as Arhoolie Records and Rounder Records) and the commercialization of orquesta tejana (later known as *música tejana,* or simply tejano) have contributed to the perpetuation of the music as "folkloric" and increasingly "regional."

What Peña leaves out of this discussion, however, is the continued "Mexicanization" of the border region and the impact the surge of Mexican migration into the United States had on Mexican immigrant popular music, particularly after the end of the Bracero Program in the mid-1960s. While Tejanos and Chicanos were establishing a place for themselves within North American culture and society, increasing numbers of new Mexican immigrants were coming into the United States each year, many of them illegally, and finding work beyond the Southwest (e.g., in Chicago, Michigan, Oregon, Washington State). These migrants represented a new labor class, discriminated against by both North American employers and bilingual, upwardly mobile Chicano/Tejano residents. While the Chicano movement brought about numerous educational, socio economic, and cultural reforms (e.g., bilingual and bicultural education, recognition that the United States is a multicultural society, Chicano and Latino university programs, farm labor reforms, recognition of Chicano arts and artists), many of these benefits did not affect the lives of new Mexican immigrants and eventually contributed to further divisions within the ethnic Mexican community at large, divisions based on education level, language skills, immigration status, and class distinctions. It is clear that while the advancements brought about by the movement established a vibrant Mexican presence and cultural heritage that has maintained a high profile in North American society since the 1970s, the increasing numbers of undocumented immigrants have generated a negative reaction (Gonzales 1999, 223). And as the general population grew apprehensive about these numbers, it began to blame Mexican immigrants for everything from job shortages to increases in drug-related crime. In many regions of the Southwest, attitudes toward Mexican immigrants grew hostile. Fearing a return to the discriminative and oppressive atmosphere experienced by their parents and grandparents, many Chicanos and Tejanos sought to distance themselves from this new "Mexican" population, only further marginalizing the latter as impoverished laborers and "second-class" residents.

During this period norteña emerged as the popular music associated with this growing and doubly marginalized community. While Texas-Mexican conjunto became detached from the migrating Mexican and the increasingly "Mexicanized" border community, norteña emerged as a distinct genre with its own style. Though conjunto and norteña featured the same working-class instrumental core (accordion and bajo sexto) and had assimilated from rock and roll such modern instruments as the electric bass, drum set, and occasionally the saxophone, they grew apart stylistically. While conjunto became a dance hall phenomenon that increasingly showcased the accordion (now a symbol of Tejano and Chicano identity) and relied more on English-language lyrics, norteña groups, who typically sang in Spanish, focused more on the corrido and traditional rhythms such as the European-derived polka and waltz and the regional Mexican *huapango,* a dance rhythm with rapidly alternating patterns. For many migrating Mexicans, the corrido evoked the Revolution (a time when peasants and bandit heroes changed the course of Mexican history); the fetishized and eternally macho Norteño cowboy; and the humiliating and, now increasingly dangerous, border-crossing experience.

Unlike the Texas-Mexican conjunto, norteña represented neither a working-class past nor a constructed Mexican heritage; rather, it represented the present-day experiences of a Mexican laborer community that confronted racism and disenfranchisement in the struggle to better the lives of its families and communities. These immigrants—in part because of the overwhelming percentage of undocumented workers among them and because they formed distinct communities and Mexican enclaves throughout the United States—have tended to sustain stronger ties to their communities of origin; they have not assimilated and have lower naturalization rates than any other immigrant community in the United States and have maintained a profound sense of Mexican identity. Norteña music has perpetuated this immigrant notion of mexicanidad through songs that invoke solidarity and collective identity by means of musical documentations of "real life" immigrant experiences and both documented and fictive exploits of the modern-day border cowboy, the narcotraficante.

As a popular music form rooted in a race- and class-based community in North American society, norteña has grown into a transnational popular music phenomenon that has also penetrated the U.S. Latino popular music industry, albeit via strikingly independent and individualistic means. Norteña's popularity and dissemination throughout an expanding Mexican diaspora has been fueled by the ability of the immigrants in this community to imagine themselves as Mexican no matter where they have settled. In this imagining, history and experience take precedence over place (Appadurai 1996; Bhabha 1994). The popularization and perpetuation of norteña music, along with a clearly defined notion of a global Mexican nation, have helped the Mexican immigrant (particularly the undocumented) to rise above the class-based discrimination, oppression, and displacement imposed by a North American government that continues to criminalize its border zone and blame immigration problems on the migrating Mexican.

REFERENCES

Appadurai, Arjun. 1990. "Disjuncture and Difference in the Global Cultural Economy." *Theory, Culture, and Society* 7 (2–3): 295–310.

Appadurai, Arjun. 1996. *Modernity at Large: Cultural Dimensions of Modernity.* Minneapolis: University of Minnesota Press.

Arizpe, Lourdes. 2004. "Migración y cultura. Las redes simbólicas del futuro." In *Los retos culturales de México,* edited by Lourdes Arizpe, 19–42. Mexico City: Centro Regional de Investigaciones Multidisciplinarias, Universidad Autónoma de México.

Astorga, Luis. 1996a. *Mitología del narcotraficante en México.* Mexico City: Plaza y Valdés.

Astorga, Luis. 1996b. *El siglo de las drogas.* Mexico City: Espasa Calpe.

Bhabha, Homi K. 1994. *The Location of Culture.* London: Routledge.

Carrizosa, Toño. 1997. *La onda grupera: Historia del movimiento grupero.* Mexico City: Edamex.

Durand, Jorge, Douglas S. Massey, and Emilio A. Parrado. 1999. "The New Era of Mexican Migration to the United States." *Journal of American History* 86 (2): 518–536.

Duvalier, Armando. 1937. "Romance y corrido." *Crisol: Revista de Crítica* (June): 35–43, (September): 8–16, and (November): 35–41.

Edberg, Mark Cameron. 2004. *El Narcotraficante: Narcocorridos and the Construction of a Cultural Persona on the U.S.-Mexico Border.* Austin: University of Texas Press.

García, Mario T. 1996. "La Frontera: The Border as Symbol and Reality in Mexican-American Thought." In *Between Two Worlds: Mexican Immigrants in the United States,* edited by David G. Gutiérrez, 89–118. Wilmington, Del.: Scholarly Resources.

García Hernández, Arturo G. 2005. "Prejuicios e ignorancia detrás del llamado a censurar antología de corridos." *La Jornada* (Mexico City), April 7.

Gonzales, Manuel G. 1999. *Mexicanos: A History of Mexicans in the United States.* Bloomington: Indiana University Press.

Gutiérrez, David G. 1999. "Migration, Emergent Ethnicity, and the 'Third Space': The Shifting Politics of Nationalism in Greater Mexico." *Journal of American History* 86 (2): 481–517.

Hernández, Guillermo E. 1999. "What Is the Corrido?" *Studies in Latin American Popular Culture* 18:69–92.

Herrera-Sobek, María. 1979. *The Bracero Program: Elitelore versus Folklore.* Los Angeles: UCLA Latin American Center Publications.

Herrera-Sobek, María. 1990. *The Mexican Corrido: A Feminist Analysis.* Bloomington: Indiana University Press.

Herrera-Sobek, María. 1993. *Northward Bound: The Mexican Immigrant Experience in Ballad and Song.* Bloomington: University of Indiana Press.

Hobsbawm, Eric J. 1983. "Introduction: Inventing Tradition." In *The Invention of Tradition,* edited by Eric Hobsbawm and Terrence Ranger, 1–14. Cambridge: Cambridge University Press.

Limón, José E. 1992. *Mexican Ballads, Chicano Poems: History and Influence in Mexican-American Social Poetry.* Berkeley and Los Angeles: University of California Press.

Lipsitz, George. 1994. *Dangerous Crossroads: Popular Music, Postmodernism, and the Poetics of Place.* New York: Verso.

Malkin, Elizabeth. 2008. "Mexicans Barely Increased Remittances in '07." *New York Times,* February 26.

Manuel, Peter. 1993. *Cassette Culture: Music and a People's Medium in North India.* Chicago: University of Chicago Press.

Martínez, Glenn A. 1998. "Mojados, Malinches, and the Dismantling of the United States/Mexico Border in Contemporary Mexican Cinema." *Latin American Issues* 14:31–50.

Massey, Douglas, Jorge Durand, and Nolan J. Malone. 2002. *Beyond Smoke and Mirrors: Mexican Immigration in an Era of Economic Integration.* New York: Russell Sage Foundation.

McDowell, John Holmes. 1972. "The Mexican Corrido: Formula and Theme in a Ballad Tradition." *Journal of American Folklore* 85:205–220.

McDowell, John Holmes. 1981. "The Corrido of Greater Mexico as Discourse, Music, Event." In *"And Other Neighborly Names": Social Process and Cultural Image in Texas Folklore,* edited by Richard D. Bauman and Roger D. Abrahams, 44–75. Austin: University of Texas Press.

Mendoza, Vicente T. 1954. *El corrido mexicano; antología.* Mexico City: Ediciones de la Universidad Nacional Autónoma de México.

Mendoza, Vicente T. 1964. *Lírica narrativa de México: El corrido.* Mexico City: Universidad Nacional Autónoma de México, Instituto de Investigaciones Estéticas.

Nicolopulos, James. 1997. "The Heroic Corrido: A Premature Obituary?" *Aztlán: Journal of Chicano Studies* 22:115–138.

Paredes, Américo. 1958. *"With His Pistol in His Hand": A Border Ballad and Its Hero.* Urbana: University of Illinois Press.

Paredes, Américo. 1976. *A Texas-Mexican Cancionero: Folksongs of the Lower Border.* Austin: University of Texas Press.

Paredes, Américo. 1993. *Folklore and Culture on the Texas Mexican Border.* Austin: University of Texas Press.

Passel, Jeffrey S. 2005. "Estimates of the Size and Characteristics of the Undocumented Population." *Pew Hispanic Center Online,* March 21, http://pewhispanic.org/reports/report.php?ReportID=44 (accessed April 14, 2005).

Peña, Manuel H. 1985. *The Texas-Mexican Conjunto: Music of a Working-Class People.* Austin: University of Texas Press.

Peña, Manuel H. 1999a. *Música Tejana: The Cultural Economy of Artistic Transformation.* College Station: Texas A&M Press.

Peña, Manuel H. 1999b. *The Mexican American Orquesta: Music, Culture, and the Dialectic of Conflict.* Austin: University of Texas Press.

Pérez-Reverte, Arturo. 2002. *La Reina del Sur.* Miami: Santillana USA Publishing.

Quiñones, Sam. 2001. *True Tales from Another Mexico: The Lynch Mob, the Popsicle Kings, Chalino, and the Bronx.* Albuquerque: University of New Mexico Press.

Ramírez-Pimienta, Juan Carlos. 1998. "Corrido de narcotráfico en los años ochenta y noventa: Un juicio moral suspendido." *Bilingual Review* 23 (2): 145–156.

Ramírez-Pimienta, Juan Carlos. 2004. "Del corrido de narcotráfico al narcocorrido: Orígenes y desarrollo del canto a los traficantes." *Studies in Latin American Popular Culture* 23:22–41.

Ramos, Mario Arturo. 2002. *Cien corridos: Alma de la canción mexicana.* Mexico City: Editorial Océano.

Rouse, Roger. 1991. "Mexican Migration and the Social Space of Postmodernism." *Diaspora* 1 (1): 8–23.

Smith, Robert C. 2000. "How Durable and New Is Transnational Life? Historical Retrieval through Local Comparison." *Diaspora* 9 (2): 203–234.

Smith, Robert. 2003. "Migrant Membership as an Instituted Process: Transnationalism, the State, and the Extra-Territorial Conduct of Mexican Politics." *International Migration Review* 37:297–343.

Wald, Elijah. 1998. "The Ballad of a Mexican Musical Tradition: Corridos Are Still Celebrating Outlaws, Even in the Age of the War on Drugs." *Boston Globe,* January 18.

Wald, Elijah. 2001. *Narcocorrido: A Journey into the Music of Drugs, Guns, and Guerrillas.* New York: Rayo.

Questions for thought:

- What are some characteristics that connect Mexican musical genres?
- How has migration and immigration had an impact the development of music such as música norteña, the son complex, and mariachi?
- What national and ethnic groups had an impact both coming to and leaving Mexico, and how has this changed the musical landscape?
- How has slavery impacted Mexican music?
- Does the politics of immigration have effect on Mexican music on both sides of the border?
- What are the connections between Northern European music and Mexican music? How are these connections manifested?

Activity

Search YouTube for two música norteña groups (Los Tigres del Norte and Enigma Norteño, for example) and mariachi bands (Mariachi Vargas de Tecalitan and Mariachi Nuevo Jalisco, for example). After viewing several videos of each genre, see if you can generate a list of characteristics for each genre. Then compare mariachi and música norteña. Can you hear any connections between both genres? How are they similar and how do they differ visually? Musically?

Figure Credits

CHAPTER FIVE

Latin American Music: Salsa Picante with Rice and Beans

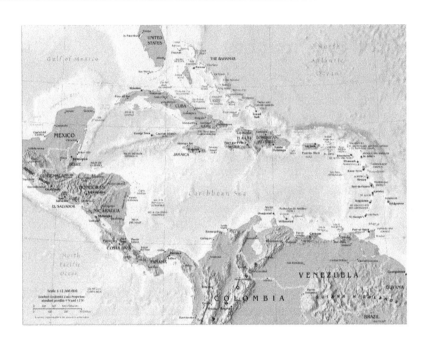

FIGURE 5.1 *Map of Central America and the Caribbean*

Introduction

Salsa is a relatively new word for a music that has been vibrant and popular for many decades. It has been known as Latin music, Cuban or Puerto Rican dance music, and many other names. It brought together genres such as rumba, merengue, bomba, plena, and others in dance-driven presentations throughout the Spanish-speaking Caribbean, Central and South America, and the many Latin communities in the United States. In the 1980s the name salsa came to be used for this mix of music, and the name stuck. It is as if this body of music and dance were waiting for a name

100

like salsa to coalesce into a powerful cultural force. Salsa today is one of the most recognized musical traditions in the global musical market; it can be heard in its traditional homes in the Americas, as well as venues in Europe, Asia, and the rest the world. The roots of salsa are similar to other music of the Americas. Salsa represents a blending of different musical ideas from the Old and New World, as well as Africa, mixing together in unique ways.

As was stated in elsewhere in this anthology, the polka was one of many European dances that became popular in the Americas, having come to the New World in the 1840s with a large immigrant population from Germany and Eastern Europe. These Eastern Europeans migrated to many parts of the New World, including many parts of the United States, Mexico, Central and South America. The polka, which featured European harmony, melody, and instruments, formed a hybrid with African dance traditions, drums, and rhythms, varying throughout the Americas, depending on slave and former-slave populations and colonial influences. The resultant hybrids are the most important dance genres in the Americas:

- tango (Argentina)
- plena and bomba (Puerto Rico)
- ragtime (United States)
- rumba (Cuba)
- beguine (Martinique)
- maxixe and choro (Brazil)

All of these dances appeared at approximately the same time in the 1870s and share similar characteristics. They were originally part of black culture that moved gradually into the mainstream. The differences in these dances reflect the differences in language and culture in different places throughout the Americas. Among the Latin American dances that followed this model are the tango (Chapter 4), the plena and bomba (Puerto Rico) and the rumba (Cuba), which contributed to what we now call salsa.

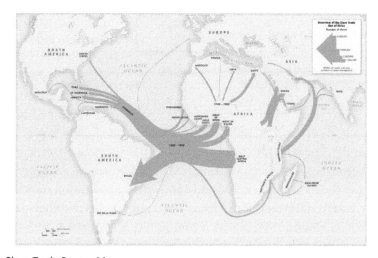

FIGURE 5.2 *Slave Trade Routes Map*

Salsa

To understand the development of salsa and the other dances mentioned above, one must understand slavery in Spanish Latin America and how the influences of slave and colonial cultures merged. The differences among these dances, and indeed the differences among all polka-derived dances in the New World, reflect the differences in language and culture both on the part of slaves and colonial populations. For example, slavery in much of Latin America lasted two generations past emancipation in the USA; in Cuba, slavery was abolished in 1880, the slave trade having lasted until 1867; in Brazil, slavery lasted until 1888. In the Dominican Republic and Haiti, slavery ended earlier, largely due to slave revolts in the 1820s. Unlike the United States, slaves were able to keep much of their culture intact, with many cultural practices remaining much closer to their African roots, including music, drums, language, and religion. This was because the numbers of slaves taken to the Caribbean were much larger than to the United States (see the map above), there was somewhat less control of slave culture by the colonial overseers, and slavery and the slave trade lasted much longer.

Son	Originated in the Oriente (eastern) province of Cuba. One of the foundation dances of Salsa
Rumba	Drumming, dancing and call-and-response in Spanish and African languages. From Son
Guarija	Derivation of Son, which is slower. "Guantanamera" is a Guajira
Conga	Cuban Carnival music
Pilón	Dance based on pounding sugarcane in a mortar and pestle (pilón)
Timba	"Salsa on steroids," mixing Brazilian music, R & B, hip-hop and Salsa. Developed in Cuba in the late 1980s, sometime called Cuban Salsa
Reggaetón	Reggae, Hip-hop, plena and other genres mixing. Developed in Panama by Jamaican immigrants, biggest in Puerto Rico and Cuba
Danzón	Derived from European dances, with African-influenced rhythms, led to Mambo
Bomba and Plena	From Puerto Rico, originally slave celebrations, feature call-and-response. The terms today are virtually interchangeable.
Cha-cha-chá	A derivative of danzón and Mambo
Mambo	Can have many meanings, from danzón, blending Latin music with American Jazz

FIGURE 5.3 *table of Latin dances*

Although most slaves in the New World were obliged to adopt the religions of their slave masters, in some parts of the Americas slaves were able to maintain many of their religious traditions, often mixing several traditions from different language groups and tribes into hybrid religions, often either mixed with Catholic elements or using Catholic symbols to hide these religions from their slave masters. In Cuba and other parts of the Caribbean such as Puerto Rico, this developed into *Santeria*, also known as *La Regla Lucumi*. Based largely on polytheistic religious practices brought from slaves from the *Yoruba* tribe (from the area of what is now Nigeria and Benin), it blends elements from other African traditions. Originally practiced in secret, Santeria includes possession rituals in which music and dance induce possession trances by initiates trained to be the traditional vessels for *Orishas*, the deities in this polytheistic system. It is a social as well as a religious system in which community is important, and rituals involve the sharing of food and blessings, as well as communal dancing. There are variants of

Santeria throughout the Americas; in Brazil the tradition is known as *Candomblé*, and *Voudou* (or *Voundun*) in Haiti.

Visually, Santeria blends Catholic and African elements, and dance is the most important part of the liturgy; it demands different kinds of music for different parts of the ceremonies. Drums provide most of the accompaniment, although bells may also be used. Santeria's drumming and rhythm is the base of many Latin American dances, many of which are the basis of what we now call salsa.

Unifying Elements

These genres all have some unifying elements, the most important of which is the clave pattern, which is the rhythmic foundation of all Afro-Cuban music and many other music traditions throughout the Americas. It is sometimes referred to as the key or guide pattern, and in some African-American genres

FIGURE 5.4 *Claves with other percussion instruments*

it is known as hambone. The pattern is found in many sub-Saharan musical traditions, and it probably came to Cuba and the Caribbean with Yoruba slaves, who were taken from the area around modern-day Nigeria and Benin. This pattern is typically played

on claves, two wooden sticks, usually made of hardwood, which are struck together. It can also be sounded by hand claps and is incorporated into the rhythmic patterns of drums and other instruments in the modern salsa band.

There are two basic types of clave, the son and the rumba patterns, with many variations. The pattern is an alternation of three notes followed by two, or vice-versa. They are very similar; the only difference is in the three-note sequence, with the third note in the rumba pattern delayed as compared to the son pattern.

Another unifying element in this music is call-and response, an element in much African-derived music. Although call-and-response can be found throughout the world, it is very common in most African music cultures and can be found throughout the Americas,

FIGURE 5.5 *Son and Rumba clave patterns*

regardless of the slave-group origins of musical traditions. In Spanish it is known as *coro-pregon*.

Drums also are a unifying factor in this music, again coming from African musical traditions. Slaves throughout the Americas used many types of drums, again reflecting the diversity of tribes, language groups, and music cultures. As stated above, Santeria uses drums and other percussion instruments as the musical base of rituals. Because of the large numbers of slaves and the relatively small number of colonial supervisors in the Caribbean and Brazil, slaves were able to maintain more of their cultural, musical, and religious traditions than in the United States. A major manifestation of these traditions is the use of drums and African-derived drumming, which found its way into most Afro-Latin music.

Two other unifying elements in much of this music are *montuno* and *tumbao*. Montuno is a repeated two-measure rhythmic and harmonic figure, usually played by the piano or the guitar. It was derived from the call-and-response present commonly at the end of a son. It has become one of the most prevalent features of salsa and other Latin genres. Tumbao is a rhythmic bass figure played by the electric bass or piano, derived from the clave rhythm. Montuno and tumbao are often combined in the piano part of a tune. Together, these elements help define salsa and other Latin music.

Hybrid Dances

As is the case with music, dance traditions in Latin America also reflect a measure of hybridity. The dance roots of many modern Latin dances are from both Europe and Africa. One of the European roots is the *contradance*, the basis of many dances for couples, including square dancing in the United States. This couples dance, combined with African rhythms, led to the first important Latin dance, the habanera (from Havana), which became the basis for many dances including the Argentine tango. *Danzón* also combines Afro-Cuban rhythms with European dancing and also features clave rhythms mixed with European wind and string instruments. It became very popular among black and mulatto populations in Cuba and Puerto Rico in the late 19th century. The most important dance genre in Cuba is the *son*, which blends Spanish and African characteristics. As it evolved throughout the 20th century, horns, the drum set, and other instruments were added, leading to what we now call salsa.

The *guajira* is a slower version of the son. The most-heard and most famous Cuban song is "Guantanamera," composed in 1929 by Joseito Fernández. The lyrics are from a poem by José Marti (1853-1895), the Cuban national hero and literary figure. His writings and political activity made him a symbol for Cuban independence from Spain. He was later an inspiring figure for Fidel Castro's Cuban revolution in the 1950s; he remains one of Cuba's most honored heroes.

Three Stages of Latino Music Assimilation in the United States

Latin American music is very popular in the United States; it has been so for quite some time. Latin American music was assimilated into American culture in three separate stages: exotic novelties and dance fads, hybrids, and dominant styles. The exotic novelties and dance fads stage of Latin music assimilation can be traced to the late 19th century, a time during which polka-derived dances were popping up throughout the Americas. One such dance was the habanera, which developed in Cuba in the 1870s. It quickly spread and was influential in many places, including Argentina where it had an impact on the development of the tango. By the 1910s, the tango itself was a major dance fad in the United States and in Europe (See Tango chapter). In the U.S., it first appeared in New York City but quickly spread throughout the country. It was one of the most identifiable and popular dances in the Roaring Twenties and found its way into silent movies and early talkies. Tango gave way to another dance fad, the rumba, which came to Miami and New York in the 1930s, accompanying Cuban dance band leaders such as Xavier Cugat and Desi Arnaz, among many others.

Tango and rumba, along with other dances, influenced jazz and American popular music in a phenomenon known as the *Latin Tinge*. Latin dances and rhythms became part of early jazz and the blues. A good example of this incorporation is in the "St. Louis Blues" by W.C. Handy. This song is a typical twelve-bar blues in the first, second, and fourth verses. The third verse is a tango that is 16 bars long, usually played with a typical tango bass line.

The second stage of Latino music assimilation is the hybrids of the 1950s and 60s. This stage began with *mambo*, which took Latin rhythms and forms and added the

FIGURE 5.6 *Tito Puente playing timbales in the 1960s*

instruments and harmonies of the American big band. It merged the son with jazz horns and jazz riffs, creating a Latin big band sound. It also represented a backwards motion of influence since it is the first instance of American music influencing Latin music. It was the first iteration of Latin jazz, and its influence can be heard in subsequent jazz-based genres such as *cubop*, which takes Cuban music blended with bebop rhythm and harmonies. The most important performer of mambo was band leader and timbale player Tito Puente (1923-2000), who was born to Puerto Rican parents in Spanish Harlem in New York City. Puente added timbales, tunable drums common in Latin music, to the American big band, and he came to be known as the King of the Timbales and the King of Latin Music. He produced some of the biggest mambo hits during his fifty-year career.

In the 1960s, another Latin-American hybrid came onto the music scene both in the United States and in Brazil: *bossa nova*. The name of this genre means new style, or new way, in Portuguese, referring to a new way to play and dance samba. Bossa nova took the rhythms of samba and mixed it with the harmonies and instruments of American bebop jazz. Brazilian musicians, who had come to the United States with Brazilian bands during and after World War II, picked up the forms and harmonic sophistication of bebop, taking that sound to Brazil. Unlike the samba, this hybrid uses piano as the harmonic and rhythmic base of the sound.

The final stage of Latino music assimilation is the dominant styles, including the merengue, the dance form from the Dominican Republic that has become pan-Latino in its reach and influence. The most important Latin dominant style is what we now call salsa, although the name did not come into use until the late 1970s. Salsa got it start in Latin communities of New York, most notably the South Bronx and Spanish Harlem, and Miami, taking Cuban and Puerto Rican music, blending it with mambo, and creating a new style that became the dominant Latin music that can be heard throughout Latin America and the world.

Why Salsa?

Salsa is a return to the roots movement that has been the dominant Latin music since the late 1970s. It is a distillation of Latin and Afro-Cuban dances, combining a variety of music and dances from several countries, mixing to form salsa. Some of these dances were able to maintain some of their identity, merengue for instance, but they took on a new instrumentation from mambo. The roots are in the son, but in the Puerto Rican plena and bomba as well. Indeed, many first generation *salseros*, or salsa musicians, were Puerto Rican, and some claim salsa is more Puerto Rican than Cuban. Originally found in the centers of Latin population in the United States, it has become pan-Latin, and indeed a global genre. Although it retained much of its Cuban core, it was increasingly performed by non-Cubans, and today is played by non-Latinos.

FIGURE 5.7 *Salsa band playing on the street in Havana, Cuba, 2012*

Afro-Cuban and Puerto Rican music and American elements combined to form salsa, which is faster and more rhythmic than the son. As a consequence, it is less romantically expressive than the son. It features dense rhythmic textures, the clave rhythm as its base, and also includes polyrhythms. Combined with montuno piano patterns and tumbao bass, as well as American horns and jazz-based improvisation, salsa has become part of the American and global soundscape.

The roots of salsa, and the name itself, are in dispute. The great Celia Cruz, the Queen of Salsa, said: "From 1960 to around 1973, our music was in the doldrums. But when we started calling it 'salsa,' our young people sort of liked the name and from then on, thanks to salsa, a lot of things started to happen." Many artists did not like the name. Tito Puente stated that "for me, salsa is the ketchup you put on French fries." Some believe that the name had little to do with the music. Cuban musician Mario Bauzá said, "In fact, what they call salsa is nothing new ... it is nothing more than a publicity stunt." Puerto Rican musician Ray Baretto said that "the term salsa is a new invention which allows people who do not know it very well to identify a musical style. It's simply a marketing tool."

Salsa came full circle in the 1980s when some salseros performed in Cuba, which had a music scene that had waned due to the American boycott of the island. Cuban musicians embraced salsa and developed their own version called timba. This development helped revitalize the Cuban music industry. It also provided a new source of revenue as timba bands started touring the world in the 1990s, bringing hard currency back to Cuba.

Reading

The reading for this chapter, "Situating Salsa: Latin Music at the Crossroads," places salsa in a global context. Salsa can be found around the world, in unexpected places such as Japan, Africa, and India, throughout Europe and in the Americas, both North and South. The market for salsa, both music and dance, is global, but this global genre has local connections, connotations, and meanings. Salsa's roots are Cuban and Puerto Rican, but it has become pan-Latin as it has grown in Latin American communities and was later embraced as the most identifiable and popular Latin American musical genre.

SITUATING SALSA: LATIN MUSIC AT THE CROSSROADS

Lise Waxer

"Echale Salsita." Put a little sauce on it. When Cuban composer Ignacio Piñeiro wrote this song for his Septeto Nacional in 1933, little did he know that he was setting the precedent for use of a term that would later be synonymous with an internationally popular Latin sound. Salsa, with its roots in the Cuban and Puerto Rican cultural diaspora to New York City, has now grown into a global musical phenomenon with audiences and practitioners ranging from Tokyo to Dakar. Today's salsa market offers Latin dance lessons, several Internet websites, touring dance competitions sponsored by Bacardi rum, and even "salsa cruises" with nightly performances by leading stars.

In Spanish, "salsa" literally means "sauce," with a culinary metaphor that evokes images of a spicy concoction—somewhat mirroring the music's own hybrid origins and infectious appeal. As the authors in this volume discuss, salsa means many things to many people, but a basic part of its attraction has been its ability to make people move together—to dance. Here, everyday troubles are forgotten in the "everynight life" of dancing bodies (Fraser Delgado and Muñoz 1997). The social interaction of salsa dance is mirrored and reinforced by the dynamic exchanges of the musicians themselves. For those of us who find our way into salsa as listeners, following the complex polyrhythmic conversations of salsa performance can be as exhilarating as getting down on the dance floor. For many of its new audiences, salsa is also a gateway to the cultural Other, a fascinating and often exotic world where new selves find liberation from cultural strictures.

Salsa developed in the Latino barrios of New York City during the 1960s and '70s. Based largely on Cuban forms of the 1930s, '40s and '50s, salsa also incorporated Puerto Rican elements and influences from North American jazz and rock. Salsa's Cuban and Puerto Rican antecedents were themselves a fusion of African and European elements[1] (see Alén 1984, Echevarría Alvarado 1984, and Dufrasne-González 1994 for more information on these forms). Cuban musicians in the first half of this century frequently used to say "toca con salsa!" (roughly, "hit it!" or "swing it!") when the excitement and energy of the music began to rise. This metaphor was inferred by Ignacio Piñeiro in his famous composition "Échale salsita." Many observers agree that a Venezuelan radio disc jockey, Phidias Danilo Escalona, was among the first to use the term "salsa" to denote Latin dance music in the early 1960s (Rondón 1980:33), although New York publisher Izzy Sanabría claims to have coined the name himself, at the end of the decade (Roberts 1979:187). Certainly, by the early 1970s, salsa had become the standard term of reference throughout Latin America, owing in large part to its use by Fania Records as a commercial label with which to market this music.

Given that the New York community in which salsa developed was strongly Puerto Rican, during the 1960s and '70s salsa became a potent emblem of Puerto Rican identity both for islanders and for those living in the mainland United States (Duany 1984; Padilla 1990), helping underpin nationalist sentiment against the specter of U.S. colonial domination. The use of the ten-stringed Puerto Rican cuatro, an icon of island culture, by Willie Colón and the Fania All-Stars during the early 1970s further underscored salsa's Puerto Rican affiliations.[2] The music's own interracial heritage was mirrored by the strong interethnic participation that marked the New York scene, with Jewish and African-American musicians performing in several bands. Jewish pianist Larry Harlow even became an important bandleader and producer in the New York scene. During this same period, salsa music also spread to other parts of Latin America, especially Venezuela, Panama, and Colombia—countries with close geographic and economic ties to the Caribbean. Significantly, salsa's lyrics reflected the experiences of the Latino and Latin American black and mixed-race working class, and—in distinction to its Cuban antecedents—songs mirrored the violence and discontent of the inner city. When salsa's exuberant beat and social message caught on with Latin American leftist intellectuals from the middle and upper-middle classes in the 1970s, salsa music shed its lower-class associations to establish a devoted following not only across national boundaries, but across social ones. By the 1980s, salsa was firmly entrenched as a transnational musical genre, with followers throughout the Americas and also in Europe, Africa, and Japan.

Salsa's complex history and international spread have given rise to much debate about its genesis and legitimacy as a musical category. Cuban specialists and musicians, in particular, have long contested the use of the term, claiming that salsa is nothing more than "Cuban music in new clothes." Marisol Berríos-Miranda and other authors in this volume, however, demonstrate that there are significant stylistic and ideological distinctions that mark salsa as a musical style distinct from its Cuban ancestors. Even a casual listening to salsa from the 1960s and '70s (e.g., Eddie Palmieri) and its Cuban antecedents from the 1940s and '50s (e.g., Arsenio Rodríguez) provides empirical grounds for distinguishing between the two. While the rhythms and forms are the same (e.g., *son*, *guaracha*, *mambo*, *cha-cha-chá* and *bolero*), the stylistic treatment is quite different. Salsa uses more percussion and larger horn sections than its Cuban antecedents.[3] The arrangements are more aggressive, and in the classic *salsa dura* ["hard/heavy" salsa] from the 1960s and '70s, the lyrics refer to a social and cultural milieu different from that of Cuba.

"Salsa" is a term that overlaps significantly with an earlier catchall, "Latin music." The very fluidity of the label "salsa" mirrors that of its predecessor. "Latin music" was a term applied primarily to Cuban and Puerto Rican dance genres in the 1930s, '40s and '50s, although it was occasionally used to denote other Latin American styles such as Argentine *tango* and Brazilian *samba* and *bossa nova*. Similarly, while salsa is generally understood to refer to popular dance styles with a Cuban and Puerto Rican musical base, other Caribbean styles, such as the Dominican *merengue* and Colombian *cumbia* have sometimes—and incorrectly—been thrown into this category, usually by outsiders to these traditions (see, e.g., Manuel 1988:46). As I argue elsewhere, the ambiguity of the term "Latin music" reflects its shifting, transnational character. While the term "Latin" tends to collapse difference in a way that can perpetuate oppressive stereotypes, such as the notion that Latins are all the same, it does point to a notion of Latin popular music as a stylistic complex that cannot be reduced to one specific location (Waxer 1994:140). Latin music and salsa, despite their clear reference to Cuban/Puerto Rican-based styles, have evolved into a musical expression with multiple sites of articulation. Salsa's transcendence of geographic and cultural boundaries has been central to its affective power—its capacity to literally move thousands of people. In a recent essay, Mayra Santos Febres refers to this process as "translocation"—the emergence of a globalized musical community from among its different locales of production and reception (1997).

Despite the fluid and rather slippery usage of the term, "salsa" clearly refers to much more than a specific musical form. Willie Colon notes, "Salsa is not a rhythm, it's a concept" (1999). Angel Quintero Rivera and Luis Alvarez similarly observe that salsa is a "way of making music" (1990). For this reason, some writers choose to capitalize the word as "Salsa," to emphasize its importance and its distinction from mere "salsa." [...] Wilson Valentín [...], Tite Curet Alonso [...] and Medardo Arias Satizábal [...] maintain this emphasis. Our volume does not pretend to resolve the debates concerning salsa's exact origins, or to fix its specific taxonomic location in the terrain of Latin American popular music. Rather, it is concerned with situating salsa as a musical *style*, wherein—as Colón and Quintero and Álvarez suggest—a social and cultural way of looking at the world (concept) is welded to praxis (making) through the creation and reception of musical sound. Style, in other words, becomes intrinsically bound up with larger social values, beliefs, and practices, not only reflecting but actively shaping human experience (Turino 1989; Keil 1985; Feld 1988; Meintjes 1990). Importantly, style and meaning are contingent to local historical processes. We cannot assume that salsa sounds the same or means the same thing everywhere it is played. The diverse and nuanced cases presented by the authors in this book clearly demonstrate that salsa's multiple transnational contexts have given rise to a number of different practices in salsa performance and salsa consumption.

This volume contains recently published and original new research on salsa and salsa-related styles (such as son, boogaloo, Latin jazz, and *timba,* or "Cuban salsa"), in global perspective. Our aim is to enlarge the scope of salsa research, which has concentrated primarily on salsa's Afro-Cuban roots and its New York and Puerto Rican creators. In her landmark study *Listening to Salsa* (1998), Frances Aparicio discusses the need to understand salsa as an emergent musical style whose meaning is being renegotiated by production and consumption in several different parts of the world. Indeed, the chapter in which she analyzes this issue is also titled "Situating Salsa" and serves as a point of departure for this anthology. By including chapters that explore salsa's adoption and localization not only in other Latin American countries (Colombia, Venezuela) and Latino communities in North America, but also in England and Japan, we have attempted to provide a truly international purview of contemporary salsa.

A central theme of this anthology concerns local-global links in Latin American and Caribbean popular music, exploring the constant circulation of people, ideas, sounds, and musical commodities among salsa's transnational sites. Although the Puerto Rico–New York–Cuba nexus remains a central axis for the creation and commercial production of salsa, the music's strong reception in several other global sites points to a dynamic process of globalization and relocalization that greatly expands salsa's popular significance. Several of these chapters examine the ways in which multinational economic flows and structures of power actually play out and are felt in people's daily lives. As Patria Román-Velásquez points out in her essay on salsa in London [...], "the local is treated not as self-contained and bounded, but understood in terms of its interaction with global processes." This observation is underscored by Shuhei Hosokawa, who notes "that the global and local cannot be considered as a pair of opposites but rather as an interwoven nexus shaped by the contours of history" [...].

The collection marks an overdue musicological nod in the direction of Latin American and U.S. Latino cultural studies. Much of the current literature in this field has been concerned with nonmusical expressive forms, such as literature, the plastic arts, and theater (García Canclini 1989, Rowe and Schelling 1991). Even the provocative and influential recent anthology *Everynight Life: Culture and Dance in Latino/a America* (Fraser Delgado and Muñoz 1997) does little to address specific musical concerns, leaving readers with little sense of how salsa—as sound and not only movement—operates in everyday experience and cultural performance. Being a hybrid musical expression, salsa has much to teach us about the dialectic between tradition and modernity in Latin America, and the effects of social diaspora and culture industries in overlapping and expanding contexts. It is also a tremendous laboratory in which to examine the role of musical expression in shaping individual subjectivities and social identities. For example, as Marisol Berríos-Miranda discusses in "Is Salsa a Musical Genre?" [...], the ways in which salsa represents national identity for Puerto Rican listeners are marked through subtle but essential variations in rhythmic phrasing and ensemble playing that differentiates Puerto Rican salsa from its Cuban antecedents—elements usually overlooked in most writing on salsa. In another case, as I discuss in "Llegó la Salsa" [...], for Venezuelan and Colombian listeners salsa has marked a cosmopolitan sensibility that ties local performers and audiences to the sphere of transnational culture, becoming a vehicle for them to "be in the world" when barriers of class and race prevent them from accessing elite forms of cosmopolitan culture.

Spurred by increased transport and communications links, mass media, and transnational economic flows, the rapid diffusion and relocalization of salsa points to important cultural processes of our times. Paralleling other styles such as rock and reggae, salsa's transnational popularity clearly illustrates the mechanics of hybridization and globalization that characterize popular culture in the twentieth century. Significantly, salsa has provided an alternative transnational popular style to the hegemony of U.S./British rock music and its association with U.S. political and economic domination. This has been important not only in the Latin American context but in other parts of the world as well. Our project of "situating salsa" arises from the need to reconsider the complicated and shifting trajectories of one of the most important global popular styles of our time.

GLOBAL MARKETS

Recent scholarship on globalization has questioned classic core-periphery models of international relations and development. Arjun Appadurai notes,

> The new global cultural economy has to be understood as a complex, over-lapping, disjunctive order, which cannot any longer be understood in terms of existing center-periphery models (even those that might account for multiple centers and peripheries). . . . The complexity of the current global economy has to do with certain fundamental disjunctures between economy, culture and politics which we have barely begun to theorize. (1990:296)

Certainly, the proliferation of hybrid popular musics on the world landscape during the late twentieth century has blurred any rigid notion that these developments occurred as a direct project of enterprises located in the "Western" or Euro-North American center. A series of essays published as a special edition of *World Music* in 1993 explored this emergent process. The authors call attention to the increasing "transversality" (Erlmann 1993:13) and "polylateral" or "multilateral" (Guilbault 1993b:39, Pacini Hernández 1993:49) flows of contemporary popular music, in diverse ways that shatter any notion of core-periphery movement.

Salsa's rapid spread through Latin America during the 1970s, followed by its adoption in Europe, Japan, and Africa during the 1980s and '90s, has similarly posed the need for considering this genre in terms of multiple sites of production and reception. Though salsa's diffusion to these places does not quite fall into the category of globalization along the lines of McDonald's, MTV, Microsoft, and Michael Jackson, the distinction between "transnational" (cutting across national boundaries) and "global" (truly worldwide) is not always clear in salsa's case. Although salsa's spread to different countries within Latin America might best be classified as transnational, its adoption in Europe, Japan, and West Africa certainly approaches global proportions. Furthermore, the increasing presence of Big Five record companies—especially Sony and BMG—in the salsa industry during the 1990s clearly ties salsa to globalizing forces in the music business, even when salsa is not necessarily promoted with the same emphasis in different world markets. The dozens of salsa-related websites that have emerged on the Internet also speak to increasing globalization along this medium.[4]

Certainly, the burgeoning Latino population in the United States has strongly affected salsa's production and distribution in the multinational music industry since the late 1980s. Keith Negus traces the complex ways in which new "Latin divisions" were established in the major companies—Sony/CBS, EMI, Polygram, BMG, and Warner/WEA—during this period, in an attempt to capture the growing Hispanic market. Ironically, despite the initial presence of salsa as a "domestic" genre in the U.S. market (which includes Puerto Rico), virtually all major companies, with the exception of EMI, farmed their Latin Music divisions out as subsidiaries of their international operations, with the resulting paradox that salsa became an "international" or "foreign" genre within the U.S. market. Even EMI and RMM (which is part of MCA's operations in the United States) were set up as separate divisions segregated along ethnic and language lines within the national market. The lines of communication within these networks are extremely complicated—for example, WEA Latina and Polygram Latina both report to their Latin American divisions, which in turn report to head offices in London. Furthermore, the Latin departments of all these companies maintain production studios in Miami but are controlled by financial offices in New York and Los Angeles (1999:142–45).

Most major salsa artists in the United States, the Caribbean, South America, and Japan—and even some local salsa labels, such as Venezuela's Rodven, picked up by Polygram—are or have been represented by one of the Big Five record companies. The complex and impersonal structure of these enterprises, however, means that the interests of local artists and, often, local audiences are left out of the picture when it comes to production and marketing decisions. As in the early 1980s, when several New York salsa artists began moving out from under the control of Fania Records, artists and producers are now contesting the hegemony of multinational record labels—often as a response to being shut out from access to the major companies in the first place. In the past decade, small independent labels have released numerous productions and compilations of material deemed commercially unviable for mass global markets, often distributed by independent companies such as Descarga Records in New York or local specialty shops. Other international salsa artists whose contracts with the majors terminate for various reasons are also sidestepping the corporatism of the music industry. Colombia's Grupo Niche, for example, represented by Sony throughout the 1990s, released its last album under the self-produced PPM (Productores Profesionales de la Música or Professional Producers of Music) label.[5] Willie Colón, who claims to have been blacklisted in the U.S. Latin market (2000), released his last album on the self-produced Azteca Music label,[6] distributed in Mexico by Polygram Latino América. More ethnographic research is needed to document these relationships and the effects of the global music industry on salsa performance and production.

Notably, during the late 1980s and early 1990s, salsa played a surprisingly marginal role in the "world beat" boom that spurred the global spread of several other international popular styles. According to Deborah Pacini Hernández, this may be explained partly by subtle yet pervasive anti-Latino racism in the U.S. markets where much of the "world beat" hype was promulgated—particularly against Puerto Ricans and Dominicans, commonly portrayed as drug dealers, pimps, and hot-blooded vixens in the U.S. media (1993b:57). Indeed, in her essay [...] on salsa clubs in London [...], Patria Román-Velásquez notes that a British entrepreneur similarly associated Puerto Ricans with an image of violence and delinquency that he wanted to avoid, preferring instead to cultivate an exotic tropical paradise closer to the stereotype of Miami's Little Havana. On the other hand, Latin American and U.S. Latino sensitivity to U.S. domination may have made artists and promoters reluctant to pursue the "melting pot" of the world beat industry, preferring to maintain a separate identity (Pacini Hernández 1993b: 57). Certainly, as Pacini Hernández notes, several recent currents in Spanish Caribbean music themselves point to internal regional dynamics that play into and off of larger global trends. The rise of Spanish reggae and hip-hop, for instance, while influenced by the worldwide impact of these styles, has developed without top-down domination of multinational record companies.

Currently, there are five principal "schools" or transnational styles of salsa performance: New York, Puerto Rican, Venezuelan, Colombian, and Cuban, with the development of *timba* or "Cuban salsa" in the 1990s. Some observers also add Miami to this list, although—as Christopher Washburne points out in his essay on *salsa romántica* [...]—the common pool of arrangers and studio musicians used in New York, Miami, and even Puerto Rico has made much contemporary salsa produced in these places sound very similar. Crosscutting these transnational schools is another stylistic matrix that correlates to salsa's historical development. Negus (1999:138–39) characterizes these as: (1) the "old school" (salsa dura, or "hard/heavy salsa"), following the New York, Puerto Rican, and Venezuelan sound of the 1960s and '70s; (2) salsa romántica, a continuation of the *salsa erótica* (sensual salsa) developed in the 1980s; (3) "soulful salsa," incorporating Top 40 pop, rhythm and blues, and soul harmonies and arrangements (e.g., Luis Enrique, Victor Manuel); and (4) "dance club salsa," which fuses salsa romántica with elements of hop-hop, r&b, and Cuban *timba* (e.g., Marc Anthony, La India).

The history of salsa's Cuban roots and its development in New York and Puerto Rico is well documented in several studies (Blum 1978; Roberts 1979; Rondón 1980; Arias Satizábal 1981; Singer 1982; Duany 1984; Alén 1984; Padilla 1989 and 1990; Gerard 1989; Arteaga 1990; Boggs 1992; Santana 1992; Manuel 1991, 1994, 1995; Quintero Rivera 1998; Washburne 1999). A smaller body of research by Venezuelan and Colombian scholars documents the rise of salsa in those countries (Rondón 1980; Baéz 1989; Arteaga 1990; Ulloa 1992; see also Waxer 1998). Very little work has been published on the rise of Cuban salsa or *timba* in the 1990s, although the strong commercial success of this sound in international markets will no doubt result in a spate of studies in the near future. Robin Moore provides an exploration of salsa and socialism [...].

Less understood are the sites outside of Latin America where salsa has also spread. The emergence of Japanese salsa bands in the 1990s sent profound waves through the international salsa scene, especially because these performers subverted Eurocentric stereotypes about what "Oriental" musicians should look and sound like. As Shuhei Hosokawa notes [...], the rise of Japanese salsa was marked by a complex negotiation of ethnic and exoticized identities. Notably, however, this development pointed to an important new trend in the globalization of popular music: the adoption of a non-Western style by another non-Western country, without the necessary intervention of North American or European influence. Hosokawa criticizes the ethnocentrism of studies that ignore this trend and offers a detailed analysis of Orquesta de la Luz's success at home and abroad. Current work in progress by Junko Oba suggests an even more nuanced approach to our understanding of salsa's "globalization" in this case, since the shift from regional/transnational audiences to a larger, global public market was precisely what led to the demise and eventual breakup of Orquesta de la Luz:

> A major cause of its poor sales and of the *subsequent collapse of the band* itself was that the promotional strategies of their new record company [from RMM to BMG], which aimed at capturing a larger global market with Orquesta de la Luz, inevitably de-localized the band and dissociated them from the salsa communities evolved around their music. In hindsight, the failed venture revealed how significantly the previous popularity and international success of Orquesta de la Luz had been grounded on and supported by the skillful local marketing operations designed specifically for the respective local markets in Japan and the Americas.

On another front, Senegalese salsa singers have been recording with Puerto Rican and Cuban musicians in New York, beginning with Laba Sosseh in the early 1980s and intensifying with Pape Seck, Sekouba Diabate, and other artists of the popular group Africando in the 1990s. These pan-Atlantic collaborations mark a new transnational dynamic in salsa's development. Their emergence, in turn, grows from the steady influence of Cuban and salsa recordings in West and Central Africa since the middle of the century (Graham 1988; Collins 1992; Stewart 2000), giving rise to "re-Africanized" Cuban-based styles such as the Zairean *rumba congolaise* and shaping the early sounds of Ghanaian and Nigerian highlife and urban dance band music in Mali and Senegal. Indeed, Africando's founder and producer, Ibrahim Sylla, grew up listening to and collecting imported salsa records in his native Dakar, and the influence of these classic sounds is apparent in the group's performance. Notably, the rise of *salsa africaine,* or African salsa, points not so much to a return of salsa to African soil (Steward 1999:157) but to a complex process of cultural appropriation between two regions of the so-called Third World. As in the case of Japan, this process has emerged without the direct domination of North American or European culture industries, which were focused on rock music. Although I have heard that surplus recordings of Cuban music were allegedly dumped on African markets by U.S.-controlled record companies in the 1930s and '40s,[7] I have not been able to confirm this claim. Certainly, it seems that in the absence of direct international distribution networks for New York labels such as Tico and Alegre in the 1960s, salsa recordings arrived in countries like Senegal through indirect routes—quite possibly through the same process of merchant sailors via which salsa arrived in South America (see Waxer, chapter 10).[8] More research is needed in this area, which remains a fertile but neglected field.

Other regions have given rise to salsa bands and audiences, particularly in areas where Latin Americans from salsa-producing countries have migrated. Virtually every country in Europe has a salsa scene; some of them even have renowned salsa bands. The founding of Conexión Latina in Munich in the early 1980s, for example, emerged from the collaboration between German jazz musicians and Puerto Rican *salseros* stationed on duty at a U.S. Army base in Germany. Their recordings have earned international acclaim. In this volume, Patria Román-Velásquez discusses the "routes and routines" through which English and Latin American entrepreneurs and customers have established a salsa club scene in London [...]. Her findings are similar to research I conducted in my hometown of Toronto, Canada, in the late 1980s (Waxer 1991). Brigido Galvan is conducting current research on more recent developments in salsa and Latin popular music in Canada.

The theme of global markets and the transnational music industry crosscuts several of the essays in this volume. Although, as Oba cautions, it is crucial to distinguish between regional and global levels in the music business, it is certain that the rise of the recording industry and the transnational diffusion of its products through formal and informal channels have been central processes in salsa's development. The production of Latin popular music, furthermore, has often developed in dialectical relation not only to different regional or global markets, but also musical production in other commercial styles. Christopher Washburne, for example, offers an "inside" view of the recording process, noting the ways in which distinctions between the New York and Puerto Rican schools of salsa affected the creation and production of a typical contemporary salsa tune [...]. In another essay, Juan Flores explores the fascinating history of the boogaloo fad in the 1960s, and the ways in which this early form of salsa was informed by trends in African-American popular music [...]. Robin Moore explores the influence that the transnational salsa industry had in revitalizing popular music production by the state-owned Cuban music industry during the 1990s, helping to spur the development of a new commercial style [...]. The commercial success of timba and traditional Cuban music in Europe and North America during the 1990s has had profound ramifications for this socialist country. Not only has it provided a much-needed source of income for the beleaguered nation, it has also obliged the Cuban state to adopt certain mechanisms of the capitalist global music industry.

Despite the strong presence of industry mechanisms at virtually every stage of salsa's history, however, the spread of salsa to different parts of the globe has not necessarily been conducted with its direct administration. Medardo Arias and I [...] look at the ways in which sailors served as an informal but vital link in the diffusion of Cuban, Puerto Rican, and salsa recordings to Colombia from the 1940s through the 1960s, before formal networks of record distribution were established in the 1970s. Patria Román-Velásquez [...] explores the way in which Latin American migration to England also introduced salsa to the country in the 1980s, before industry-controlled channels were consolidated to tap this growing market.

Tied to the notion of global markets is the issue of movement and cultural diaspora, particularly in the case of the Puerto Rico-mainland U.S. migrations that gave rise to salsa in the first place. Ángel Quintero Rivera, for instance, positions salsa as a style rooted in a tradition in which the theme of movement and labor migration have been present since the early twentieth century (1998). He sees many of the topical themes and musical elements articulated in 1970s and 1980s Puerto Rican salsa to be similar to those already expressed in the 1920s Cuban son which is salsa's principal musical predecessor. [...] focusing on the career of legendary salsa vocalist Héctor Lavoe, Wilson Valentín explores the concept of "trans-*Boricua*" identity and the affirmation of

Puerto Rican migration and subjectivity through music [...]. According to Valentín, the memory of Lavoe (who died in 1993) has become an arena in which cultural identity continues to be negotiated across different geographical and social spaces.

Salsa's transnational diffusion has facilitated a cross-pollination of musical styles, not only with elements of its own Afro-Cuban and Afro-Puerto Rican ancestry, but also with jazz and other Latin American traditions. Steven Loza explores the fusion of Cuban son and jazz in the music of Poncho Sánchez, a successful Chicano percussionist and bandleader [...]. Marisol Berríos-Miranda notes that salsa's localization in different Latin American countries has been marked by the fusion of salsa with national musical styles [...]. In my essay on Venezuelan and Colombian salsa, I briefly touch on some of the fusions between salsa and traditional regional musical genres such as *gaita*, *joropo*, *cumbia*, and *currulao* [...].

Also significant is the way in which salsa's global diffusion has masked a gender ideology that constructs Latin popular culture in terms of male superiority. Women have long been present as dancers and listeners in salsa's transnational diffusion, and during the late 1980s and 1990s, women in several countries (including the United States, Cuba, Colombia, Canada, Japan, and Denmark)[9] have made important contributions as salsa and Latin jazz musicians. Yet, the images promoted by the music industry continue to highlight men over women. In an important extension of her earlier work on salsa and gender (1998), Frances Aparicio here offers a cogent critique of the ways in which women and "feminized salsa" have been consistently subordinated in salsa discourse [...]. Her feminist genealogy of three of salsa's most prominent women performers—Celia Cruz, La Lupe, and La India (all vocalists)—is framed as a step toward understanding how Latino/a cultural politics and transnational identities have been constructed through music.

LOCAL MEANINGS

While a look at salsa's global spread is essential to understanding its significance, focusing on its ability to transcend geographic and cultural boundaries runs the grave risk of depoliticizing the structures of power and ethnic/cultural difference that gave rise to this music in the first place. Aparicio cautions us not to ignore "salsa's value as a historically oppositional expression within the larger tradition of Afro-Caribbean music" (1998:68). In her view, "border crossing" does not automatically assume equality. In his essay "Whose World, What Beat?" Reebee Garafolo similarly observes that the reconfiguration of global political and cultural economies that has led to globalization in popular music has also spawned more complex systems of capitalist oppression and control (1993). In some cases, salsa's history as a countercultural expression made it an ideal voice for people living in similar contexts, such as Panama, Venezuela, or Colombia. In these countries, salsa emerged as an expression of an urban, working-class, black and mixed-race culture in several cities whose histories were similar to that of Cuba and Puerto Rico. In other places, such as Japan and Europe, the political and ethnic elements have been modified in order to make salsa a more "universal" expression—but at the same time, one removed from salsa's roots as a voice for social opposition.

The essays […] pay careful attention to salsa's ties to local and regional meanings and structures of power. It is only in local contexts that we begin to understand the ramifications of salsa's spread to different parts of the world. Here, we begin to see the distinct practices that enabled salsa to be used as a vehicle for cultural values in countries as distinct as Puerto Rico, Colombia, and Japan. The strong ethnographic basis of most of the studies contained in this volume further underscores the local meanings and uses of salsa in its diverse transnational sites.

The contributions of Tite Curet Alonso […] and Medardo Arias Satizábal […] are perhaps the most "local" in their location, since they present very personalized perspectives of the impact of salsa on their own life experiences. Curet Alonso is a prolific composer, journalist, and sociologist (among other careers, including postman), and is one of the most revered composers in salsa today. His vignettes of various artists and producers with whom he has worked offers a unique insider's perspective on the salsa world. Arias Satizábal is a renowned author and poet in Colombia, who won the prestigious Simon Bolívar Award for Journalism in 1982 for his ten-part series on the history of salsa (1981)—a work written parallel to but without knowledge of César Miguel Rondón's acclaimed volume which appeared in Venezuela during this same period (1980). His chapter provides an evocative text recalling a childhood and adolescence growing up to the sounds of Cuban music and salsa in the Colombian Pacific port of Buenaventura.

Marisol Berríos-Miranda […] and Wilson Valentín Escobar […] also speak from their own subject positions as Puerto Rican scholars, and their exploration of salsa as a simultaneously national and transnational style is unmistakably rooted in their own personal experiences of salsa as an emblem of Puerto Rican identity. Berríos-Miranda criticizes the oft-cited view of salsa as "just Cuban music," analyzing the articulation of musical expression and ideological categories that makes salsa a distinct voice for Puerto Rican cultural sensibilities within the context of colonial subordination. Valentín Escobar, similarly, looks at the ways in which Puerto Rican salsa, while speaking to issues of transnational diaspora and movement, is also rooted in an emergent and constantly negotiated sense of place and cultural roots in the island itself.

Juan Flores, Frances Aparicio, and Patria Roman-Velasquez extend this purview to a study of salsa within minority Latino ethnic communities. Flores traces the development of boogaloo as not only an important moment in salsa history, but also an important chapter in black and Latino cultural collaborations mirrored a generation later in the rise of hip-hop culture in New York City […]. He positions boogaloo as a creative response to cultural and economic circumstances, within the context of minority ethnic struggles in this city. Similarly, Aparicio focuses on salsa in the U.S. Latino/a context, exploring the ways in which competing gender ideologies have intersected with those of race and ethnicity to frame the performance and reception of salsa's three principal female artists: Celia Cruz, La Lupe, and La India […]. Roman- Velasquez, in a different sphere, looks at insider and outsider perceptions of Latin dance clubs, and the role of London's burgeoning Latin dance scene in shaping Latino ethnic identity in England […].

In other essays, salsa's local-global links are explored for their impact on local musical practice and meaning. Robin Moore, for example, analyzes Cuban life after the revolution, and the ways in which musicians have responded to local situations […]. Timba, or "Cuban salsa," while a product of transnational commercial influence, has also acquired local potency for the ways in which it comments upon the return of capitalism and prostitution to the island. In my essay on salsa's adoption in Venezuela and Colombia [...], I explore salsa as a musical lingua franca for the rapidly expanding, heterogeneous urban environments of Caracas and Cali, where local and regional musical traditions no longer served to express new cultural sensibilities and experiences. In these cities, although Puerto Rico and New York continued to serve as central point of reference for salsa performance, practices of consumption often differed quite radically from their original counterparts—this is especially evident in the rise of the record-centered dance scene and *salsotecas* in Cali. Shuhei Hosokawa presents a similar instance in which salsa served as a vehicle for expressing the rapid changes and disjunctures of contemporary Japanese society, while reaffirming traditional cultural values [...]. Indeed, it is through exact mimicry of New York and Puerto Rican salsa bands that Orquesta de la Luz, Japan's most successful group, has upheld the traditional educational process of *kata* learning. Hosokawa also analyzes the ways in which geographical and cultural distance between Japan and the Americas actually promoted the success of Orquesta de la Luz, in a complex process through which cultural Others were negotiated and embraced through particularly local values on both sides.

Most of the authors represented in this volume approach local-global links through a historical perspective, analyzing salsa's global spread and local meanings in terms of specific historical conjunctures and contexts. This diachronic approach (Quintero Rivera 1998:40) is strongly influenced by the interdisciplinary field of cultural studies. As Quintero Rivera points out, however, a synchronic approach is also necessary for understanding music's impact in actual real-life moments. Such a perspective is represented [...] in Washburne's examination of the mechanics of a typical *salsa romántica* tune [...], and Loza's study of two Poncho Sánchez compositions [...]. Berríos-Miranda [...] also presents a methodical outline of the key elements and musical values that musicians and listeners expect to hear in a "good" salsa performance.

The essays in this volume have been organized along general topical lines that anchor this book's broad look at global markets and local meanings. The essays in the first section, "Locating Salsa," explore salsa as a simultaneously national (i.e., Puerto Rican) and also transnational (pan-Latino) musical style. While my central concern as editor of this volume has been to break away from the Cuba–New York–Puerto Rico focus of most salsa research to date, this is grounded in the philosophy that understanding salsa is fruitless if we forget its initial emergence as a vehicle for Puerto Rican and Nuyorican cultural identity and resistance against U.S. cultural domination. Salsa's initial Puerto Rican creators—Tito Puente, Eddie Palmieri, Willie Colón, Héctor Lavoe, Ismael Rivera, Ray Barretto, Tite Curet Alonso, Papo Lucca, Willie Rosario, and others—remain pivotal icons for contemporary salsa musicians and audiences around the globe. Although salsa's contemporary significance cannot be reduced to Puerto Rico alone, it certainly loses meaning if the dynamics of this fundamental location are ignored.

The second section, "Personalizing Salsa," looks more closely at individual artists and their musical and social impact. Among those profiled in this section are Celia Cruz, La Lupe, La India, Héctor Lavoe, and Poncho Sánchez. Also included are Tite Curet's autobiographical vignettes of Rafael Cortijo, Cheo Feliciano, Ismael Miranda, and Rubén Blades. The essays in this section outline various ways in which salsa has served as vehicle for expressing social identity at several levels, demarcating categories of race, class, ethnicity, community, gender, and generation. Their biographical orientation casts an important perspective on the complex conjunctures among salsa performance, production, reception, and consumption.

The third section, "Relocating Salsa," provides case studies of salsa's impact in different parts of the world, particularly where these shed light on local-global links at different levels, within and beyond translocal Latin American communities. Though we can certainly perceive what Appadurai refers to as "deterritorialization" (1996) at work in these cases, we also see an equally strong current of relocalization or, as some scholars are starting to put it, "glocalization" of salsa in different sites of the world (Robertson 1995; Kraidy 1996; Swyndegouw 1997). The multiple uses and meanings that salsa has given rise to in diverse places North and South, East and West, are a key part of the reconsideration of salsa's contemporary significance […].

Included in the volume are two essays […] that analyze salsa from a more systematic musicological examination of salsa performance and sound structure. These chapters, while certainly accessible for a general reader, are aimed particularly at musicians and specialists—an audience whose interests in musical structure are bypassed in most salsa scholarship.

The articles collected in *Situating Salsa* represent some of the best current scholarship on salsa. Clearly, as we move into a millennium in which Latin Americans and U.S. Latinos are posed to become major figures on the global cultural landscape, salsa's worldwide impact will increase in stature and complexity. This volume will probably raise as many new questions as those we have attempted to answer here. Certainly, we have not been able to address all the issues raised by salsa's current diffusion, and we hope that this volume will help to spur continued research. As salsa continues to reach into new locales in Europe, Africa, Australia, and South America, the significance of its origins as a contestatory Afro-Caribbean style will become increasingly complicated.

Despite the diversity of agendas that have accompanied salsa's adoption in different countries, its overarching nature as a joyful and exuberant musical style seems to be a constant in all its transnational and global contexts. In the introduction to his recent seminal work, *¡Salsa, sabor y control!*,[10] Ángel Quintero Rivera says that his objective is to formulate a new approach to sociological studies of Latin America and the Caribbean, one that focuses not on prevalent media images of underdevelopment, hunger, drugs, corruption, dicatorships, and human rights abuses, but rather on *"las contribuciones del Caribe a la alegría en el mundo"* [the contributions of the Caribbean to joy in the world, author's emphasis].

> [This] means not only a thematic innovation, but also a relocation of perspectives. To conceptualize joy also means, necessarily, to speak of sadness, but from the perspective of happiness; to meditate and research and reflect upon those processes that make happiness difficult, and the possible avenues of its future development. *¡Salsa, sabor y control!* trys to broach these complex social processes—communal, national, regional, and global—around one of our great delights. (1998:10)

Quintero Rivera's radical proposition informs the spirit of our project here. Like the beat of the clave, or rhythmic time line, that propels salsa's impelling groove, the element underscoring each of these essays is salsa's power to raise voices and move joyful bodies within and across cultural boundaries. Our aim is not only to shed new light on current debates about race and ethnicity, class hierarchy, gender roles, and generational differences, in multiple transnational contexts. Like the legions of fans and aficionados worldwide who know what it is to be carried away by a night of *descarga* and dancing, our own "salsa jam session" aims to convey some of our own passion for salsa's dynamic *afinque* (swing) and *sabor* (essence). I think Ignacio Piñeiro had it right all along. *Échale salsita.*

NOTES

1. Minor vestiges of the extinct Siboney and Taino Indian cultures have also been retained, most notably in the notched scraper known as *güiro,* a percussion instrument made from an elongated gourd.

2. A dearth of research exists on the Puerto Rican *cuatro,* owing in large part to the sensitivity of its nature as an icon of Puerto Rican culture—and hence, nationalism—within the current colonial regime. Attempts to showcase cuatro history by local cultural organizations and even by the Instituto de Cultura Popular have been repeatedly squelched by the government. In this regard, recent work by the Cuatro Project, an independent research consortium, has been especially valuable. See website: www.cuatro-pr.org, and its recently completed documentary film, *Nuestro Cuatro: Los puertorriqueños y sus instrumentos de cuerda, vol. 1,* available in Spanish and English versions.

3. With the exception of some Cuban big bands of the 1940s and '50s such as La Gigante de Benny Moré, the Orquesta Casino de la Playa, and the Orquesta Riverside. These big bands paralleled the New York mambo orchestras of Machito, Tito Puente, and Tito Rodríguez that directly preceded salsa in the New York scene.

4. Salsa-related websites include Latin Music On-line, OasisSalsero, the Willie Colón Website and Forum, Descarga Records, San Francisco/Bay Area Salsa and Latin Jazz, Salsa Web, Picadillo, Latin Dance, Der Salsaholic, Hot Salsa (Le Guide de la Salsa), Musica Salsa Forum, Salsa Jam, Salsa Brasil, SalsaJazz, Jazz con Clave, Salsa con Cache, Noti-Salsa, Salsatecas, Bamboleo, Sonero, SalsaNet, Latino, Cadena SalSoul, Dimensíon Latina, Salsa in Finland, Samurai Latino, NYC Salsa, Salsa em Brasil, Master Timbaleros, Timba Website, Richie Blondet's Montuno Papers, and Nestor Louis's webpage. Most commercial salsa artists also have their own website, as do Fania and RMM Records.

5. Grupo Niche (1999) *A Golpe de Folklore* (PPM 0001).

6. Willie Colón (1999) *Demasiado Corazón* (Azteca Music 2-1719[24]). Colón also spoke about his blacklisting to a small group of students at Trinity College, Hartford, Conn., November 11, 1999.

7. Jay Nash, personal communication, November 1991.

8. Deborah Pacini Hernandez (1993a) describes a parallel process in the other direction, via which records of Afro-pop, South African *mbqanga* (township jive), Zairean *soukous* and Caribbean styles such as *soca* and *zouk* were introduced into the Colombian port of

Cartagena in the 1970s and '80s, where they were adopted as an emblem of Afro-Colombian identity in a localized sound known as *champeta* or *terapia*.

9. These include contemporary all-women salsa bands such as Anacaona (Cuba), Son de
Azucar (Colombia), and Perfume de Salsa (Denmark), and musicians such as Rebeca
Mauleón-Santana (U.S.), Sheila Escovedo (U.S.), Jane Bunnett (Canada), and Nora of
Orquesta de la Luz (Japan). During the early to mid-1990s, both Havana and Cali had
more than ten *orquestas femeninas* or all-women bands. I analyze the rise of all-women
salsa bands in Colombia elsewhere (Waxer 2001).

10. Awarded the 1999 Casa de Las Americas Prize and 2000 Latin American Studies Association
Award for Best Book on Latin America.

BIBLIOGRAPHY

Alén, Olavo. 1984. *De lo afrocubano a la salsa: géneros musicales de Cuba.* San Juan: Cubanacán.
[Reprinted in English as *From Afro-Cuban Music to Salsa,* with accompanying CD. Berlin: Piranha
Records BCD-PIR 1258, 1998.]

Aparicio, Frances R. 1998. *Listening to Salsa: Gender, Latin Popular Music and Puerto Rican Cultures.* Hanover, N. H.: Wesleyan University Press/University of New England Press.

Appadurai, Arjun. 1990. "Disjuncture and Difference in the Global Cultural Economy." In Mike
Featherstone, ed., *Global Culture: Nationalism, Globalization and Modernity.* London: Sage,
pp. 295–309.

_____. 1996. *Modernity at Large: Cultural Dimensions of Globalization.* Minneapolis: University
of Minnesota Press.

Arias Satizábal, Medardo. 1981. "Esta es la verdadera historia de la salsa." Printed as an eleven-part
series in *El Occidente* newspaper. Winner of the 1982 Premio Simón Bolívar for Journalism.

Arteaga, José. 1990. *La Salsa.* Bogotá: Intermedio Editores. 2nd rev. ed.

Baéz, Juan Carlos. [1985] 1989. *El vínculo es la salsa.* Caracas: Fondo Editorial Tropykos.

Blum, Joseph. 1978. "Problems of Salsa Research." *Ethnomusicology* 22(1):137–49.

Boggs, Vernon, ed. 1992. *Salsiology: Afro-Cuban Music and the Evolution of Salsa in New York
City.* Westport, Conn.: Greenwood Press.

Collins, John. 1992. *West African Pop Roots.* Philadelphia: Temple University Press.

Colón, Willie. 1999. Jacket cover to *Demasiado Corazón* (Azteca Music 2–1719[24]).

_____. 2000. "The Latin Grammies: Is There no End to the Egotism of the Miami Mafia?" Inter-
national press release, published simultaneously in English and Spanish by several media.

Duany, Jorge. 1984. "Popular Music in Puerto Rico: Toward an Anthropology of Salsa." *Latin American Music Review* 5(2):186–207.

Dufrasnes-González, Emanuel. 1994. *Puerto Rico también tiene ¡tambo! Recopilación de artículos
sobre la plena y la bomba.* Río Grande: Paracumbé.

Erlmann, Veit. 1993. "The Politics and Aesthetics of Transnational Musics. *World Music* 35 (2): 3–15.

Echevarría Alvarado, Félix. 1984. *La plena: origen, sentido y desarollo en el folklore puertorriqueño.*
Santurce: Express.

Feld, Steven. 1988. "Aesthetics as Iconicity of Style, or 'Lift-up-over Sounding': Getting into the Kaluli Groove." *Yearbook for Traditional Music* 20:74–113.

Fraser Delgado, Celeste and José Esteban Muñoz, eds. 1997. *Everynight Life: Culture and Dance in Latin/o America.* Durham, N. C.: Duke University Press.

Garafolo, Reebee. 1993. "Whose World, What Beat: The Transnational Music Industry, Identity, and Cultural Imperialism." *World Music* 35(2): 16–32.

García Canclini, Nestor. 1989. *Culturas híbridas: Estrategías para entrar y salir de la modernidad.* Mexico City: Grijalbo.

Gerard, Charley. 1989. *Salsa!: The Rhythm of Latin Music.* Crown Point, Ind.: White Cliffs.

Graham, Ronnie. 1988. *The Da Capo Guide to Contemporary African Music.* New York: Da Capo.

Guilbault, Jocelyne. 1993. "On Redefining the 'Local' through World Music." *World Music* 35(2):33–47.

Keil, Charles. 1985. "People's Music Comparatively: Style and Stereotype, Class and Hegemony." *Dialectical Anthropology* 10:119–30.

Kraidy, Marwan Michael. 1996. "Towards a Semiosphere of Hybrid Identities: A Native Ethnography of Glocalization." Ph.D. dissertation, Ohio University.

Manuel, Peter. 1988. *Popular Musics of the Non-Western World: An Introductory Survey.* New York: Oxford University Press.

_____. 1991. "Latin Music in the United States: Salsa and the Mass Media." *Journal of Communication* 4(1): 104–16.

_____. 1994. "Puerto Rican Music and Cultural Identity: Creative Appropriation of Cuban Sources from Danza to Salsa." *Ethnomusicology* 38(2):249–280.

_____. 1995. *Caribbean Currents: Caribbean Music from Rumba to Reggae.* Philadelphia: Temple University Press.

Meintjes, Louise. 1990. "Paul Simon's *Graceland,* South Africa, and the Mediation of Musical Meaning." *Ethnomusicology* 34(l):37–73.

Negus, Keith. 1999. *Music Genres and Corporate Cultures.* London: Routledge.

Oba, Junko. (n.d.). "Making and Selling Japanese Salsa: Orquesta de la Luz and the (Re)imagining of Salsa." Unpublished manuscript.

Pacini Hernández, Deborah. 1993a. "The *picó* phenomenon in Caragena, Colombia." *América Negra* 6:69–115.

_____. 1993b. "A View From the South: Spanish Caribbean Perspectives on World Beat." *World Music* 35(2): 48–69.

Padilla, Félix. 1989. "Salsa Music as a Cultural Expression of Latino Consciousness and Unity." *Hispanic Journal of Behavioral Sciences* 2(l):28–45.

_____. 1990. "Salsa, Puerto Rican and Latino Music." *Journal of Popular Culture* 24(1):87–104.

Quintero Rivera, Ángel. 1998. *¡Salsa, sabor y control! Sociología de la música "tropical."* Mexico City: Siglo Ventiuno Editores. Reprinted by Casa de Las Americas, Havana.

Quintero Rivera, Ángel, and Luis Manuel Álvarez. 1990. "La libre combinación de las formas musicales en la salsa." *David y Goliat* 57:45–51.

Roberts, John Storm. 1979. *The Latin Tinge: The Impact of Latin American Music on the United States.* New York: Oxford University Press.

Robertson, Roland. 1995. "Glocalization: Time-Space and Homogeneity-Heterogeneity." In Mike Featherstone, Scott Lash, and Roland Robertson, eds., *Global Modernities.* London: Sage, pp. 25–44.

Rondón, Cesar Miguel. 1980. *El libro de la salsa: crónica de la música del caribe urbano.* Caracas, Venequela: Editorial Arte.

Rowe, William, and Vivian Schelling. 1991. *Memory and Modernity: Popular Culture in Latin America.* London: Verso.

Santana, Sergio. 1992. *¿Qué es la salsa?: Buscando la melodía.* Medellín: Ediciones Salsa y Cultura.

Santos Febres, Mayra. 1997. "Salsa as Translocation." In Celeste Fraser Delgado and José Esteban Muñoz, eds., *Everynight Life: Culture and Dance in Latin/o America.* Durham: Duke University Press, pp. 175–88.

Singer, Roberta. 1982. "'My Music Is Who I Am and What I Do': Latin Popular Music and Identity in New York City." Ph.D. dissertation, Indiana University.

Steward, Sue. 1999. *Musica! The Rhythm of Latin America: Salsa, Rumba, Merengue, and More.* San Francisco: Chronicle Books. Published simultaneously in England as *Salsa! Musical Heartbeat of Latin America*, London: Thames and Hudson.

Stewart, Gary. 2000. *Rumba on the River: A History of the Popular Music of the Two Congos.* London: Verso.

Swyndegouw, Erik. 1997. "Neither Global nor Local: 'Glocalization' and the Politics of Scale." In Kevin R. Cox, ed., *Spaces of Globalization: Reasserting the Power of the Local.* New York: Guilford, pp. 137–66.

Turino, Thomas. 1989. "The Coherence of Social Style and Musical Creation among the Aymara of Southern Peru." *Ethnomusicology* 33(l):l–30.

Ulloa, Alejandro. 1992. *La salsa en Cali.* Cali: Ediciones Universidad del Valle.

Washburne, Christopher J. 1999. *Salsa in New York: A Musical Ethnography.* Ph.D. dissertation, Columbia University.

Waxer, Lise. 1991. "Latin Popular Musicians in Toronto: Issues of Ethnicity and Cross-Cultural Integration." Master's thesis, York University.

_____. 1994. "Of Mambo Kings and Songs of Love: Dance Music in Havana and New York City from the 1930s-1950s." *Latin American Music Review* 15(2): 139–76.

_____. 1998. "*Cali Pachanguero:* A Social History of Salsa in a Colombian City." Ph.D. dissertation, University of Illinois at Urbana-Champaign.

_____. 2001. "Las Caleñas Son Como Las Flores: All-Women Salsa Bands in Cali, Colombia." *Ethnomusicology* 45(2):228–259.

Questions for thought

- What are the unifying elements of salsa? How important is rhythm to salsa music and dancing?
- What is the connection between Santeria and salsa? Compare this to the relationship between samba and the Brazilian version of Santeria. How are samba and salsa connected? Why did these two musical traditions both draw from similar African religious practices? How are they different?
- What are the three stages of Latino assimilation in music?
- What is the origin of the name salsa?
- What are the five principal schools of salsa? Should Miami be on that list?
- What has remained constant in salsa as it is adopted in different countries and contexts?

Activity

Search for salsa recording and dance performances on YouTube, focusing on salsa in the 1960s, 70s, 80s through salsa today. How is salsa from the 1960s different from salsa in the 1970s, from the 80s, and salsa today? What has changed? What has stayed the same? Then compare salsa from Miami and New York. How is salsa in these two American cities similar? Different? Which do you prefer?

Figure Credits

Fig. 5-1: Source: https://commons.wikimedia.org/wiki/File:CIA_map_Central_America_%26_Caribbean.png.

Fig. 5-2: Copyright © Flikr (CC by 2.0) at https://www.flickr.com/photos/45803876@N00/31911547722/in/photostream/.

Fig. 5-4: Source: https://commons.wikimedia.org/wiki/File:(Portrait_of_Noro_Morales_and_Humberto_López_Morales,_Glen_Island_Casino(%3F),_New_York,_N.Y.,_ca._July_1947)_(LOC)_(5062524130).jpg.

Fig. 5-6: Source: https://commons.wikimedia.org/wiki/File:TitoandRogerDawson.jpg.

CHAPTER SIX

Caribbean Music: Reggae, Rumba, and Riddims

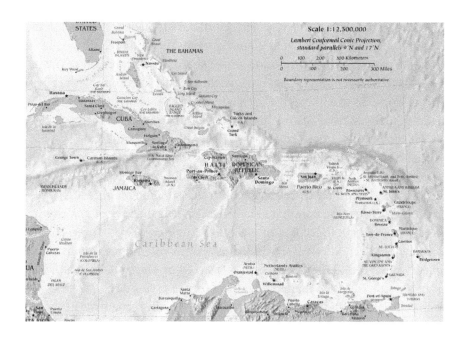

FIGURE 6.1 *Map of the Caribbean*

Introduction

Caribbean music has had a major impact on world popular music. When most people think of Caribbean music, Jamaican *reggae*, Cuban and Puerto Rican salsa and Trinadadian calypso often come to mind. Reggae is the latest in a series of genres that developed in Jamaica since the 1940s, from *mento* to *ska* and *rock steady*, all leading to reggae. Calypso's legacy resulted in *soca*, which remains a popular dance genre.

1940s Trinidad, CALYPSO → Jamaica, MENTO	Late 1950s/60s Jamaica, SKA →	mid-1960s Jamaica, ROCK STEADY →	1970s Trinidad, SOCA Jamaica, REGGAE

FIGURE 6.2 *Caribbean music timeline*

Jamaican Music

Mento

Mento is the first of a progression of genres that led to reggae. Unlike other Jamaican genres, which are urban in origin, mento was formed in the rural countryside. It first appeared in the late 1940s and early 1950s and used instruments that were readily available, including guitar, banjo, various hand drums, and a rumba box, a large version of the thumb piano, or mbira, that often provides the bass line. Mento is often confused with calypso, a similar genre from Trinidad and Tobago. They share some characteristics, but each is a separate and distinct genre. (Mento is sometimes referred to as Jamaican calypso). Mento's lyrics tend to be topical and humorous, at times rife with sexual innuendo.

As is the case with most genres in the New World, at least those with significant slave populations, mento's roots are both West African and European. These two sources combined to form a unique genre, reflecting both slave and colonial culture. Mento was the first Jamaican genre to be dominated by what is now called the *skank* rhythm, in which upbeats are stressed in the accompaniment, forming a one-TWO-three-FOUR feel. By the 1950s many Jamaican artists were recording mento, often marketed as calypso. A good example of this is the "Banana Boat Song" (Day-O) by Harry Belafonte, a New Yorker of Jamaican descent. Many conflate calypso and mento to this day.

Mento enjoyed a revival in the 1980s and was eventually recognized as the root of Jamaican popular music. Thanks to groups like the Jolly Boys, who toured the United States and released many recordings in the late 1980s and early 1990s, mento was reestablished as an important popular genre and remains popular today.

Ska

In the 1960s, another popular music genre developed in the Jamaican dance halls of Kingston and other cities known as ska. Although it shared some characteristics with mento, the focus in ska was dancing, and it quickly became Jamaica's most important dance-oriented popular style. It combined elements of mento and calypso with American influences, most notably from rhythm and blues. It developed when Jamaican musicians started building elaborate sound systems to play R&B, jump blues, and other American genres;

these musicians started recording their own versions of this music, taking on Jamaican characteristics, most notably the skank rhythm of mento.

Ska features repetitive themes and improvised solos, and it quickly found its way into dancehalls in Kingston and London, where a large number of Jamaicans settled in the later 50s, and by the early 60s it was the dominant musical genre of Jamaica. The dance featured skanking, a dance move in time with the skank rhythm so prevalent in mento but at a much faster tempo.

Rock Steady

Rock steady is a musical movement that reflected the Jamaican politics of the 1960s, becoming a musical outlet to express civil discontent. The British government had pulled out of Jamaica in 1962, leaving a political and economic void. With little time to prepare the country for the changes that the British leaving caused, there was a great deal of chaos in the country, and poor Jamaicans were left with few resources and fewer recourses. This led to large number of disaffected Jamaicans, resulting in a struggle for survival and a decade of major problems for the country. Street gangs, made up of disaffected youths known as Rude Boys, developed in the ghettos of Kingston and other cities. One result of this political stress was a protest music movement that lasted more than a decade: rock steady.

Compared to ska, rock steady was more relaxed, slower, more streamlined, and as might be expected, replete with political lyrics and attitudes. It moved at a slower tempo, but still with the dominant skank rhythm. It also featured the "one-drop" drum beat, which has a heavy accent on the third beat of the bar. The slower tempo also allowed for more complex bass rhythms. The same musicians and producers were playing ska and rock steady, the main difference being in tempo and lyrics. Rock steady's characteristics were carried forward in the 1970s as the foundation of reggae.

Reggae

Reggae is Jamaica's most important musical genre, which has developed since the 1970s as a global genre with great influence on the music of many countries, including the United States, Brazil, much of Europe, and Asia. It has a more polished sound than ska or rock steady, reflecting the innovation and creativity of recording studios and their use of technology, leading directly to developments in hip-hop and rap a few years later. The same engineers and DJs that developed the sound of reggae developed the techniques and sound of rap, mostly among the immigrant Jamaican populations in the South Bronx, the birthplace of rap.

FIGURE 6.3 *Bob Marley in concert*

As was the case with rock steady, the lyrics of reggae often deal with the political and social conditions in Jamaica. They were a means of expressing the frustration of Jamaicans with the worsening conditions in Jamaica following the British leaving and the political vacuum they left; a socially conscious message is an important aspect of reggae. The leading record label for reggae was Island Records, a company that supported the message of reggae.

An important component of reggae was the embracing of the Rastafari lifestyle and philosophy. This Afrocentric religious movement developed in Jamaica in the 1930s. It holds that blacks are the chosen people and that blacks will eventually return to Africa. Rastas believe that Haile Selassie (1892–1975), the Emperor of Ethiopia, was the Messiah, and have a belief system that is based on a particular interpretation of the Bible. According to the Oxford Living Dictionary, a Rastafarian is "a member of the Rastafarian religious movement. Rastafarians have distinctive codes of behavior, dress [and social markers], including the wearing of dreadlocks, the smoking of cannabis, the rejection of Western medicine, and adherence to a [restricted] diet."

The most important musician in reggae was Bob Marley (1945–1981), the son of a white Englishman and a black Jamaican woman. By the age of fourteen, Marley began exploring the music studios and dancehalls of Trenchtown, a rough neighborhood of Kingston and in many ways the home of reggae. His music is infused with Rastafari religious ideals, which are embedded in the lyrics, delivering a socially conscious message. His music was heavily influenced by American rhythm and blues and the Jamaican genres that preceded reggae, first expressed with his band, Bob Marley and the Wailers. The group disbanded in 1974, at which time Marley focused on a solo career and relocated to England. He died of cancer in 1981 at age 36. Marley's music, and reggae in general, still features the skank rhythm of the preceding Jamaican genres. It tends to move at a slow pace and is known for its "slackness" or vulgarity. In addition to skank, it is rhythmically active, with rhythms referred to in the Creolized version "riddims."

Reading #1

One of the readings for the chapter, "How Reggae Defeated Mambo," looks at reggae as the most important and influential Caribbean musical genre. Cuban music was extremely popular in the Americas in the 1950s, but with Castro's revolution and the subsequent void left by the isolation of the newly communist island, Cuban music lost its dominance and fell into decay; Jamaica and reggae were poised to fill this void. The booming tourist industry in Jamaica and the collapse of tourism in Cuba helped spark worldwide interest in reggae and Jamaican music in general.

HOW REGGAE DEFEATED MAMBO

When communism squelched popular music in Cuba, Jamaica took over as cultural capital of the Caribbean

Chris Kjomess

Havana in the 1950s was Las Vegas with beaches. Affluent North Americans escaped to Cuba to indulge in cigars, sex, rum, and affordable luxury. Leading hotels and casinos boasted of dance halls and large orchestras. Modeled after popular New York orchestral combos, these tourism-generated bands infused popular music from the United States with the instruments and rhythms of Cuba, Africa, and the Caribbean.

The result was explosive. The mambo quickly busted out of the glitzy cabarets and into the buzzing streets of Havana. Small, private social clubs, of the type immortalized in the 1999 documentary *Buena Vista Social Club*, began springing up on every street corner. Organized by neighborhood, by occupation, and by social status, these clubs helped nurture a strong community-based sense of the new Cuban music.

Like so much Cuban-American culture before the two countries became bitter adversaries, Havana's mambo craze leapt back across the Florida Straits to a willing United States. New York Jazz musicians began incorporating Cuban elements into their music. Pop singers such as Nat "King" Cole began recording with musicians in Cuba and singing in Spanish. Cuban artists such as Beny Moré and Celia Cruz found themselves at the fore of a new, syncretic movement in pan-American popular music.

FIGURE 6.4

And decades before cultural observers would enthuse over the "crossover" appeal of Jennifer Lopez and Shakira, Yankee audiences threw their arms around Cuban percussionist Desi Arnaz, whose mambo band-leader character Ricky Ricardo co-anchored the most popular show on American television, *I Love Lucy*.

At the height of '50s mambo fever, you would have been laughed out of the room had you predicted that comparatively tiny and impoverished Jamaica would soon become a dominant force in global music, while the Caribbean's longstanding cultural capital of Havana fell into irrelevance and decay. But the rise of communism and its attendant cultural protectionism soon choked off mambo and Cuban creativity at the source, while Jamaica's economic boom and unfettered recording industry uncorked a revolutionary new music called reggae.

The glossy exterior of Havana's nightlife concealed something much darker. Dictator Fulgencio Batista demonstrated little regard for the constitution he had created more than a decade earlier. Racial and social divides ran deep, free speech and assembly were severely curtailed, and the wealth brought in by the booming tourist trade was seen as benefitting only the well connected.

On July 23, 1953, a group of revolutionaries led by Fidel Castro attacked the Moncada Barracks in Havana. While easily thwarted, the attack marked the beginning of what would be the Cuban Revolution. After a brief prison stint, the bearded revolutionary fled to Mexico, then returned in December of 1956 with Argentinean physician and military strategist Che Guevara and

80 men. Taking to the Sierra Maestra Mountains, and shoring up support from rural workers and farmers, Castro and company began what would be a two-year war against the Batista regime. On New Year's Day 1959, Batista fled to the Dominican Republic, and Fidel Castro began his long victory march to Havana.

FIGURE 6.5

Initially, many musicians were optimistic about the new Cuba. At last they would be able to explore their craft free from the constraints of the market. Class and race would no longer divide people, and artists would now be able to freely connect with all Cubans instead of merely catering to visiting Americans. Most non-headlining musicians saw an initial increase in income, and composers were afforded the security of a regular salary. Cultural education programs strove to valorize domestic music and raise the musical literacy of all Cubans.

But this new musical economy was unsustainable. The casinos were looted and shuttered within days of the revolution. Hotels were commandeered, and tourists stopped coming. With the engine of the economy cut, more and more clubs found it impossible to stay open. By January 1960, the government had taken over most performance venues. And by the summer of 1960, Cuba's numerous radio and television networks were nationalized.

Disaster Diet

Thanks to *The Prepper's Cookbook* (Ulysses Press), the next political upheaval or natural disaster could be surprisingly delicious. Tess Pennington's book, designed for people fearing social and economic collapse, provides diverse recipes for food made from nonperishable items, such as shepherd's pie, beef and potato tacos, and breakfast quinoa. It also explains vital safety practices, such as how to ensure that you have clean water and how to store your packaged food supplies.

While Pennington is not explicitly motivated by a lack of faith in government, she does note how long many people had to wait for assistance after Hurricane Katrina. She also says that her suggestions will prepare you not just for unexpected natural disasters but for economic ones, such as inflation. *The Prepper's Cookbook* is a welcome reminder that humanity, with proper preparation, can not only survive disaster but can do so while enjoying tasty meals.

—*Matthew Feeney*

A musician wishing to be heard in Cuba now required government approval. Opportunities to perform abroad were limited to state-sponsored tours, and formal approval was required even to travel anywhere on the island. Cuban musicians, who once roamed as far as their talents could take them, now found their ability to share their works dependent upon the state's assessment of their loyalty to the Revolution. And it was not only professional musicians who were silenced: The Social Clubs, so vital to the musical soul of the island, were declared unegalitarian and abolished.

By 1961, all production facilities had been nationalized. State approval was required for any new recording. Censorship and bureaucratic red tape frustrated artists. Reduced tourism and trade cut Cuba off from its most lucrative markets, and the lack of profit motive meant that no one stood to make money by pushing new music or reissuing perennially popular recordings. Meanwhile, the deteriorating economy (exacerbated by the U.S. embargo) made money still more scarce. By 1966, Cuba, which used to press millions of records a year, only managed to eke out 184,000.

FIGURE 6.6

As his country moved much closer to the Soviet Union, Castro soon adopted Moscow's model of arts production. To be a musician in socialist Cuba, one had to audition for a panel of conservatory-trained professionals who assigned the would-be performer a letter grade of A, B, or C. Given the background of the panel, it was only natural that those most proficient in classical European styles were assigned to the highest class, while those proficient in folk or popular styles would be diverted into lesser pools.

Popular styles of music such as jazz and early rock 'n' roll were tolerated in the early days of the Revolution, but later years saw them labeled as imperialist, and effectively banned. (Even the Beatles were banned for several years on grounds of cultural imperialism.) Artists attempting the Cuban tradition of incorporating new rhythms and instruments into their styles were blacklisted from state radio and TV.

In 1968, a prohibitionist "Dry Law" closed Cuban clubs, leaving 40 percent of Cuban club musicians with no place to perform. In 1970, most were forced into the sugar fields as part of the communist state's *zafra de los 10 milliones*, a desperate plot to save the Cuban economy with a massive, one-time sugar haul. Musicians had their instruments ripped from their hands and replaced with machetes. In just one decade, Havana went from being the wellspring of popular pan-American music to a desert of rigid, top-down culture.

The colonial island 90 miles south of Cuba had a much more modest musical pedigree at the time of the mambo boom. The first popular music documented in Jamaica was *mento*. Played on homemade string, wind, and percussion instruments in rural parts of the country as early as the 19th century, mento featured an even, playful gait and cheeky lyrics about daily life. Sounding similar to Trinidadian calypsos, mento did not start appearing on record until the 1950s, when entrepreneurs such as Ken Khouri and Ivan Chin sought to jump-start a domestic recording industry.

These early mento recordings did not sell particularly well in the face of regional competition from Cuba and Trinidad. The biggest hit of the era, Alerth Bedasse's "Night Food," caught the attention of the colonial government (Jamaica was ruled by Great Britain for three centuries until its independence in 1962) due to its provocative lyrics about a young man who is confused when an older woman invites him to sample the warm sweet night food, even though the room they are in is pitch black and he has no utensils. Trade and Industry minister Willis O. Isaacs personally attacked the song in an address to parliament, raising concerns about censorship, further discouraging investment in domestic recording.

But the 1950s would be a time of economic and political change in Jamaica. Global demand for aluminum was growing; the miracle metal was being used in everything from airplanes to TV dinner trays. By the end of the decade Jamaica would be the world's leading producer of aluminum's raw material of bauxite. Less labor intensive than farming, bauxite mining created a labor surplus and young Jamaicans poured in from the countryside in search of better opportunities.

Jamaicans began leaving the island to work on sugar and cotton plantations in the United States, replacing southern blacks who had left during the Great Migration. An estimated 174,000 Jamaicans also moved to the United Kingdom between 1953 and 1962, after which the British government abruptly cut off immigration from the newly independent state. Millions of pounds in remittances were sent to Jamaica every year.

Limited transportation and infra-structure had long handcuffed the country's tourist industry. But after World War II, commercial travel and newly built hotels helped spur three decades of consistent economic growth. Jamaican GNP nearly doubled between 1952 and 1962. The years between 1940 and 1960 saw significant reductions in illiteracy and infant mortality, and a 10-year jump in life expectancy.

Speculative Science

Randall Munroe, the NASA roboticist cum artist behind the webcomic *xkcd*, has a weekly column (what-if.xkcd.com) answering reader's "What if?" questions about science and technology.

With the clever Munroe as your guide, even the most seemingly absurd speculations lead to valuable insights. We learn why solar cars don't work via an explanation of why cows don't photosynthesize, for example. He also plays with pop perceptions of tech fears—he's sure a robot revolution wouldn't get anywhere because most don't work accurately for long and would likely end up stuck against walls.

Munroe's research rediscovers some wild flights of fancy from the past, as when governments wondered how nuclear weapons might be used in the ocean to create waves extending 300 miles inland. And he also describes amusing examples of government overreach: The Soviets made a machine gun too powerful to work in an airplane, while the U.S. points Hubble-type telescopes from orbit at Earth every day.

—*Ed Krayewski*

Jamaica was in the process of becoming urban and modern, and the young people who found themselves in the capital of Kingston were no longer interested in the "country" music of their past. Retailers began setting up speakers in front of their business in hopes of luring customers inside. Entrepreneurs such as hardware store owner Thomas Chin started renting out mobile sound systems for parties.

By the mid-1950s the sound system was the center of Kingston nightlife. Hotels and tourist clubs did not welcome locals, and state radio catered to a conservative affluent audience, so the sound-system dance was the place most Jamaicans went to show off their wares and hear new tunes. An underground economy grew around the dances: Organizers charged admission, DJs received a fee, and food and alcohol vendors lined the streets around the venue.

Competition between DJs was intense, and customer feedback immediate. The hottest music in 1950s Kingston was American jazz and rhythm and blues. DJs paid a premium for records by artists such as Rosco Gordon and Fats Domino. Records were imported or bought off boat workers coming from the United States. Many DJs actually got their start working as migrant laborers in the United States, using the money they earned to collect equipment and records. A new breed of music entrepreneurs was just beginning to build the infrastructure needed for Jamaican music to flourish.

FIGURE 6.7

While popular music was withering in Cuba, it was beginning to bloom in Jamaica. The growth of Jamaican tourism, in part spurred on by the collapse of Cuban tourism, created plenty of opportunities for musicians. Given the high rates of youth unemployment, joining a hotel band was a good career option.

The island was also beginning to discover its own great pop singers. Vere Johns, a Jamaican journalist and well-traveled entrepreneur, began hosting a talent show on RJR radio, broadcast from the Palace Theater. Singers battled it out over pop and R&B songs, and the crowd, composed of Jamaicans from all classes (due to the availability of cheap seats), would pick the winner through their cheers. The show launched the careers of many important artists, including the eventual king of ska Derrick Morgan, who went on to record Jamaica's first international hit record; Millie Small, and even the band from which The Legend himself, Bob Marley, would emerge, The Wailers.

Mobile DJs, always looking to stay ahead of the competition, began recording their own music. At first they tried to mirror the rhythm and blues records—particularly the jerking piano boogies of artists like Rosco Gordon and Professor Longhair—that were so popular at sound system dances. Soundman Clement "Cox- some" Dodd originally recorded Theo Beckford's classic "Easy Snappin'" in 1956 as a "sound system special"—a song you'd only hear live at the dance. Coxsome didn't release the record for sale until 1959, at which point it instantly topped the Jamaican charts.

Exclusive recording contracts and publishing rights were nonexistent at the time, leaving plenty of artists disgruntled about never getting their due or proper compensation. But the anarchistic sound wars produced some of the most important recordings in Jamaican musical history.

One of the transformational figures in 1960s Jamaican music was Cecil Bustamente Campbell, better known as Prince Buster. An accomplished boxer and unflappable tough guy, Buster caught the attention of Coxsome, working not only as a strongman for the DJ turned producer, but also as a curator, who with one listen could name the artist and title of rival DJ's selection.

Around this time many unemployed youth had begun hanging out in a Trenchtown yard with a group of mystics known as Rastafarians. Many musicians who played on early ska records began bringing their horns to the yard to jam with the rasta drummers, who performed layered, syncopated rhythms in a West African style. While a Muslim, Buster appreciated the new possibilities brought on by the inclusion of African drumming, and in 1960, while recording the vocal group The Folkes Brothers, he invited rasta drum guru Count Ossie to join the session. The resulting record, "Oh Carolina" was an immediate hit and a turning point in Jamaican music

Ska began sounding less and less like Jamaican imitations of music from New Orleans and more like something altogether unique. The rigid, offbeat "ska-ska" of the guitar and piano that gave the music its name became looser, and the bass abandoned its supporting role to become the prime mover behind the sound systems' massive walls of speakers. Jamaica was a new nation, with a unique identity and its own new popular music.

As the Kingston music scene grew, musicians from throughout the Caribbean found their way to Jamaica. Trinidadian guitarist Lynn Taitt advocated for the exploration of different tempos and began incorporating counter lines common to calypso music. The bouncing bass, slower tempo, and bubbling guitar line heard on Hopeton Lewis' 1966 hit "Take It Easy" would usher in the beginning of rocksteady. This music, with its layered guitars (one chunking out chords, while another provided dancing, muted melodies), its free, earthshaking bass, and popping, syncopated drums, laid the foundation for reggae.

While the political wars between the island's two union-based parties (the Jamaica Labour Party and the People's National Party) was threatening the stability of the fledgling nation, Jamaican music continued to evolve and respond to the times. Musicians and producers—particularly Rastafarians who had a long tradition of political cynicism—turned out anthems criticizing the political turmoil and violence. People began using the word *reggae* to describe the scruffy, loose music of the late '60s produced by a new generation of artists ready to challenge the old sound-system guard. The 1970s would see the audience for Jamaican reggae music explode, changing popular music around the globe.

Gay Denial

Journalist Jonathan Rauch has written movingly about many personal topics, from caring for his infirm parents to being an introvert. But his latest book—ebook, actually—is his most confessional and compelling yet. *Denial: My 25 Years Without a Soul* (Atlantic) is Rauch's account of his first quarter century, in which he was unable to come to grips with the fact that he was gay.

Borrowing an old-fashioned psychiatric term, Rauch describes himself as an "invert": His life, he says, was like "a photographic negative." Despite teen puppy love, a tingly interest in male musculature, a profound lack of interest in sex with women, and no particular anti-gay animus, Rauch concluded only that he was "a monster," destined to be cut off from the pleasures of intimacy and family.

What a strange and wonderful world we live in where a D.C. think tanker can pour out this tortured tale (with a mercifully happy ending!), make it instantly available for $1.99 on Amazon, and be greeted with applause.

—Katherine Mangu-Ward

The man who brought Jamaican music to the world was Chris Blackwell, a British citizen whose ties to Jamaica dated back to the 17th century. Blackwell had been recording Jamaican music as early as 1958, and was one of the most prominent record distributors in the burgeoning days of the sound system. As a producer, Blackwell would score his first international hit with Millie Small's "My Boy Lollipop," a record that not only sold well within the U.K.'s West Indies community, but found crossover success, with Small even sharing a TV spot with The Beatles.

Blackwell felt that the world was ready for a global reggae mega-star, and saw potential in The Wailers, particularly their charismatic frontman Bob Marley. Jamaican music had been on the verge of breaking internationally for a few years, but Blackwell realized that the popular audience for the music would not be found in the black community, but rather the white counterculture.

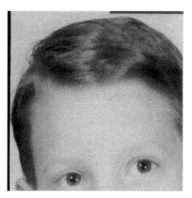

By adding a few distorted guitars and marketing the Wailers as a rock band, Blackwell thought his hand-picked group could cross over to international superstardom. The Wailers 1973 *Catch A Fire* was indeed an instant classic, introducing much of the world to the music that had been shaking Jamaica for the past decade. By the mid-'70s reggae had a firm foothold in the U.S. and the U.K. as both a high-valued import

FIGURE 6.8

product and a style worth mining by acts like The Clash and even The Rolling Stones.

What accounts for the major divergence between Cuban and Jamaican popular music in the 1960s and beyond? Control. The socialist government of Cuba set out to preserve and promote culture through top-down programs that stifled competition and expression, providing little incentive to cater to anyone other than those in power. In Jamaica, popular opinion drove the sound systems and fierce competition between musicians and producers led to a tremendous period of innovation. Cuba created an orderly system for music education that produced little of lasting value; Jamaica's disordered economic growth produced a global phenomenon whose reverberations are still being felt.

While sound system dances, like Jamaican life itself, were not free from police harassment, the culture continued and was never banned outright the way Cuban social clubs were. Travel restrictions, bans, and embargos cut Cuban musicians off from their regional audience and the Cuban diaspora, and even the most popular Latin American musical genre of the '60s and '70s—salsa—excluded the country whose *tresillo* rhythm (three notes in a long-long-short pattern) provided its backbone. Jamaica, on the other hand, maintained steady lines of regional and international trade, consistently seeding the island with new music and equipment, while building a strong market abroad.

In December 2012 Raul Castro, ruling the island after his ailing brother Fidel, announced that reggaeton—the Spanish language rap style set to Jamaican dance hall beats that has come to dominate Latin America in recent years—would be banned from the public places. Once again the Cuban people are being protected from popular music deemed to be imperialist and debasing.

But as the example of Jamaica reveals, music cultures can thrive in competitive environments. And personal and economic freedom can strengthen local culture rather than debase it, creating music so unique and infectious that imitators will spring up on the other side of the globe.

Chris Kjorness (ckjorness@gmail.com)
teaches music at Longwood University in Farmville, Virginia.

Trinidadian Music

Calypso

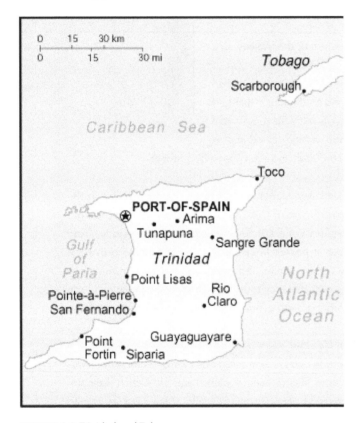

FIGURE 6.9 *Trinidad and Tobago map*

A Caribbean genre that is in many ways related to Jamaican music is from the island nation of Trinidad and Tobago. It is calypso, a genre that developed in the 1920s and has its roots in the call-and-response singing of African slaves. Its name comes from *Kaiso,* or *Kal Iso* (Lets Go!) a big hit in 1910s. Calypso traditionally features a *chantwell,* or song leader, who improvises verses for call and response. An example of calypso is the hit "Rum and Coca-Cola" by the singer known as Lord Invader, a big hit in the 1940s that spoke to the influences of American music and servicemen on the islands during World War II. Calypso is often confused with mento, which is occasionally referred to as Jamaican calypso.

Soca

Soca developed in the 1970s and soon was the featured music in Trinidadian Carnival. The name comes from soul-calypso, a mix of traditional calypso with disco, rhythm and blues, and soul. The topics of the lyrics tend to focus on partying, dancing and love, with an emphasis on the melodic line. Soca encourages group participation and remains an important genre for Carnival in Trinidad. The biggest soca hit was "Hot Hot

Hot," a song that has been covered many times by artists such as Buster Poindexter, Bina Mistry (in Hindi), and Sebastian from *The Little Mermaid*.

Reading #2

The other reading for this chapter, "Five Themes in the Study of Caribbean Music," looks at aspects of unity and diversity in Caribbean music and culture. It poses a fundamental question: To what extent does the Caribbean constitute a unified musical area? Although differences in music and language are obvious, there are connections between the disparate cultures and sounds throughout the region. It explores the African connections between the different sounds of the Caribbean and focuses on the themes of race and ethnicity, music, sex, and sexism in the music of this "island continent."

FIVE THEMES IN THE STUDY OF CARIBBEAN MUSIC

Peter Manuel, Kenneth Bilby, and Michael Largey

UNITY AND DIVERSITY IN A CONTINENT OF ISLANDS

[...] we briefly looked at some aspects of unity and diversity in Caribbean culture and music. Having, surveyed the region's individual music styles, we may now be better poised to tackle some fundamental questions: To what extent does the Caribbean constitute a unified musical area? Is Caribbean music just a colorful collage of diverse genres, without any pan-regional continuity? In what sorts of ways has music been able to transcend linguistic boundaries?

The Caribbean has always been culturally and politically divided by geography, language, political dominion, and ethnicity. The linguistic and colonial boundaries are the most obvious, and to some extent one can divide the area into three major cultural zones—that is, Spanish, English, and French. However, even these subregions are in some respects internally fragmented in terms of rivalries as well as musical traditions. Residents of the nearby French islands of Martinique and Guadeloupe manage to look down on each other, and the calypso line "Small island, go back where you really come from" long expressed Trinidad's attitude toward its neighbors. The end of colonialism has only exacerbated such fragmentation. The pan–West Indian federation fell apart in 1962, and a few years later, tiny Anguilla seceded from St. Kitts-Nevis, even though it had no telephones, power, or paved roads. (As calypsonian Wrangler Wynne sang, "I caught a Barbadian in my room last night, he said he was lookin' for the Federation site.") In what ways, then, have musical tastes and traditions reflected such divisions, and in what ways has music transcended them?

The parallels between musical and linguistic boundaries are obvious. A Martinican feels closer to France than to nearby Barbados. Similarly, despite Cuba's proximity to Jamaica, its similar history, and its overwhelming musical influence on the Spanish Caribbean, Cuban music does not seem to have much impact on Jamaican popular music. Linguistic fragmentation reaches an extreme in the southern Caribbean Basin, where the national languages of the adjacent Venezuela, Guyana, Suriname, French Guiana, and Brazil, are, respectively, Spanish, English, Dutch, French, and Portuguese.

However, such disparities represent only part of the picture. For one thing, [...] the entire region shares a set of basic sociomusical attributes, including the presence of an Afro-Caribbean cultural common denominator; a history of musical syncretization; the strength of oral traditions; and the emergence of lower-class, African-influenced work songs, religious musics, Carnival traditions, and creole, duple-metered dance-music genres. Further, even the boundaries between the Spanish, French, and English zones have often been fluid and permeable. The French creole zone formerly extended to eastern Cuba, Trinidad, and elsewhere in the present Anglophone realm (including New Orleans), and in terms of language and musical tastes, Dominica and St. Lucia still straddle the two.

Internal migrations have also left musical traces that traverse linguistic barriers. Haitian culture and music pervade eastern Cuba, just as Cuban dance music heavily influenced the 1950s Haitian konpa. West Indian migrants to southern Puerto Rico appear to have contributed to the emergence of plena, and the Trinidad calypso was enriched by melodies brought from throughout the region. The Afro-Curaçaoan tambú, as brought to Puerto Rico by immigrants, appears to have been the source of the bomba rhythm called *holandés*, while the tambú of modern Curaçao bears obvious influence of the Cuban rumba, presumably deriving from the guest workers who resided in Cuba. Descendants of Afro-American migrants from the southern United States preserve their own traditions in the Dominican peninsula of Samaná, and laborers from just about everywhere migrated to Panama to work on the canal. Internal migrations have continued in recent decades as Haitians seek work in the Dominican Republic, Dominicans flock to Puerto Rico, and small-island West Indians migrate to prosperous Trinidad (while everyone migrates to New York). Similarly, despite strained relations between Haitians and Dominicans (including disputes about the origin of the *méringue*/merengue), the two nations' musical histories are inseparable. [...] the mid-twentieth century Haitian konpa emerged to some extent as a local variant of the Dominican merengue, while modern Dominican bandleaders like Wilfrido Vargas have mercilessly plagiarized Haitian hits.

Since the 1950s, the conflicting trends toward unity and diversity have acquired a new dimension with the spread of the mass media. It may seem contradictory to speak of simultaneous homogenization and diversification, but that is in many ways what has happened, especially as the sheer amount of musical production and recording increases. One common denominator has been popular music from the United States, which now pervades the entire region. Rap, rock, and R&B have their own undeniable appeal and vitality, and when backed by powerful multinational record companies, they can tend to put local musics on the defensive throughout the Caribbean. In many countries, local broadcast media are so poorly funded that they can barely compete with the United States. In some smaller countries, there is hardly any local TV at all. Instead, everyone watches pirated satellite transmissions from the United States, complete with New York City news and ads for products that are unavailable as well as unaffordable. So it is not surprising that rap and R&B have a strong presence in West Indian airwaves, constituting a new sort of musical lingua franca. The presence of these cosmopolitan musics may at once enrich local music scenes by broadening horizons and impoverish them by displacing and devaluing local musics.

A new and distinctly Caribbean sort of pan-regional common denominator has been dancehall reggae and its Spanish-language variant, reggaetón. The international popularity of dancehall, indeed, has transcended language barriers and provided a kind of cultural unity and contact that is unprecedented in the Caribbean. In general, the mass media, together with interaction of migrant communities in New York and elsewhere, facilitate all sorts of musical cross-fertilization and fusions, from Garifuna punta-rock and Spanish-language soca to Fulanito's fusion of merengue, rap, and house. Many of these hybrids are just ephemeral gimmicks and fads, but others may be more than that. Indeed, in an age of multiple identities and crisscrossing media networks, some of the most vital and dynamic artistic creations may be coming from the borders and interstices rather than the stylistic hinterlands. The borders can of course be virtual rather than geographical, for this is the era of the remix, in which fusions of languages, styles, and genres can operate both as statements of social solidarity and as postmodern pastiches.

RACE AND ETHNICITY

The history, styles, and meanings of Caribbean music are intimately linked to issues of race in several ways. Musical genres are often associated with or claimed (plausibly or not) by specific ethnic groups; alternately, they may be celebrated as national patrimonies whose appeal transcends such boundaries. Throughout the region, song texts chronicle and articulate popular attitudes regarding race. Perhaps most significant are the ways in which music not only passively reflects race relations but actively influences them. In some cases, it serves as a powerful symbol of racial syncretism and harmony, often situating local versions of Afro-Caribbean music in the mainstream of national culture.

It is impossible to generalize about race relations and attitudes in the Caribbean, except to say that they are complex, diverse, and often different from those in the United States. Thus, for example, throughout the West Indies black people may historically have internalized colonial prejudices, but because they generally constitute demographic majorities, unlike many North American blacks, they are less likely to regard themselves as members of an alienated and marginalized minority. Race relations in the Spanish-speaking Caribbean are generally more fluid and flexible than in the English-speaking world. For many Puerto Ricans, this tradition of tolerance and mixing has been a source of nationalistic pride vis-à-vis the United States. Certainly, North American and English racial ideology, which traditionally recognizes only black and white, is relatively unusual in the Spanish and French Caribbean, especially since so many people are of mixed ancestry. Instead, people may be highly conscious of shades of coloring. Even within Afro-Caribbean communities, social preferences for lighter skin, thin noses, and straight ("good") hair remain widespread, although they have been much challenged—including by music—in recent decades. For North Americans, understanding such attitudes is complicated by the entirely different norms of discourse about race. Especially in the Hispanic Caribbean, people simply do not talk about race in the same ways that Americans do.

In some cases, racial attitudes are expressed openly in song, as in the '50s chachachá "Negra bembon," in which a black man chides a *mulata* for thinking herself superior. At the same time, one must be careful in trying to draw conclusions from song texts. For example, in Latin music, innumerable songs portray the ideal woman as a *mulata*. This convention could be interpreted as an indication of racial openness on the part of the singer, or a black preference for lighter skin, or, perhaps most often, a white stereotype of *mulatas* as hot and sexy—a stereotype that at once exoticizes mixed-race women and devalues the sexuality of others.

In general, the styles, associations, and breadth of individual music genres tell us much about the racial and cultural composition of Caribbean societies as a whole. Most Caribbean musical cultures exhibit a continuum of genres, ranging from the African-derived to the European-derived. The proportions vary considerably from island to island, however. An obvious contrast is between some smaller West Indian countries, where neo-African cult musics are relatively weak and marginal, and Cuba and Haiti, where they are extremely widespread. Even in Trinidad, for example, Shango worship has remained a private subculture to such an extent that calypsonians have traditionally portrayed it as an exotic and bizarre cult, to be feared or ridiculed. By contrast, innumerable Cuban popular songs refer with easy familiarity to the orishas (spirits) whose religion pervades lower-class Afro-Cuban life. Similarly, one can trace a direct evolution from Congolese secular dances through the traditional rumba and on to modern Cuban dance music and salsa, as reflected, for example, in modern salsa versions of old *sones* like "Kikiribú mandinga" (That's the End of That!), with its combination of African words and colloquial Spanish. By contrast, the weakness of such threads of continuity in the West Indies led Trinidad's Prime Minister Eric Williams to speak, however exaggeratedly, of Afro-Trinidadians as a "deracinated" people with "nothing indigenous."

Throughout much of the Caribbean, the emergence of creole popular musics has involved a process of accepting and legitimizing local forms of Afro-Caribbean music. This process occurred in different forms and in different stages throughout the Caribbean. It happened especially late in the British West Indies, where colonial masters had so successfully instilled ideas of black racial inferiority among their Afro-Caribbean subjects. Hence, many colonial-era calypsos mocked people with negroid features, and the waves of the French and Spanish Caribbean *negritud* movement seemed to bypass the English-speaking islands. It was not until the 1970s that a black pride movement—in the idiosyncratic form of Rastafari—forced a reassessment of such colonial prejudices. Since then, roots reggae songs have explicitly and defiantly celebrated Africa and blackness, and self-denigrating racist calypsos have gone out of style. In subsequent decades, dancehall songs have voiced popular Jamaican attitudes with particular frankness. After the singer Buju Banton was criticized for his "Love me Browning," which eulogized fair-skinned girls, he released his own rejoinder, "Love Black Woman."

In Cuba and Puerto Rico, the local version of the *negritud* movement generated a degree of white bourgeois interest, however qualified and obscurantist, in local black music and culture. In *negrista* poetry, this often took the form of white poets writing verse in colloquial *bozal* (fresh-off-the-boat slave) speech and "oogah-boogah"–type, African-sounding mumbo-jumbo. In early–twentieth-century Cuba, white composers wrote many theater songs that eulogized blackness in a somewhat sentimental, exoticizing fashion. In Puerto Rico, where white literati had traditionally ignored black traditions, the essayist Tomás Blanco took a step forward in a 1935 article declaring his island's culture to be mulatto, as best embodied in the plena. Still, this formulation neglected bomba, which is thoroughly Afro-Puerto Rican rather than mulatto. In the '40s and '50s, the Afro-Cuban bandleader Arsenio Rodríguez could draw on his own family heritage to present a more authentic black perspective, as in "Bruca Maniguá," with its mixture of Spanish and Congolese words:

Yo son Carabalí, negro de nación

sin la libetá, no puedo viví

Mundele caba con mi corazón

tanto matrata, cupo van filirí

chechere bruca maniguá, ae!

I'm a Carabali, a black man from Africa

Without freedom I can't live

The white man is breaking my heart

From so much abuse my body is dead

Powerful witch from the bush!

In the same period, Afro-Puerto Rican singer Ruth Fernández liked to remind listeners of the island's African heritage in the song "¿Tu abuela, dónde está?" (Where's Your Grandmother?), addressed to a negrophobic man who denies his mixed racial ancestry:

You like the foxtrot, and me, "Bruca Maniguá"

If you're so proud of looking white, "¿Tu abuela, dónde está?"

You're a polished *blanquito* [a pass-for-white snob] and among high society,

you don't want anyone to see your mother's mother

But I know her well, her name's Siña Tatá

You hide her in the kitchen, because she's a genuine negress

Here, whoever doesn't have Dinga [blood] has Mandinga.

While some Dominicans have tried to deny the African-derived elements of merengue, in most countries, the Afro-Caribbean elements of modern popular musics are now recognized and celebrated. Reggae, the Cuban *son*, the plenas and bombas of Puerto Rican bandleader Rafael Cortijo, and even the imagery in Tego Calderón's reggaetón videos are all so overtly Afro-Caribbean that their popularity has at once reflected and helped create a wholesale mainstreaming of black identity.

However, developing an inclusive sense of national identity involves more than a simple, unidirectional acceptance of black culture. It may also demand a new sort of openness on the part of Afro-Caribbeans. The Trinidadian Denyse Plummer, as a fair-skinned teenager of biracial parents, sought to blend in with the predominantly white community she was raised in, and when she later started singing calypso, she was heckled and pelted by black audiences who resented her for being whitish, bourgeois, and female. But both through her prodigious talent and through the advent of a less proprietary public sense of popular culture, by the '80s she was well accepted by Afro-Trini audiences and went on to win the Calypso Monarch prize repeatedly. Similarly, while the Rasta aspect of roots reggae celebrated Africa and black nationalism, dancehall culture has become a remarkably open arena in which the ethnicity of Super Cat (an Indo-Jamaican) or David Rodigan (a white Brit) is essentially a non-issue.

The modern tendency to celebrate Afro-Caribbean culture as national culture is naturally complicated by the presence of other ethnic groups. Even leaving aside Cuba and Puerto Rico, with their substantial white populations, many West Indian islands have significant East Indian, Chinese, Syrian, and European communities. [...] the identity question is particularly marked in Trinidad and Guyana, where East Indians outnumber blacks. The oft-heard saying, "All ah' we is one"—which could be taken to imply that everyone should conform to a creole mainstream—is giving way to a more explicit multiculturalism. Although ethnic stereotypes still abound, and communities are often polarized by politics, the norm remains one of interracial courtesy and tolerance, not Balkan-style fratricide. And typically, the contradictions raised by Afrocentricism are expressed not in violence but in whimsical songs, like the calypso "Split Me in Two," by Mighty Dougla. Dougla, whose sobriquet denotes an Indian-African mulatto, contemplates his fate under an imaginary law repatriating all Trinidadians to their ancestral homelands:

> Can somebody just tell me
>
> where they sending poor me?
>
> I am neither one nor the other,
>
> six of one, half dozen of the other.
>
> If they serious about sending back people for true,
>
> they got to split me in two.

Such complexities and contradictions are reflected in the ethnic associations of musical styles in general. Many music genres remain identified with particular communities, with tastes and affiliations serving as boundary markers. For example, one Indo-Guyanese youth told me, "I like all kinds of Indian music, and nothing else." However, what is perhaps more marked is the tendency for Afro-Caribbean popular musics—*son*, reggae, soca, and konpa—to become integrating symbols, uniting audiences of all communities. In such cases, music serves less as a flame beneath a melting pot than as a dressing poured over a mixed salad, integrating its diverse elements into a coherent whole.

Meanwhile, the entertainment industry does not hesitate to foreground—or, in some cases, obscure—a performer's ethnic identity for its own commercial purposes. Since the 1990s, in mainstream U.S. pop culture, being Latino has become fashionable—in certain contexts and to certain degrees. Although Jennifer Lopez's music has no particular Latin stylistic flavor, her Puerto Rican ancestry is certainly part of her image, and, like Christina Aguilera, she does sing in Spanish as well as in English. Similarly, Ricky Martin's music, whether sung in English or Spanish, falls into the pop rather than Latin category, and he is successfully promoted to the Anglophone market as a sexy Latino (Latin, but not too Latin). For his part, Marc Anthony more overtly embodies "crossover" marketing; much of his repertoire is mainstream English-language pop, but he also sings straight-ahead salsa, draping himself in the Puerto Rican flag in his Latino-oriented concerts. And although he complains about the term "crossover," there may be no better term to describe his dual target audiences and his release of songs like the *son–montuno*–flavored "I Need to Know/Dímelo" in both Spanish and English versions.[1]

MUSIC, SEX, AND SEXISM

In the Caribbean as throughout the world, love and male–female relationships have always been favorite song topics. Throughout the region, music relates the perennial themes of love, betrayal, and loss. Caribbean men, especially in the Spanish-speaking areas, often use songs to convey their feelings, singing softly in a lover's ear, playing a romantic record over and over for a beloved woman, or even giving a sweetheart a chosen recording. In a lighter vein, songs throughout the region display an uninhibited delight in sexuality, typically expressed in whimsical, thinly disguised puns and double entendres. Beyond this level, however, the particular sentiments expressed in Caribbean music reflect the attitudes and values in the region, many of which, rather than being universal, are products of specific sociohistorical conditions.

It is difficult to generalize about gender relations in the Caribbean, as in most complex societies. Throughout the region, for example, one finds nuclear families as well as strong extended family structures. Kinship networks help provide stability and cohesion to families in situations where the men are absent or peripheral, for whatever reason. In the twentieth century, it has become quite common for men to have only loose ties to their children and partners. To a considerable extent, this condition is a legacy of slavery, which undermined the role of the male provider and, more significant, destroyed traditional African kinship structures, which had to be rebuilt afresh after emancipation.

With modernization, familial ties have been further strained by urbanization and greater mobility, which disrupted village kinship networks, and above all by poverty and unemployment. As traditional men's occupations like cutting sugarcane have been mechanized, the role of the male breadwinner has been increasingly weakened. In some cases, women stand better chances than men do of finding jobs, whether as domestics or as workers in factories whose managers prefer women because they are less likely than men to organize. Such conditions can put a tremendous strain on family cohesion. The devoted but unemployed father unable to feed his children can suffer unbearable grief and guilt, as chronicled in Zeigfield's 1938 calypso "Depression":

> Five children and a wife and myself to mind,
>
> but to me the world is so unkind.
>
> No work, no food, no clothes to wear.
>
> If things go on, I'll die in despair.

Such a father, however well-meaning, may even be ejected by a wife who, out of duress, finds a better provider or who is herself employed but unable to feed a dependent man. Alternately, the man may simply avoid responsibility, going from one mate to another, ignoring whatever children he sires, and hoping ideally to shack up with some woman whom he can charm into supporting him. Thus, throughout the Caribbean, as elsewhere, many lower-class men and even women have tended to avoid marital or even emotional ties that may become burdensome and frustrating. When relationships become mediated primarily by money, some employed women shun male hangers-on, and unemployed women accept men's advances only if they get something tangible in return. As Growling Tiger's calypso "Money Is King" (1935) relates:

> If you have money and things going nice,
>
> any woman will call you honey and spice.
>
> If you can't give her a dress or a new pair of shoe,
>
> she'll say she have no uses for you.

At worst, the women struggle to support the children, and the underemployed and demoralized men hang out in bars, listening to songs that pump up their egos and soothe their frustrations.

Music is part of this condition, but on the whole it reflects not universal feelings but predominantly male viewpoints, in accordance with male domination of most aspects of the music world and of public culture in general. Many modern Caribbean songs articulate the most self-indulgent forms of male boasting and its flip side, self-pity. Such songs may be extremely influential in presenting a certain male ideal, that of the swaggering macho stud who attracts women by his charm alone and promises nothing more than a good time. Some songs offer specific advice to other men, like the several old calypsos warning against marriage (for example, Atilla's "I'll Never Burden Myself with a Wife"). In genres as disparate as calypso, bolero, and reggae one finds denunciations of women for their alleged faithlessness, moral degeneracy, and ugliness.[2] While men boast of their sexual conquests and demand that women submit to them,[3] they denounce promiscuous women and rail against supposedly false accusations of paternity.[4] Men's irresponsibility is celebrated, and women are repeatedly portrayed as valuable only for sex.[5] Jamaican dance-hall deejays often clarify that they offer women only sex, rather than commitment, while at the same time deriding as prostitutes women who demand some material compensation for their favors.[6] Traditional calypsos, plenas, and other songs have portrayed women as trying to tie men down with black magic (obeah, brujería).[7] A few songs have urged men to keep their women in line and even to gain their love by beating them.[8] Many songs have articulated a paradigmatic dichotomy between the respectable yet devalued wife and the sexy and seductive mistress—in West Indian parlance, the wifey vs. the matey or deputy, or in Spanish, the señora vs. the mujer de la calle (woman of the street, quintessentially a mulata).[9]

Portrayals of women in Caribbean music vary according to individual genres and their social backgrounds. Overtly sexist songs are relatively unusual in the Spanish Caribbean, perhaps due to the persistence of Hispanic ideals of family honor—ideals that many West Indian women might find repressive in their own way. The norm in most Latin music, whether sentimental boleros or upbeat salsa songs, is a genteel sentimentality, often idealizing women, however unrealistically. There are, however, plenty of boleros and bachatas that denounce women as mentirosas, traidoras, and abusadoras (liars, cheats, and abusers).

Such song lyrics may seem sexist to some. But interpreting their social significance may be far from simple and may involve recognizing the contradictory relationships between expressive discourses like popular song and actual gender relations and attitudes. Most Caribbean popular music is dance music, in which the literal meaning of the text may be less important than the purely musical aspects. Accordingly, many listeners are easily able to ignore or shrug off the verses' problematic aspects, especially in the ideal listening context of the dance floor. One female West Indian college student told me, "I like dancehall, and I don't mind the sexist songs; I just don't take the words seriously."

Another concurred: "I like this music because of how it sounds, not because I agree with the message it sends." Even in word-oriented dancehall, the text may be valued less for its message than for the way its rich alliterations, internal rhymes, and rhythmic delivery contribute to the kinetic drive of the music. The danger, however, is that among some listeners, the sexism and homophobia of the lyrics may be so rampant and ingrained that they are taken for granted.

As for the many bachatas and boleros in which broken-hearted men bitterly denounce women as liars and traitors, the innumerable female fans of such songs, rather than taking offense, may appreciate the vulnerability the male singer expresses and, in listening, can easily identify with the abstract emotions of longing and heartbreak he voices. The listener's ability to relate in this "transvestite" manner may be conditioned by the way and the extent to which a song is identified with a particular gender, depending on grammar, the sex of the singer, and other factors. Sentimental love songs are particularly likely not to be strongly gendered in their text content, such that listeners can easily transcend the overt and superficial gendering that is present. By contrast, a female listener might well have difficulty assuming the subject position in Beenie Man's "Yaw Yaw," in which the deejay boasts of having impregnated several women and sings admiringly of a friend who has twelve children who are still teething.[10]

One factor that is changing the gender dynamics of Caribbean music is the increasing ability of women to voice their own viewpoints. Women have always played important roles in performing certain kinds of Caribbean music, from domestic lullabies to church hymns, but in the Caribbean, as elsewhere, the worlds of professional folk music and commercial popular music have traditionally been dominated by men. Women have entered these genres, but they often have to contend with predominantly male personnel and male-oriented performance norms (and the producers' habit of putting a bikini-clad bimbo on album covers). Moreover, in patriarchal societies, any woman who expresses her sensuality in public runs the risk of being perceived as a sex object by men, especially in a genre so oriented toward "slackness" as Jamaican dancehall. Thus, for example, the flamboyantly sexy dancehall performers Patra and Lady Saw are seen by some West Indian women as embarrassments who reduce women to the status of bimbos and sex toys and cater to the male deejays' degrading stereotypes. Other West Indian women, however, resent the traditional double standard that allows men but not women to flaunt their sexuality, and they enjoy how the new breed of liberated women like Lady Saw, rather than being passive sex objects, can present themselves as fully in control of their exuberant sexuality. They ask, "If men can act that way, why can't we?" One female West Indian student told me, "My sisters and I were raised in a fundamentalist Christian family, and we were taught to be ashamed even to see our own naked bodies in the mirror. But Lady Saw and Patra changed all that for me!"

Other female performers, from salsa's Celia Cruz to reggae's Tanya Stephens, manage to find ways to constitute female role models without portraying themselves as boy-toys. Latin women have been able to find particular inspiration in songs like La India's "Ese hombre" (That Man) and Olga Tañón's merengue "Es Mentiroso" (He's a Liar), which turn the tables on men by denouncing duplicitous and philandering former partners. Merengue singer Lidia de la Rosa resignified the evergreen "La Chiflera," with its denunciation of duplicitous women, by adding her own verses, "If the man is going to have a good time, the woman will, too."[11]

In many cases, however, female performers have relied on male producers and composers. The all-female merengue group Las Chicas del Can showed that women could play and sing just like men, and their songs included some witty feminist manifestos, such as that presenting a woman getting back at her cheating man by doing the same ("It wasn't one man, nor two, it was three"). Some people, however, felt that the band's ability to serve as female role models was compromised by the fact that Las Chicas, from its compositions to its skimpy "jiggle-show" outfits, was overwhelmingly the creation of a male producer, Wilfrido Vargas. To what extent, and in what way, does the gender of the author matter? Does it matter that Cuban singer La Lupe's moving and poignant neo-feminist song "La Tirana" was written by a man (Tite Curet Alonso)? Or, for that matter, that Aretha Franklin's liberated–soul-sister anthem "Respect" was also written by a man and earlier recorded by Otis Redding?

In many cases, more important than a song's lyrics are the dynamics of how the song is used, especially in terms of what is happening on the dance floor. Whether in a reggae club or Trinidad's Carnival procession, it often seems that, regardless of the song lyrics, women are ruling the scene, flaunting their sensuality in a way that is more for their own enjoyment than aimed to entice men. Hence, while a dour critic might regard the words of the merengue "La Tanga" (The Thong) as "objectifying," when that song is performed in clubs women love to jump to the stage and strut their stuff to wild applause. Similarly, a Jamaican college student emphasized to me how the sexy, hedonistic lyrics of dancehall songs are perfectly suited to the party and club milieu. She wrote, "As couples gyrate against a wall to lyrics like 'Wine pon me Gal' and 'Flex Girl Time to Have Sex,' the content of the song is not offensive, but necessary. If dancehall performers began to base the contents of their songs on world peace, family life, or even the sweetness of falling in love, the music would lose its edge and popularity."

A disparaging voice might argue that the celebration of sexuality for its own sake can serve to reduce individuals to bodies and body parts and encourage the sexual exploitation of women and the failure of men to take responsibility for the children they sire. These are not merely narrow, puritanical concerns in societies or subcultures where the weakness of the institution of the family places great burdens on women and children. At the same time, it could well be argued that the dance floor is the one arena in which sensuality can be celebrated in a controlled and even artistically creative context. It is clear that millions of women in the Caribbean and elsewhere experience popular music as a liberating and even exhilarating force precisely because it allows them to experience and, through dancing, express their own sexuality, free from the traditional constraints of family, religion, and patriarchy in general. In that sense, the open eroticism of much Caribbean dance music, however rampant with objectification and hedonism, may constitute an essential and arguably liberating aspect.

CARIBBEAN MUSIC INTERNATIONAL

Liberty Avenue in Queens and Brooklyn's Nostrand Avenue typify the new kind of polyglot Caribbean migrant neighborhoods that have emerged in New York City and elsewhere. West Indian snack bars offering calaloo and roti adjoin Chinese-Cuban eateries, while groceries hawk coconuts, curry powder, fresh fish from Guyana, cassava, and day-old Caribbean newspapers. On the sidewalk, one hears a

Babel-like chatter of Spanish, Jamaican patwa, Haitian creole, Afro-American jive, and even standard English (though usually with a Caribbean lilt). Meanwhile, ghetto-blasters, car stereos, and storefront cassette players boom out the throbbing rhythms of merengue, salsa, soca, and reggae, which intertwine like some perpetually changing postmodern polyrhythm.

New York has become a Caribbean city, especially since the 1980s, when its Caribbean population reached a sort of critical mass of more than 2 million. As of 2005, more than a third of the city's 8 million residents are Caribbean immigrants or their children. New York is now the biggest Caribbean city and the second biggest Jamaican, Haitian, and Guyanese city. There are more people from Nevis in New York than there are in Nevis itself. Dominicans, numbering more than 800,000, have become the dominant community in Washington Heights ("Quisqueya Heights") and parts of Queens and Brooklyn, as have Puerto Ricans in Spanish Harlem and the Lower East Side ("Loisaida") of Manhattan, and English-speaking West Indians elsewhere in Brooklyn and Queens. While other North American cities like Cleveland and Detroit have degenerated into depopulated rotting shells, New York's economy has been revitalized by Caribbeans who bring their traditions of initiative and self-reliance. As the saying goes, when a West Indian gets ten cents above a beggar, he opens a business—and adds color and vitality to the city's street life and culture.

The vicissitudes of the immigrant experience—especially to New York—have been voiced, whether poignantly or humorously, in dozens of plenas, *aguinaldos*, merengues, calypsos, and dancehall songs. Taken retrospectively, many of these can be seen to articulate a loosely sequential set of stages, or what Juan Flores, in reference to Newyorican identity, calls "moments,"[12] in terms of their attitudes toward New York vis-à-vis the island former homeland. The starting point for these is the immediate reality of the forsaken homeland and the difficult and often hostile new urban environment. In this initial stage, the immigrant community is an isolated "island in the city," whence the singer longs to return home: "Yo me vuelvo a mi bohío" (I'm going back to my hut). The harshness of the dislocation engenders Flores's second "moment," an enhanced and often idealized appreciation of the Caribbean homeland, which is eulogized as a place of physical and emotional warmth, in contrast to cold and unfriendly New York. As Flores points out, this new appreciation of the homeland, although nostalgic and utopian, can extend to its Afro-Caribbean aspects. It can also constitute a necessary step toward the next "moment" or state of mind, in which immigrants—or, more typically, their children—transcend sentiments of despair and loss, embrace their new homeland, and assert the legitimacy of their own culture therein. Thus, in the '70s, New York *salseros* saw themselves not as some voiceless, disempowered minority, but as the musical messengers of a new sense of Latino pride which, like salsa, emerged in New York, while drawing from island tradition. Hence, Bobby Rodriguez could sing:

> I bring you a message . . . . It's the *clave* of the *guaguancó* rhythm
>
> the modern sound from the enchanted isle (Puerto Rico)
>
> I sing to my Puerto Rico and to Los Angeles as well
>
> to Venezuela and Santo Domingo.[13]

This dynamic and transplanted modernization of island-based music paves the way for the culminating "moment," in which Caribbean-Americans actively and selectively embrace other aspects of mainland (perhaps especially Afro-American) culture, along with other Caribbean cultures. This process is nowhere more apparent than in music, when local performers freely combine salsa, merengue, and reggae with rap and R&B, and with each other. And as Flores stresses, such hybrids should no longer be seen as a case of Caribbean Americans passively assimilating to the hegemonic mainland culture, but rather as dynamic artistic collaborations enacted from a position of cultural strength and confidence.

Many Caribbean immigrants keep closely in touch with their homelands by way of cut-rate phone cards, satellite TV, faxes and modems, camera phones, and frequent visits. With their dual senses of loyalty and their networks of families and friends in both places, they constitute transnational communities that are economically, emotionally, and culturally as much "there" as they are "here." For others, "home" is a distant island that they may have never seen, barely remember, or remember in a way that hasn't existed for decades. Homeland ties may be particularly poignant for undocumented workers who are unable to return home, except to leave the United States for good. For all of them, music and food can assume new significance as symbols of identity; curry goat and reggae music can represent Jamaica, just as roti and calypso signify Trinidad. Caribbean migrants and their descendants develop complex and multiple senses of identity, so that a second-generation Jamaican may see himself or herself in various contexts as Jamaican, West Indian, Afro-Caribbean, Afro-American, Brooklynite, or just plain American. Most Caribbeans, rather than wishing to assimilate totally, want to retain some sense of their origins, and their musical tastes generally reflect these cosmopolitan and overlapping senses of identity.

Emigration has mixed effects on musical culture in the homelands. Emigrants can enrich island culture by sending money home and by serving as conduits for new trends and ideas. Haitians in the United States, for example, send considerable money back home to support Rara festivals. At the same time, the tendency for the best and brightest to emigrate can deplete the ranks of talented musicians on the islands. Lesser folk-music genres that fail to thrive in emigrant communities can decline altogether. For example, folksong traditions formerly maintained in lively "tea meetings" on islands like Nevis and St. Vincent have been eclipsed markedly because most of the creative performers have left.[14] Islanders left behind express their demoralization in songs like the early 1990s calypso from Dominica "Dominicans Come Home."

Such instances of cultural impoverishment are to some extent counterbalanced by the thriving of Caribbean culture abroad. As we have seen, New York, with its media infrastructure and concentrated Caribbean enclaves, has been a center for Caribbean music for many decades. From the 1920s, most of the leading Puerto Rican composers and performers, from Manuel "Canario" Jiménez to Rafael Hernández, came to live in the city, and much of the evolution of Latin dance music took place here. The mambo evolved mostly in clubs like the Palladium, and salsa emerged as a barrio reinterpretation and resignification of Cuban dance music in the late 1960s. New York continues to be the center of the recording industries for Haitian and West Indian music, and record piracy throughout the Caribbean makes it the biggest record market. Other cities, like Toronto, Birmingham, and Paris, have played similar roles in the development of modern Caribbean music, collectively hosting more clubs, record producers, and top groups than the islands themselves.

Of course, the international presence of Caribbean music has never been limited to immigrant communities. In the nineteenth century, the habanera charmed European salon dancers, and Jamaican regiments brought by the British to their West African colonies introduced not only European brass band music but also their own syncretic "goombay." Since then, Caribbean commercial popular-music styles have found their own international audiences, often in accordance with the eccentricities of the global music industries. In some cases these may be motivated by the sheer power of the music. In the 1950s in the United States, the mambo was, by any standards, some of the hottest dance music around. In other cases, Yankee demand for some sort of superficially exotic, sensuous, and tropical beat has generated ephemeral fads of various bowdlerized versions of Caribbean music. Hence, the first LP in the world to sell a million copies was not by Elvis, or the Beatles, but Harry Belafonte's 1956 *Calypso*, which spawned a brief but furious fad of ersatz calypsos and shaped the repertoire of West Indian tourist music for generations. As Belafonte often pointed out, most of the songs on the LP, like "Day-O," were not calypsos at all, but the vogue led to corny "calypsos" subsequently being recorded by such aspiring entertainers as Louis Farrakhan, Maya Angelou, Robert Mitchum, Alan Arkin, Jack Lemmon, and Rita Hayworth. (Said Trinidadian scholar Keith Warner of Hayworth's "calypso" dancing in the film *Fire Down Below*, "It just looked to us like another white person who can't dance.")

Some of the most significant disseminations of Caribbean music have largely bypassed the developed West, with the mass media allowing Caribbean musics to spread way beyond the reach of Caribbean musicians themselves. Thus, for example, Cuban dance music became a dominant urban popular music in Africa during the mid-twentieth century, providing, among other things, a model for the composition and performance of horn-based dance musics, which later evolved into the more distinctively local genres like Congolese soukous. Since the 1970s, roots reggae came to enjoy phenomenal popularity in African countries like Gambia, whether in the form of old Bob Marley records or new songs in local languages by performers like Alpha Blondy (Ivory Coast) and Lucky Dube (South Africa). With the added input of dynamic groups like Steel Pulse in Great Britain, roots reggae in many respects came to flourish outside the Caribbean more than in its homeland, Jamaica. For that matter, dancehall has also become a global style, easily adapted to local languages everywhere from Malawi to New Zealand. Similarly, zouk—or "Cabo zouk"—sung in Cape Verdean creole has become the dominant dance music in Cape Verde and its diasporic communities in Europe and New England.

In general, musics like salsa, reggae, and zouk have taken on lives of their own outside the Caribbean, becoming truly international. This process, however, does not signify a global cooptation of Caribbean music, for the region itself and its émigré musicians continue to be sources for the most dynamic innovations. For the most creative artists, Caribbean music now involves combining international sounds and Caribbean cross-fertilizations while often reaching deep into local traditions for inspiration.

MUSIC AND POLITICS

The Caribbean has long served as a vacation retreat for many foreigners; Caribbean people themselves, however, have historically had to contend with toil, relative poverty, and repressive and corrupt governments that have often been imposed by outside forces. One function of music in the Caribbean, as elsewhere, has always been to provide some sort of escape from such adversity. In dancing and singing, people can temporarily forget their woes, reaffirm community ties and values, and cultivate their own artistic creativity. But it has also been the nature of music and verse to express the full range of human emotions, including those related to sociopolitical conditions. Through music, men and women can voice aspirations and ideals, strengthen group solidarity, and transcend adversity by confronting it and transmuting it into song. Accordingly, music in the Caribbean has often been explicitly linked to sociopolitical struggles.

Local music genres, whether overtly political or not, can be important symbols of nationalistic pride and identity. In the nineteenth century, both Cuban habaneras and Puerto Rican danzas, aside from being fashionable dances, were celebrated as symbols of bourgeois and petty bourgeois opposition to Spanish rule. The unofficial Puerto Rican anthem, "La Borinqueña," is a gentle danza rather than a military march. Many other songs and *décimas* of this period also explicitly celebrated the independence struggle and, later, nationalistic opposition to Yankee domination. Populist dictators like Trujillo have also promoted local musics for their own propaganda purposes.

Some musicians themselves have entered the realm of politics. Harry Belafonte, however maligned for his commercialization of calypso, was a fervent champion of progressive causes and a critic of racism and American imperialism. Merengue innovator Johnny Ventura was an outspoken opponent of the Balaguer dictatorship in the Dominican Republic and held important political offices, while salsa artists Ruben Blades and Willie Colon both ran energetically, if unsuccessfully, for political office. While Colon has composed songs dealing with everything from military despots to AIDS, he said during his 1994 campaign for the U.S. Congress, "Sometimes writing a song is not enough."

In the twentieth century, one of the greatest challenges for Caribbean countries has been to ameliorate poverty by gaining control over their own natural resources and by creating social justice. North American imperialism has in many cases impeded such progress. Virtually whenever a Caribbean state has attempted significant reform—redistribution of wealth, land reform, or nationalization of resources—the United States has intervened, often by overthrowing governments in the name of "safeguarding American interests" and "fighting communism." Aside from the numerous regional military occupations in the early twentieth century,[15] the CIA destabilized elected governments in Guatemala (1954) and Guyana (1962–64), effectively replacing them with corrupt and brutal dictatorships. In 1964, the U.S. Marines invaded the Dominican Republic to restore the Trujillo elite to power. In the 1970s, U.S. hostility helped undermine the reformist People's National Party (PNP) government in Jamaica, leading to its defeat in 1980 by the more pliant Jamaican Labour Party. In 1991, U.S.-trained Haitian generals on the CIA payroll ousted elected Prime Minister Jean-Bertrand Aristide and instituted a reign of terror. While American intervention in 1994 nominally restored Aristide to office, it has served to sustain the infrastructure of military and paramilitary repression, and in 2004 Aristide was again pressured by the United States—albeit in complex circumstances—to abdicate. Since 1959, the Cuban people have had to endure all manner of Yankee hostility, including armed invasion in 1962, ongoing CIA-backed sabotage and terrorism,[16] and a crippling embargo.

During this period, much of the Caribbean music industry has been dominated by North American–owned multinationals with a vested interest in maintaining the status quo. There has also been a marked tendency—and often explicit pressure from producers—for musicians in the industry to avoid controversial song lyrics and stick to stock romantic or sexual themes. Nevertheless, different forms of Caribbean music have, in their own way, confronted social reality and reflected, however idiosyncratically, the demand for social justice. Such uses of music were particularly prominent in the 1960s and '70s, which were a period of sociopolitical ferment, mobilization, and optimism throughout the region, as in much of the world. The Cuban Revolution was thriving, the Dominican dictator Rafael Trujillo was dead at last, and the newly independent West Indian states thought that they could for the first time control their own national destinies. As Bob Marley sang (ambiguously, to be sure): "If you are the big tree, we are the small axe, ready to cut you down." In the United States, this was the era of the youth counterculture and the Black Power movement, whose influence spilled over into the Caribbean. And last, even if the Soviet bloc itself did not constitute an attractive model, at least its existence and the aid it could provide implied the possibility of an alternative to Yankee domination and cultural "Coca-Colonization."

The *nueva canción* of Cuba and, to a lesser extent, of Puerto Rico and the Dominican Republic was one form of music explicitly linked to the optimism and idealism of the era. Other genres have mirrored the spirit of the age in their own ways. Salsa of the 1970s emerged as the youthful voice of the barrio, self-consciously assertive and optimistic, chronicling the vicissitudes of lower-class urban life with a dynamic exuberance. In Jamaica, the sociopolitical ferment of urban youth found expression in roots reggae, which was linked not only to Rastafari but also to the activism and idealism of the 1970s PNP government. Calypsos by Black Stalin, Chalkdust, and others also reflected the influence of the Black Power movement and the broader political consciousness of the period.

In subsequent years, however, political developments frustrated most of the aspirations of the 1960s and '70s, leading to the decline of the utopian idealism expressed in that period's music. By the 1980s, the American youth counterculture had declined, and the Civil Rights Movement, having achieved some important goals, dissipated in the face of more intractable problems of economic equity. In the Latino community, the Young Lords self-destructed, and salsa lyrics withdrew from barrio assertiveness to the safe common-denominator topics of romance and melodrama. The years around 1990 found the Cuban Revolution in crisis, the Trujillo–Balaguer elite back in power, and the Puerto Rican independence movement marginalized for good. The *nueva trova* movement seemed to sputter out accordingly. In Jamaica, the PNP experiment collapsed under hostility from the United States and the International Monetary Fund, leading to a return to the status quo of multinational exploitation and laissez-faire capitalism. Accordingly, roots reggae's militancy has largely given way to the boasting and slackness of dancehall, and Bob Marley's "Redemption Song" has given way to Mad Cobra's "Flex, Time to Have Sex."

In retrospect, the 1960s and '70s, with their exuberant optimism and idealism, seem like a passing revolutionary historical moment, at once admirably idealistic and naively utopian. In the globalized "New World Order," with its absence of clear imperialist antagonists, singing of revolution and redemption has become like spitting into the wind, and popular music seems to have retreated into sensuality, sentimentality, and lumpen nihilism. Perhaps it may be inappropriate to expect dance music to do more than entertain, although the music of Ruben Blades and Juan Luis Guerra, and songs like Buju Banton's "Untold Stories," suggest ways of transcending the norms of commercial entertainment. And there is something to be said for dancing through adversity, in a way that combines both escapism and affirmation of life, community, and hope.

NOTES

1. Marc Anthony (born Marco Antonio) has stated, "This crossover thing really displaces me. Like I'm coming in and invading America with my music. I was born and raised in New York,

man" (as quoted in Licia Fiol Matta, "Pop *Latinidad*: Puerto Ricans in the Latin Explosion," *Centro de estudios puertorriqueños Bulletin* 14, no. 1 [2004]: 40).

2. For example, Mighty Sparrow's 1950s calypso "Jean Marabunta" (see Keith Warner, *Kaiso! The Trinidad Calypso* [Washington, D.C.: Three Continents, 1985], 100); Rafael Cortijo, "Severa" (1950s Puerto Rican *guaracha*).

3. For example, Buju Banton, "Have to Get Your Body Tonight" ("...even by gunpoint"), or Bounty Killa's "Stucky" (1980s dancehall).

4. For example, in El Gran Combo's "Me dicen papá" (1970s Puerto Rican salsa), the singer complains about all the multiracial children who call him "Papa" and whom he must support, noting that some of them resemble his friends who hang around, and one of them looks like the bolero singer and famed ladies' man Daniel Santos. Other songs in this vein include Mighty Terror's "Chinese Children" and Sparrow's "Child Father" (calypsos; see Warner, *Kaiso!* 97–98); and Bounty Killa's "Living Dangerously" (dancehall).

5. For example, Atilla's "I'll Never Burden Myself with a Wife" (1930s calypso).

6. For example, Beenie Man, "Old Dog" and "Nuff Gal" (1990s dancehall); Coupé Cloué, "Fem colloquint"; and Miami Top Vice (T-Vice), "Yo tout pou Zin" (Haitian konpa). In "Old Dog," Beenie Man states that it is simply his nature to need many women, often two or three at a time, and that he even intends to seduce his mother-in-law.

7. For example, Cortijo's "Huy que pote" (1950s Puerto Rican plena) and the colonial-era calypsos cited in Gordon Rohlehr, *Calypso and Society in Pre-Independence* Trinidad (Port of Spain: G. Rohlehr, 1990), 258–63.

8. For example, Mighty Sparrow, "Turn Them Down" (calypso); Hector Lavoe, "Bandolera"; Johnny Pacheco, "Préstame los guantes" (salsa); Daniel Santos, "Yo la mato" (bolero); and Johnny Ventura, "Dále un palo" (merengue).

9. For example, the recent Dominican merengue "La Grua (The Tow Truck)," which depicts the possessive wife dragging her husband away from his girlfriends at the dance club.

10. During an interview with one of my students, Sabrina Hannam, Beenie Man stated that he was in fact a monogamous, devoutly religious family man, and that the playboy image was merely a commercial pose. He further asserted that he sang because God told him to, although, as she observed, "God did not specify what type of song should be sung."

11. "Si el hombre se divierta, la mujer también vacila" (pointed out to the author by Sydney Hutchinson).

12. Juan Flores, "'Qué assimilated brother, yo soy asimilao': The Structuring of Puerto Rican Identity in the U.S.," in idem, *Divided Borders: Essays on Puerto Rican Identity* (Houston: Arte Público Press, 1993), 182–95.

13. "El Mensaje" (1975): "Te traigo un mensaje. . . . Es que tengo la clave de este ritmo guaguancó, sonido moderno de la isla del encanto, Yo le canto a mi Puerto Rico y a Los Angeles también, a Venezuela y Santo Domingo."

14. Roger Abrahams, *The Man-of-Words in the West Indies* (Baltimore: Johns Hopkins University Press, 1983), 12, 16.

15. These include occupations of the following countries: Nicaragua (1910, 1912–33), Honduras (1903, 1907, 1911–12, 1919, 1924–25), Cuba (1906–09, 1912, 1917–20, 1933–34), Mexico (1913–17, 1918–19), Panama (1921, 1925, 1989), the Dominican Republic (1916–24), and Haiti (1915–34).

16. In 1976, for example, the CIA-trained terrorist Orlando Bosch blew up a Cuban civilian airliner, killing all seventy-three people aboard. Bosch has lived in Miami since 1990, when President G. H. W.

Bush intervened to terminate his short U.S. prison sentence. See, for example, Ann Louise Bardach, *Cuba Confidential: Love and Vengeance in Miami and Havana* (New York: Vintage, 2002), chap. 7.

Conclusion

This chapter delves into the music of the Caribbean, but it is in no way inclusive. There are many other genres in the many music cultures. Jamaica and Trinidad share many connections and commonalities, perhaps having to do with their large African-derived populations and connections to England. In both island nations, socio-economic conditions had a strong influence on music development, lyrics, and the shaping of the genres. Recent technologies also shaped the modern musical styles and means of delivery. One can hear the connections in the sound and in the lyrics.

Questions for thought:

- How is the "skank" rhythm a unifying element in Jamaican music?
- What is meant by the term riddims?
- What is the relationship between reggae and Rastafarian culture?
- Do you agree with using "Caribbean music" as a general term? If so, what musical and cultural forces unify music from this part of the world?
- How do you think politics affected the development and dissemination of Caribbean music? What impact has migration and immigration had on the body of music?

Activity

Listen to the following music on YouTube:
Mento: Harry Belafonte, "Banana Boat Song" and The Jolly Boys, "Woman's Smarter"
Ska: The Ethiopians, "Train to Skaville"
Rock steady: The Paragons, "Mercy, Mercy"
Reggae: Bob Marley, "No Woman, No Cry" and "One Love"
Calypso: Lord Invader, "Rum and Coca-Cola"
Soca: The Merrymen, "Hot Hot Hot!"

What are the unifying elements of mento, ska, rock steady and reggae? What are the unifying elements of calypso and soca? Are there any unifying elements between the four Jamaican genres and the genres from Trinidad and Tobago? How are they similar? How are they different?

References

"Rastafarian." Accessed March 17, 2018. *Oxford Living Dictionary.* https://en.oxforddictionaries.com/definition/us/rastafarian

Figure Credits

Fig. 6-1: Source: https://commons.wikimedia.org/wiki/File:CIA_map_of_the_Caribbean.png.

Fig. 6-3: Copyright © Ueli Frey (CC by 3.0) at https://commons.wikimedia.org/wiki/File:Bob-Marley-in-Concert_Zurich_05-30-80.jpg.

Fig. 6-9: Source: https://commons.wikimedia.org/wiki/File:Td-map.png.

Fig. 6-10: Source: https://commons.wikimedia.org/wiki/File:(Portrait_of_Calypso,_between_1938_and_1948)_(LOC)_(5189344885).jpg.

CHAPTER SEVEN

AfroPop: Highlife, Tip-toe Guys, and Graceland

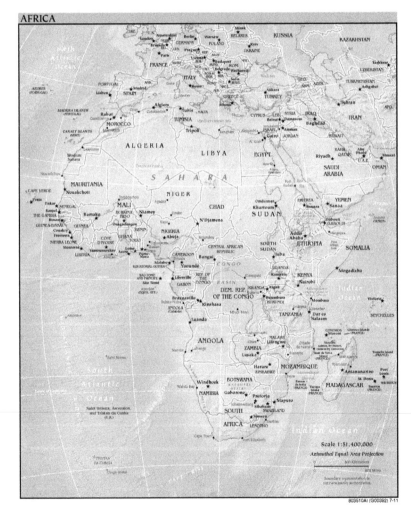

FIGURE 7.1 *Map of Africa*

Introduction

In world music circles, people often refer to "African Music." That begs many questions from ethnomusicologists: What part of Africa? Sub-Saharan or the *Magreb*, the Arabic part of Africa? Are you referring to traditional or popular music? If Sub-Saharan, which region of the continent to you mean? Are you referring to a country, which is a recent classification, or a tribe/language group? Is it music of worship, of work, or entertainment? Do you mean historically or modern music? The same can be said for studying any region of the world: What do you mean by American music? Latin American? European? There are some characteristics that apply to any of these regions, and the same is true with African music.

Musically, African music can be divided into five musical regions: North Africa, where music is of Arabic and Islamic origin; West Africa, which has many traditional and popular genres such as highlife; Central Africa, where soukous, which is also known as rhumba, is popular; East Africa, where Swahili sounds dominate; and South Africa, from which a cappella traditions have taken on world significance.

Although African music varies from region to region, there are some commonalities in much music on the continent. Due to the fact that all of Africa was colonized by European countries, there are many European influences in much African music. Among these characteristics are duple meter, which was not common before European occupations, melodies based on the European major and minor scales, and western harmonies. There are also commonalities in terms of stylistic features in much African music, including polyrhythm and other complex rhythms, repetition, and improvisation. In this chapter, we will look at two genres from different regions that serve as models that demonstrate the similarities and differences between music from different regions, different language groups, and different countries.

Highlife

African-American music was highly influenced by several music cultures from West Africa, from which most slaves taken to the United States/British North American originated. The music of Latin America also had strong influences from West Africa. The movement of music across the Atlantic, however, was not a one-way street. In the 20th century, as American music became available around the world, African music started demonstrating influences of music from the United States and Latin America, including samba from Brazil, rumba and the son from Cuba, and American genres such as jazz, rock and hip-hop. As early as the 1940s, with the movement of men and material throughout Africa during World War II, many West African genres started changing. Much of this music was a hybrid of African and European music due to the colonial period, but as colonial powers started withdrawing from Africa, music in the newly independent African countries started expressing a new, global hybridity. Nowhere was this more the case than in Ghana and Nigeria, where this hybridization was expressed in the music known as *highlife*.

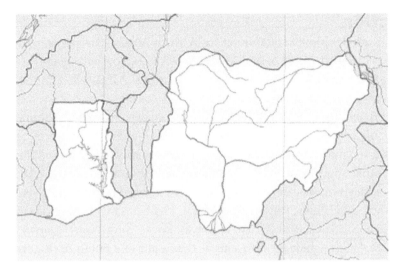

FIGURE 7.2 *Ghana and Nigeria*

Highlife was one of the earliest successful fusions of European, West African, and New World music. It is a transnational genre, most popular in Ghana and Nigeria, reflecting the fact that the borders of African countries, decided by European colonial rulers, are political, not cultural boundaries. (The same is true of the Rio Grande, which separates the countries of the USA and Mexico, but not the music of either country.) It was the most popular dance genre in West Africa until the 1970s, and it remains popular in Africa and in the diaspora. There are two streams of highlife, the dance band stream, following the model of American swing bands, and guitar bands, embracing influences from guitar-driven genres from Cuba. It developed in the 1920s as Ghanaian and Nigerian musicians, whose music already fused African music with European instruments and melodic and harmonic ideas, started incorporating foreign influences from genres like the foxtrot. World War II brought even more influences from American pop music, calypso, the Cuban son and others.

The most important highlife musician was E.T. Mensah (1919–1996), a Ghanaian band leader and instrumentalist who was known as the "King of Highlife." Born in Accra, he started studying flute when he was in school and went on to be known mostly for playing trumpet and saxophone, as well as other instruments. In the 1940s he joined a band called the Tempos, of which he became the leader early on. The band performed songs in English, Twi, Ga, Fante, Ewe and other African languages, reflecting the artificiality of the borders of Africa. The band garnered international attention in 1956 when it performed with Louis Armstrong on his African tour.

In Nigeria, guitar highlife was more popular than dance band highlife. This guitar-driven highlife grew out of an older acoustic genre called igbo, another local guitar tradition called palm wine, and the blues. In 1976, at the end of Nigeria's civil war, a band called Rocofil Jazz, led by Prince Nico Mbarga, had a huge hit with "Sweet Mother," which sold more than 13 million copies and remains the best-selling African record in history.

(The guitar was introduced by the Portuguese early in the colonial period; it became, and remains, the most important European instrument in Africa. There are many guitar-like instruments in Africa, and African musicians use the African-blended, European, and African string instrument styles. Most instruments were imported from Europe and the Americas, but in recent years locally-made instruments became popular.)

FIGURE 7.3 *Ebo Taylor Highlife band*

Highlife remains popular in Nigeria and Ghana, as well as in the diaspora, notably in England and Germany. Highlife in recent years blended traditional highlife sounds with hip-hop and dancehall reggae, among other genres. There is even gospel highlife in Accra, meaning that highlife spans from the nightclub to the church. It made it to England in the 1920s, when highlife clubs opened in many cities. The 1930s saw the birth of the West Africa Students Union, a group that included highlife in its celebrations. The 1940s and 50s saw a great deal of highlife activity in England, including many bands and clubs. In the 1970s Ghanaian musicians started mixing into the London highlife scene, and by the 1980s there were many independent highlife record labels in England.

Reading #1

The first reading for this chapter, "First Fusions—Orchestras and Brass-Bands: E. T. Mensah, the King of High Life, and King Bruce," explores the history and development of this genre, which fuses African musical ideas in terms of rhythm and form with European melodic ideas and hymn-type harmonies. This kind of fusion had taken place before, but through the mix of European instruments and American popular music, a new hybrid, highlife, was formed. There had been other dance music traditions in Africa playing American and European music, but these were for the most part large orchestras that had lost their popularity by the beginning of World War II. They were replaced by smaller jazz combos playing jazz and swing, mixing with African ideas and forming highlife, pioneered by E. T. Mensah. Highlife, which continued to evolve in Ghana and Nigeria, remains part of the African musical scene today.

FIRST FUSIONS—ORCHESTRAS AND BRASS-BANDS

John Collins

E. T. MENSAH, THE KING OF HIGHLIFE, AND KING BRUCE

Traditional African music is flexible and ever-changing. There have been cross-overs and feedback, Western influences on African music and African influences on Western music.

John Collins, "First Fusions--Orchestras and Brass-Bands: E T Mensah, the King of High Life, and King Bruce," *West African Pop Roots,* pp. 17-31. Copyright © 1992 by Temple University Press. Reprinted with permission.

Modernised traditional music and dance-styles that developed along the West African coast m the nineteenth century demonstrate the subtlety of the interaction between black and white music—styles such as gome (or goombay), ashiko (or asiko), timo, and osibisaaba rhythms that later were incorporated into highlife and juju music.

Even though no European instruments were used in these first fusions, the songs were sung in hymn-type harmonies European carpentry techniques were used for the construction of new brands of African drums, such as the square tambourines and the giant gome-drum. Another type of drum that was much simpler to make than the local hand-carved drums was the barrel-drum, made by coopers with planks and iron hoops.

While some African musicians started to incorporate new ideas into their music, others began playing in brass-bands, regimental bands, and dance orchestras.

In the poorer areas of port towns, local musicians learned to play sailors' instruments and created a blend that became known as palm-wine music, ragtime, or "native blues." This developed into guitar-band music.

Brass-bands go all the way back to military brass and fife bands associated with the coastal forts European, West Indian, and African musicians were employed at these forts. They played military marches, polkas, waltzes, and fusions of their own.

KONKOMBA MUSIC

About a hundred years ago, a type of African brass-band music called adaha became very popular with the many brass-bands in the Fanti areas of Ghana. Within a short time the whole of the south of Ghana was swinging to this music, and every town of note wanted to have its own brass-band.

When local musicians couldn't afford to buy expensive imported instruments, they made do with drums, voices, and plenty of fancy dress. This poor man's brass-band music, which included drill—like dances, became known as konkomba or konkoma music.

BENI AND DANCE ORCHESTRAS

FIGURE 7.4 *Ghanaian regimental band, around World War I*

A similar thing happened in East Africa when, around the turn of the century, military brass-band music was taken up by local people. They combined African and European drums, bugles, and brass instruments with military parade-type dances and called it "beni." This beni ngoma, or beni dance craze, was spread around the rural hinterland of East Africa by the askaris, local African troops during the First World War period. It became progressively Africanised. For instance, the trumpet was replaced by the gourd kazoo. This led to a whole number of even more Africanised dance-styles, like the mgonda, kalela, and chikosa.

Another popular type of music around the turn of the century was performed by the African dance orchestras, complete with brass, woodwind, and stringed instruments. The black and mulatto elites in the towns especially liked this music. There were orchestras such as the Lagos City Orchestra in Nigeria, the Excelsior Orchestra in Accra, the Don't Worry Entertainers of South Africa and the Dapa Dan Jazz Band of Sierra Leone.

These large, prestigious orchestras played waltzes, foxtrots, quicksteps, ragtimes, and other ballroom dance numbers for their top-hatted audiences. Then, they began to orchestrate the local melodies and street music. That's how highlife got its name.

These stylish orchestras went on playing up until the Second World War, and then died out. During the war, tens of thousands of Allied troops were stationed in Africa, and African soldiers fought in Burma and elsewhere. All this affected the popular music scene in Africa. Jazz and swing became all the rage.

FIGURE 7.5 *Surviving members of the Excelsior Orchestra (formed in Accra in 1914), 1959*

So the huge orchestras gave way to the smaller jazz combos of the postwar period. The man who pioneered this breakthrough was E T. Mensah.

E. T. MENSAH

E. T. Mensah, or E. T. as he is known, was born in Accra in 1919. It was his band, the Tempos, that pioneered urban highlife played by dance-bands. E. T. started his musical career when, as a small boy, he joined the Accra Orchestra as a flute player. The Accra Orchestra was formed by Teacher Lamptey around 1930, based on a schoolboy band.

Teacher Lamptey, the headmaster of a James Town elementary school, had been a member of one of the first dance orchestras in Ghana, the Jazz Kings, formed in the early 1920s. But it was his Accra Orchestra that became the best-known prewar orchestra, and many of Ghana's top musicians played in it, including E. T., Joe Kelly, and Tommy Gripman.

E. T. and his older brother Yebuah went on to form their own Accra Rhythmic Orchestra, which won the Lambeth Walk Dance Competition in 1939 at the King George Memorial Hall (present-day Parliament House).

FIGURE 7.6 *The Accra Orchestra was formed in 1930 out of this school brass-band. The founder, Teacher Lamptey, is seated and wearing a police-type hat.*

Yebuah Mensah comments on the origin of the term "highlife".

During the early twenties, during my childhood, the term "highlife" was created by people who gathered around the dancing clubs such as the Rodger Club (built in 1904) to watch and listen to the couples enjoying themselves. Highlife started as a catch-name for the indigenous songs played at these clubs by such early bands as the Jazz Kings, the Cape Coast Sugar Babies, the Sekondi Nanshamang, and later the Accra Orchestra. The people outside called it "highlife" as they did not reach the class of the couples going inside, who not only had to pay a, then, relatively high entrance fee of 7s 6d, but also had to wear full evening dress including top-hats.

E T Mensah was self-taught at first.

He taught himself music, starting with the flute. During World War Two, saxophonist Sgt Leopard of the British Army in West Africa, looking for musicians, took him under his tutelage. From him, E. T. learnt how to play the alto saxophone. He took to playing the trumpet and later led the Accra Tempos Band. E. T. claims that it was watching and listening to Eddie Calvert play Cherry Pink and Apple Blossom that encouraged him to play the trumpet the way he does now. Many musicians in Ghana have passed through his hands, many more extending outside Ghana have modelled their style on his. His music was recorded by Decca (West Africa) and admirers gave him the title "King of Highlife."

—(record notes, Mensah's African Rhythms)

The high-class dance orchestras were eclipsed during the Second World War, when American and British troops were stationed in Ghana. They brought in jazz and swing. Night-clubs and dives were opened with names like Kalamazoo, Weekend-in-Havanna, and the New York Bar. They also set up dance combos and played with local musicians.

JAZZ AND SWING

The first combo was the Black and White Spots, set up by Sergeant Leopard. E. T. left his brother's orchestra and joined up with Leopard's jazz combo as sax player in 1940. Sergeant Leopard, a Scot, had been a professional saxophonist in England. According to E. T., it was Leopard himself who taught them jazz techniques.

It was Sergeant Leopard who taught us the correct methods of intonation, vibrato, tongueing, and breath control, which contributed to place us above the average standard in the town.

Just after the war, E. T. joined the Tempos, set up by Ghanaian pianist Adolf Doku and English engineer Arthur Harriman. At first the band included some white soldiers but after the war, when the Europeans left, the band became completely African and E. T. became

FIGURE 7.7 *Right to left E. T. Mensah and J. Mallet, members of the Accra Rhythmic Orchestra, 1937*

its leader. It was a seven-piece band with E. T. doubling on trumpet and sax, Joe Kelly on tenor sax, and Guy Warren on drums.

Guy Warren made an important contribution as he had been playing Afro-Cuban music and calypsos in England. So the Tempos not only played with a jazz touch, but incorporated calypsos into their repertoire and added the bongos and maracas to the lineup.

It was the Tempos' style of highlife that became all the rage; by the early 1950s the band started touring West Africa and recording for Decca. E. T., who had been a pharmacist, was able to go fully professional.

It was during the 1950s that E. T. was acclaimed the king of highlife throughout West Africa, for although the palm-wine variety of highlife was popular in the rural areas of West Africa, ballroom music and colonial-type orchestras still dominated the urban dance scene.

FIGURE 7.8 *E. T. Mensah (seated, centre) and his Tempos dance-band, early 1950s*

In Nigeria, highlife music like konkomba, juju, and palm-wine was left to the rural and low-class urban night-spots. High-class clubs featured dance-bands like Bobby Benson's, Sammy Akpabot's, and the Empire Hotel Band, which played only swing and ballroom music. But E. T.'s style of highlife soon began to influence them and create a whole new generation of Nigerian dance-band musicians like Victor Olaiya, Eddie Okunta, Arinze Rex Lawson, Charles Iwegbue, Victor Chukwu, Chief Billy Friday, Enyang Henshaw, King Kennytone, and Roy Chicago.

The Tempos influenced not only these mature Nigerian dance-band musicians, but also the young Victor Uwaifo As Dan Acquaye, one of E. T.'s musicians, recalls from one of the many of the Tempos' tours of Nigeria.

> In Benin City, Victor Uwaifo, then a schoolboy, would rush down to our hotel after school to watch my cousin Dizzy Acquaye on the guitar. He was determined to play the guitar and used to help Dizzy clean his instrument.

FIGURE 7.9 *Bobby Benson's band.*

Victor Uwaifo corroborates this story.

> I used to see E. T. Mensah and his Tempos play whenever they were in Benin and I went to see their guitarist, Dizzy Acquaye, to put me through a few chords. I had a guitar book but I didn't understand the chord drawings Dizzy helped me.

Many musicians passed through the tutelege of the Tempos—Joe Kelly, Tommy Gripman, Saka Acquaye, Spike Anyankor, Ray Ellis, and the first female vocalist Juliana Okine (all from Ghana); and Zeal Onyia and Babyface Paul Osamade from Nigeria.

E. T. ON TOUR

During the 1950s, the Tempos toured West African countries, where there were no highlife bands. In Sierra Leone there were local palm-wine music and meringue (or maringa), but this was never played by the dance-bands there. So E. T.'s music was an instant success. They played at a party for the prime minister, Doctor Margai, and toured the country. By the early 1960s, dance-bands like the Ticklers were in full swing, playing both highlifes and meringues.

FIGURE 7.10 *The Tempos dance-band, mid-1950s*

In Liberia, too, local music was not being played by the dance-bands. They were playing the quadrille, a refined Creole music that the American Liberian freed slaves brought over from the southern states of America. In fact, the Tempos were so popular in Liberia that President Tubman invited them to his inauguration. He sent them the following telegram:

I am very pleased to note that you and your band have safely arrived in Accra. We enjoyed the melody, rhythm and tempo of your band and this telegram constitutes an invitation to you and your band to return for the inauguration.

In the French-speaking countries of Guinea and the Côte d'Ivoire, E. T. did not come across an African dance-band or orchestra, let alone one playing indigenous music In the night-clubs of Conakry and Abidjan he heard white groups playing French music. The Tempos had to show the people there how to dance highlife.

E. T. Mensah's Tempos spread highlife far and wide, until E. T. retired in the 1970s.

FIGURE 7.11 *Temple House, James Town, Accra*

When I wrote *E. T. Mensah, the King of Highlife* (published by Off the Record Press, 116 Whitfield Street, London WIP 5RW, in 1986) I was living at Temple House, James Town, in downtown Accra (1974–1979). On many occasions E. T. visited me. He told me he remembered coming to the place as a boy with Teacher Lamptey's Accra Orchestra, which played for Ghanaian "big people" with top hats and tails at balls held in the old tennis courts at the back of the house (now a factory). Oddly enough percussionist Kofi Ayivor also lived there in the 1960s. When I left, Kris Bediako, the leader of A Band Named Bediako and the Third Eye group, moved into my flat.

The house was built around 1900 by a black lawyer named Thomas Hutton-Mills who sponsored the balls. His daughter Violet was a brilliant classical pianist who reluctantly had to give up a professional musical career to become her father's secretary. She died in 1971 and it was her son and daughter-in-law, Tom and Balbil Whittacker, who told me the house's history. They were my landlords. Because of their musical heritage, they never minded my band rehearsing in the house.

KING BRUCE AND THE BLACK BEATS

An award was given to Ghanaian musician King Bruce by the Entertainment Critics and Reviewers Association of Ghana (ECRAG) on April 30, 1988, for his "immense contribution to the development of Ghanaian art and culture in the field of highlife music." This musician's career in dance-band music spans nearly forty years.

My first contact with King Bruce was in the mid-1970s, when I hired equipment from him for my own band. For a while we were both on the executive board of the Musicians' Union of Ghana (MUSIGA). In August 1987 King gave a number of interesting presentations at the conference of the International Association for the Study of Popular Music (IASPM) held in Accra (of which I was on the local organising committee) with its theme of "Africa in the World of Popular Music." Since then I've recorded four songs for him—"Esheo Heko" (There Comes a Time), "Onyiemo Feo Mi Feo" (Walk Beautiful), "Ekole" (Perhaps), and "Tsutsu Tsosemo" (Old Time Training)—that King has released locally on cassette.

King Bruce, a Ga, was born in James Town, Accra, in 1922. His musical experiences started early and were varied. His mother belonged to a traditional women's singing group called Etsi Penfo, his eldest brother Kpakpo Thompson taught him piano, another brother, Eddie Bruce, played palm-wine guitar-styles like "fireman" and "dagomba wire" in a group of seamen called Canteen. At the same time, and much against his parents' wishes, King was a keen follower of the Accra street music, such as the alaha, kolomashie, tsibode, koyin, and other popular dance-styles played by the local Ga drumming groups.

At the prestigious Achimota College, King continued to be inspired by music, particularly by some of the teachers who taught there. These included Phillip Gbeho, who composed Ghana's national anthem, and Doctor Ephraim Amu, who, King explains, "was my house-master as well as my music teacher and taught us his Twi and Ewe songs. He had come to Achimota after he lost his appointment as a teacher at the Akropong Training College because of his strong African tendencies. He didn't believe in the idea of going to classes or church in Western-style suits, but always wore traditional kente cloth or batakari. He had these strong feelings about African culture as far back as the 1930s and was welcomed at Achimota, as the founders of the school—Guggisburg, Fraser, and Aggrey—were strongly interested in promoting African ways."

It was at the end of his schooldays at Achimota that King developed a taste for swing and dance-band music, for these "were the war years and we had British and American army units stationed here. They had bands for their entertainment and so ballroom music progressed very much. The airport was virtually taken over by the Americans and one wing of Achimota College itself was taken over by the British resident minister, who was taking care of the British war effort here. So this was the time of musicians like Glenn Miller, Benny Goodman, and Artie Shaw, so by the time I left Achimota I had a definite liking for jazz and swing."

FIGURE 7.12 *King Bruce's Black Beats, 1952 King Bruce (far left) is playing trumpet*

King did not actually start playing in a dance-band, however, until he had spent a couple of years in England studying to be a civil servant with the P&T (Posts and Telegraphs) and learning to play the trumpet. On returning to Accra in 1950, he hung around for a while with top musicians like Adolf Doku, E. T. Mensah, Kofi Ghanaba (Guy Warren), Joe Kelly, and Papa Hughes. He occasionally played clips (claves) for Ghana's leading highlife dance-band, the Tempos. When King felt he was ready to go on stage with his trumpet, he joined Teacher Lamptey's Accra Orchestra.

King stayed with this group until 1952, when he and tenor saxist Saka Acquaye formed the Black Beats band. This name, according to King, "just came out spontaneously. One evening when we were coming home from rehearsals Saka asked me what name we were going to use. Without hesitation I said Black Beats. The reason was that Doctor Amu at Achimota had impressed on us the necessity for doing things African. At the same time as a group we were very much enamoured with jazz, swing, and music with a beat. So we were all interested in playing good dance-band music, but keen on giving everything a recognisable African beat."

Unlike the other Ghanaian dance-bands, the Black Beats vocalists (the Black Birds, Lewis Wadawa, and Frank Barnes) dominated the instrumental lineup—and in this they were influenced by the swing and "jump" music of Afro-American Louis Jordan. It was with this format that the Black Beats began to release a string of highlife hits for HMV, Senophone, and Decca composed by King, like "Teeman Sane" (A Confidential Matter), "Laimomo" (Old Lover), "Nkuse Mbaa Dong" (I'll Never Return), "Nomo Noko" (A Thing of Joy), "Srotoi Ye Mli" (Distinctions), and "Agoogyi" (Money—this song being composed by Oscarmore Ofori).

In 1961 disaster struck the band. Alto saxist Jerry Hansen and nine musicians left the semiprofessional Black Beats to form the fully professional Ramblers dance-band. Nevertheless, within a few months King had reorganised his band and with this second-generation Black Beats began releasing more hits for Decca, like "Se Nea Woti Ara" (I Love You Just as You Are), "Kwemo Ni Okagbi" (Take Care You Don't Dry Up), "Odo Fofor" (New Love), and "Nkase Din" (I Am Quietly Poised).

During the whole period when King was running the Black Beats he was slowly working his way up the civil service ladder, but getting a lot of criticism from his superiors for playing on stage. As King comments, "At first the opposition from my employers came in hints. Then in 1967 the opposition came in black and white as a result of a letter I received from the government. It was from the head of the Administrative Civil Service and they told me that I had now got to the stage where I was due for promotion from assistant to full principal secretary and that the only thing that stood in my way was my dance-band playing. So I had to decide whether to continue playing or accept promotion. So

I replied that I got commitments to play up to Easter 1968, but that from April and thereafter I would comply with the undertaking and wouldn't play in public anymore."

I asked King how he felt about this. He replied, "I was very much annoyed because I had always believed that it was the actual playing in a band that sharpens your faculties and brings new ideas. When you sit down doing nothing you don't create new music. So the ban on my playing hurt me very much as I had to sacrifice a lot to play music and had always wanted to pursue it and make something out of it."

To keep his band running King handed the Black Beats' leadership to Sammy Odoh. Instead of playing King started managing the band—plus others that became based at his house in James Town. During the 1970s he was running eight "BB" bands the Black Beats, Barbecues, Barons, Bonafides, Barristers, Boulders, "B" Soyaaya, and Blessed Apostles.

Besides being a senior civil servant, composer, band leader, manager, and teacher of the hundred or so musicians who have passed through his groups, King Bruce has also found time to help organise all three of Ghana's music unions: the 1950s' Gold Coast Association of Musicians, the short-lived (1960–1966) Ghana Musicians Union, and the present-day MUSIGA.

In 1977 King Bruce retired from the civil service. He still actively pursues his musical career. He runs two "BB" bands (the Black Beats and Barristers), has begun to rerecord some of his old hits, is active in MUSIGA, and was involved in the recent changes in the copyright law that now make infringement a criminal offence. In the latest phase of his musical career, he became for a while the manager of the sixteen-track Elephant Walk recording studio in Kaneshie, Accra.

South African Choir Tradition: Ladysmith Mambazo and the Tip-Toe Guys

An African genre that has been on the world stage for many years is the a cappella choir tradition from South Africa, best represented in a global context by the group Ladysmith Black Mambazo. Although this group and others enjoy great popularity, and there are many full-time musical groups, the tradition actually developed among migrant workers in the diamond and gold mines of South Africa. The original choral tradition is known as *mbube* (lion in Zulu), a name that came from one of the first popular songs in the tradition. This song became interna-

FIGURE 7.13 *Ladysmith Black Mambazo*

tionally famous in the 1940s when it was recorded by the Weavers, with the title "Wimoweh," and in the 1960s when recorded as "The Lion Sleeps Tonight" by the Tokens.

The genre has been around since the 1920s and developed into its current version known as *isicathamiya*, sometimes translated as *"tip-toe guys"* or "walking softly," referring to the synchronized dancing that is now part of the performance practice. The genre developed when young Zulu men started to flock to mines and factories, often very far from home, where they would spend most of the year. They lived in group lodgings where they passed their time, and preserved their culture, by singing and dancing. Over time, these groups started competing within each mine or factory; these competitions helped the genre become more popular. The genre spread to Johannesburg and other cities and became a fixture in South Africa's music culture. As is the case with much music in Africa, isicathamiya represents a blending of African and European music, in this case, Zulu call and response and melodic and harmonic forms from Christian hymnody and other European music, which came to South Africa with the Dutch and English colonizers.

Graceland

The most famous group in this tradition is Ladysmith Black Mambazo, the four-time Grammy-winning group, which takes its name from Ladysmith, the home town of most of the group's members, Black, referring to the black ox, the strongest of farm animals, and the Zulu word for axe, referring to the power of the group and their ability to chop down opponents in competitions. Made up mostly of bothers and cousins of their leader, Joseph Shabalala, they formed in the 1960s, started competing with other groups, and developed into full-time musicians. In 1986, Ladysmith Black Mambazo performed on Paul Simon's album *Graceland*, which helped make them international stars, a status they enjoy until today. This album helped introduce world music to mainstream audiences and was the first of several albums Paul Simon made with world music artists.

PAUL · SIMON
GRACELAND

FIGURE 7.14 *Cover of Paul Simon's album Graceland*

Reading #2

One of the readings for this chapter, "Graceland (1986): World Music Collaboration," takes a close look at the political context in which this collaboration was released at a time before the end of Apartheid. It explores the ways in which musical ideas and traditions were mixed in the process of composing and recording this album; it also looks at the responses from musicians to the album and the idea of this collaboration.

GRACELAND (1986) WORLD MUSIC COLLABORATION

Carol A. Muller

INTRODUCTION

In the minds of many involved in the production of South African music in the late twentieth century, longtime American **popular musician Paul Simon's *Graceland*** album (1986) was a turning point in South African music history. A collaborative recording project between South Africans and the American singer-songwriter, the *Graceland* album **showcased** South African music to a worldwide popular music market at a critical moment. The (mostly Black) South Africans included in the project were **Joseph Shabalala** and his unaccompanied *isicathamiya* group **Ladysmith Black Mambazo**, guitarist **Ray Phiri**, bass player Bakhiti Khumalo, drummer Vusi Khumalo, percussionist Makhaya Mahlangu, singers General MD Shirinda and the Gaza Sisters, piano accordionist Forere Motloheloa, and the township group, Boyoyo Boys. White South African pennywhistle player Morris Goldberg appeared on a couple of tracks, and exiled South African musicians Miriam Makeba and Hugh Masekela joined *Graceland* for the African Tour. There is no doubt that for Black South African music in particular, the *Graceland* album opened the doors to the world and popular music marketplaces in ways few other recordings have.

And yet, despite the positive outcomes of collaborative effort between these two constituencies of musicians—African and American—the *Graceland* album incited outrage from many around the world, particularly those who were aware of the struggles of Black South Africans against the apartheid regime.

In this chapter we take a closer look at both the political context in which this collaborative project was produced and released to the world—a political context shaped in part by another recording that urged foreign musicians *not* to work in South Africa; we examine the ways in which different musical ideas and traditions were used in composing the songs that constitute the *Graceland* album; how the re-release of the album ten years later changed its tone; and finally, we take a brief look at some of the responses from musicians to the album and the spirit of the project itself.

1980S POLITICS: "RHYTHMS OF RESISTANCE"

The mid-1980s in South Africa were the most repressive years in apartheid history, a period in which the government expelled foreign journalists and declared numerous "states of emergency" because political resistance to apartheid, inside and outside of the country, was at an all-time high. As a result, state security forces were ever-present in Black townships and White urban areas, and thousands of mostly Black South Africans, including hundreds of children, were arrested and detained without access to legal representation, let alone a free and fair trial. It was also the era of the mega **"charity rock"** concerts like Live Aid, Farm Aid, and We Are the World,[1] which were beamed by satellite to the world from London and the United States. In these events the stars of the entertainment world presented themselves, and were marketed as, socially conscious musicians. This was the moment in which American rock musician and producer **Little Steven** released the collaboratively created *Sun City: Artists United Against Apartheid video*, album, and book package.[2] The music video had been made with MTV audiences in mind and aired on that channel (the American Public Broadcasting Services, PBS, had refused to air the video for fear of alienating its largely White viewers, and there was no Black Entertainment Television BET; at the time). *Sun City* was not just a moneymaking event; it was designed to raise people's consciousness and to get them to think about South African policies of apartheid and reflect on parallel experiences of racism in their own countries.

To comprehend the controversy generated by *Graceland*, we must consider four points: (1) the international cultural boycott that had been called for by South Africans in exile in Europe and the United States and applied against South Africa—its government and its people; (2) **"Sun City,"** the entertainment center in South Africa that symbolized the evil of the apartheid regime; (3) *Rhythm of Resistance*, a video documentary on Black South African music directed by British filmmaker Jeremy Marre in 1979 and aired publicly in many live and mediated places; and (4) the musical **collaborations** across racial divides that had begun to form inside South Africa in the 1980s.

CULTURAL BOYCOTT

The history of **cultural boycotts** against South Africa reaches back beyond apartheid to the 1940s. As early as 1946 the American Actor's Equity resolved to discourage its members from working in South Africa because of racial discrimination. India initiated the first boycott in 1947. It was an Anglican priest, Father Trevor Huddleston, who had worked in Sophiatown, Johannesburg, a community destroyed by the government, who called for a boycott against South Africa that achieved international media attention in the 1950s. The poignancy of his message was reinforced with the Sharpeville Massacre in March 1960. In response, Equity, the British Actors' Union, and the British Musicians' Union refused to allow their members to perform in South Africa from the late 1950s. Nobel Peace Prize winner (1960) Albert Luthuli invoked **United Nations Organization** principles to call for an even larger boycott in the 1960s. In 1965, sixty-five performers and actors pledged to refuse to perform in apartheid South Africa (1948–1990), including Harry Belafonte, Sammy Davis, Jr, and Nina Simone.

In 1969, the United Nations resolved to encourage member states to suspend all ties with the South African government: political, sporting, and cultural. When television was introduced to South Africa, no British shows were aired because of the boycott. By the 1980s, South Africa had become quite isolated from the international cultural and sporting arenas.[3] In the early 1980s the United Nations declared that it would blacklist any performer who traveled to South Africa. Essentially, the United Nations cultural boycott meant that there would be no exchange of performers or performances between that country and the rest of the world. (Nevertheless, since the boycott could only be policed in terms of entertainers traveling in person, recordings of many famous artists continued to be sold in South Africa through the 1980s.)

By traveling to South Africa in 1985, at the height of public awareness of the evils of apartheid, Paul Simon broke the terms of the cultural boycott, which was supported not only by the United Nations, but also by numerous arts organizations the world over. Simon had not acquired permission to travel to South Africa from either the United Nations or the African National Congress, the two organizations at the forefront of the boycott. The international anti-apartheid community feared that if someone as powerful as Paul Simon did not abide by the principles, the struggle against the South African government would crumble. It was a struggle that had gained momentum with the political messages of another group of British and American musicians—the musicians who called themselves **Artists United Against Apartheid**, led by rock guitarist Little Steven (Steven van Zandt) who a year earlier had released a song about boycotting South Africa.[4]

SUN CITY: ARTISTS UNITED AGAINST APARTHEID

Sun City is the Las Vegas-style casino and entertainment center created by Sol Kerzner, funded in part by the South African government. South Africa's equivalent to Donald Trump, Kerzner built the casino in what was then the "independent" homeland of **Bophutatswana**,[5] north of Johannesburg. It was opened in 1979. There was no international political acknowledgment of these homelands. Nevertheless, overseas entertainers were lured to the site with offers of significant financial packages and the assurance that Bophutatswana was not part of South Africa, but rather, an independent state. The problem was that Bophutatswana was just one of the official Bantustans into which Black South Africans had been relegated, so most of the Black residents of the homeland lived in dire poverty, in contrast to the significant resources the South African government covertly poured into the entertainment oasis.

In 1985 American and British musicians worked together to create the MTV-targeted music video *Sun City: Artists United Against Apartheid*, and a series of other recordings made in the spirit of the international anti-apartheid movement. Recordings included the song "Biko" by Peter Gabriel, "Apartheid is Wrong" by Stevie Wonder, "Nelson Mandela" by Youssou N'Dour, "Tutu" by Miles Davis, and "No Easy Walk to Freedom" by Peter, Paul, and Mary.[6] The music video, book, and record package articulated the collective resolve of musicians not to be coerced into playing at Sun City. *Sun City* was issued in 1985, the same year that Paul Simon quietly traveled to South Africa to record tracks with three groups he had heard on a cassette titled *Gumboots: Accordion Jive* Hits Vol. II, given to him by a friend. Many considered Simon's project to be a blatant disregard for the cultural boycott, action interpreted as a lack of concern for the suffering and plight of the same Black South African musicians and their communities. The negative media attention did not hinder record sales—*Graceland* has sold millions of copies the world over. South African guitarist Ray Phiri claimed in 1998 that 13 million copies had already been sold.[7] As I comment at the end of this chapter, in retrospect, there have been many positive outcomes for the project.

RHYTHM OF RESISTANCE

In an effort to build sympathy for Black South African performers abroad, British filmmaker Jeremy Marre traveled to South Africa in the late 1970s to make a documentary film for the BBC titled *Rhythm of Resistance: Black South African Performance*. Produced before the cultural boycott, Marre's documentary fleshed out the politics of musical performance and production in the apartheid period. Ladysmith Black Mambazo was one of the groups featured on this documentary, a film frequently shown at anti-apartheid gatherings especially on college campuses in Britain and the United States in the 1980s.

Marre's agenda in *Rhythm of Resistance* was clearly to expose the hidden forms of street and studio performance of Black South Africa, labeled "tribal" music, that were used by performers and their audiences as acts of resistance to apartheid […]. Marre later produced the video/DVD documentary (discussed below) about the *Graceland* album as a collaborative project, in which clips from *Rhythm of Resistance* were inserted, visually connecting the two documents and the stories behind the music in each. Paul Simon claims that it was this documentary that inspired him to travel to South Africa and record with local musicians.

DOCUMENTING SOUTH AFRICAN MUSIC

The thirteen-part video series *African Wave: South African Music and Its Influences* [...] tells the stories of thirteen South African musicians/groups whose lives intertwine in the aftermath of the *Graceland* album. Countering the separate development/apartheid images of South African performances under apartheid, this series stresses the "multicultural music of South Africa, its major musicians, and the traditional and contemporary influences that color their work" (see video cover for Bowey 1998). Included in the series are those who have recorded with Gallo Records: township pop singer Brenda Fassie; the contemporary queen of popular music in Africa Yvonne Chaka Chaka; African Jazz Pioneers leader Ntemi Piliso; Ladysmith Black Mambazo; Ray Phiri, Sipho Hotstix Mabuse (the latter three all participants in the *Graceland* recording); White rock copies Little Sister; South African reggaeman Lucky Dube; Mango Groove; hybrid Soweto duo Marcalex; hip hop artists Prophets of da City, and the late great Zulu dancer and growler Mahlathini. The most pervasive themes in the series are (1) market cross-over, which in South Africa means racial and genre cross-over—that is, groups that sell to more than one group of consumers defined by race/culture and language; (2) covering and borrowing sounds and styles from abroad; and (3) the significance of *Graceland* to their music.

COLLABORATIONS ACROSS THE RACIAL DIVIDE

Rhythm of Resistance provides the first glimpses of the kinds of musical collaborations that South Africans themselves had begun to form anew in the late 1970s, such as that of the singer-songwriter duo of White South African Johnny Clegg and Black migrant worker Sipho Mchunu. I remember discovering the music of the duo, called Juluka, and the band they subsequently formed—and dancing the night away with my friends to recordings of this music in the mid-1980s. But I also recall attending one of their performances in the Durban City Hall at about the same time—the sheer presence of Black and White men performing together in public was reason for the stage to be guarded by South African police, who stood in the wings the entire performance to quell any public unrest that might be generated by the interracial group. Fortunately, the only thing generated by the performance was huge enthusiasm for the sounds streaming from the stage.

Soon other groups also began to transgress the racial ideologies of apartheid. Later in the 1980s, Mango Groove, an interracial ensemble, recorded and performed South African popular music, integrating the sounds of *kwela* and *marabi*, sounds that evoked a deep nostalgia for a bygone, pre-Grand Apartheid era (see *African Wave, Part Seven: Mango Groove*). The African Jazz Pioneers was another popular group, made up largely of Black South African musicians who had played jazz in the 1950s but who re-formed as an interracial group. They included a White trombonist in their group in the 1980s (see *African Wave, Part Ten on African Jazz Pioneer Ntemi Piliso*).

THE *GRACELAND* ALBUM

A great deal has been written about the *Graceland* album since its release in 1986—much of it in response to the controversy itself.[8] But since the recording and the controversy were recorded more than two decades ago, my purpose here is to use *Graceland* to flesh out the many meanings and interpretations that are generated by a single musical recording. The *Graceland* case study should enable you to reflect on the relationship between South African music history and that of the United States, on one hand, and more generally on some of the issues raised by the *Graceland* collaboration and the production of "world music," on the other.

At its core, *Graceland* is a musical collaboration between Paul Simon and a host of other musicians. These included Cajun zydeco music of Rockin' Dopsie and the Twisters, the Chicano Rock of Los Lobos, the Everly Brothers in the United States, as well as a large contingent of South Africans, with Joseph Shabalala and Ladysmith Black Mambazo, and Ray Phiri and Stimela in the foreground. The *Graceland* album included a different set of musicians than did *Graceland: The African Concert* (presumably for logistical reasons, but the changing personnel and the difference between studio production and live performance are important in coming to terms with the ownership of *Graceland*).

Like so many recordings, including *Sun City*, the *Graceland* album was the result of numerous studio recordings creating multiple tracks of sound that were then combined to create the single texture we now hear as the final *Graceland* product. And these recordings occurred in Johannesburg, London, Los Angeles, and New York City. One of the criticisms of the album is that even though Simon was showcasing musicians to the world, they were not properly credited for their creative contribution. By all accounts they were well paid as studio musicians but were not compensated as artists. Responding to this accusation in Marre's video, Paul Simon talks not so much as a musician but as a producer, shifting the idea of musical collaboration to one where he and his engineer collected raw materials in South Africa that required the vision of the producer to bring it all together and "refine" it for the popular market.

There are eleven tracks on the CD, to a greater and lesser degree incorporating or shaped by South African vocal and/or instrumental performances. Excluding the Zulu texts of Joseph Shabalala, the words of all the songs are attributed to Paul Simon. A number of tracks are discussed in detail on the Marre DVD (1998), *Paul Simon's Grace-land: Recounting the Journey of a Legendary Music Recording*. These are: track 1, "Boy in the Bubble"; the least South African in sound of all tracks, track 2, "Graceland"; track 8, "Homeless," which is the most easily identifiable as a South African sound; four more tracks discussed and showcased are track 9, "Crazy Love Vol. II," track 7, "Under African Skies," track 6, "You Can Call Me Al," and track 5, "Diamonds on the Soles of her Shoes." Five of the eleven tracks are analyzed to varying degrees below.

Marked differences are contained in the liner notes inside the 1986 original and 1996 reissue. The 1996 notes are considerably expanded. They are written by *Billboard* magazine's editor-in-chief, Timothy White, who discusses how the album was produced and the shifting political context of its production and reception since 1985. The photographic image of Paul Simon leaning against a wall, alone, which was originally on the front of the album, is moved to the back in 1996; the "more African" image, the Ethiopian print of King George on a horse, has moved from back to front. All the musicians who contributed in some way to *Graceland*, and their record companies, are carefully listed and acknowledged in the same way in both sets of notes. What has changed significantly is the discussion of the political significance of *Graceland* in light of the new South African democracy, a change few in the 1980s had imagined would be possible just a few years later. In short, a recording made and distributed globally in 1986 primarily as an American masterpiece written in the first person by Paul Simon, with a brief personal narrative of how it all came about, is completely reframed in 1996. The emphasis on a personal journey is gone. In its place is a politically informed story that relates the *Graceland* album and its production more intimately to South African music and political history, and places Paul Simon firmly into that archive, along with the South Africans who worked with him. Even if our response two decades later is to shrug our shoulders and say "So what?" to 1980s racial politics, it is clear that the controversy generated by *Graceland* in 1986 forced Paul Simon and Warner Brothers to reevaluate and reconfigure the presentation of the product for the global marketplace.

THE PAUL SIMON VIDEO: MAKING *GRACELAND*

Unlike the *Graceland* album, which was made in the apartheid era, Jeremy Marre's video, *Paul Simon's Graceland: Recounting the Journey of a Legendary Music Recording* (1998), was released well into the post-apartheid era. Its contents, like the liner notes of the 1996 *Graceland* release, are far more politically engaged. In this environment musicians like Paul Simon—those Western popular musicians who have collaborated with those from less powerful places in the global economy—have become far more aware of relationships of power, the need for mutual respect between all musicians, appropriate payment and accreditation for multiple layers of musical sound that collectively constitute the final product, and the proper acknowledgment of musical collaboration. Since the mid-1980s, the view of third-world musicians as sources of inspiration has shifted to viewing them as co-creators. One might argue that the *Graceland* controversy not only raised awareness of the political plight of Black South Africans, but also highlighted issues of African creativity and the need for proper compensation. Although some cynically call it an atmosphere of political correctness, the present era is at least characterized by a heightened sensitivity to the politics of musical production, especially those between so-called first-and third-world musicians.

The brief recording chronology runs like this. Paul Simon spent several weeks listening to a cassette, a copy of *Gumboots: Accordion Jive Hits, II*, given to him by a friend, Heidi Berg, in the summer of 1984. Simon, then in something of a creative slump, was looking for personal and compositional renewal. He heard in this music a certain kind of familiarity, a resonance with popular music of the 1950s—hearing the familiar in the different would in fact come to be a defining characteristic of 1990s world music consumption (Taylor 1997). Simon asked Warner Brothers to track down the source of the cassette. They made contact with record producer Hilton Rosenthal in Johannesburg, who sent about twenty recordings of the gamut of contemporary Black South African performance. Simon listened closely and repeatedly to these recordings, allowing them to shape his musical thinking. Producer Hilton Rosenthal set up a recording date with Paul Simon and three groups that performed on Simon's cassette: Tao Ea Matsekha, General MD Shirinda and the Gaza Sisters, and the Boyoyo Boys bands. (Clips from these recording sessions are included in the Marre video.) Paul Simon and his engineer, **Roy Halee**, quietly traveled to South Africa in February 1985.

Soon after the Johannesburg recording session Paul Simon sent a letter and tape to Joseph Shabalala with some compositional ideas drawn from previous Mambazo recordings, to shape what became Simon's contribution to "Homeless." Then Shabalala and Ladysmith Black Mambazo traveled to London to record with Simon. Simon returned to New York and over the next few months invited several other musicians, including Nigerian pedal steel guitarist Demola Adepoju and Senegalese singer Youssou N'Dour, to record rhythmic and vocal tracks that would be dubbed into the recording mix. Some of this recording took place in Los Angeles. Although the album was scheduled for release in the summer of 1986, Warner Brothers delayed until the fall. South African musicians were in New York City because Ladysmith Black Mambazo and the Soweto Rhythm Section were to appear on *Saturday Night Live*. The South Africans went into the studio with Paul Simon in New York City and recorded in a few takes "Diamonds on the Soles of her Shoes," which was never intended to be on the original album.

Two ideas form the core of Marre's video on the making of *Graceland*: **collaboration** (see Meintjes 1990 for a thoughtful exploration of this idea in *Graceland*) and **composition** in the artistic sense. These two concepts work in tension with each other because a truly collaborative project would have required Simon to give artistic (and royalty) credit to the other artists, whereas the composition of a work of art by an individual composer enabled Simon to take the credit and royalty checks. Like the montage of musical traditions that defines the *Graceland* project, Marre integrates video footage from a range of sources: live interviews with musicians and technicians; footage from his own archive as used in *Rhythm of Resistance*; excerpts of *Graceland: The African Concert* (filmed in Zimbabwe in the late 1980s); news footage of political turbulence under apartheid; still images of 1950s Black South African performance, particularly of pennywhistle *kwela*; studio footage from Johannesburg, London, and New York; footage taken from *Saturday Night Live*; and several music video clips that both illustrate the words of the songs and present a single track ("You Can Call Me Al") with Chevy Chase lip-synching the words in a humorous rendition of the song.

ANALYZING *GRACELAND*

There is a pervasive sense in Marre's documentary on *Graceland* that when Paul Simon initiated contacts with and traveled to South Africa in 1985, he was on a personal journey as an artist out to expand his creative resources, and as such, was largely concerned with essentially musical and creative processes. Paul Simon's travel to record in South Africa does not appear to have been a journey with a political motivation, as Marre's *Rhythm of Resistance* video so clearly was. His was a musical journey, a singularly artistic process—initially, anyway—one in which art/music and politics did not have to mix. Simon's position is not that unusual amongst creative people—who often argue that they simply want their music to speak for them, that politics is not their mode of engagement. What Paul Simon would quickly discover is that it was impossible for him to separate the musical, political, and even the personal because in the South Africa of the late twentieth century, the personal, political, economic, and even musical were inextricably intertwined.

In addition to telling of the politicized character of the "journey of a legendary music recording," Marre's video contributes to an understanding of South African music in the global economy in ways that are important to ethnomusicologists. First, it provides rare footage of the inside of a recording studio, and not just one but several studios. Second, the video reveals the complex layers of compositional process, from Paul Simon's jotting of words onto paper, to the "jam" sessions held with South Africans, to the careful crafting of the final mix. Third, we witness some of the interaction between Paul Simon and the South African musicians as the tracks are laid. The voices of the musicians are woven into a narrative that provides different perspectives on a single process and portrays the complex negotiation that occurred as *Graceland* came together. Finally, the footage of engineer Roy Halee provides a rarely heard voice from inside the industry itself. Both men, Simon and Halee, are presented as thoughtful and frank in their discussion of the musical and traveling experiences that ultimately resulted in the *Graceland* recording.

Simon's narrative of how he came to make *Graceland* and the processes by which he selected and multi-tracked the final product are key organizational nodes in the film. About halfway through the video an educational segment on South African music deconstructs the layers of South African sounds in the musical product. Perhaps the most useful information we glean from the video is how specific musical tracks were created, what parts were specifically South African, and what parts came directly from Paul Simon. Let us take a more in-depth look at three of these.

"THE BOY IN THE BUBBLE"

The opening measures of the album not only introduce to the audience strands of the familiar-but-strange sounds of Southern African migrant worker performance; they also represent the whole concept of *Graceland* sonically. It was a social and musical experiment, collaborative to its very core, inspired by the sounds of **accordion**, guitar, drums, and bass on the *Gumboots: Accordion Jive Hits, II*. The song starts out with several measures of solo piano accordion playing, and the powerful beats of the drum enter to place the beat firmly in its 4/4 frame. For almost eight measures these two instruments establish the groove that carries Paul Simon's voice and lyrics through the remainder of the track.

"I think we always knew that this would be the start of the album. It began so unusually, and the sound of those drums sounded so 'African.' It was really an announcement that said you haven't heard this before . . ." Simon says. For engineer Roy Halee the song suggested the uncertainty of the moment, musically and politically. "It represents that whole experience: a very dark, very brooding quality about it. It most represents the whole trip, the whole concept, the recording in that studio" (Marre DVD 1998).

The song text, particularly in its refrain, explains the recording project as a connection created between the center and its "distant constellation," a "long distance call," urging its mainstream audience to think globally, to extend their listening ears to the place of "lasers in the jungle" (even though there is no "jungle" in South Africa). Retrospectively, the stress upon "miracles and wonder" has an eerie prophetic sense to it. But as Paul Simon remarks on the video, he knew that political change would eventually come to South Africa, but it seemed, in the mid-1980s, a very remote possibility. It is significant that the narrative about the radical political transformation of South Africa in the 1990s also used words like "miracles" and "wonders."

"HOMELESS"

The most removed in sound and musical arrangement from the experience of mainstream popular music audiences is the eighth track of the *Graceland* album, "Homeless." This is the track that most powerfully demonstrates the possibilities of musical collaboration between South African musicians and Paul Simon, even though they come from extremely different musical traditions. This track is also the most authentically "South African" in its sound—dear to many South Africans, but certainly the most remote to cultural outsiders because of its Zulu language text, which is not translated for the listener, and the sound of the Zulu language (and its clicks).

The song begins with Joseph Shabalala intoning the "call" and Mambazo men "responding" in traditional African style. They sing Simon's original ideas in Zulu but do not directly translate his words. Of all the South African musical traditions represented on *Graceland*, the unaccompanied four-part harmony vocal arrangements of *isicathamiya* is the one most flexible in meeting the requirements of the recording while remaining faithful to the tradition. *Isicathamiya*, which means "to walk stealthily, like a cat," or "to walk on tiptoes," traces its roots to mission hymnody (the four-part—soprano, alto, tenor, bass or **SATB format**) and the visit of African American performer Orpheus McAdoo and the Virginia Jubilee Singers to South Africa in the 1890s.[9] As the performance aesthetics of *isicathamiya* shifted in the twentieth century, so has its name. From *mbube* (discussed in Chapter 1) it was subsequently called *ibombing* because of the loud, near shouting style of its performance. Under Joseph Shabalala it has assumed a softer, sweeter, more harmonious sensibility, and is now performed with *isteps*: soft, stealthy dance routines reminiscent of nineteenth-century minstrel performances that took place all around South Africa.[10] Joseph Shabalala has frequently explained that performers learned to step lightly to avoid drawing police attention to their song and dance activities at night in the townships.[11]

As you listen to "Homeless," try to separate the distinctly "African/South African" aspects and those that are more familiar, more "mainstream" in American popular music. In thinking about the idea of familiar but different, an idea that characterizes the music on this album, and indeed the central characteristic of the success of "world music," think first about language (Taylor 1997). While Mambazo and Simon both sing in English, listen to the intonation of Black South African English. How does it differ from the American accent? The structure of the piece is largely sung in a call and response format—sometimes Joseph Shabalala is the leader, calling for a response; at other times Paul Simon assumes leadership, and Shabalala's voice is subsumed into the larger choral response.

Isicathamiya, as we have seen, is about four voices—soprano, alto, tenor, and bass—in harmony. Is this texture African or Western? This is an important question. Because of the long history of European, and more recently American, colonization of South Africa (largely through the missions and more recently through the entertainment industry), the musical texture of the mission hymn has become so much a part of Black South African performance practices, not only in *isicathamiya* but also in other styles of choral music, that it is now considered African. Clearly, **borrowing**, **assimilating**, even **appropriating** musical styles and ideas across the oceans has not been a one way process—Africans of European traditions, White Americans of Black African styles, for example—but is indeed an ongoing feature of the musical exchange between the two continents throughout the twentieth century, and in some cases, even earlier.

But as it has been indigenized, the SATB texture has taken on its own peculiarities. In the *isicathamiya* context, the soprano and alto voices usually sung by women are missing—the women are back at home in the rural areas, left behind by men who migrated to the cities for work. When migrant men began to form vocal groups and sing in the mission style, they adjusted the sound to a bass-heavy texture. In *isicathamiya* most voices sing bass, then tenor. Typically only one or two higher male voices sing alto, and the leader sings the soprano line. This is what you hear in Ladysmith Black Mambazo's singing both on *Graceland* and numerous other recordings they have made over the last four decades.

Finally, notice the creative, perhaps unusual use of the human voice on this track. Near the beginning of the song, we suddenly hear something that sounds like "rrrrrp rrrrp shek shek" in one of the voices. These are vocal imitations of sounds Joseph Shabalala recalls hearing in his childhood on his family farm. A little later one of the men, perhaps Shabalala, ululates—a high-pitched articulation typically done by women to express approval and joy in performance. Near the end of the song, the English phrase "Somebody say" is juxtaposed with alternating English words and syllables that are purely rhythmic in function: "ih hih hih ih." In all of these instances the human voice is used both melodically and rhythmically—a key feature of much vocal performance in South Africa. These are the familiar but different elements of *isicathamiya* performance that Tim Taylor, author of *Global Pop: World Music, World Markets*, argues appeal to world music consumers (1997). If you listen carefully to the Zulu lyrics near the end of the song you will hear a "click" sound in the middle of the word "*omanqoba*." (The letter "q" represents the click.) The Zulu language actually uses three different click sounds, the letter "c" is a soft click; "q" is a harder click, almost like the sound of horses galloping one can make with the mouth; and the letter "x" represents a click created at the back of the cheeks. South African singer Miriam Makeba popularized the Xhosa-language "Click Song" in the late 1950s and early 1960s when she sang with Harry Belafonte in New York City. The clicks clearly represent the exotic for those of us who speak English.

When listening to the "Homeless" track we might be tempted to presume that the marriage of cultures, languages, and voices was a happy one from the beginning, because its final product works so beautifully. But in the Marre video, Joseph Shabalala comments on the struggles that Ladysmith Black Mambazo had working with Paul Simon's initial ideas for the song. Simon sent his ideas to Shabalala before they met together to work out the song more fully. Shabalala recalls that he liked Simon's lyrics very much, but making the music work was far more of a challenge.

> It's a little bit difficult to blend the voices, the American voice, the African voice. The first day we were just touching, many people were trying to help us, and I just said, OK. Even the producer ... was there, trying to teach us. That was confusing me, it was his first time to teach us: we didn't know him. We are used to working together alone, and come with something solid and good. (Shabalala in Marre DVD 1988)

There may have been some misgivings among the group, too, because Shabalala remembers having reassured the group that Simon was a good and a polite man. Roy Halee agreed. "At the beginning it felt a little strange, [Ladysmith Black Mambazo] are tricky to record because they don't produce a lot of sound, those bass voices are very soft " (Halee in Marre DVD 1988).

When the group returned to their hotel, they prayed. They decided that they would just give Paul Simon what they knew and not try to do what he wanted. Mambazo would give what they knew, and Paul Simon would give what he had. The plan worked, and the next day the "Homeless" musical collaboration began to take shape.

"GUMBOOTS"

This track on *Graceland* is composed using the music on the cassette that Simon first listened to in 1984. The original tracks were performed by a South African band, the Boyoyo Boys, now overlaid with the wailing saxophone sounds of South African jazz performed principally by Barney Rachabane. These saxophone sounds are clear signifiers of the sounds of South African jazz, harking back to the excitement that African jazz produced for South Africans in the 1940s and 1950s—sounds that were silenced by the apartheid regime, particularly if they brought people of all races together in a single place.

Missing from the recording, but included in Marre's *Graceland* video, are the actual sounds of **gumboot** dancing, the boot dance of migrant workers from southern KwaZulu Natal who worked both in the port city of Durban and on the mines in Johannesburg. I have a peculiar attachment to gumboot dancing: I learned to perform the dance in 1985, trained by a migrant worker, Blanket Mkhize, and his team. When I visited the United States in early 1986 and told people that I gumboot danced, I would regularly be confronted with blank stares. "You mean Gumby?" people would laugh. But by 1987, *Graceland* had been released to the world, and far more people signaled recognition when I mentioned that I was a gumboot dancer—oh, from the *Graceland* album, people would inevitably remark. […]

SOUTH AFRICAN RESPONSES TO THE *GRACELAND* RECORDING

Several musical responses to the plight of Black South Africans in the mid to late 1980s were generated both inside and outside of South Africa by the publicity associated with *Sun City: Artists Against Apartheid*, and the *Graceland* project.

SARAFINA

Out of the workshop-style theater training identified with protest-theater in the 1970s and 1980s, South African playwright Mbongeni Ngema created a Broadway musical, **Sarafina! *The Music of Liberation***. It tells the story of Sarafina, a woman who teaches history at a school for Black South Africans in the township of Soweto. Sarafina seeks to teach history in a way that the South African government disapproves of, so she is arrested and put in prison. In the stage production, Sarafina symbolically represents Mandela—a man emasculated and feminized by his imprisonment. At the end of the production, Sarafina returns from her imprisonment as a man—the male figure of an imagined Nelson Mandela (he was still in prison at the time, and all visual representation of his face was banned in South Africa until his release in 1990). The Broadway production of *Sarafina* was subsequently produced for a popular audience in Holly-wood, starring Whoopi Goldberg as

Sarafina (Singh n.d.). A documentary film on the making of *Sarafina* from the perspective of its performers/co-creators was also made in the late 1980s (Noble 1988). There are several aural connections created between *Graceland* and *Sarafina* in the video made about the production of *Sarafina*. It opens with the South African performers standing close to one of Manhattan's famous bridges singing "Homeless." And *mbaqanga*, the popular musical style used in *Sarafina*, was introduced to the world by the *Graceland* album.

FIELD RECORDING, MARCH 1988, AMAOTI, KWAZULU NATAL

One of the first local responses to the *Graceland* recording I heard in South Africa was in an informal township school in AmaOti, in the Durban Metropolitan Region, in March 1988. (This is close to where the Shembe community [...] has its headquarters.) My husband, a US citizen, was teaching in the school and had been called to an all-day parents' meeting. At the time, Inanda, the area in which the AmaOti school was located, was a hotbed of student protest against the apartheid government, school boycotts, and political instability. Partway through the performance, the choir suddenly moved from a series of religious and gospel style songs to a version of "Diamonds on the Soles of Her Shoes." I recall the sense of amazement I felt at the relative speed with which the *Graceland* album had rooted itself in this community. Even more amazing was that these students were clearly politically aware—and yet they sought to emulate the music of the recording that had generated so much heated debate elsewhere in the world. They could have refused to sing the song because of its use of South African musicians despite the cultural boycott. Instead, they sang the song with enormous pride and satisfaction on that Sunday morning in 1988. In a recent documentary titled *On Tip Toe* (2002), Joseph Shabalala claims that he had not even heard about the United Nations cultural boycott when Paul Simon invited him to collaborate on the *Graceland* project. Clearly, Radio Zulu was effectively screening out international concerns about apartheid.

SOWETO STRING QUARTET, ZEBRA CROSSING (1994)

This album features the *Graceland*-inspired track "The Paul Simon *Graceland* Collection" which includes excerpts from four songs, "Homeless," "Diamonds on the Soles of Her Shoes," "Graceland," and "You Can Call Me Al" arranged to sound like a single piece.

The **Soweto String Quartet** hails from Johannesburg's largest and best-known Black urban township, Soweto. It has clearly established itself in an attempt to give respectability to the traditional and contemporary music of Black South Africans—to "classicize" the music. This is a recording made by Gallo (Africa) Records, the White-controlled commercial record company that is the dominant force in the South African recording industry. There is a dual signification in the title, "Zebra Crossing." On the one hand, the black and white of the zebra represent a kind of racial mixing, the zebra symbolizes Africanness, and the unity of Black and White in a single space; but the Zebra Crossing also resonates with global popular culture, referencing the Beatles' *Abbey Road* cover imagery from three decades earlier!

Distancing the group from the cloud of controversy that hung over the release of the recording, the author of the liner notes for this recording celebrates Paul Simon's intervention in

South African music history by showcasing South African music and musicians. The collaborative project is justified by the already hybridized nature of *mbaqanga* music—adding a little more to the *mbaqanga* pot where "the rich flavors of South African black music culture simmer" (Soweto String Quartet 1994, liner notes). The notes convey appreciation to Paul Simon and the *Graceland* project for opening the ears of the world to South African music, and for "stirring up" the *mbaqanga* pot once more.

DAVID KRAMER (1996), KLASSIC KRAMER

David Kramer is a South African singer and writer of protest song and theater. Born in England, he immigrated to South Africa many years ago and now lives in Cape Town. He is well known in the Cape for his depictions of the Afrikaans poor and working class (largely White) in the Western Cape. On his CD *Klassic Kramer*, he tells a story to a live audience about the time he met Paul Simon in 1985 when Simon visited South Africa to record what became the *Graceland* album. The story he told in 1991 at the Dock Road Theater in Cape Town, South Africa begins with a song he calls "Weskusklong," sung in Afrikaans that I have translated into English here.

> The earth is large and the stars are small
>
> Only lizards in the desert
>
> Deer and thorn and the bitter aloe
>
> I know the "East Coast," but its not the same
>
> Biscuits and biltong, I am a West Coast Khoi
>
>
> Give me a whip, give me a stick
>
> Give me a wife in a red floral dress
>
> Give me the open veld where the deer pasture
>
> You'll find me there between the stones
>
> Biscuits and biltong, I am a West Coast Khoi.

Kramer's narrative is significant for the way in which he positions himself in the relationship between the powerful American music industry, represented by Paul Simon, and South African musicians. It revolves around being invited to the studios in Johannes-burg (Marre's documentary provides a series of clips of these recording sessions, though none has Kramer in the frame) to witness Paul Simon and the South African musicians collaborating. Though Kramer is himself a popular musician in South Africa, he is not asked to collaborate with Paul Simon. Instead, at the studio in Johannesburg he invites Paul Simon and Roy Halee to visit him in Cape Town, a place many in South Africa consider the treasure of the country. He never thought Paul Simon would actually come, but it turns out he decided to after all.

So Kramer took the popular American musician to the Cape Point, the place where one can see both the Indian and Atlantic Oceans simultaneously, a place of great beauty and a popular tourist destination for foreign and local visitors. While they were there, Kramer was standing next to Paul Simon when a busload of tourists arrived and disembarked from the bus. When the tourists saw the two men, they came rushing towards them, asking Kramer for his signature. Nobody seemed to recognize Paul Simon, though they probably knew his voice and his music. So there Kramer stood, signing autographs, while Paul Simon, the powerful international star, stood to the side. It was an extraordinary example of the power of being known in the local context, over being the more widely known, but less recognized international name.

That night Paul Simon and David Kramer shared songs and stories at Kramer's home. Simon sang for Kramer, and then asked Kramer to sing for him. And the song he sang was "Weskusklong." As Kramer tells the story, Paul Simon took a copy of Kramer's song back to New York with him, and a little while later he had a call from Bob Dylan asking permission to do a cover version of the song. Kramer asks Bob Dylan to send him a cassette of the cover version. And he ends his story by imitating Bob Dylan's distinctive voice singing "Weskusklong."

David Kramer's spoken narrative is remarkable for the way in which it generates ideas about how the margins and centers operate, not from the perspective of global centers, but indeed, from the margins. In this narrative, the focus has shifted from the global star to the local: rather than the unknown international star, at least a star known only in voice and not in body, the tourists flock to the person they know from live performance and television commercials (Kramer did a commercial for Volkswagen on national television). Then of course, there is the lovely idea of a famous musician like Bob Dylan not being able to sound like anything other than his own voice, not being able to cover the music of others, even though they have been covering his songs for decades. Finally, Paul Simon, the famous musician, is unable to categorize David Kramer's music because he doesn't recognize it. The joke is on him, because it derives from the singer-songwriter tradition shaped by Paul Simon himself, just in another language. Ultimately Kramer's narrative is a discourse about shift s in the balance of power: who holds the power depends on what your perspective is.

LEEUKOP PRISONERS' CHOIR (C. 1996) "HOMELESS"

The recording of "Homeless" by the inmates of a Pretoria prison provides a poignant example of the way in which the words represent the real experience of not having a home for many South Africans. In this context, however, "Homeless" comes to mean something very particular: men in a high security prison, trained by two White choral directors, express anxiety about the possibility of having no home when they are released from prison. Once again, a close copy of the original version, but without the White voice of Paul Simon, the **Leeukop Prisoners' Choir** extends the *Graceland* archive deeper into South African musical history and experience.

KHAYELITSHA UNITED MAMBAZO

Geared toward the tourist market, **Khayelitsha United Mambazo** is a look-alike and sound-alike group modeled on Ladysmith Black Mambazo. They were selling this CD at the edges of their performance space while they sang at the Victoria and Albert Waterfront, a popular tourist destination in Cape Town's harbor, in July 2002. The disc has two songs sung in *isicathamiya* style. This group has clearly identified themselves as part of the larger Mambazo musical network, hoping to sell copies of their CDs to tourists for whom the name "Mambazo" and the sounds of the group will probably ring a bell. Copies and imitations are the ways in which South Africans have learned the repertories of the global entertainment industry. These actions foster a sense of connection to the centers of power. Imitation has long been a tradition in South African performance. In the past African people copied the sounds and gestures of animals and birds to harness their power; in the nineteenth and twentieth centuries, the model shifted to recorded objects and radio programing when the performances originated elsewhere in the world, though they relished imitations of local acts as well.

INSPIRATION'S "HOMELESS"

Established in 1989 at the University of Pennsylvania, **Inspiration** is a student a cappella group that celebrates the power of Black music, by singing the music written and performed by people of the African diaspora.

CONCLUSION

Part I begins and ends with discussion about two important moments in twentieth-century South African music history that involve the recording and global travel of South African music: the "Mbube"/"Wimoweh"/"Lion Sleeps Tonight" recording and the *Graceland* collaboration. In between, we examined in some detail twentieth-century South Africa's political and media history. We began with the story of "Mbube," because in many ways, it bookends two very different political contexts, particularly for Black South Africans. In the first, the late 1930s, the years of segregation and before the extreme years of apartheid (1948–1990), Black South Africans were not considered citizens of what was then the Union of South Africa. They were simply uneducated "natives" with no rights in a nation-state. So, Solomon Linda, "Mbube's" composer, ceded his composer rights time and again, because in reality, he didn't really have any. He was not considered part of the modern South African nation—a nation conceived under apartheid, as including only people of European descent. By the early 2000s, when the Linda family came to a legal agreement with George Weiss's Abilene Music Company, about royalty payments for the melody of "The Lion Sleeps Tonight," South Africa had been radically transformed: in 1994 it had become a democratic nation—all South Africans over the age of eighteen were entitled to vote for the people they wished to govern them. Along with the right to vote came a range of constitutional, economic, and human rights. Righting the wrongs of the past included fighting for royalty payments denied in an unjust social system.

We ended this section with a discussion of *Graceland*, the collaborative musical project produced by American Paul Simon with among others, several South African musicians in the mid-1980s. Once again, we examined political contexts and transformations, but this time in a very particular historical moment—the mid-1980s when political oppression of Black South Africans by the apartheid government was at its peak, and resistance (both internally and internationally) to apartheid was mounting. We have seen that the *Graceland* recording, while extremely contentious at the time, in retrospect played a key part in putting South African music into the hearts and minds of consumers around the world. It put South African music on the popular music map. But, *Graceland* also conveyed to South Africans in a slightly more symbolic way, that it was possible to work together, to create something new, across racial and cultural divides. The musical experiment that *Graceland* represents could become a model for wider social, political, and cultural experiments. *Graceland* as a project also outlines an important process in the creation of "world music"—ultimately, it is a highly successful story about the capacity of very different musical practices to find a way to blend, harmonize, to become palatable to a wide range of musical tastes both in South Africa and the world at large. Ultimately, the *Graceland* project put on display through musical composition and collaboration a range of traditional South African genres, many formed through internal musical migrations in the twentieth century. In Part II we will take a closer look at several of these, most especially gumboot dance, *maskanda* guitar traditions, and the globally renowned *isicathamiya* styles popularized by Joseph Shabalala and his Ladysmith Black Mambazo.

KEYWORDS

accordion musical instrument played in many parts of the world, with keyboard/buttons for pitch played on the right and left sides, and a middle that expands and contracts to create the air on metal reeds that produces the sound

appropriate an important concept in the study of world music—pronounced in one way and used as an adjective, it means something done in accordance with expectation; used as a verb it means almost the opposite—something taken without permission

Artists United Against Apartheid a 1980s political group formed around Little Steven, the rock musician, who urged musicians and entertainers to refuse to play in South Africa until apartheid was dismantled

assimilation to take on the ways of others in order to fit in

Bantustan homeland created by apartheid government, not recognized internationally

borrowing a process in which one musician uses the materials of another, but with permission

Bophutatswana the independent homeland where Sun City, the casino and entertainment complex, was located

charity rock rock concerts and musicians who perform at specific venues and events to raise money and awareness about poverty, starvation, and other humanitarian causes

collaboration the word used to describe the process of song-creation on *Graceland*, whereby musicians work together to create new music

composition the creative process involved in producing new songs

cultural boycott a movement in which musicians and artists refused to send their work or travel themselves to South Africa while apartheid was in place

David Kramer a British-born South African singer-songwriter who met Paul Simon when he was in South Africa recording tracks for *Graceland*

Graceland even if this was not Paul Simon's explicit intention, *Graceland* refers to both his collaborative album with South Africans and other musicians, and the home of rock'n'roll star Elvis Presley (who was strongly criticized for appropriating and profiting off Black American music)

Gumboots the name of the recording that inspired Paul Simon to record with South African musicians, but also a category of migrant worker boot performance […]

isicathamiya means to walk on tip toe, or stealthily like a cat; is the quieter version of "mbube" styled close-harmony singing from South Africa, made famous by Joseph Shabalala and Ladysmith Black Mambazo

Inspiration the student ensemble at the University of Pennsylvania that recorded a version of "Homeless" from the *Graceland* album

jive lively dancing between a man and a woman, with the man "swinging" the woman, accompanied both by jazz and then rock music; very popular in Black communities in the 1940s and 1950s in South Africa; often called "Zulu jive" or "sax jive" for example.

Joseph Shabalala leader of Ladysmith Black Mambazo

Khayelitsha United Mambazo copycat group of *isicathamiya* singers who perform for tourists at the Victoria and Albert Waterfront in Cape Town, South Africa

Ladysmith Black Mambazo the *isicathamiya* group who performed on *Graceland*, literally means the "black axe from Ladysmith" (KwaZulu Natal), so-named because they won all the choir competitions

Leeukop Prisoners' Choir a South African choir formed in the Leeukop prison, and who performed the song "Homeless" in reference to those who would be homeless when released from prison

Little Steven rock musician who created the *Sun City: Artists Against Apartheid* film and song collaboration

Paul Simon American folk rock singer-songwriter who collaborated with South Africans on the *Graceland* album

popular musician a musician who is recorded, marketed, and distributed by the global entertainment industry and sells thousands of records

Ray Phiri South African guitarist and leader of Stimela, a popular South African band

Rhythm of Resistance the film produced by British filmmaker Jeremy Marre for the BBC that inspired Paul Simon's project

Roy Halee Paul Simon's recording engineer, who traveled with Simon to South Africa in 1984

Sarafina! The Music of Liberation a Broadway production of South African protest musical theater written and directed by Mbongeni Ngema in the late 1980s

SATB format four-part harmonizing

showcased *Graceland* put on display, through the compositional and collaborative processes, the sounds of South African music for popular music consumers. This becomes an important mechanism of musical display for those who might not have access or typically choose to listen to "world" music

Soweto String Quartet an important post-apartheid string quartet that has "classicized" much South African music by arranging and performing it in a quartet environment

Sun City the casino opened by South African developer Sol Kerzner that continued to host foreign entertainers when the United Nations Organization had called for a boycott of such activity while the apartheid government stayed in power

Sun City: Artists United Against Apartheid the documentary video made for MTV urging American and British artists to boycott South Africa

United Nations Organization a transnational organization headquartered in New York City that works to protect people or countries under siege, and to act on behalf of those whose human rights are violated by states or parastatal organizations

NOTES

1. Each of these events, and more, are all well-documented on the worldwide web: Google keywords, e.g., "Live Aid," "Farm Aid," or "Live Eight" for example.
2. You can find video clips of the *Sun City: Artists Against Apartheid* song on YouTube, keyword: Sun City.
3. South African Rob Nixon has written concisely about the sports and cultural boycott (1994: 131–174) against South Africa.
4. Check YouTube for video footage of the Sun City song. "Ain't Gonna Play Sun City" is the name of the collaboratively produced song calling for a boycott.
5. These "homelands" were not recognized as "independent" of the South African government by any organization or country, including the United Nations Organization. It was only the apartheid government and the "puppet" black political leaders in the homelands who thought of them as such.
6. These and similar songs can all be found on iTunes.
7. The *Graceland* album is currently available for purchase on tune lists like iTunes and in CD format.
8. See for example Garafalo 1992, Lipsitz 1994, Nixon 1994, Erlmann 1999, Meintjes 1990, and Hamm 1995. At the time the international press, including *Newsweek*, *Time*, the *Village Voice*, the *New York Times*, and other media were also deeply engaged with the controversy.
9. See Erlmann 1996 for extensive discussion of this history and its performance.
10. See Erlmann 1991 and 1996 for further explanation.
11. See Erlmann's 1988 reissue of *mbube* recordings, *Mbube Roots: Zulu Choral Music from South Africa, 1930s–1960s*. Cambridge, MA: Rounder Records, ROUNDER CD 5025.

REFERENCES

Erlmann, Veit. *Music, Modernity, and the Global Imagination*. New York: Oxford University Press, 1999.

Erlmann, Veit. *Nightsong: Performance, Power, and Practice in Black South African Performance*. Chicago: Chicago University Press, 1996.

Erlmann, Veit. *African Stars: Studies in Black South African Performance*. Chicago: Chicago University Press, 1991.

Garafalo, Reebee. *Rockin' the Boat: Mass Music and Mass Movements*. Boston: South End Press, 1992.

Hamm, Charles. *Putting Popular Music in Its Place*. Cambridge: Cambridge University Press, 1995.

Lipsitz, George. *Dangerous Crossroads: Popular Music, Postmodernism, and the Poetics of Place*. New York: Verso, 1994.

Meintjes, Louise. "Paul Simon's *Graceland*, South Africa and the Mediation of Musical Meaning." *Ethnomusicology* 34 (1990): 37–73.

Nixon, Rob. *Homelands, Harlem, and Hollywood: South African Culture and the World Beyond*. New York: Rout-ledge, 1994.

Questions for thought

- How has African-based music from the Americas—samba, reggae, salsa—impacted African music such as highlife? In what ways did highlife fuse African and Western musical and cultural ideas?
- How did E.T. Mensah and King Bruce shape the sound of highlife?
- How were different musical ideas and traditions used in the compositional process for the album *Graceland*?
- How do isicathamiya and Highlife represent a blend of African and non-African music?
- How was *Graceland* a reaction to Apartheid and the cultural boycotts of South Africa in the 1970s and 1980s?
- Although *Graceland* is usually remembered as a collaboration between Paul Simon and Ladysmith Black Mambazo, what other musicians and musical traditions went into the making of this album?

Activity

Listen to the album *Graceland*, which can be accessed through YouTube or many streaming services. Pay particular attention to the sound of each song and try to distinguish the American and African elements and performers for each selection. Then search "Highlife Music Ghana" on YouTube and listen to several selections. Again, pay attention to how African and Western musical ideas are combined. Can you discern any common elements between highlife and the music of *Graceland*? Both sets of music represent African/Western fusion, but how do they differ? How are they similar?

Figure Credits

Fig. 7-1: Source: https://commons.wikimedia.org/wiki/File:AfricaCIA-HiRes.jpg.

Fig. 7-2: Copyright © Faycal.09 (CC by 3.0) at https://commons.wikimedia.org/wiki/File:Ghana_and_Nigeria_location_map.jpg.

Fig. 7-3: Copyright © Schorle (CC by 3.0) at https://commons.wikimedia.org/wiki/File:Ebo_Taylor_13.JPG.

Fig. 7-13: Source: https://commons.wikimedia.org/wiki/File:Ladysmith_Black_Mambazo_2008.JPG.

Fig. 7-14: Source: https://commons.wikimedia.org/wiki/File:Graceland_cover_-_Paul_Simon.jpg.

CHAPTER EIGHT

Bollywood and Bhangra:
Indian Music in the Diaspora

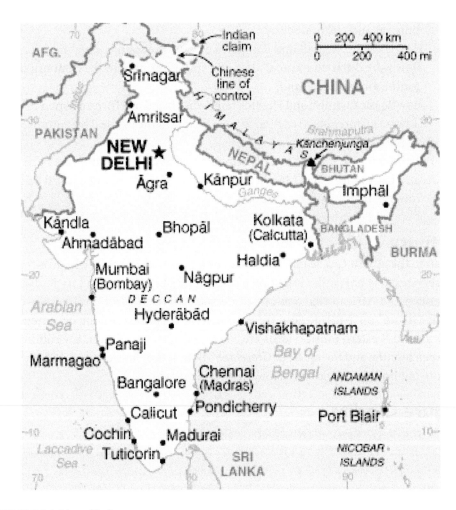

FIGURE 8.1 *Map of India*

Introduction

Throughout its history, India has been a land of traditions and changes. It has been a crossroads of cultures, a mixing of East and West, absorbing invasions and ideas since Alexander the Great until it dislodged its role as the jewel in the crown of the British Empire. There have been many migrations—Aryan, Islamic, British, and many more—that brought ideas and traditions, making the country a blend of these ideas, contributing to what is India today. The country is a mix of old and new; nowhere is that clearer than in music, where Indian classical and popular music merged with European and later American music to form the musical hybrid that is Indian music today.

India is a country of more than 350 languages and dialects, largely divided from north to south. It embraces many religious traditions, including Hinduism (the largest), Islam, and Sikhism, and is the birthplace of Buddhism. Musically, it is equally diverse. Traditional music is divided along the same geographic lines as languages, north and south, along the Indus Valley of the north and the Carnatic Plains of the south. The country is a juxtaposition of seemingly contradictory images and ideas, with old and new occupying the same space: the Taj Mahal and other traditional architecture are found near modern skyscrapers; traditional poetry and art sit next to cinemas and dance clubs; Indian instruments such as *sitars* and *tablas* as well as guitars and pianos are part of the soundscape that is India.

India's governmental system, bureaucracy, transportation, and educational systems are legacies of the British, who ruled India from the 17th century until 1947, when the country was divided into Hindu-dominated India and predominately Islamic Pakistan (originally East and West Pakistan, a country divided by thousands of kilometers; East Pakistan later became the independent Bangladesh). The British also left a legacy in music, with European musical instruments coming into common use, both for Western music, but also for Indian; the violin is one of the most important instruments in Indian classical music. Later, in the 20th century, another musical tradition became important that changed the face of Indian popular music: American musical genres, such as jazz, the blues, rock and roll, and later hip-hop, which can be heard in the most important Indian popular music genres at home and in the diaspora: bhangra and film music.

FIGURE 8.2 *The Taj Mahal*

Bollywood and Bhangra

Bollywood

More films are produced in India every year than anywhere else in the world. The part of the film industry based in Mumbai is known collectively as *Hindi* cinema, or popularly as Bollywood, although it is part of the larger Indywood, which also encompasses other film centers in places such as Calcutta and Chennai, producing films in other Indian languages such as Tamil. The Bollywood name was coined in the 1970s and comes from a mix of Bombay, the former name of Mumbai, and Hollywood (Rajghatta, Chidanand 2008). Most of the films are musicals, and song-and-dance numbers are often woven into the script; a film's success often depends on the quality of the production numbers (Kalita 2005). The music in these movies is a blend of East and West, which is entirely consistent with everything Indian. This film tradition is highly influenced by many Indian musical traditions, popular and classical, and owes a great deal to Hollywood as well.

Much of the music is in many ways reminiscent of early rock and roll: similar instrumentation (with the addition of Indian percussion); simple harmonies based on rock progressions; similar forms including the ubiquitous 12-bar blues form; and similar vocal styles, albeit with a decidedly Eastern twist. It also uses many of the musical and visual ideas of MTV in the 1980s, with the visual cuts and camera angles as well as the musical/choreographical character of American music videos. Videos from Bollywood movies are extremely popular on Indian television, as well as in Indian communities in the U.S., Britain, and elsewhere. They tend to be visually dynamic, with lots of colorful lighting and costumes, with tightly choreographed dancing presented with lots of cinemagraphic cuts and juxtapositions.

The music from the Indian film industry is highly influential; it is the dominant popular music in India. Music from films is often released before the film, with the goal of creating interest in the music and increasing the audience; the music is often more popular than the movie. The trend recently is to release videos from the film early as well. The music, known locally as *filmi,* is usually recorded by studio musicians and lip-synched by on-screen actors. Songs are very important to a movie's success, and films are rarely successful if they do not feature at least one musical hit. With the globalization of Bollywood and its popularity in the Indian diaspora in Europe, Africa, and the United States, the lyrics are often a blend of Hindi and English. Globalization also has led to great influences from global trends such as salsa and hip-hop (Rao, 2010).

FIGURE 8.3 *Bollywood show in Bristol, England*

Reading #1

The first reading for this chapter, "India's Music: Popular Film Songs in the Classroom," discusses the history of Indian classical music, its characteristics, and its influence on film music. The author goes on to cover the place of film in Indian culture, including in her discussion the instruments used in this music, from both traditional Indian and western sources, as well as the context and meaning in Indian film music. The article also provides a guide to resources on Indian music and suggests ways in which Indian film songs can be taught in American classrooms.

INDIA'S MUSIC: POPULAR FILM SONGS IN THE CLASSROOM

Natalie Sarrazin

Is it possible that the most popular music in the world has been left out of most American music classes? While many in the United States have never heard of it, the Indian film industry is the largest film industry in the world, with an output roughly three times that of Hollywood.[1] It is estimated that 3 billion tickets are sold annually, including 25 million sold to Indians living in Britain, the U.S., and elsewhere.[2] This popular world music could easily be an exciting part of a multicultural music education curriculum. Including this music not only exposes students to an entirely new musical genre and cultural industry, but can also change their perception of our own film industry, popular music, and values as students explore how another culture makes and enjoys music.

Most music educators are eager to learn about and incorporate the music of other cultures in their classroom. Despite this enthusiasm, teachers' low comfort level with some non-Western music, their unfamiliarity with the music, and the difficulty of accessing authentic examples can make it hard to incorporate music from different cultures.[3] While there may be an abundance of materials for some regions, many others, such as India, are underrepresented in the curriculum.[4]

Even as Indian music is left out of many American music classrooms, increasing numbers of South Asian Indians have come into our society. They represent the fourth-largest immigrant group in the U.S., with more than 1 million immigrants counted in the 2000 Census.[5] Whether you teach in an urban or a rural area, chances are that you've had children of Indian descent in your classroom.

Besides a dearth of teaching materials, Indian music presents a variety of challenges for the music educator. India is a complex, ancient culture with a long history and a classical music tradition involving music that many Westerners find difficult to listen to, let alone teach, because of its unfamiliar language, instruments, timbres, forms, and styles. However, Indian film music, which blends Indian classical and Western pop styles, can be a more accessible introduction to the music of South Asia.

BACKGROUND: INDIAN CLASSICAL MUSIC

Before looking at any Indian music, it's important to become familiar with the musical and cultural basics. Indian classical music is seen as the root of all Indian musics and remains an important part of all other Indian musical genres. The sidebar titled Basic Characteristics of Classical Indian Music lists some of the principal elements of the classical tradition that guide all Indian music traditions, be they popular or classical.

Many teachers' familiarity with Indian classical music may be limited to the sound of a sitar and the music of Ravi Shankar that influenced the Beatles and other popular musicians of the 1960s. However, Indian music is becoming a larger part of the American musical tapestry, and it's becoming more accessible. Indian instruments such as the tabla no longer sound exotic to Western ears, as they are prominently featured in TV commercials and films. Movie hits like *Monsoon Wedding* (2002), the Oscar-nominated *Lagaan: Once Upon a Time in India* (2001), and the Jane Austen adaptation *Bride and Prejudice* (2004) have crossed over into Western markets. Indian folk music is influencing Western popular music. For example, bhangra, a style of music from the Punjabi region, is a staple of many Western dance clubs, where DJs mix Indian music with disco and hip-hop.

INDIAN FILM MUSIC AND CULTURE

Although some in the industry consider the term to be derogatory, the Indian film industry is popularly known as "Bollywood," which is short for "Bombay Hollywood." The industry produces eight to nine hundred films per year, while Hollywood's output is about only about five hundred films per year.[6] Bombay (now called Mumbai) is generally considered the center of the industry, but Calcutta (Kolkatta) and other major cities in South India also produce films.

The Indian music industry is the second largest in the world after that of the U.S., with film music making up 70 percent of all music sales.[7] Film music dominates the music industry largely because almost every Indian film contains six to nine song-and-dance numbers. This fact alone speaks volumes about the demand for music in India and its importance as a form of expression.

FIGURE 8.5 *Indian films such as the 1976 hit* Kahbi, Kahbie *(pictured above) offer abundant examples of songs that blend Western and Indian musical styles.*

You might want to introduce Indian film music by asking students what it would be like if every Hollywood film of every genre (westerns, action films, etc.) contained song-and-dance sequences. Music's influence on a film's success is significant. Sometimes, the soundtrack sales alone can make a film a moneymaker, regardless of the plot, acting, or directing

Film music is the musical lingua franca that most nonresident Indians (NRIs) in the U.S., Britain, and many other countries share. The reasons behind film music's popularity outside India, particularly among students, are its entertaining quality and its ability to help nonresidents stay connected with their Indian culture and identity. When students of Indian descent in universities meet, they can often build relationships through their common interest in Indian films, actors, and especially film songs, regardless of their parental languages (Punjabi, Gujarati, Bhojpuri, etc.) or region of origin.

Web sites, MP3s, and distribution of films in Indian markets and online make it relatively easy for those outside India to keep up with new film releases and songs. Many theaters in the U.S. now show Indian films, and actors and playback singers often perform to full stadiums in large U.S. and European cities.

BASIC CHARACTERISTICS OF CLASSICAL INDIAN MUSIC

- Emphasis on melody and rhythm
- Use of drone
- Little or no harmony or harmonic progression (although film songs often employ harmony)
- Strong solo tradition (single vocalist or instrumentalist)

Natalie Sarrazin, "India's Music: Popular Film Songs in the Classroom," Music Educators Journal, vol. 93, no. 1, pp. 26-32. Copyright © 2006 by SAGE Publications. Reprinted with permission.

- No head voice or falsetto in singing (chest voice used in all ranges)
- Use of ornamentation
- Improvisation that extends brief compositions based on the rules of the raga
- Expression of one or more of the nine moods (rasas, or "essences") considered vital to music, art, and drama and associated with extra musical concepts such as season, time of day, and region
- Aural transmission and memorization of music, little use of notation
- An introductory section (alap) without percussion instruments (which join in later)

Natalie Sarrazin is an assistant professor of music at SUNY College at Brockport in New York. She can be reached at nataliesartazin@hotmail.com.

PLAYBACK SINGING

Actors and actresses in Indian films typically don't sing their characters' songs. The people who sing for them are known as playback singers. Playback singers record the songs offscreen in studios, while the actors and actresses lip-synch to them onscreen.

Many Westerners frown on the practice of having an actor mime a song. This isn't an issue for Indians, who are not only fully aware of playback singers, but consider them as famous as the actors themselves. Indians believe that playback singers are an asset to a film because they divide up the labor so that people who can act, act, and people who can sing, sing. The Indian film industry doesn't demand that actors learn to sing, thus keeping the song quality and musicality high.

One of the most famous female playback singers is Lata Mangeshkar, who is listed in the 1991 *Guinness Book of World Records* as the most recorded artist in the world, with thirty thousand solo, duet, and chorus backed songs recorded in twenty Indian languages between 1948 and 1987.[8] Other well-known playback singers include female singers Asha Bhosle and Alka Yagnik and male singers Kishore Kumar and Udit Narayan.

SOUND AND MEANING OF INDIAN FILM MUSIC

Film music, as part of the larger Indian musical tradition, sometimes uses traditional instruments such as the tabla and sitar. But film musicians have also assimilated sounds, styles, instruments, rhythms, and melodies from all over the world. These include the Latin rhythms especially prominent in the 1950s films of director Raj Kapoor and the more recent additions of techno, pop, and hip-hop. Some of this musical borrowing can be controversial, particularly when entire melodies are used outright. It's interesting to listen to an Indian take on such familiar Western melodies as "My Favorite Things" and "I Am Sixteen" from *The Sound of Music* or "Cotton-Eyed Joe," all of which have been used in Indian films.[9]

While musical borrowing may make some film songs sound familiar to Westerners, much about them is different. The most obvious difference is the language. Indian film songs are typically sung in Hindi or Urdu, though Tamil, Telegu, and other local Indian languages are commonly heard in regional films. The sound of the music will also seem strange to many Western listeners. The fundamental difference that strikes most Americans is the vocal timbre. The vocals, especially of female playback singers such as Lata Mangeshkar, have a particular sound that dominates almost every recording. Indian film vocals use a lot of ornamentation, have a high and thin timbre, and don't involve the head voice. (Most Indian singing extends the chest voice into the upper registers.) Functional Western harmony plays almost no role in traditional Indian music, but it's increasingly present in film songs.

Song and Sentiment. The number of songs produced over the almost ninety years of Indian popular cinema hovers in the tens of thousands. However, like classic American films such as *Singing in the Rain* and the accompanying standards featured in them, certain films and songs are perennially popular. One of the industry's most enduring songs is "Mera Joota Hai Japani" ("My Shoes Are from Japan") from Raj Kapoor's 1955 classic *Shree 420 (Mr. 420)*.[10] The film's title refers to the number assigned to cheats and con artists in the Indian penal code. The song, sung by playback singer Mukesh, is one in which country bumpkin Raju (played by Raj Kapoor) travels by foot along a country road to the big city of Bombay. Kapoor intentionally imitates Charlie Chaplin in his demeanor and dress—revealing his innocence before he becomes corrupted by Bombay's high life. The song's refrain (see song example 1) expresses the sentiment that despite his outward appearance (wearing clothes made in different countries), Raju's heart still belongs to India.

The Hindi text for this refrain isn't difficult for English speakers to understand because it includes cognates for Japan, pants, England, and Russia. The word *mera* means "my," and *hai* is a form of "to be"; in this case, it means "are." As with most film songs, the melody is catchy and easy to learn. This refrain is in a minor- sounding mode while the verses have a more major sound. This song has become an Indian standard, capturing the sentiment of many Indians at home and abroad that India is in their heart. It's a simple but appropriate introduction to India's film music and cultural outlook. See the list of Resources for ideas of where you can find recordings of the song so you can introduce it to your students.

SONG EXAMPLE I. REFRAIN OF "MERA JOOTA HAI JAPANI"

Mera joota hai Japani	My shoes are from Japan
Ye pantaloon hai Inglishtani	My pants are made in England
Sir pe lai topi Russi	On my head is a red hat from Russia
Phir bhi dii hai Hindustani!	But still my heart is from Hindustan (India)!

Source: From the 1955 film *Shree 420*, directed by Raj Kapoor (Mumbai: R. K. Films, 1955). Songs by Jaikishan Pankaland and Shankarsink Raghuwanshi.

The majority of Indian popular films are romantic, with a hero and heroine as lead characters. These leads sing the bulk of the songs. The films tend to be melodramatic, heavy on emotion, and full of conflict involving a villain. One interesting note is that the film's villains *never* sing. Music has a humanizing effect, and the humanizing of villains would contradict the moral order of the universe depicted in Indian popular cinema.

Family ties are emphasized and often play a significant role in the leading couple's life. Arranged marriage is a cultural institution in India, but films often portray love marriages or some type of middle ground where the couple meets, falls in love, and then tries to persuade their parents to agree to the union.

Instruments. Since the beginning of recorded film soundtracks, many Indian film songs have had Western orchestrations. Pianos, large string orchestras, and Latin American instruments are quite common. The popular song "Kahbi, Kabhie," discussed later in more detail, uses maracas, a marimba, flute, violins, and chimes. The only indigenous Indian instruments in the song are the tabla and the *shehnai*. This use of Western music is typical of songs from the '60s, '70s, and '80s, although other songs from the period do include more traditional Indian instruments.

Song Structure. Although Indian film songs have their roots in folk and classical music, they have a pop-song style and format that will seem familiar to Westerners. The basic song form for Indian films differs only slightly from its Western pop counterpart. Pop songs in the West typically have verses and a refrain (see the Song Forms sidebar). Often, a bridge with different rhythms and lyrics inserted after one refrain temporarily changes the mood.

In Indian film songs, the refrain is first, followed by the verse and instrumental interlude. The typical film song form alternates between refrain, verse, and interlude, as seen in the sidebar. Keep in mind, however, that the terms verse and refrain are Western. The Indian musical predecessors of verse and refrain are *sthai* and *antara*, which are found in the Indian classical music tradition and have a slightly different function than a Western verse and refrain.

A refrain in Indian film music is similar to a refrain in Western pop music. The refrain contains the main idea of the song and often the title. Interludes, an important structural aspect of the songs, are rooted in semiclassical songs, such as the Urdu Persian *ghazal* form. Interludes in film songs often feature solos of different instruments (e.g., flute, shehnai), but they can also keep the same instruments throughout the song.

Indian film songs tend to run five minutes or longer, while the typical Western pop song is three minutes. If you introduce Indian film music to your students, be sure to plan for class length and student attention span.

TEACHING WITH A TYPICAL INDIAN FILM SONG

The song "Kabhi, Kabhie" (see song example 2 for translated lyrics) is a typical romantic song. It's from the 1976 hit film *Kabhi, Kabhie* directed by Yash Chopra, known for his romantic films. The film stars Amitabh Bachchan, a giant in the industry and possibly the world's best known actor. Although the film's date might make it appear old, this is a familiar and beloved classic, and its form and sound are typical of the thousands of songs that have appeared in the past six decades of Indian film music. You can find the song on soundtracks of the film, available at the online stores listed in the Resources sidebar, or on some Indian film music compilations, such as *Rough Guide to Bollywood*.

Context. This is a love song about a poet and his beloved who must marry others. The lyrics of this very romantic song express the couple's belief that they were destined to fall in love, though a relationship never materializes. Since arranged marriage is the norm, the idea of choosing your own spouse is merely broached in this song. The couple falls in love, but they don't marry each other and instead have arranged marriages. Both decide, however, to allow their children to have love marriages.

SONG FORMS

TYPICAL HINDI FILM SONG

Intro., Refrain, Interlude,
Verse I, Refrain, Interlude,
Verse 2, Refrain, Interlude,
Verse 3, Refrain, Interlude, etc.

WESTERN POP SONG

Intro.
Verse I, Refrain
Verse 2, Refrain, Bridge
Verse 3, Refrain

"KAHBI, KAHBIE"

Intro., Refrain
Verse I, Interlude, Refrain
Verse 2, Interlude, Bridge
Verse 3, Interlude, Refrain
Verse 4, Refrain

RESOURCES

General Information on India

- www.culturopedia.com. Excellent Web site for all things Indian, including music, dance, architecture, Indian symbols and anthems, languages, theater, people, and sports.
- www.kamat.com/kalranga/timeline/timeline.htm. Historical timeline of India.

Classical Indian Music

- Arnold, Alison, ed. South Asia: *The Indian Subcontinent* Vol. 5, *The Garland Encyclopedia of World Music and Dance*. New York: Garland Publishing, 1997.
- http://chandrakantha.com/articles/indian_music/. An excellent overview of Indian classical music. Includes examples of and details on musical genres, instruments, CDs, and books.

Indian Film and Film Music

- Ganti,Tejaswini. *Bollywood:A Guidebook to Popular Hindi Cinema*. New York: Routledge, 2004. A general introduction to the Hindi film industry. Covers history, major films, and personalities, and the inner workings of how a film is made.
- Rajadhyaksha, Ashish, and Paul Willemen. *Encyclopaedia of Indian Cinema*. London: British Film Institute, 1999. Exhaustive compendium of Hindi film material. Includes chronological summaries of some of the best films and lists the greatest names in the industry.
- *There'll Always Be Stars in the Sky: The Indian Film Music Phenomenon*. DVD. Directed by Jeremy Marre. Newton, NJ: Shanachie, 2003. A dated but excellent documentary introducing the film music industry.

- www.bollywhat.com. A site with basic information and translated film lyrics of dozens of recent film songs. Includes all of the lyrics for songs from *Kahbi, Kabhie; Dil Se; and Dil Chahta Hai.* (Be sure to learn about copyright regulations before sharing complete song lyrics with students. See www.menc.org/copyright for more information.)
- www.uiowa.edu/~incinema/.Web site from the University of Iowa. Contains information on *Shree 420.*
- www.upperstall.com.Web site dedicated to analysis of classic Indian films.

Sources of CDs and DVDs

- www.indiaweekly.com. This site often runs sales and specials. Many items go in and out of stock quickly, so check back often.
- www.nehaflix.com. This site often runs sales and specials. Many items go in and out of stock quickly, so check back often.
- www.amazon.com. The prices here tend to be a bit higher than the other sites mentioned. Carries most, but not all, of the CDs and DVDs mentioned in this article.

Film Music CD Soundtracks

- *Bride and Prejudice.* Casablanca, 2005.
- *Dil Chahta Hai.* T-Series, 2001.
- *Dil Se.* Venus VCDSP-722, 1998.
- *Kabhi, Kahbie.* RPG. (May be listed as *Silsila/Kabhi, Kabhie* or with the alternate spellings *Kabhi, Kabhi* or *Kabhie, Kabhie.*)
- *Koi Mil Goya.* Tips, 2003.
- *Lagaan*: Once Upon a Time in India. Sony Music, 2001.
- *Monsoon Wedding.* Milan Records, 2002.
- *Shree 420.* RPG. (May be listed as *Awara/Shree 420* or with the alternate spelling *Awaara/ Shree 420.*)

Film Music CD Compilations

- *Beginner's Guide to Bollywood*, Nascente, 2003.
- *I Love Bollywood*, Manteca, 2001.
- *Rough Guide to Bollywood*, World Music Network 1074, 2002. (Includes the song "Kabhi, Kabhie.")

Bhangra CDs

- *Bhangra: Original Punjabi Pop.* Arc Music, 2003.
- *Bhangra Beatz.* Naxos, 2000. (Contains examples of dance bhangra, which mixes in hip-hop and other dance and club styles)

SONG EXAMPLE 2. "KABHI, KABHIE"

Refrain	(Male, then female) Sometimes a thought comes to my heart
Verse I	(Female) That you were made just for me
	Before now, you lived somewhere in the stars You were called to earth just for me
Interlude I	Strings, chimes
Refrain	(Female) Sometimes a thought comes to my heart
Verse 2	(Female) That this body and these eyes belong to me That the dark shadow of your hair is for me alone That these lips and these arms belong to me
Interlude 2	Chimes, strings, flute
Bridge	(Female) Sometimes a thought comes to my heart
	As the *shehnai* plays along the way
	(Male, then female) It is my wedding night and I'm lifting your veil (Female) In my arms you blush and become shy
Interlude 3	Strings, chimes
Refrain	(Female) Sometimes a thought comes to my heart
Verse 3	(Female) That you will love me like this forever You will always look upon me lovingly (Male) I know you're a stranger, but even so,
Refrain	(Male, then female) Sometimes a thought comes to my heart

Note: This title also often appears as "Kabhie, Kabhie."
Source: Kabhi, Kabhie (Sometimes). Directed by Yash Chopra, music by Khayyam, lyrics by Sahir Ludhianvi. Mumbai, India:Yash-Raj films, 1976. Playback singers, Lata Mangeshkar and Mukesh. Reproduced courtesy of Saregama India, Ltd. Lyrics by Sahir Ludhanvi. Translation by Anand Dwivedi and Natalie Sarrazin.

Duet Structure. "Kahbi, Kahbie" is a typical Indian duet, which differs from Western duets in that the singers almost never perform at the same time; instead, they alternate singing. This reflects a controversy from very early in Indian cinema about the negative implications of having women involved in the film industry in the first place. It also reflects the gender segregation often found in the culture.

Musical Storytelling. The storytelling aspect of film songs is very important and tells us a great deal about the culture. This love song is about two people who have only just met but are daydreaming of being together. The instruments tell us what the words don't explicitly say For example, in the bridge section, the singers are imagining a wedding. The instrument playing at that point is a *shehnai*, an instrument that looks and sounds like an oboe and is traditionally used for weddings. The sound of the shehnai makes listeners think of weddings, and because the shehnai appears in the middle of a line sung first by the female singer and then by the male, the sound joins them together.

Teaching Ideas. You can use "Kahbi, Kahbie" in the classroom in several ways. First, have students listen to the song and tap or cover their hearts when they hear the word for heart (*dil*) in the song's refrain. This action will emphasize the importance of the word "heart" in the song and the importance of emotion in almost all Indian film songs. You might also teach students to sing through the refrain of the song ("kahbi, kabhie, mere dil men khyal ata hai," pronounced "cub-hee, cub-hee, meh-reh, dill meh key-ahl ah-tah heh").

Here are a few questions you can use to stimulate discussion of "Kahbi, Kahbie" and how Indian film music compares to Western popular music:

- Who is singing (male or female)? Who sings more often? When during the song do they sing? Do they ever sing together? (Males and females were segregated in traditional Indian society, so they tend to not sing together.) What are some gender divisions in Western music? (singing versus instrument playing, types of instruments)
- Describe the sound of the male and female vocal timbres. (Female vocals in Indian films until the 1990s required a high, thin, light, and girl-like sound that lacks vibrato. The male sound is more familiar to us.) Describe the timbre of Western popular singers, both male and female. What sounds do we prefer in our culture?
- Based on who's singing, what type of a song do you think it is? (romantic)
- What instruments do you hear? (maracas, tabla, flute, marimba, violins, shehnai) Did you hear any familiar or unfamiliar instruments?
- Is this music familiar? How is it the same or different from popular music you know?
- Discuss the importance of the heart in love songs in Western and Indian cultures.

ENDLESS POSSIBILITIES

I've suggested just a few starting points for introducing Indian popular film music in your classroom. Other possibilities include recent soundtracks that have incorporated even more Western instrumentation, sampling techniques, a heavy rock beat, and Western timbre. I recommend anything by film music composer A. R. Rahman, (sometimes spelled Rehmen), particularly the song "Chaiyya, Chaiyya" from Mani Ratnam's 1997 film *Dil Se* or the 2001 soundtrack to *Lagaan*. Other recent films with excellent soundtracks include *Dil Chahta Hai* (2001) and *Koi Mil Gaya* (2003), which is loosely based on E.T. and is one of India's first forays into science fiction film.

Teaching Indian music doesn't have to start with classical traditions. Before getting discouraged about becoming familiar with an entire classical tradition or the daunting array of folk music styles in local languages, consider Indian popular film music as an alternative that provides students with an accessible and fun portal into India and its rich musical and cultural offerings. It also presents a distinctive art form that influences the musical and daily life of a subcontinent and millions of people in dozens of countries beyond its borders.

Notes

1. Alison Arnold, "Film Music: Northern Area" in *South Asia: The Indian Subcontinent, vol. 5, The Garland Encyclopedia of World Music and Dance,* ed. Alison Arnold (New York: Garland Publishing, 1997), 537.
2. Eric Pfanner, "India's New Cinema Has a Global Script," *International Herald Tribune,* May 22, 2006, www.iht.com/articles/ 2006/05/21/yourmoney/movies22.php.
3. Bennett Reimer, ed., *World Musics and Music Education: Facing the Issues* (Reston, VA: MENC, 2002).
4. Joyce Jordan, "Multicultural Music Education in a Pluralistic Society," in *Handbook of Research on Music Teaching and Learning,* ed. Richard Colwell (New York: Schirmer Books, 1992), 738.
5. U.S. Census Bureau, *The Foreign-Born Population: 2000* (Washington, DC: U.S. Census Bureau, 2003), 5. Available at www. census.go v/prod/2003 pubs/c2kbr-34.pdf.
6. "Indian Cinema Statistics 1995-2000," *Screen International,* July 12, 2001; Motion Picture Association of America, *2005 Theatrical Market Statistics* (Encino, CA: MPAA, 2006), 10.
7. India Infoline, "Indian Corporates: Analyst Meet," www.indiainfoline.com/ meet/me216.html.
8. Upperstall, "Lata Mangeshkar," www. upperstall. com/people/lata.html.
9. For a list of copied songs, see "Copied Hindi Songs," www.angelfire.com/music4/sangeet/ copiedsongs.html.
10. See the Resources list for Web sites with more information on this film as well as purchasing information. Please note, however, that the spelling of transliterations vary widely in Hindi, making Internet searches difficult. The double "ee" in *shree,* for example, is also commonly written as a long "i." Likewise, the double "oo" in other titles may also be a "u."

Bhangra

Another Indian music that blends Indian and Western music is bhangra, originally a dance music tradition from the North Indian state of Punjab usually associated with weddings and festivals. Traditional bhangra was danced in India and Pakistan, whereas modern bhangra developed mostly in the Punjabi diaspora, most notably in England. This modern bhangra has its roots in the 1970s, when Punjabi groups started experimenting with the fusion of Western and Punjabi music, and immigrants started using Western instruments to play their traditional music. Indian music had been influential in England since the Beatles, who studied Indian philosophy as well as music, incorporating this influence in albums such as *Sgt. Pepper's Lonely Hearts Club Band*, which used sitars and other Indian instruments, and songs such as "Norwegian Wood," which is based on a traditional Indian melody.

Although bhangra was being heard and indeed was popular in England since the 1980s, it was only recently that this music started appearing on the English music charts, despite the fact that this music often outsold British artists. This was a reflection of the means of distribution of bhangra music: it was rarely sold in British music stores, and store sales were what was used to determine the places on the charts. It was rather sold privately, in clubs and other venues, at times out of trunks of cars and on the street, usually in the form of cassettes. All of this changed with the Internet, which leveled the playing field for bhangra artists (please see the chapter on Radiohead).

FIGURE 8.4 *Traditional Punjabi Bhangra dance*

Reading #2

In the other reading for this chapter, "Bhangra Boomerangs," the author places bhangra in the mix of globalization of music, beginning the discussion with American cultural imperialism, which is defined as the worldwide diffusion of American products and ideas, focusing on American music as a force for homogenizing global culture. Bhangra is a music that blended Punjabi festival music with Western rhythms and ideas, forming a hybrid that exploded onto the world music scene in the 1990s. The article goes on to discuss bhangra as a force that proves that local cultures not only encounter this global imperialism but can appropriate it for reinventing themselves.

BHANGRA BOOMERANGS

Anjali Gera Roy

RE-IMAGINING APNA PUNJAB

Cultural imperialism, defined as the worldwide diffusion of American products, life-styles, and ideas, is predicated on an elision between americanization, McDonaldization, and globalization. There is no denying the fact that America, as the sole superpower in the present globalized context, occupies a dominant position and that global consumerist flows largely emanate from the North American continent.[1] American cultural products such as the Hollywood film, TV programmes, sports, music, fashion, and food undoubtedly constitute America's largest exports to the world. American popular music, in particular, is considered a prime instrument in the homogenization of global culture by the American 'superculture'. But the cultural-imperialism thesis is predicated on contested models such as the nation-state, the broadcast-theory of media, one-way information

---

1   Alex Seago, "'Where Hamburgers Sizzle on an Open Grill Night and Day': Global Pop Music and Americanization in the Year 2000," *American Studies* 41.2–3 (Summer–Fall 2000): 121.

flows, the centre and the periphery. As a consequence, opposition to 'cultural imperialism' also continues to be defined in terms not in tune with ground realities. Recent critiques of the theory have convincingly argued against reducing contemporary global hegemonies to a national cultural hegemony. Even if one were to read globalization simplistically as americanization, the nightmare of indigenous cultures driven out by an American cultural blitzkrieg denies receiving cultures agency and underestimates their capacity for appropriating alien cultural inputs to their own needs.

Through tracing the reverse musical flows of bhangra, a North Indian performance tradition, this essay juxtaposes 'the boomerang effect' against the American cultural-imperialism thesis in order to unpack the workings of new global hegemonic structures and resistances. 'The boomerang effect' is defined as receiving cultures' selective appropriation of alien cultural elements, which are re-exported to the invading culture in an altered form so as to modify its character. The Punjabi harvest dance bhangra, re-invented in the mid-1980s in Britain through its hybridization with black sounds by British Asian youth, was hailed as Asian dance music by the British media and 'returned back' to India, where it was being modernized as bhangrapop through its integration of Western rhythms.[2] Thus, instead of the Indian skies being deluged by alien 'American images' and sounds after India's 'satellite invasion' as apprehended, the Indian popular music scene was taken over by a regional folk-performance tradition.[3] Disproving those who detected a grand American impositional design of a global monoculture engulfing autochthonous India cultures, the bhangra resurgence appears to have ignited a folk-cultural revival. Bhangra's re-emergence proves that local cultures are equipped not only to counter global monocultural invasion but also to appropriate it for reinventing themselves.

The bhangra explosion of the 1990s forces us to view hegemony in ways other than as national dominance. Bhangra is an example of a 'third culture' marked by multidirectional flows across all bhangra sites that cut through national boundaries. It signals a folk-music revival ushered in by the combined impact of global media, transnational musical corporations, advanced communication technologies, and multicultural politics. Ulf Hannerz's concept of creolization is particularly relevant to the complex interaction of bhangra music and local identities in the context of globalization. The music is hybridized with other musical sounds to make it palatable to a westernized audience and marketed as exoticized music.[4] The transnational corporations involved in producing and marketing bhangra are less interested in promoting any national agenda than in maximizing their profits. Bhangra practitioners, both folk and modern, are complicit with market forces in

2   It is interesting that, even though Bhangra was resignified as British-Asian popular music, its return to India in the wake of globalization led to its being confused with American popular music.

3   Bhangra 'returned back home' to India after becoming a rage in Britain, crossing linguistic, regional, and class barriers to win itself a national constituency. Going by the number of Bhangra competitions held in US colleges and universities in the last few years, Bhangra promises to be as much a part of multicultural USA as it is of India or the UK .

4   Rupa Huq believes that Bhangra does not fall strictly into the world-music category. See "Asian Kool? Bhangra and Beyond," in Disorienting Rhythms: The Politics of the New Asian Dance Music,

the reification of their music and their bodies. Yet, despite the mutual co-option of all bhangra participants in the space of Indian public culture, resistance of a passive nature is still visible on several levels in bhangra production and consumption. As folk tradition, it contests national/classical domination; as indigenous Indian music, it resists the homogenizing impact of global monoculture; as popular culture, it participates in the low/high opposition. Punjabi speakers, at home and in the diaspora, continue to perform this harvest ritual to re-enact their collective memories. In the UK and the USA, it serves as the most visible signifier of ethnocultural Asian identity while global youth converge on it to constitute a different youthful subjectivity. But the reification of ethnic difference in bhangra's marketing, in which music companies, television channels, and bhangra practitioners are equally complicit, is a serious cause for concern.

Why do fears of an impending global culture invariably manifest themselves as a suspicion of americanization? Are there sufficient grounds for the elision between American and the global? Richard Pells celebrates the essential features of American popular culture, which make it truly global in character and scope. Arguing that America has been the largest importer and re-distributor of foreign cultures, Pells depicts the American cultural space, having been constructed by multiple immigrant traditions, as highly eclectic in its borrowings. He attributes American popular culture's global appeal to its multicultural character. "Its incorporation of foreign styles and ideas', he says, has "made it popular for so long in so many places,"[5] Pells also attempts to explain why American popular culture came to be identified with global culture.

> Americans have specialized in selling the dreams, fears and folklore of other people back to them. That is why a global mass culture has come to be identified, however simplistically, with the United States.[6]

Alex Seago, however, puts the blame on US pop music's dominance in the multibillion dollar communications industry, which causes it to be regarded as "a prime culprit in the homogenization of global culture."[7] This negative identification of American popular with global culture results in anxieties about an alien cultural invasion in the wake of globalization in India that translates as americanization. India's occidentalizing tendencies are apparent in its lumping together all European traditions as the West, which denotes America in the contemporary Indian imaginary.

---

ed. Sanjay Sharma, John Hutnyk & Ashwani Sharma (London: Zed, 1999): 61–80. But Bhangra is often classified as world music. Punjabi MC was awarded the Club Global Award for World Music 2004. Although I accept Huq's distinction, I believe that Indian audience receives most Western popular music as American/Western popular, where finer distinctions are lost. Bhangra returns to India along with other ethnic music packaged as world music as well as Western popular.

5 *Richard Pells, "American Culture Goes Global, or Does It?" Chronicle Review (12 April 2002): B1.*

6 *Pells, "American Culture Goes Global, or Does It?" B1.*

7 *Alex Seago, "'Where Hamburgers Sizzle on an Open Grill Night and Day'," 119.*

Reinhold Wagnleitner's contention that "without the global diffusion of popular culture there would be no Beatles" may be modified with respect to bhangra.[8] Without the global diffusion of popular culture there would be no Apache Indian. Bhangra's return to India was really initiated in British popular culture, where second- and third-generation diaspora Punjabis hybridized the Punjabi harvest ritual with reggae and hip-hop beats to invent a new genre. But its inflow to India was channelled after the privatization of the Indian skies by a mega-media machine concentrated in America and dominated by American popular culture.[9] "What Americans have done more brilliantly than their competitors overseas," Pells asserts, "is to repackage the cultural products we receive from abroad and then retransmit them to the rest of the world."[10] Brit-Asians might have re-invented bhangra, but Americans repackaged it and re-transmitted it back to India and the rest of the world.

Since 1995, when it was being hailed as a primarily British-Asian act, bhangra has travelled all the way back to India even as spills over into the USA and Canada. Its ubiquity has robbed it of its specific location in Punjabi folk-regional and black-British cultural politics. It returns to the subcontinent not only divested of its Punjabi or British Asian specificity but repackaged as American popular culture, which is at once the source of its appeal and its denigration. Its re-transmission through American media and circulation networks requires that it be repackaged to suit the tastes of a global audience literate in American popular cultural lingua. Bhangra's distinctive local dialects are overwritten by a familiar global American slang to make it audible to an Americanized global audience. This is illustrated by Punjabi MC's celebrated crossover success by giving American listeners what they were ready for. The rapper gave the song a certain familiarity, but the traditional Indian breakbeats were something new. "It's different, and it doesn't hurt that Jay-Z is on it," says Dana Hall, former r&b editor at *Airplay Monitor*. "It's just the right combination of him [Jay-Z] and a new, interesting beat that is exciting for programmers to play."[11] The global domination of this voice is asserted through the implicit understanding that local cultural forms must be recast in the predominantly americacentric format normative in the contemporary

8   Reinhold Wagnleitner, "'No Commodity Is Quite So Strange As This Thing Called Cultural Exchange': The Foreign Politics of American Pop Culture Hegemony," *Amerikastudien/American Studies* 46.3 (2001): 454.

9   Despite refuting the cultural imperialism thesis, Alex Seago concedes that US pop music is "a prime conduit of cultural globalization" ("'Where Hamburgers Sizzle on an Open Grill Night and Day'," 119). Though contemporary popular culture is global rather than American, it continues to be equated with American popular culture for various reasons. I have used the term American popular culture to denote this space. "Bhangra doesn't come from India anymore. Actually, I think of bhangra as British music," says the New York DJ Rekha; "It's not really fair to lump bhangra together with Indian music that comes out of India," she explains. "It's more accurate to say it's Punjabi music than Indian, because Punjabi is India and Pakistan."

10   Pells, "American Culture Goes Global, or Does It?" B1.

11   Steve Jones, "Jay-Z remix spices interest in Panjabi MC," *USA Today* (21 May 2003), http://www.usatoday.com/life/music/news/2003-05-19-panjabi_x.htm (accessed 18 July 2005).

global culture and media industry. Local musical genres are transmitted and retransmitted to the world and the sending areas as an identifiable American package.

Apart from demanding that local content be adjusted to American popular cultural preferences, American popular cultural space also alters their character through its technologies such as format, programming, marketing, and advertising. Local musics are inserted into programmes with a clear American slant, which might now have become the shared culture of certain kinds of global viewers. They are introduced by deejays or veejays, raised on a standard American musical diet, who approach all local musics with a characteristic American enthusiasm for exoticized local cultures. Thus, the repackaging of local cultures that Pells celebrates defamiliarizes them for the local audience. Pells' contention that the success of the American popular cultural machine lay in its skill in "selling" the "folklore of other people back to them" is precisely the way bhangra was sold back to India. The American popular-culture machine employs the mediascape of MTV, which, until its recent weakening into insignificance thanks to YouTube, was seen to symbolize the McDonaldization of the cultural sphere. MTV is a multicultural *mela* or fair, which brings together the world's diverse musical traditions packaged in American costume under a single *shamiana* or marquee. Local music traditions, decontextualized and deterritorialized, are made to tango together under this pavilion. Algerian rai and Mexican salsa, American rap and West Indian reggae, Pakistani qawwali and British pop are let loose in a multiracial, multi-ethnic, multicultural nightclub mediated by American popular cultural terminology and politics. The role of American popular cultural space in enabling widely disparate local cultures to encounter one another cannot be denied. This space makes room for all, from Björk to Nusrat Futeh Ali Khan, who are willing to submit to the laws of popular cultural commerce.

Bhangra's return as American popular culture accounts for its contemporary popularity as well as denigration. Due to its imbrication in the discourses of globalization, postmodernism, and hybridity, its reception in India was coloured by a suspicion of the global. Bhangra hybrids were dubbed alien cultural imports and became the target of resistance to 'American cultural imperialism'. The americanization thesis has dominated cultural nationalist opposition to globalization exhibiting an elision between American and the global. 'Americanization' is interpreted as commercialization of a folk tradition through its contamination by alien cultural elements. Resistance to bhangra converges on the issues of hybridity, vulgarity, and foreignness as it earns the wrath of the *swadeshi* or the nativist brigade intent on evicting all foreign cultural imports. While one may concede that the explicit sexuality of some bhangra albums crosses permissible Indian 'decency' limits, the charge of vulgarity and reification is really contingent on the musical location in which bhangra is received. Although the Indian audience, accustomed to a popular Indian musical grammar, might find hybrid bhangra music videos offensive, they are no more or less 'vulgar' than others circulating through American popular cultural space. The pornographic camera gaze, the sexualized body and bodily movements, the genre-mixing, the reification of music—this is all part of the music-video grammar routinely employed in American popular culture. The moment bhangra consents to its insertion in this space, it is forced to compromise by participating in its economics and politics, including the system propped up on stars, bestsellers, fans, promotionals, and ratings. The blasphemy occurs, not through the exposure of the female body or overt display of sexuality, but though the desacralization of the harvest ritual through its insertion in a field of commerce.

Puritan resistance to imported bhangra music itself became the source of bhangra's irresistibility to Indian teens, particularly urban middle class. Urban middle-class Indian youth, schooled to reject anything traditional, vernacular, and folk as 'native', embraced folk music with alacrity when it 'returned back' as American popular from Britain across music television and the internet. Generation X, keen to keep up with global sonic trends, was more than willing to lap up Punjabi peasant fare so long as it was packed by transnational music giants as world music or American popular music. One is forced to concede that 'American cultural hegemony', if there be one, was a "hegemony by invitation."[12] The answer to the question "Why is American Popular Culture so Popular" is provided by Berndt Ostendorf:

> the success of American popular culture lies not in any of its individual formal or aesthetic properties, but in its overall design which is that of a consciously constructed liberal New World utopia.[13]

The association of America with wealth, power, youth, and consumption is perhaps the reason why popular culture comes to be regarded as an exclusively American product. Reinhold Wagnleitner offers a slightly different explanation:

> the major attraction of an opposition to American popular culture for young people lies in the fact that it always contains an element of rebellion: a rebellion against the tastes of politicians, priests, the military, and teachers.[14]

Both these impulses could explain middle-class urban youth's espousal of a marginalized folk tradition even as the parental generation denigrated it. American culture signifies, for Indian youth, modernity and "a pursuit of happiness" in "its most up-to-date pursuit of consumption," but also rebellion. Its packaging as American popular culture makes bhangra partake of features the youth associates with American culture. It matters little whether the signifiers denoting Americanness refer to any signified in real America. America has invaded Indian youthful subjectivities, as a brand image, signifying freedom and opportunity. In switching over to bhangra, they believe themselves to be tuning in "to the alluring messages of western consumerism's chief propagandist, American popular culture."[15] In spite of the dilution of "the link between pop music and an Anglo-American cultural axis" that Seago speaks of, popular culture continues to be identified with an essentialized Americanness in several parts of the world, including India, and is loved and hated for the same reason. Indian puritanism's fixation on bhangra's alien mixes and semiclad

12 Reinhold Wagnleitner, "'No Commodity is Quite so Strange as this Thing called Cultural Exchange'," 450.

13 Berndt Ostendorf, "Why is American Popular Culture so Popular? A View from Europe," Amerikastudien/American Studies 46.3 (2001): 339.

14 Wagnleitner, "'No Commodity is Quite so Strange as this Thing called Cultural Exchange'," 447.

15 Wagnleitner, "'No Commodity is Quite so Strange as this Thing called Cultural Exchange'," 448.

female bodies in the music videos also makes it blind to bhangra's resistive character. Bhangra is denigrated for the wrong reasons. Bhangra's *denigration,* its 'blackening' through its being mixed with Black-Atlantic musical beats like rap, reggae, and hip-hop, goes completely unnoticed in the Indian fetishization of American popular culture.

Paul Gilroy points out that American popular culture is composed of the musical legacy of the descendants of slaves from Africa.[16] Neil Lazarus agrees that the black core that modern African music co-opts is essentially Africa's contribution to the shaping of American popular culture.[17] Pells turns this argument around to refute the American cultural-imperialism thesis.[18] He regards American popular culture as a space constituted by immigrants contributing their unique talents to the vast melting pot. Pells argues that this space, far from promoting any nationalist agenda, acts as a hub where the world's cultural diversity is stored and disseminated. American popular culture, disseminated through transnational media networks, has undoubtedly become the meeting-ground of cultures not even remotely connected. Bhangra became fused with Afro-rhythms in the real British and the virtual American popular cultural space, propped up on a black musical base. The politics and economics of the British Empire created the proxemics resulting in the evolution of hybridized bhangra. But the black/brown global youthful dance, in the diaspora and homeland, now occurs in a popular cultural space that emancipates and indentures both black and brown bodies in unpredictable ways. American popular culture adds a different slant to the politics of immigration within the Empire, which inflected black/brown relations in a certain direction. As George Lipsitz puts it in his introduction to the German edition of *Dangerous Crossroads,*

> The popularity of contemporary bhangra music in Britain reveals another instance of how commercial culture can bring into focus previously blurred histories of imperialism.[19]

The popular cultural space initiates a conversation between black and brown unshackled for the first time from essentialist self-definitions. The space of popular culture proves to be emancipatory here, to the extent that it enables a dialogue between two local cultures hitherto oblivious or suspicious of one another. The borrowing from the black core of American popular that was also the bedrock of black-British culture leads to a meeting of two orally oriented cultures in Britain's Afro-bhangra fusion. Bhangra, reggae, rap, and hip-hop are all diasporic voices whose roots go back to the rich oral cultures of Africa and India. The global diffusion of American popular culture sets off a hitherto unheard duet between orally oriented local cultures.

---

16 Paul Gilroy, *The Black Atlantic: Modernity and Double Consciousness* (London: Rout-ledge, 1993): 208.

17 Neil Lazarus, *Nationalism and Cultural Practice in the Postcolonial World* (Cambridge: Cambridge UP, 1999): 198.

18 Pells, *"American Culture Goes Global, or Does It?"* B7.

19 George Lipsitz, *"Dangerous Crossroads,"* introduction to the German edition of *Dangerous Crossroads* (September 1998), http://www.translocation.at/d/lipsitz.htm (accessed 12 February 2004).

One needs to understand that cultural battles in India are not restricted to the high/low, classical/popular cultural binary. Popular culture itself is a contested zone. The high/low dichotomy has been visualized in India as an interdependency of Great and Little Traditions. The Indian cultural master-narrative projects India's multiple Little Traditions as feeding into the Great Indian Tradition. But the Great and Little Traditions interdependency is essentially hierarchical, because the Little Traditions have always occupied the low end of the scale. Indian popular cultural space reveals a similar asymmetry between the national and the regional. The film-dominated Indian popular cultural scene is defined almost completely by Hindi film music. Regional film music is popular in small linguistic pockets, and non-film music has a minute share of the music market. Popular culture space, inherently suspicious of modernity's high/low opposition, has interrogated its privileging of high cultures by breaking down the boundaries between high and low. Bhangra, a marginalized folk tradition, re-entering Indian cultural space via this popular cultural space, is thereby able to challenge traditional hierarchies. Its acquisition of global visibility, as it is circulated through this space, destabilizes the Indian cultural master-narrative in which regional and folk-cultural traditions are relegated to a secondary status. The global space has thus proved to be beneficial to local vernacular traditions, which had remained buried under the national master-narrative. In destabilizing traditional boundaries and hierarchies, it has redefined the Indian cultural sphere in which regional and folk cultures now play an increasingly important role. Therefore, the global visibility accorded to a regional folk culture in this global space has facilitated its nationalization. The willingness of non-Punjabi speakers in different parts of India, who were introduced to bhangra through MTV, to sing along and dance to bhangra tunes accords it a national character. Bhangra's incorporates 'American' inputs to re-invent itself as a national music, in the process de-stabilizing the Indian cultural master-narrative. Bhangra hybrids integrating American popular cultural elements have become a national music which goes by the name of bhangrapop.[20] Although a room might have been created for bhangra by British-Asian bhangra on the national cultural landscape, bhangrapop has taken over the national popular consciousness. Bhangrapop circulates through the music videos of stars like Daler Mehndi but is also mainstreamed though its large presence in popular Hindi film. Its popularity is reflected as much in the number of albums sold as in the impact it has had on other regional musics. Surfing through multiple regional language channels, one is greeted with Tamil, Telugu, Bengali or Oriya imitations of Hindi-film-influenced bhangra. Bhangra's popularization has deconstructed the Hindi

---

20 I have used the term 'Desibhangra' to describe bhangra hybrids with a pan-Indian appeal instead of 'bhangrapop'. They may be distinguished from British bhangra or 'Vilayetibhangra' or the music produced in or targeted at Punjabi 'Punjabibhangra'. The best known practitioner of bhangrapop is Daler Mehndi, whose bhangra album was the first to break the national mainstream charts. Daler stormed the Hindi film music dominated popular culture industry with his eclectic blend of Punjabi with 'American' popular culture. Unlike British bhangra practitioners, whose mixings are with specific forms of American popular music such as reggae or dancehall, Daler and other bhangrapop practitioners based in India mix bhangra at random with whatever appeals to them in American popular music.

national hegemony by inserting a regional culture into the popular space of the nation, thus opening a path for other marginalized regional cultures.

John Tomlinson defines cultural imperialism as a discourse in which resistance to such imperialism is also outlined in terms familiar to the West.[21] But native cultures have always possessed the means and capacity to transform themselves by appropriating alien cultural elements to their own needs. Bill Ashcroft calls this postcolonial transformation.[22] It is interesting that he should name Bollywood's appropriation of Hollywood formulae as an example of postcolonial transformation.[23] Indian popular music might be added to this list in which bhangra takes the lead. Transformations in the reception, production, transmission, and consumption of bhangra reappropriate it for the folk and alter the character of contemporary global/American popular culture.

Seago asks "whether or not the global presence of MTV in itself signifies the development of a uniform Americanized capitalist monoculture."[24] Warning against conflating the simple presence of cultural goods with the attribution of deeper cultural effects, Seago shows that apprehension about the birth of an americanized global MTV generation was refuted by the indigenization of contemporary pop culture, and he cites India as one of the most obvious examples. That might be true, but a MTV generation was certainly born after India's 'satellite invasion', which regularly tunes in to the commodified images of American culture.[25]

Bhangra retains in India only a generational and low-cultural rebelliousness, losing the class, gender, race, and ethnic resistance it performs in Britain. Indian youth subcultures mimic American counter-cultural angst sans its affluence. While Indian middle-class youth might affect American counter-cultural postures, the background of poverty and unemployment nips potential revolt in the bud. Produced on the boundaries between compliance and resistance, middle-class Indian youth subcultural resistance assumes less overt forms marked along generational rather than class, race or ethnic markers. Deprived of opportunities for overt political action, middle-class Indian youth subcultures resist by acts of petty rebellion such as expressing a preference for a life-style that the previous generation disapproves of. Since the parental generation is committed to a nationalist agenda, the generational war on the Indian subcontinent is fought over the selective adoption of 'Western' lifestyles—language, dress, music. As Ulf Hannerz has noted in the

---

21   John Tomlinson, *Cultural Imperialism: A Critical Introduction* (Baltimore M D: Johns Hopkins UP, 1991): 6.

22   Bill Ashcroft, *Post-Colonial Transformation* (London & New York: Routledge, 2001).

23   Ashcroft, "Resistance," in Ashcroft, *Post-Colonial Transformation*, 32. A fuller account (from a 2009 paper given at a National University of Singapore conference on South Asian film) can be found in Ashcroft's "Bollywood, Postcolonial Transformation," chapter 1 of *Travels of Bollywood Cinema: From Bombay to LA*, ed. Anjali Gera Roy & Chua Beng Huat (Oxford & New York: Oxford UP, forthcoming 2012).

24   Alex Seago, "'Where Hamburgers Sizzle on an Open Grill Night and Day'," 125.

25   M T V India managing director Alex Kuruvilla claims that M T V India reaches 25 million homes. "An Interview with MTV India managing director Alex Kuruvilla" (19 July 2002), http://www.indiantelevision.com/interviews/y2k2/executive/alex.htm (accessed 5 February 2004).

case of Nigeria, middle-class, urban Indian youth aspire in this way to participate at the centre.[26] Unlike British-Asian youth, they do not use the space created by world music to assert ethnic difference but to participate in metropolitan culture. The poignant incongruity brought out by Arjun Appadurai in the replication of cosmopolitan cultures on Third-World sites may be seen in the imitative gesture of middle-class urban Indian youth's turning to world music. Indian youth turns to its own music with the gaze of the Western Self that imbues Indian music with an exotic otherness. It reproduces the Self's exoticization of the Other, unaware that it occupies the Other's space in the Western imagination. While British bhangra or Vilayetibhangra draws on ethnic differ-ence in forming British-Asian subcultures to separate itself from white cultural hegemony, Indian bhangra or Desibhangra exoticizes difference to identify with the dominant culture. Middle-class urban Indian youth cultures 'other' regional ethnic cultures just as white American youth coun-terculture valorized and othered non-Western cultures. For middle-class urban Indian youth, folk music is the zone of pleasure that it accesses as a spectacular costume party. In an ambivalent fascination for 'authentic' values of the 'folk' similar to American countercultures, it succumbs to the authenticity-narrative with which world music is underwritten. In the imaginary of middle-class urban Indian youth, folk cultures are imbued with a vitality and authenticity that parental cultures are believed to lack. It opposes these parental cultures through a metropolitan appropriation of 'folk' values. Thus, middle-class urban Indian youth culture constitutes a "different, youthful, sub-jectivity" along generational lines rather than those of class or ethnicity, unlike British-Asian youth subcultures. But a move away from cultural essentialism in favour of elective identities similar to Vilayetibhangra may also be observed in the formation of middle-class urban youth subjectivities. As in Vilayeti-bhangra, middle-class urban Indian youth demonstrates that you don't have to be Punjabi to dance to bhangra. Besides, middle-class urban Indian youth, without intending to, deconstruct the cultural narrative of the nation and reverse its high/low hegemony. They displace nationalist projections of cosmopolitanism and regionalism by espousing the regional as both local and cosmopolitan. They thus oppose high-cultural hegemony with the folk-popular. In contrast to British bhangra, Indian bhangra's resistivity is restricted to a generational revolt against both the high and the popular cultural preferences of their parents. Inadvertently, it ends up dismantling several hegemonic centres. While its appropriation of American popular music in generational resistance would reconstruct the binary division of American/Indian, modern/ traditional, popular/high, middle-class urban Indian youth's espousal of MTV-routed indigenous musics like bhangra embroils it in a national cultural politics.

The appeal of the American Dream is not restricted to urban middle-class Indian youth. 'The soteriological aura of American goods" has been as seductive to those faking want as those "who suffer from actual material want."[27] The images of abundance and material aspirations inscribed in American popular culture, circulated over MTV India, are shared by all regions and sections where they awaken a sensory response. Others access them indirectly through national channels and

---

26   Ulf Hannerz, *Transnational Connections: Culture, People, Places* (London: Routledge, 1996), in
     Christopher Pinney, Pleasure and the Nation (Delhi: Oxford UP , 2001): 11.

27   Berndt Ostendorf, "Why is American Popular Culture so Popular? A View from Europe," 362.

Hindi film music. In the process, bhangra reaches the majority of Indians as a hybridized music. If urban middle-class Indian youth turn to an exoticized bhangra as folk authenticity, working-class rural and urban youth recognize in it the vernacular voice, albeit defamiliarized. In a strange case of mutual cannibalization, as American-popular-culture-directed urban middle-class Indian youth turn to folk as authentic and natural, youth in both urban and rural working-class neighbourhoods mimic their movements in an attempt to appropriate privilege and status. Unlike middle-class urban Indian youth emulating an 'American' life-style, these youth repeat 'americanized' gestures in the process of imitating their urban, privileged counterparts. As working-class youth parody hybridized bhangra movements on Mumbai's streets and Bhatinda's wheatfields, they repeat them with a difference that reappropriates bhangra from its popular cultural location.

The cultural-imperialism thesis, in positing local audiences as mute spectators, denies them agency. Bhangra's marketing in the West depends on the exoticization of ethnicity and rusticity, which results in its being 'othered'. Middle-class urban Indian youth, too, become complicit in auto-exoticization, approaching bhangra as they do through the frame of American popular culture. The appropriation of elements of American popular culture in working-class youth's per-formance of indigenous folk traditions, on the other hand, reverses the process of exoticization. The folk's incorporation of American cultural vocabulary in their repertoire makes a mockery of myths of purity and origin. Hybrid bhangra performed at the Ganesha festival or at any other celebration on a Mumbai street recovers for the folk tradition the robust energy and harvest-song origin that it loses as the global city's dance music. Thus, the mute object of cultural imperialism gains agency not only through the exercise of choice but also through use. Bhangra returns to India othered by American packaging. Working-class Indian youth open the same package, recovering it as its own. In the process, it transforms traditional culture as well as the invading alien culture. One would find as many working-class imitators of American youth subculture, rural and urban, as middle-class. But working-class earthiness recovers in bhangra the subcultural resistance attaching to American youth cultures as they reply to the classical, national narrative in a folk vernacular. While middle-class urban Indian youth might converge on bhangra in search of a lost folk 'authenticity', working-class youth redefine it in both a contemporary rural and an urban context. Middle-class urban Indian youth, in opposing received parental culture with an 'americanized' indigenous tradition, inadvertently collaborates with it in reinstating a marginal-ized regional vernacular, destabilizing national cultural hierarchies.

Simon Philo examines MTV against the cultural-imperialism debate, "Does MTV's near global reach necessarily signal the end for local, regional or national differences"? he asks, and sets out "to challenge the still widely-held premise that MTV's now global reach makes for a kind of Invasion of the Body Snatchers-scenario."[28] Agreeing with Seago that an americanized MTV culture has not been able to make inroads into the heart of India due to stiff competition by homegrown music channels, I would add that MTV itself has been forced to indigenize for the

28   Simon Philo, "Getting Dumber and Dumber: MTV's Global Footprint," *Proceedings of the Second Cultural Studies Seminar, Ege University İzmır, Turkey, May 1997*, MTV Online, http://members.tripod.com/~warlight/P H I L O.html (accessed 12 February 2004).

same reasons. MTV India, launched in 1994 as part of MTV Asia, has capitulated to Indian taste by switching over to a format dominated by Hindi film and peppered with small doses of regional and non-film music, much to the dismay of a segment of 'americanized' Indian youth. Except for the standard *Select* and the American show *Love Line*, MTV focuses on the homegrown music scene and local practitioners rather than Western stars. Fears of an American cultural invasion have been allayed by indigenous music channels' continuing domination of the popular-music sphere. Instead, the prime instrument of 'americanization', MTV, as "both symbol and carrier of an all-pervasive global pop culture dominated by Anglo-American products and tastes," has inadvertently become an agent of the reinvention of traditional Indian cultures. The arrival of MTV and the Star package caused regional and national indigenous channels to reinvent themselves and revamp their programming. Most of these channels appropriated Star and MTV's American format for an Indian audience and conditions in Indian languages.

When the satellite channels were introduced in the mid-1990s, it was assumed that globally focused, English-aspiring Indians would prefer to view Western-style programmes. This predicted viewership model directed MTV, the global music channel, to beam international pop and rock content. But MTV broadcasts turned out to be a major flop, compelling a shift in policy. Dominique Jackson in the *Guardian* in August 1994 suggested that its "new policy of tailoring output more closely to national markets" was the inevitable result "of commercial considerations, themselves born of sea-changes in political mood."[29] The Viacom-owned MTV's initial unwillingness to localize led to its parting ways with Star TV. MTV was forced to indigenize after competition from Rupert Murdoch's Channel V, which had abandoned the global pop ideology and announced its arrival in pure Hinglish "We are like this only." While condescending to play Indipop, MTV still refused to play Hindi film music. The sole winner in this was the low-budget Indian channel Zee TV, which captured the market because of its Hindi slant.[30] When MTV returned on its own, "it was western, but it did a flip and went Hindi," as Channel V Asia's managing director Steve Smith put it.[31] MTV localized by getting the right Hindi English mix and gained critical mass. By 1999, seventy percent of its music was Hindi film music and the MTV success story was being hailed as a case study in *adaptation*, or a generic strategy against semi-globalization. David Flack, Senior Vice President of MTV Asia's Creative and Content Division, had learnt to sing the glocalization tune the hard way by the end of the century.

> Despite MTV being a global brand, we are local in approach. We reflect
> the taste and demands of our viewers and this differs in each market. Thus
> the need to create specific channels (in each country) that meet the needs

---

29   Simon Philo, "Getting Dumber and Dumber."

30   *By early 1994, Zee's prime-time audience share in three metropolitan cities was up to 37%, compared to 39% combined share of Doordarshan National Network and Metro Channel, and a meager 8% combined share of the STAR platform.*

31   *Steve Smith, interview with Channel V Asia Managing Director Steve Smith, "I Expect a New Look Channel V by May 1999," Indian CAB and SAT Reporter 1.20 (8 February 1999), http://www. indiantelevision.com/newsletter/080299/interview80299.htm (accessed 11 February 2004).*

of our target audience," he bravely announced at the C21 World Marketing Conference in 2000.[32]

MTV was revitalized with the infusion of local culture; its accessibility to different audience catapulted its ratings. IRS (Indian Readership Survey) 2002 revealed an impact on the MTV's viewership and reach, which turned out to be thirty-six percent more than the second-placed channel. By 2003, MTV had gone completely 'filmi' and reportedly was not making much profit. One can visualize Vir Sanghvi's trademark smirk when he asks, "What happened to global rock and roll? What happened to Baywatch and The X Files?" He himself provides the answer: "India ignored all existing models of TV development and evolved its own."[33] Today, the programming on MTV is hardly different from that on other music channels, with the exception that the programmes are in English or Hinglish rather than Hindi or other regional languages. MTV also appears to be showcasing local, previously obscure, practitioners, which brings them mass popularity and helps the domestic music industry flourish. It not only brings local music out of obscurity locally, but also brings global visibility and recognition through events such as the MTV Asia awards. Kenny Santana begins with a teaser: "MTV is American? Think Again," and concludes: "It's a global brand that has turned local and is helping local music turn global."[34] Does the Birmingham-based bhangra practitioner Malkit Singh, who was recently knighted by the Queen, agree?

The thesis of American cultural globalization is also premised on a globalized market's appropriation of local voices and control of local industry through its vast resources. But 'the duped-native' theory appears too simplistic in this situation. On the face of it, diasporic practitioners might appear to be collaborating with a global music industry in cannibalizing the folk for self-promotion or anthropologizing it for Western consumption. But the sonic collaborations between diasporic metropolitan and Punjabi folk practitioners reveal a mutual co-option that demystifies the 'duped-native' myth. Folk practitioners willingly consent to the hybridization of their music by diaspora practitioners in the hope of gaining global visibility. If the diasporic practitioner or global music industry appropriates folk voices as exotic or authentic, the native practitioner seems only too happy to play along and be party to his self-exoticization as a marketing move. Bhangrascape is a space of mutual co-option and cannibalization refuting the victim and victimizer fallacy. Bhangra practitioners resist within and despite their participation in global sonic commerce.

The postmodern space has made room for native voices. But the native is allowed to speak only as the Other. A new ethnography is at work, often replicating the ethnographer/native collaborator nexus, in anthropologizing and archaizing the native. The native is once more subjected to the ethnographic gaze, which renders him speechless by appropriating or mediating his voice. The bhangra practitioner is 'the native in his frame' defamiliarized by being plunged into a foreign

---

32 Kenny Santana, "M T V goes to Asia," Yale Global (12 August 2003), http://www.globalpolicy.org/ globaliz/cultural/2003/0812mtv.htm (accessed 12 February 2004).

33 Vir Sanghvi, "Inventing Our Own Model," www.india seminar.com/2003/521/521 %20vir%20sanghvi. htm (accessed 12 February 2004).

34 Kenny Santana, "M T V goes to Asia."

setting that essentializes his difference. The camera juxtaposes him with these images and de-contextualizes the native practitioner to articulate his foreignness. The turban, the beard, and the bhangra costume are obvious ethnic signifiers standing out against the metropolitan ambience of the setting. In the absence of these visible identity-markers, skin colour and bodily structure are highlighted to signify ethnic difference. The subordination of the lyrics to the sound and the beat in contemporary bhangra texts inserts Punjabi into an alien context that proclaims its foreignness. As lyrics cease to signify meaning, they can safely be replaced in the remixes with English.

Bhangra legends locked in their frames and silhouetted against a modern Euro-American background appear to be denuded of dignity and interiority. Embedded in a discourse of otherness to pander to the West's fantasies of the self, the native practitioner redefines the self within this space. He follows a smart strategy for resisting his objectification. By doing the unexpected, by refusing to remain 'within the frame', he inserts himself forcefully in the global cultural space. Although the folk practitioner might participate in the game of the American popular-culture industry, he makes sure that the game is played on his terms. The folk practitioner uses the outsider's ignorance to protect his personal space. Consenting to play the game by its rules, he nevertheless exploits the outsider's ignorance of native traditions to set new rules. He might insert a pure folk composition in a hybridized setting or compose a hybridized text when required to pander to metropolitan yearnings for purity. Singing in his own language and improvising his own dance steps, the folk practitioner exploits the global space made available to him to gain global visibility for himself and his music. Having gained a foothold in this space by agreeing to hybridize, it is not long before he has the world dancing to pure folk tunes. The myth of the native practitioner exploited by global musical giants is refuted by the practitioner's manipulation of the global popular cultural space to corner a larger share of the market than his regional location would allow. The practitioner, while making cosmetic alterations to adapt to global tastes, remains grounded in a specific indigenous musical heritage. The American popular-cultural format attempts to contain the native's voice in the discourse of otherness. But this voice breaks through at several moments to insert itself powerfully into the spaces of the self as an otherness redefining the self. The American popular cultural format has made him sound like an exotic curiosity, but the native is certainly speaking to those who can understand his language. Bhangra beat sounds inclusive, but bhangra's Punjabi lyrics lock into a Punjabi space protected from the outsider's profane gaze. Placing Punjabi difference in lyrical untranslatability, the bhangra practitioner speaks to the Punjabi folk. The outsider eavesdrop on Punjabis 'talking that talk', in which the outsider becomes the object of the native's gaze. Despite the attempt to recast bhangra in an American vocabulary, bhangra retains its folk and regional specificity in its Punjabi lyrics and ritualized movements, and continues to speak to the folk.

The prospect of a global musical conglomerate driving local competition out of business is reversed by the emergence of a local music industry cashing in on bhangra's popularity. The model of a single producer imposing national cultural agendas on many gullible consumers is disturbed by the presence of a strong local music industry controlling and dominating the Indian music market. Like MTV, transnational musical giants like Sony control a very small proportion of the huge Indian music market. The signing of bhangra stars by such international giants might have converted them into global brand names. But it was also feared that they would sacrifice artistic and musical integrity in the interests of marketability. As pointed out earlier, native practitioners managed to retain their integrity within the constraints imposed by a gigantic music mart. But they also found an alternative to their commodification and anthropologization by launching their own labels. Bally Sagoo, often accused of complying with international music trends and markets, not only promotes his own music under his label ishqrecords but also showcases new ethnic talent in a move to sidestep the music market's hegemonic structures. If a practitioner like Bally Sagoo manages to resist within the market system, the music market itself demonstrates democratizing trends. The bhangra music market today is dominated by a virtual newcomer in the Indian music industry called T Series, which broke into the monopolistic Indian music market by creating and exploiting a niche for regional music and musical genres neglected by the music industry leader SAREGAMA HMV. Although T Series is often accused of indulging in unethical practices, its growth path charts a musical success story which challenged other national and global monopolistic structures. While SAREGAMA HMV concentrated on traditional Hindi film music segment, T Series India diversified into new popular music segments led by bhangra. Before SAREGAMA could say *shava shava*, T Series had created and cornered a huge regional music market. T Series' strategy for taking on the national behemoth was large volumes and low pricing as a step toward musical democraticization. T Series' low-priced cassettes, which brought recordings (copied or printed) of global as well as Indian practitioners within the reach of the average Indian consumer, percolated through to the working classes as 'americanized' regional music. Few Indians could afford to buy Nusrat Futeh Ali Khan under the world music label. But they could listen to his re-recorded mixes as well as those of other world-music practitioners in a single music cassette for a fraction of the cost. Thus, the diffusion of American cultural values in India took place though a little-known Delhi-based music company owned by a former owner of a fruit juice stall.

T Series' marketing strategy, like youthful preferences, disturbed several hegemonic structures. Its turning to regional and folk music to capture a niche market heralded the arrival of regional folk, primarily bhangra, on the national cultural scene, giving Hindi film music a run for its money. Its cost saving measure of avoiding stars made the reputations of numerous little known bhangra practitioners. Finally, its uncanny ability to tune in to the musical tastes of the Indian masses translated hybrid popular musical genres into a familiar popular dialect. In this process, T Series reclaimed the 'othered' bhangra of American popular cultural space for the Indian masses making it its own, albeit transformed by alien influences. Having instilled in the Indian masses a taste for both folk and hybrid bhangra mutants, T Series today is seen experimenting with bhangra remixes to grab a share of the global remix industry. In providing visibility to practitioners better known in India than globally, T Series also defeats the authenticity cult promoted by the global music industry by privileging practitioners who fit in with global trends and agendas. T Series, like the native practitioner, enters the global space to wrest 'othered' indigenous cultural forms back for the Indian masses and disturbs the space through its economics rather than politics. The fear of an alien cultural invasion proves unfounded because indigenous music companies like T Series defeat the global giants' hegemonic intentions by undercutting their prices. The flooding of the Indian market by music produced by indigenous companies deconstructs the model of one global producer and many local consumers and the notion of unidirectional flows. The availability of locally produced music ensures that the tastes of the Indian masses are not dictated by a multi-billion-dollar American conglomerate. Instead, the local market shapes the global market, altering global taste-hierarchies in the process. The professed localization of American transnationals translates into a true indigenization as local musical preferences influence the composition of American popular culture. The presence of a vibrant local industry also ensures its autonomy. A transnational American popular culture would remain confined to certain local taste groups while the masses would remain free to exercise their preference for particular forms of music and stars through their purchasing power. Apache Indian and Bally Sagoo would have to play second fiddle to homegrown stars like Daler Mehndi or Pammi Bai.

Though bhangra has played a crucial role in the redefinition of Asian ethnicities in the UK, Canada, and the USA, it can redefine the popular cultural space only after its mainstreaming. As Andy Bennet points out, bhangra's impact in Euroamerican locations is greater in areas with concentrations of Asian immigrant populations than in the rest. It percolates through to the larger white majority and other minority groups only as it enters the mainstream. Bhangra's participation in black musical culture made it acceptable to white audiences to whom black music, as opposed to Asian music, has always seemed the core of American popular culture. Musical collaborations between bhangra and reggae, rap, and hip-hop practitioners or remixed versions of bhangra have been a major reason for its mainstreaming. Even those ignorant of its specific roots might have encountered it in reggae, rap or hip-hop remixes.

But bhangra underwent a transformation from an 'Asian noise' to an international sound when Asian bhangra practitioners became names to be reckoned with on the pop charts or were included in main, rather than special, categories. Since bhangra first resurged in Britain, the UK charts are the first reflection of bhangra's mainstreaming. The first Asian practitioner to cross over into the mainstream was Apache Indian as the first and only Asian practitioner to have ever been nominated for a National Brit Award. His Top Twenty hit single "Arranged Marriage" was voted 'Best Contemporary Song' by the British Academy of Songwriters, Composers & Authors in 1993. But bhangra's incursion into American popular culture occurred via American film and television. Apache Indian's hit "Boomschackalak" has been used in fifteen world national TV commercials (including *Lynx*, featuring Jennifer Aniston) and five Hollywood films, including *Dumb and Dumber*. The current popularity of Bollywood and Indian diasporic films has introduced the American and the global audience to filmed versions of bhangra. The three diasporic hits of a decade ago, *Monsoon Wedding* (2001), *Bend it like Beckham* (2002), and *Bollywood Hollywood* (2002), depend heavily on bhangra and other Punjabi music. Bollywood also transmits bhangra movements globally through Bollywood films' mandatory bhangra number, such as *shava shava* in *Kabhi Khushi Kabhi Gham* (2001) or *mahi re* in *Kaante* (2002). Bhangra traced a circuitous route to the USA, mostly through hip-hop. Following the influx of West Indians, desis from Trinidad and Guyana, it is not surprising that it became big at the same time dancehall broke into the USA and was assimilated into the American soundscape through sampling and remixes just as rap and dancehall was.

Bhangra's separation from black music, its acquisition of a distinctly Asian voice, and its incorporation by pop practitioners like Jay-Z, Britney Spears, and Ricky Marin signals another phase in its boomeranging on the American popular cultural scene. As Britney Spears, once the most visible icon of American popular culture, hip-hops to a bhangra tune, bhangra could be said have ingrained itself in a global American popular cultural imagination. The first bhangra hit to cross over to the mainstream in the USA was England's Punjabi MC's international hit "Mundian to bach ke." It reached the top twenty on the rhythmic Top-Forty airplay chart and was the thirty-seventh most-listened-to song in the country in mid-May 2003, moving subsequently into the top five. When Jay-Z rapping over Punjabi MC's "Mundian to bach ke" in *Beware of the Boys* is hailed as a "new sound imported to US pop airwaves" the reverse flows have truly begun. But *Beware of the Boys* is also believed to have increased the sales of Punjabi MC's album. *Beware of the Boys* was described as 'the ultimate postmodern pastiche—an americanized version of contemporary bhangra music, which is itself an anglicized version of traditional Indian folk music.'[35] This could be cited as an example of reverse flows, as a rustic Punjabi music, in the process of being americanized, returns to the American popular cultural mainstream to transform its character. Bhangra's global flows from the Punjabi village to America across the UK enable it to participate in the USA's domestic politics as Jay-Z mixes his Brooklyn braggadocio with antiwar sentiments in "Beware of the Boys." The invasion argument appears to cut both ways, because, if American popular culture has 'invaded' others' spaces, its own cultural space has also been 'othered' in the process. The coverage in *Time Out New York* of *Basement Bhangra*, a popular South Asian-oriented party started by DJ Rekha, a pioneer on the local Asian underground scene with DJ Joy, testifies to the bhangraization of the Manhattan cityscape.

> The scene inside S.O.B.'s would seem unusual even to the most been-around-the-block New Yorker: A multitude of men in traditional Punjabi turbans and Tommy Hilfiger shirts throwing down with an equal number of beautiful South Asian women to indigenous Indian music overlaid with pounding, bass heavy beats. Meanwhile, Japanese clubbers, dreadlocked hip-hoppers, art school kids and a range of other downtown types dance feverishly, with arms and legs flailing. Is this an off-the-hook mixer for the children of UN delegates? Nope. You'll find it on the first Thursday of each month at the Basement Bhangra party (the next one falls on Thursday 7).[36]

American popular culture is no longer to be confused with the Anglo-American axis; it comes from everywhere and anywhere.

WORKS CITED

Appadurai, Arjun. *Modernity at Large: The Cultural Dimensions of Modernity* (Delhi: Oxford UP. 1996).

Ashcroft, Bill. *Post-Colonial Transformation* (London & New York: Routledge, 2001).

---

35 Bas Dreisinger, "Hip-hop by Way of India," The Times (8 June 2003), http://www.calendarlive.com/printedition/calendar/suncal/cl-ca- (accessed 8 February 2004).

36 Sage Meridyth Jacobs, "The Big Bhangra Theory: A Cross-Cultural Crew Digs the Subcontinental Groove Basement Bhangra," Time Out New York 259 (September 7–14 2000), http://www.timeoutny.com/clubs/259/259.clubs.opener.bhangra.html (accessed 12 February 2004).

Bennet, Andrew. "Bhangra in Newcastle: Music, Ethnic Identity and the Role of Local Knowledge," *Innovation* 10.1 (1997): 107–16.

——. *Popular Music and Youth Culture: Music, Identity, Place* (London: Macmillan, 2000).

Dreisinger, Bas. "Hip-hop by Way of India," *The Times* (8 June 2003), http://www.calendarlive.com/printedition/calendar/suncal/cl-ca- (accessed 8 February 2004).

Gilroy, Paul. *The Black Atlantic: Modernity and Double Consciousness* (London: Routledge, 1993).

Hannerz, Ulf. *Transnational Connections: Culture, People, Places* (London: Rout-ledge, 1996).

Housee, Shirin, & Mukhtar Dar, talking to Bally Sagoo and Radical Sista. "Remixing Identitites: 'Off' the Turn-Table," in *Disorienting Rhythms: The Politics of the New Asian Dance Music*, ed. Sanjay Sharma, John Hutnyk & Ashwani Sharma (London: Zed, 1999): 81–104.

Huq, Rupa. "Asian Kool? Bhangra and Beyond," in *Disorienting Rhythms: The Politics of the New Asian Dance Music*, ed. Sanjay Sharma, John Hutnyk & Ashwani Sharma (London: Zed, 1999): 61–80.

Jacobs, Sage Meridyth. "The Big Bhangra Theory: A Cross-Cultural Crew Digs the Subcontinental Groove at Basement Bhangra," *Time Out New York* 259 (September 7–14 2000), http://www.timeoutny.com/clubs/259/259.clubs.opener.bhangra.html (accessed 12 February 2004).

Jones, Steve. "Jay-Z remix spices interest in Panjabi MC," *USA Today* (21 May 2003), http://www.usatoday.com/life/music/news/2003-05-19-panjabi_x.htm (accessed 18 July 2005).

Kuruvilla, Alex. "Interview with MTV India Managing Director Alex Kuruvilla," (19 July 2002), http://www.indiantelevision.com/interviews/y2k2/executive/alex.htm (accessed 5 February 2004).

Lazarus, Neil. *Nationalism and Cultural Practice in the Postcolonial World* (Cambridge: Cambridge UP, 1999).

Lipsitz, George. "Dangerous Crossroads," introduction to the German edition of *Dangerous Cross-roads* (September 1998), http://www.translocation.at/d/lipsitz.htm (accessed 12 February 2004).

Ostendorf, Berndt, "Why is American Popular Culture so Popular? A View from Europe," *Amerikastudien/American Studies* 46.3 (2001): 339–66.

Pells, Richard. "American Culture Goes Global, or Does It?" *Chronicle Review* (12 April 2002): B1–B7.

Philo, Simon. "Getting Dumber and Dumber: MTV's Global Footprint," Proceedings of the Second Cultural Studies Seminar, Ege University İzmır, Turkey, May 1997, MTV Online, http://members.tripod.com/~warlight/PHILO.html (accessed 12 February 2004).

Pinney, Christopher. *Pleasure and the Nation* (Delhi: Oxford UP, 2001).

Sanghvi, Vir. "Inventing Our Own Model," www.india seminar.com/2003/521/521%20vir%20sanghvi.htm (accessed 12 February 2004).

Santana, Kenny. "MTV goes to Asia," *Yale Global* (12 August 2003), http://www.globalpolicy.org/globaliz/cultural/2003/0812mtv.htm (accessed 12 February 2004).

Seago, Alex. "'Where Hamburgers Sizzle on an Open Grill Night and Day: Global Pop Music and Americanization in the Year 2000," *American Studies* 41.2–3 (Summer–Fall 2000): 119–36.

Smith, Steve. Interview with Channel V Asia Managing Director Steve Smith, "I Expect a New Look Channel V by May 1999," *Indian CAB and SAT Reporter* 1.20 (8 February 1999), http://www.indiantelevision.com/newsletter/080299/interview80299.htm (accessed 11 February 2004).

Tomlinson, John. *Cultural Imperialism: A Critical Introduction* (Baltimore MD: Johns Hopkins UP, 1991).

Wagnleitner, Reinhold. "'No Commodity is Quite so Strange as this Thing called Cultural Exchange': The Foreign Politics of American Pop Culture Hegemony," *Amerikastudien/American Studies* 46.3 (2001): 443–70.

Questions for Thought

- What are some of the basic characteristics of Indian classical music?
- What are some of the instruments used in filmi? In bhangra?
- What are the American elements of music that have been incorporated into both bhangra and Bollywood music?
- How has bhangra changed popular music culture in India?
- What importance does language play in both bhangra and Bollywood?
- How do you think African-American music has influenced bhangra, and what are the cultural repercussions of this influence?
- How have traditional Indian ideas of culture and class changed with the popularity of bhangra?
- How have bhangra and Bollywood brought American popular culture and cultural images to India?

Activity:

Search YouTube for Bollywood film music, British bhangra, and Punjabi bhangra. Make a chart comparing the music, visuals, costumes, and choreography. How are the music and images similar? How are they different? Can you identify the Western and Indian instruments used in these selections? What American elements can you identify in the music?

References

Kalita, S. Mitra. *Suburban Sahibs: Three Immigrant Families and Their Passage from India to America*. New Brunswick, NJ: Rutgers University Press, 2005.

Rajghatta, Chidanand. "Bollywood in Hollywood." *The Times of India*, July 6, 2008.

Rao, S. "'I Need an Indian Touch': Globalization and Bollywood Films." *Journal of International and Intercultural Communication* 3, no. 1 (2010): 1–19.

Figure Credits

CHAPTER NINE

K-pop: Globalization of the Asian Music Industry

FIGURE 9.1 *A map of South Korea*

Introduction

The focus of this anthology is global popular music. Recently, no music has been more global in its impact than K-pop, South Korean popular music. All South Korean popular music could fit under this label. However, since the 1990s, the term specifically refers to a modern form of South Korean popular music that embraces a number of foreign elements, including bubblegum pop, electronica, disco, hip-hop, rhythm and blues, rock and roll, and others genres. It is global in its roots and in its scope. For the most part, it is a fusion of synthesized music, sharp dance routines, and fashionable outfits.

K-pop

As is the case in the much of the post-MTV world, K-pop is audio-visual in its performance practice. It has been around since the 1990s, and the first highly successful band in the K-pop world was Seo Taiji and Boys, who hit the scene in 1992. Seo Taiji and Boys appearance on the K-pop scene marked a turning point in South Korean music: their socially-conscientious lyrics changed the model for K-pop performance. MTV stated that "K-pop music would never be the same." What set their music apart, and what remains the basis for the K-pop sound, is the extensive use of musical instrument digital interface, or *MIDI*, which has been the standard means by which computers and electronic musical instruments interface since 1983. This system specifies notation, pitch, volume (or velocity), and other aspects of musical sound production, as well as effects such as pan, vibrato, echo, reverb, etc. It remains the standard for electronic music today and is used in the production of many genres worldwide.

K-pop's focus has always been beyond the music, and performance almost always features synchronized dance. It came of age at a time when digital technology—in terms of music and communications—began to touch all aspects of music and popular culture. Were it not for social media and YouTube, it is doubtful that K-pop would have such a large following and such a dedicated fan base, who are often found in their own "performance" of their favorite music through flash mobs.

K-pop is a solo and a collaborative genre, featuring soloist and bands usually organized by gender, following the models of American and European boy and girl bands such as the Back Street Boys and the Spice Girls. The first Korean boy band was H.O.T, formed by one of the big entertainment companies, SM Entertainment. The five-member band was formed in 1996 and was popular in Taiwan and the People's Republic of China as well as South Korea. They were the first K-pop group to have a "million seller," and are often credited as the first K-pop boy band, setting the model for the such groups in South Korean music. Soon after they hit the scene, the band announced "we are the future." The future ended, however, in 2001 when the group disbanded.

A popular solo act is Kwon Ji Yong, better known by his stage name G-Dragon. He got his start the in the boy band Big Bang, which was one of the biggest selling groups in Asia, after training for six years with the YG Entertainment record label (the focus of the reading in this chapter). He went solo in 2009, and in 2013 went on an extended world

FIGURE 9.2 *Some K-pop boy bands in performance*

tour. He enjoys a global following on social media and enjoys sold out concerts everywhere. He could be seen as a model for K-pop musicians, who must go through extensive training with entertainment and record companies before they can launch their careers.

K-pop Training

K-pop training is intense and expensive, with all of the costs born by the aspiring artist. Some K-pop hopefuls run up enormous bills to pay for their training, which they have to repay to their record company regardless if they are successful musicians or not. Kids start train-

ing very young, with pre-audition training to prepare them for record company auditions. Some spend years in the pre-audition training. The next step is auditioning, and some kids will audition dozens of times. If successful, the hopeful artist will sign a trainee contract for a few years of the company's training regimen, which includes singing, acting, dance, and language lessons. Very few trainees will be offered an artist contract, compelling many to drop out of school in order to train for twelve to fifteen hours a day, plus homework such as etiquette lessons, mandatory exercise, etc.

FIGURE 9.3 *Crayon Pop at the 2015 Summer K-pop Festival in Seoul*

Only a handful of the hopeful stars are successful in the rigorous training program, and many drop out. After the debut, the competition only increases, with so many groups competing for a limited market. Successful groups have the potential for fame, marketing contracts, and an extravagant lifestyle. Regardless if they are successful or not, all trainees at all levels are financially responsible for all of the costs of training, which can run into the millions of dollars.

Busker Busker

One of the most popular groups in K-pop is Busker Busker, an unusual group in many ways. Firstly, it is an entirely acoustic band, not relying, or even using, MIDI or any other electronics. It got its start not through the standard training system that most K-pop artists have to go through, but by competing on a television show and coming in second, thereby getting the exposure that led to its popularity and success. What is most unusual, however, is that it is the only K-pop band that has a

FIGURE 9.4 *Busker Busker*

member that is not Korean. Bradley Moore, the drummer of the group, is from Fairfield, Ohio, and has no Korean roots. After graduating from Miami University in Oxford, Ohio, he went to Korea to teach English. Some of his students had a "garage" band, and the band lost its drummer due to mandatory military service. Brad had played drums in punk bands throughout high school and college, and his students asked him to sit in a few times. The band then decided to compete on a TV show, and Brad competed with them. They were offered a contract by a major entertainment company and became one of K-pop's most popular bands, constantly at the top of the charts. The rest is history.

K-pop and the Global Market

Although K-pop's greatest popularity is in Asia, it enjoys a strong following elsewhere. K-pop relies heavily on social media such as Twitter and Facebook in enhancing its worldwide exposure. K-pop is spreading through South America, the Middle East, and Europe as well as the United States; K-pop groups can be found in Turkey, Egypt, and Kazakhstan. K-pop shows have played at the MGM Grand in Las Vegas and in the Nokia Theater in Los Angeles. There are dozens of K-pop websites, and tunes can be found for purchase on I-Tunes and on streaming services such as Spotify. MTV has a K-pop website and an MTV Korean

FIGURE 9.5 *Local performers at a K-pop contest in Egypt in 2011*

Channel dedicated to Korean music, and K-pop radio shows stream on the internet. The numbers of views of K-pop videos on YouTube is staggering and is spread throughout the world. K-pop groups have performed on David Letterman and "Live! with Kelly," and much, much more, all riding the Korean Wave with no signs of slowing down anytime soon.

Reading:

The reading for this chapter, "Lessons from K-pop's Global Success," focuses on the evolution and globalization of K-pop, which started as a local Korean phenomenon in the early 1990s and rapidly evolved into one of the most important genres in the global market. It discusses the training that usually takes place for K-pop performers who may go through years of voice, dance, movement, and other lessons to hone their skills and to become marketable in the K-pop system. Recruitment is an important part of this process, and often thousands of your Koreans compete for a few spots in each company's training program. The polishing and ultimate debut of artists is discussed, as well as the financial and personal obligations that each artist assumes in this training process. K-pop has positioned itself to draw an audience from around the world, using simple melodies wrapped in a texture of Western-style pop-music conventions. It relies on tight choreography, high-energy performance, and an ever-changing fashion landscape to hold the interest of audiences.

LESSONS FROM K-POP'S GLOBAL SUCCESS

SEO Min-Soo

K-POP'S GLOBAL REACH

On the heels of the successful launch of Korean TV dramas in foreign markets, K-pop began to make inroads in China, Japan and Thailand in the early 2000s. In recent years K-pop has expanded into Europe, the Middle East and the Americas in a second "Korean Wave." K-pop's current reigning girl group, "Girls' Generation," made their nationwide US debut with an appearance on "The Late Show with David Letterman" and "Live! With Kelly" this year.

In addition to highly well-received international tours, K-pop has experienced explosive online popularity. Views for K-pop videos reached 2.3 billion on YouTube in 235 countries in 2011.

K-pop's stature now transcends economic terms; it has become a strategic asset with halo effects on Korea's brand and its products. The economic effects of the second Korean Wave are estimated at about ₩5 trillion as of 2010.[1]

FIGURE 9.6

The success of K-pop groups did not come overnight. Rather, the emergence of K-pop is the result of methodical planning and execution that offers lessons to any company setting its sights on the global market. This report analyzes K-pop's success factors, and suggests ways that Korean companies can leverage K-pop's techniques for their own benefit.

K-POP'S SUCCESS FACTORS

This report adopted a four-pointed "cultural diamond" model[2] to determine the four factors that drove K-pop to new heights: preparation, delivery, consumers and content.

In the preparation stage, K-pop's major production companies lay the groundwork for moving product overseas. The process is systematically designed, starting with selecting prospective stars, putting them

FIGURE 9.7

1   *Korea Foundation for International Culture Exchange.*

2   *Griswold, W. (1994). Cultures and Societies in a Changing World. Pine forge Press.; Alexander, V. (2003). Sociology of the Arts: Exploring Fine and Popular Forms. Blackwell.*

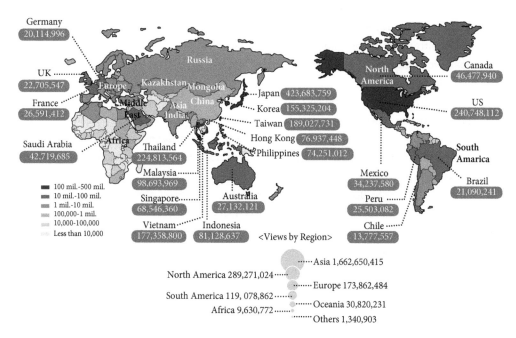

Germany 20,114,996
UK 22,705,547
France 26,591,412
Saudi Arabia 42,719,685
Russia
Kazakhstan
Europe
Middle East
Africa
Mongolia
China
Asia
India
Japan 423,683,759
Korea 155,325,204
Taiwan 189,027,731
Hong Kong 76,937,448
Philippines 74,251,012
Thailand 224,813,564
Malaysia 98,693,969
Singapore 68,546,360
Vietnam 177,358,800
Australia 27,132,121
Indonesia 81,128,637
North America
Canada 46,477,940
US 240,748,112
South America
Mexico 34,237,580
Peru 25,503,082
Chile 13,777,557
Brazil 21,090,241

100 mil.-500 mil.
10 mil.-100 mil.
1 mil.-10 mil.
100,000-1 mil.
10,000-100,000
Less than 10,000

<Views by Region>

North America 289,271,024
South America 119,078,862
Africa 9,630,772
Asia 1,662,650,415
Europe 173,862,484
Oceania 30,820,231
Others 1,340,903

FIGURE 9.8 *Number of Views of K-pop Videos on YouTube (2011)*

NOTE: GDP *based on Purchasing Power Parity per capita.*

SOURCE: JOONGANG *Ilbo. "The number of views of K-POP videos on YouTube reached 2.3 billion in 235 countries last year." (January 2, 2011)*

through a rigorous training regime, producing shows and promoting globally. Training in particular is highly engineered, with aspirants undergoing five to seven years of instruction in singing and dancing. Even after this process, there is no guarantee of actually appearing on stage. Thus, only the best of the best ever reach the eyes and ears of the public, ensuring K-pop's continuing competitiveness.

In the casting stage, production companies focus on finding bankable stars. Trainees are found through auditions or recommendations from existing celebrities. Auditions are also held overseas.

SM Entertainment, a leading K-pop producer, has been holding global auditions since 2006 in the US, Canada and Thailand, with 300,000 performers applying annually for 300 positions.

The training stage represents a long-term investment by entertainment companies. Trainees' daily regimen includes not only singing and dancing but also acting, foreign language skills and personal development. Training is conducted by teams of experts, and trainees must pass periodic evaluations to stay in the program. Performers can see their names on marquees only after several years of this regimen.

In the producing stage, companies seek out ideas from global sources. Managers work with top experts in music and choreography to perfect the appeal of their upcoming artists. Creative input is sourced globally from experts in many countries and in multiple industries.

In the global promotion stage, entertainment companies actively network with overseas partners. Companies plan overseas marketing from the earliest stages of planning, including forming partnerships with major record labels like Music Japan and Avex to reduce the risks inherent in overseas promotion. K-pop promoters also release albums specifically for local markets to overcome cultural barriers.

In delivery, K-pop now relies heavily on social networking services (SNS) like YouTube, Facebook and Twitter for worldwide exposure. The speed at which K-pop clips can go viral has significantly reduced the time and expense needed to build awareness in foreign markets. The impact of SNS is apparent when comparing the time it now takes for Korean entertainers to gain popularity compared to the pre-SNS era.

In Japan, K-pop singer Boa took five years to establish herself after her first debut in 2001. Dong Bang Shin Ki, a group which debuted in 2004, took four years to make an impression. In contrast, Girls' Generation emerged as the top band on Oricon Chart in 2011 on the day their first original album was released in Japan by riding the wave of SNS.

Information technology (IT) is also related to the consumer component of the K-pop diamond. In contrast to Korean TV dramas, whose fan base consists of middle-aged women, K-pop appeals to young people, particularly women, who are already comfortable with SNS and mobile IT. These young fans not only listen to K-pop, they also create their own K-pop-inspired entertainment. In Thailand, homemade videos of people imitating the moves of their favorite K-pop singers has become a popular trend. This viral transmission of K-pop has spread to Europe and the Americas, with fans learning K-pop lyrics and dance moves.

Lastly, from the content perspective, K-pop has assembled all the ingredients to draw fans from around the world. Musically, K-pop relies on simple melodies that incorporate western-style pop conventions. Visually, K-pop uses tight choreography to sustain high energy and interest, while an ever changing range of fashions and styles ensure that its performers remain fresh and appealing. K-pop's formula has met with broad appeal across a myriad of nationalities and languages.

APPLYING THE K-POP STRATEGY

K-pop creates direct economic value and branding effects for Korea. K-pop's songs, singers and fans provide opportunities for companies to develop new products and marketing strategies, as well as new ways to broaden their markets.

The first K-pop strategy businesses can use is launching K-pop-based products through a "one source, multi-use" method. The game and animation industries can develop characters using K-pop content and stars. K-pop songs and singers can form the basis for blockbuster theater productions, as with the hit Broadway musical "Mamma-mia," which used ABBA songs.

The second K-pop strategy Korean businesses can use is to develop tourism packages designed for K-pop fans. Tour packages that combine concerts, shopping and music locations can be developed. More than 1 million people will visit Korea to go to large events starring Korean Wave stars. This is already being arranged by Japan Travel Bureau (JTB), the biggest travel agency in Japan. JTB offers Korean Wave tour packages with concerts and shopping in cooperation

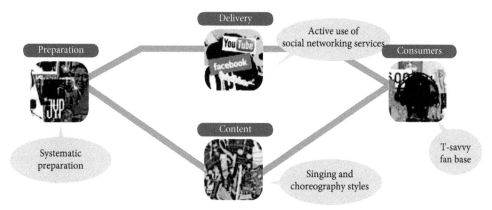

FIGURE 9.9 *K-pop's "Diamond" Success Model*

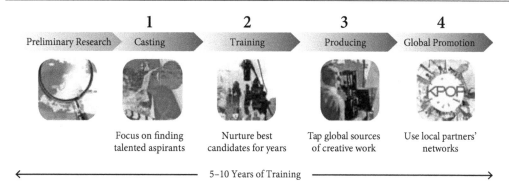

FIGURE 9.10 *Four Stages of Star Preparation*

with Korea's duty-free shopping centers. In 2011, Japan Travel Bureau organized a major concert featuring popular K-pop stars Big Bang and Kara. This two-day/three-night package attracted 2,000 Chinese tourists in 2011.

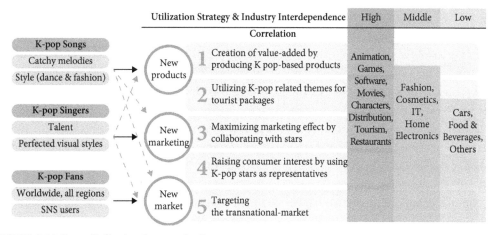

FIGURE 9.11 *K-pop Utilization Strategy by Component*

Culture clusters involving K-pop can be built around settings from two of Korea's most popular dramas—"Winter Sonata," filmed on Nami Island, and "Jewel in the Palace," filmed in Yangju, Gyeonggi Province. At the same time, exclusive spaces (K-pop theaters) for people to enjoy K-pop can attract more visitors.

The third strategy is to collaborate with K-pop idols in new product development and marketing. By connecting stars' image with product concepts, companies can enjoy substantial marketing effects. When American hip hop star Kanye West helped design shoes for Louis Vuitton, the shoes sold out immediately despite a price of $1,000 per pair. Global fast fashion company H&M and global cosmetic brand Elizabeth Arden are also collaborating with pop stars like Madonna and Britney Spears.

The fourth strategy is to use K-pop stars as models for advertising related products. Makers of food and beverages, cosmetics and clothing can bridge customers' psychological distance to products by using familiar K-pop singers that fit the product's image. Daesang Corporation, one of Korea's largest food companies, hired popular girl group Kara to model in its "Hongcho (drinking vinegar)" advertisements in Japan. After the ads appeared, Daesang achieved ₩ 47 billion in sales in the second half of 2011, 15 times as much as sales for the first half.

Lastly, companies need to turn their attention to K-pop fans in emerging market economies. Korea's exports to the Middle East and Latin America have been growing at an exponential rate. Exports of beverages to Iraq have soared 1,981 percent year-on-year. Car exports to Kazakhstan have grown 275 percent year-on-year. Mobile phone exports to Peru jumped 102 percent over last year. Korean companies hoping to capitalize on K-pop can thus devise marketing strategies that use SNS platforms. SM Entertainment President Lee Soo-Man once said that people who view its content on YouTube and Facebook are "SM citizens." Indeed, young people who listen to K-pop are often trendsetters in their country.

More specifically, companies can take different approaches in emerging markets and advanced countries when tapping the interests of overseas K-pop fans. In emerging market economies, already popular K-pop can be used to boost sales of Korean products there. In the US and European countries, rather than emphasizing national brand, K-pop stars and company brands can be linked in marketing.

IMPLICATIONS

K-pop's groundbreaking success challenges assumptions that "Korean culture," especially when presented to outsiders, must always mean "traditional culture." Korean companies can learn from this success by reassessing their existing business models and aggressively retooling them to capture overseas markets.

Companies can also pay attention to the production process in K-pop, which creates global stars by emphasizing basic skills. K-pop singers are recognized globally not only for their attractive looks but also for their excellent singing and dancing skills. This results from rigorous and lengthy training, in music, choreography, composition and foreign languages. Companies can benchmark the K-pop training system in their human resources management and instill a hiring process that focuses on basic skills and growth potential. By providing systematic education and training that maximizes individual potential, companies can produce their own global stars.

Lastly, companies should learn from the example of K-pop production companies' long-term planning, which overcame initially weak brand power. Latecomers with no name and companies targeting emerging markets can benefit by adopting K-pop's committed approach to raising customer accessibility over attaining short-term profits.

Translation: RHEE Oak-Jung

Keywords

K-pop, YouTube, Facebook, Korean Wave, Girls' Generation

SEO Min-Soo is a research fellow at SERI. His areas of expertise include art management, the culture industry and culture and art policy. He holds an MA in Psychology from Seoul National University. Contact: msoo.seo@samsung.com

Questions for Thought

- What is the artist recruitment and training like for an aspiring K-pop performer?
- What is the K-pop Diamond success model? What are the four stages of star preparation in the K-pop system?
- How are K-pop groups formed?
- What are the expectations for K-pop performers in terms of promotion and production?
- What was the Korean Wave? What is the second Korean Wave, and how are they different?
- Why has social media been important to K-pop's success?
- Why do you think K-pop has become so popular beyond the borders of Korea? What do you think of K-pop? Is it something to which you might listen in the future?

Activity:

Search YouTube for K-pop (some suggestions are K-pop girl groups, K-pop boy bands, soloist G-Dragon, Junsu, Hyuna and Ra-In). Listen to a few selections from each. What do the performances have in common? How does choreography and fashion figure in the performances? Then, search YouTube for videos by Busker Busker and compare the performances of this group to the other K-pop stars you have seen. How does Busker Busker differ from the other performers?

Figure Credits

Fig. 9-1: Source: https://commons.wikimedia.org/wiki/File:Korea,_South-CIA_WFB_Map.png.

Fig. 9-2: Copyright © A1 Candidate (CC by 3.0) at https://commons.wikimedia.org/wiki/File:K-pop_boybands.jpg.

Fig. 9-3: Copyright © Korea.net / Korean Culture and Information Service (CC by 2.0) at https://commons.wikimedia.org/wiki/File:Crayon_Pop_at_2015_Summer_K-POP_Festival.jpg.

Fig. 9-4: Copyright © CJ Entertainment.

Fig. 9-5: Copyright © Korea.net / Korean Culture and Information Service (CC by 2.0) at https://commons.wikimedia.org/wiki/File:KOCIS_K-pop_contest_in_Egypt_(6000519079).jpg.

CHAPTER TEN

How Radiohead Changed the World: A New Marketing Model

Introduction

The alternative rock band Radiohead has had many hits and has produced some very interesting music in its thirty-plus years of making music. The band also made a business decision that changed the way music is marketed, disseminated, and enjoyed, with global implications. When its recording contract expired, the group needed a means by which to distribute new music. The solution, which exploited new technologies in ways that had not been used before, created a new model for the distribution of recorded music, which did much to change the musical world.

Radiohead was formed in 1985 in Abingdon, Oxfordshire, UK. The five-piece band consists of Thom York (guitar and lead vocals), Ed O'Brien (guitar), Phil Selway (drums), Johnny Greenwood (guitar, keyboards), and his brother Colin Greenwood (bass). They also use other instruments, as well as electronic effects, in their music. Alternative and progressive bands such as Nirvana, the Smiths, the Pixies, and others were influenced by the band. Radiohead signed with EMI, one of the biggest and most important global labels in 1991, and the group released many important albums, including *Pablo Honey* (1993), *The Bends* (1994), *OK Computer* (1997), *Kid A* (2000), and *Hail to the Thief* (2003, their last album with EMI). Radiohead absorbed many styles and influences, from early rock bands to grunge to BritPop to hip-hop to electronica, and constant experimentation has kept the group's music fresh and innovative.

FIGURE 10.1 *Radiohead*

The Old Marketing Model

Radiohead had a contract with a major record label, the desire of all aspiring musicians, at the time the band formed. The marketing and distribution model for their music, and for the entire music industry, was outdated and archaic, and was rooted in the pre-Napster and pre-file-sharing era of the early 2000s. Radiohead's contract with EMI expired in 2003 with the release of *Hail to the Thief*.

The music-marketing model for bands like Radiohead was in need of a change. Artists were tied to record companies; they would tour to support record sales. For weeks or months before the release of a recording, it was publicized, with the goal of peaking excitement days before release. The idea was that on the day of release, people would go out and buy the CD. This model worked in the days of analog recordings but not so well in the digital age. The issue was leaks, which were common with digital products and the multiple ways that digital recordings could be copied and distributed. Radiohead music had been leaked beginning with *Kid A*, and all of their recordings since.

The New Marketing Model

In 2007, the band found itself without a contract, and the group had built a studio in order to have more control over recordings; the studio equipment included a server. The conditions were optimal for the band to experiment with something new. On October 10, 2007, Radiohead released the album *In Rainbows* as a digital download on its website, asking downloaders to "pay what you want" (*Huffington Post*, 2011). The results were interesting:

FIGURE 10.2 *Radiohead at Le Zénith in Paris in 2016*

- The album had 1.2 million downloads in the first month;
- 40% of those who downloaded the album paid an average of $6.00;
- $1,200,000 \cdot 40\% \cdot \$6.00 = \$2.88$ million in the first month from downloads alone.

The CD version went on sale on January 1, 2008, and hit #1 on the UK Album Chart and the U.S. Billboard 200. It sold 122,000 copies in the first week, and there were 28,000 downloads on iTunes. In total, there were three million total sales of *In Rainbows* (downloads, CDs and box sets). The pay-what-you-want download revenue exceeded revenue from CD and box set sales (300,000 box sets sold at $80 each), and pay-what-you-want download revenue exceeded total revenue from the group's pervious album, *Hail to the Thief*.

This change in music marketing had a tremendous effect on both record distribution and on the financial model for live concerts. Music release became a tool to stimulate interest in live shows. Other bands followed this new distribution and live-performance model, and it became the norm for a large portion of the music industry. In an interview with *Rolling Stone*, Thom Yorke said that "at the moment we make money principally from touring." Yorke also stated in an interview with Wired Magazine:

> *The only reason we could even get away with this, the only reason anyone even gives a shit, is the fact that we've gone through the whole mill of the business in the first place. It's not supposed to be a model for anything else. It was simply a response to a situation. We're out of contract. We have our own studio. We have this new server. What the hell else would we do? This was the obvious thing. But it only works for us because of where we are.*

Necessity Meets Technology

FIGURE 10.3 *The iPod family*

Why does this new model work? The answer is in the new and multiple ways that people listen to music, most importantly the mp3 player such as the iPod. This new portability eliminated the physical restrictions of the CD. Although there were portable music players for individual use before the iPod (the Sony Walkman, Discman, etc.), this new technology meant that listeners could have multiple copies on many devices, could listen to music in any setting they wish, and could have their music with them at all times. The downside to it is that the compression and distortion of mp3 recordings diminished the quality of the music product. Also lost is much of the social component of the music listening experience. Music technology and a new marketing model came of age at the same time. The result is new means and ideas for music distribution and music enjoyment.

Reading

The reading for this chapter, "Is Radiohead the Pink Floyd of the Twenty-First Century?" discusses Radiohead's importance as a band and the impact that its music has had on popular culture. It compares the band to another British band, Pink Floyd, one of the most important bands of the previous generation. They share much in common, and the reading argues that each occupies a similar place in the rock hierarchy of their times. The author also compares the use of technology by the bands: Pink Floyd was on the cutting edge of using technology in recording and performance for its time, with Radiohead pushing the limits of technology by breaking the mold of the music industry with the pay-what-you-want model for *In Rainbows*.

IS RADIOHEAD THE PINK FLOYD OF THE TWENTY-FIRST CENTURY?

George A. Reisch

The whole point of creating music for me is to give voice to things that aren't normally given voice to, and a lot of those things are extremely negative. Personally speaking, I have to remain positive otherwise I'd go fucking crazy.
—*Thom Yorke, Pitchfork Interview, August 16th, 2008*

All you touch and all you see is all your life will ever be.
—*"Breathe,"* Dark Side of the Moon

Watching Radiohead perform at an outdoor amphitheater, rock critic Jim DeRogatis flashed back to "Pink Floyd at Pompeii," a concert filmed inside an ancient amphitheatre near the famous village. "No other band today," DeRogatis said of Radiohead, "has the power to transport a crowd of more than 30,000 to foreboding alien landscapes and the shadowy places of their nightmares in quite the same way." Radiohead, he concluded, is "the Pink Floyd of Generation Y." Message boards and blogs are filled with similar comparisons. "Radiohead is the new Pink Floyd," they say, or, "Radiohead is *better than* Pink Floyd."

But neither Radiohead nor Pink Floyd—well, Roger Waters, at least—would agree that their music is about remote, interstellar spaces or imaginary, dreamlike experiences. These two bands have earned enormous respect and devotion because their music speaks to things in *this* world. Treating music as an escape, a mere occasion for a party, is *so* off-the-mark in Pink Floyd's case that Waters once became spitting mad at noisy, drunken fans. That episode in 1977 nudged Waters down a creative path that led to *The Wall*—a now classic, double-barreled, four-sided critique of war, cruelty, social conformity, looming madness, and alienation (not aliens).

True, there was a time when Pink Floyd was all about 'space-rock' and psychedelia. Legendary founder Syd Barrett, who died in 2006, pioneered the genre in the mid to late 1960s while Waters and David Gilmour were mainly along for the rocket ride, learning how to set the controls and write songs. Yet after Barrett's demise, Waters took the ship out of interstellar overdrive, turned it around, and headed back to the planet of his earthly obsessions.

Radiohead got their 'space-rock' reputation with *The Bends* (opening with "Planet Telex") and, mainly, *OK Computer*. Pitchfork said the album moves through "space at 1.2 light years per hour," while Qmusic said "the first three tracks (of a five-song, continuous, 25-minute suite that's as brilliant as any music of the last decade) all mention aliens or interstellar activity in some capacity." Amazon.co.uk agrees that "OK Computer heads out into the cold deep space of prog-rock and comes back with stuff that makes mere pop earthlings like Stereophonics tremble." If DeRogatis is right that Radiohead has taken over the 'space-rock' mantle from Pink Floyd, Syd Barrett's famous black cloak—the one he famously wore and sang about in "Bike"—is now draped over Thom Yorke's shoulders. Titles like "Sail to the Moon" and "Black Star" invite the comparison, while "Subterranean Homesick Alien" may even point to Barrett himself. Yorke sings about aliens who "take me onboard their beautiful ship, show me the world as I'd love to see it." When he returns to "tell all [his] friends," they would think that he'd "lost it completely"—"They'd shut me away, but I'd be alright."

But Yorke's interest in spaceships and aliens is like what Barrett said about his cloak. It's "a bit of a joke." As the chapters in this book show, Yorke's lyrics and music speak directly to our lives and times. Pink Floyd may have been "just fantastic" (as the suit in "Have a Cigar" bellowed), but Radiohead has little interest in fantasy, spaceships or aliens. These things which are "not normally given voice to" have long fascinated existentialist and, especially, phenomenological philosophers. They have to do with the world we know and experience, but they *can't* be effectively addressed using ordinary language in ordinary ways.

THE BAND IS JUST PHENOMENOLOGICAL

Why not? Because philosophical phenomenology studies first-person experience *itself,* experience that has not (or not yet) been parsed, chunked, shaded and spun into the words we use to communicate with others and think our private thoughts. Pioneered largely in the twentieth century by French and German philosophers Jean-Paul Sartre, Maurice Merleau-Ponty, Edmund Husserl, and Martin Heidegger, phenomenology studies experience in its pure forms, before it becomes reflected upon, rearranged, remembered and forced into typical models of experience (such as "good," "bad," "romantic," "exciting," "boring," "frightening," and so on). Coming *after* the original experience, all this clumsy discourse usually hides experience, or aspects of it, from our subsequent awareness and understanding. Phenomenology aims to unearth, recover, and understand was we either lose or never pay attention to in the first place.

This phenomenological bent may be familiar if you were once grabbed, startled or terrified by Radiohead's music. Most fans, I suspect, don't gradually warm up to the band. Instead, the conversion is sudden and drastic. You probably heard *OK Computer* or *Kid A* and were struck by something vague yet powerful and real—as if Radiohead presented sounds and rhythms from a hidden, subliminal soundtrack that plays just beneath the surface of life. Before I discovered the band, I thought these sounds were subjective and private—the particular sound of my own brain, I figured, humming, popping, and stuttering through life. But when *OK Computer* plays, my neurons seem to hum along with music they have *always* known. However you try to describe it, Radiohead makes sense almost immediately—musically, despite complex time signatures, and emotionally, even though the words are often obscure and drenched in sound. It also makes political sense (and I don't mean simply "*Hail to the Thief*") though I didn't realize that until reading and editing several of the essays in this book. Do you know that strangely menacing-yet-beautiful, scary-yet-uplifting sound the world makes? You're not alone.

CREEPING TOWARD PHENOMENOLOGY

If you doubt this phenomenological quality of Radiohead's music, take stock of what their major albums are *not* about. Start with their breakthrough hit "Creep" from 1992. "Creep" is about adolescent despair and alienation over a girl. Indeed, there's no phenomenology here because the song is Radiohead's rewrite of a song written many times before about an unavailable goddess. She "floats like a feather" and her skin makes Yorke cry. But once she sees him, she runs away (because he's "a creep, a weirdo"). And that's it. There's no "Pretty Woman" change of fortune here. She just keeps running and does not "come walking back" (as she does for Roy Orbison).

With one exception, "Creep" has almost nothing to do with the phenomenological tilt of post-*Bends* Radiohead.[1] In *The Bends*, they began to move away from pop's usual concerns with standard, pre-packaged experiences and emotions (romance, sex, peace-and-love (or God), rejection, denouncement, infatuation). And by *Kid A*, they had entirely abandoned them to explore the original qualities and textures of the world we live in. It was as if they opened a musical trap door, hidden to most pop bands, leading down below life's ordinary stage—on which the Beatles, Stones and Roy Orbison sang about girls and Roger Waters sang about death, money, capitalism, and madness—where we can see the wires, conduits, and neuronal loops that make it possible for us perceive and have consciousness of *anything at all*. Down here, the 'space-rock' label is meaningless. Words are meaningless.

STANDING ON THE EDGE AND LOOKING UNDERNEATH

What you hear there beneath these floorboards is often scary and intimidating. A friend of mine says the opening piano chords of "Karma Police" make the hairs on his neck stand up. I know exactly what he means. Radiohead is the only band that matters because their music, so oriented to these fundamental aspects of experience, often points to what is worrisome and foreboding in the very look and feel of modern life.

Take "No Surprises." At first, Yorke seems to offer a parody or satire, strung together out of political and cultural clichés about home, security, and routine:

> bring down the government, … they don't speak for us.

> A job that slowly kills you; bruises that won't heal.

> No alarms and no surprises; such a pretty house and such a pretty garden.

Yet wrapped in the plinkety-plink-plink music of a nursery rhyme or music box, the lyrics become less sarcastic (like The Kink's "Shangri-la") and more a study in the political infantilization—by cliché, chit-chat, conventional wisdom, and routine—of adults either unable or unwilling to live freely and

---

1   *The exception is Jonny Greenwood's brittle, abrupt, and arresting power chords that stumble into the song's chorus. Especially on first hearing, they sound as if your stereo or iPod is making strange noises. They push you closer to your original sensations to question or relocate the boundaries of the sound and your perceptions of it.*

creatively. Grant Gee's video (in which Yorke sings the song with his head inside a glass or plastic sphere—more diving bell than space suit—that slowly fills with water) shows that these voting, mortgage-holding, commuters are drowning in passivity, ignorance, and denial. The truth voiced here is breathtaking, literally, since no description or analysis can match its musical and visual punch.

SUBTERRANEAN HOMESICK TECHNOLOGY

Next to these false promises of domestic happiness, Yorke's lyrics often point to the fragility of our advanced, technological civilization. "Infrastructure will collapse," he sings in "House of Cards," while *OK Computer* begins with a car crash—

> In a fast German car
>
> I'm amazed that I survived
>
> An airbag saved my life. ("Airbag")

Midway through the album, we fight depression and alienation fed by

> Transport, motorways and tramlines,
>
> starting and then stopping,
>
> taking off and landing,
>
> the emptiest of feelings. ("Let Down")

And, near the end, we find ourselves in a crashed airplane ("Lucky").

While clearly suspicious of technology, Radiohead still has a special credibility in this arena because they have so embraced technology as a creative tool. Their tastes in musical software, hardware and even antique electronic instruments (such as the Theremin-like Ondes Martenot that Jonny Greenwood plays) are omnivorous.

Pink Floyd were also renowned for their use of technology—projectors for their light shows, echo machines, Syd Barrett's famous cigarette-lighter guitar slide, *Dark Side*'s synthesizer-based "On the Run," and lots and lots of amplifiers. Part of Floyd's early musical innovation, as Edward Macan argued (in *Pink Floyd and Philosophy*), was their commitment to electronic musical experimentation.[2] Songs like "Set the Controls for the Heart of the Sun" and "Interstellar Overdrive" build to jarring, disorienting crescendos (Macan calls them "breakthrough" moments) that take away your musical roadmaps and preconceptions in a bid to shock, awaken, and rearrange your perceptual capacities. If "Karma Police" seems scary, listen to "Careful with that Axe, Eugene!"

But the messages about modern life and technology from Pink Floyd and Radiohead point in different directions and take their logic from different cultural circumstances. Barrett's penchant for musical exploration was embraced by the emerging LSD-thirsty London counterculture not many years after postwar rationing and bread lines had finally subsided in the 1950s. In postwar England, in other words, there were plenty of reasons to musically dream about far-away, fantastic

---

2   *"Theodor Adorno, Pink Floyd, and the Psychedelics of Alienation," in Pink Floyd and Philosophy: Careful with that Axiom, Eugene! (Open Court, 2007), pp. 95–119.*

places. Barrett and his band used far-out, fantastic electronics to do just that. Under Waters, as Macan explains, Floyd's radical *musical* explorations of alienation gave way to *lyrical* indictments of education, capitalism and other human institutions. With aggressive nuclear powers to the east and west eyeing each other suspiciously through the 1970s and 1980s, Waters was less interested in conjuring psychedelic, transformative possibilities than in directly criticizing the oppressive, limiting realities he observed around him.

But these realities had vanished by the time *OK Computer* took the world by storm, some twenty-four years after *Dark Side* was released. The Berlin Wall and the Soviet Union were gone, the Balkan nations felt liberated, and many hoped that cold-war fears and insecurities would be a merely sad chapter in modern history. But new threats and demons emerged (such as war and ethnic cleansing in the Balkans and Africa, climate change, persistent disease and poverty, and new extremes in corporate greed, Enron-style). What made the post-cold-war world seem especially sinister, however, was the continued growth of a new kind of technology—information technology—that made Moog synthesizers seem quaint and harmless. The computers, networks, and databases that once may have promised greater efficiencies and global prosperity (at least until Kubrick's *2001* planted some doubt), that promised to make us fitter, happier, and safer in our homes, in our pretty little gardens, and in our selves, instead seemed to take over and reshape the way the world looks and feels.

EVERYTHING IS NOT OK, COMPUTER

Worries about the corrosive social and political effects of technology are not new. The rise of television and mass media in the 1950s caused some people to worry that democracy would atrophy if so many were exposed to information presented and controlled by so few. Sociologist C. Wright Mills delineated the tacit partnership of the military, the government, and business corporations in his celebrated book, *The Power Elite*. Herbert Marcuse's *One-Dimensional Man* argued similarly that magazines, television, and radio promoted a consumerism that suppresses genuine political freedom:

> Our society distinguishes itself by conquering the centrifugal social forces with Technology rather than Terror, on the dual basis of an overwhelming efficiency and an increasing standard of living. … In the medium of technology, culture, politics, and the economy merge into an omnipresent system which swallows up or represses all alternatives.[3]

More recently, Noam Chomsky has detailed the "manufacturing" of political consent in America and the West by elites who impose not only facts and figures on the public but that particular *feeling*, fed by technologically-enabled media, that ordinary citizens are incapable of criticism or dissent:

> It is an important feature of the ideological system to impose on people the feeling that they are incompetent to deal with these complex and important issues; they'd better leave it to the captain. One device is to develop a star

---

3   Herbert Marcuse, *One-Dimensional Man* (Beacon Press 1964), pp. x, xvi.

system, an array of figures who are often media creations or creations of the academic propaganda establishment, whose deep insights we are supposed to admire and to whom we must happily and confidently assign the right to control our lives and control international affairs. ... we poor slobs ought to just watch, not interfere.[4]

Chomsky's interest in this feeling takes him a step toward Radiohead (which is perhaps why this passage is quoted inside the *Airbag/How Am I Driving?* EP). The intellectual who has perhaps come closest, however, is Mills, who grounded his sociological and ideological analyses of modern life in what he called its "tang and feel." In a lecture from 1954, he asked his audience,

> What is the tang and feel of our experience as we examine the world about us today? It is clear that these feelings are shaping the way we ask and the way we answer all the questions of this conference.[5]

Mills had in mind two particular fears of cold-war life associated with technology and the national press—nuclear annihilation and rampant McCarthyism. But his own description of what it was like to be alive in the early 1950s expresses more broadly the anxiety of anyone who resists Marcuse's one-dimensional culture of conformity, of one who resists Chomsky's feeling that dissent implies incompetence, or of one who, like Yorke, worries that he's going crazy because important and disturbing things that *should* be said about life simply aren't. Mills said,

> We are often stunned and we are often distracted, and we are bewildered almost all of the time. And the only weapon we have—as individuals and as a scatter of grouplets—is the delicate brain now so perilously balanced in the struggle for public sanity. ... We feel that we are living in a world in which the citizen has become a mere spectator or a forced actor, and that our personal experience is politically useless and our political will a minor illusion. ... We feel that distrust has become nearly universal among men of affairs and that the spread of public anxiety is poisoning human relations and drying up the roots of private freedom. (pp. 184–85).

WHO ARE YOUR REAL FRIENDS?

Decades later, in the age of personal computers and the internet, this distrust and anxiety has found new, technology-based roots that seem to control and restrict our social, economic and emotional lives. One example is the word "friends" and the meanings, associations, and obligations lately accrued to it. Friends now refers to persons one has never seen or talked to in person. They have instead posted a few kilobytes of data or a hyperlink to the public advertisements of ourselves that most of us (under a certain age, at least) create online. To maintain those advertisements and the desirable contacts and social opportunities they bring, we must in turn

---

4   J. Peck, ed., *The Chomsky Reader*, pp. 42–43

5   *Mills and Mills, eds. C. Wright Mills: Letters and Autobiographical Writings (University of California Press, 2000), p. 184.*

maintain certain schedules (lest your inbox overflow, or friends feel unwelcome or alienated by a late response), regularly purchase (or usually re-purchase) software (since you must have an up-to-date version), wait (for batteries to recharge, operating systems to load, downloads to complete), and remain ever vigilant about being tricked or impersonated by thieves in far away places who continually scrutinize computer networks and patiently wait (like a wolf outside your door) for a slip-up, a password or credit card number revealed, allowing them to intercept your electronic payments, empty your bank account, and ruin your credit rating—essential, after all, for your continued participation in the consumer economy—that is monitored, adjusted, and sold for profit to interested parties by three large corporations known as Experian, Equifax and Transunion.

Yet, despite these and other interlinked anxieties of our internet-age (spam, phishing, cyber-stalking, cyber-bullying, and so on), very few (myself included) are willing to renounce the internet, cell phones, satellite downloads and live without the computers, email, instant messaging, countless channels of television, online games and all the other fixtures we are accustomed to. It seems, just as Marcuse predicted, that we can see no viable alternatives to the efficient, technologically rational system of life we are caught up in.

Paranoid or not, we may already be androids. One of phenomenology's basic insights is that the conscious self is connected to, shaped by, and possibly even *constituted by*, the intentionality and purposiveness of first person experience. We—our selves, our souls, our minds—do not exist independently of our bodies and our material experience in the world. Descartes, for instance, was wrong to reason as he did in his *Meditations* that "I exist" and *then, subsequently*, convince himself that the exterior world he saw around him was in fact real and that his senses could be trusted. Instead, the "I" that experiences the world is always embodied. Being, Heidegger insisted, must always be understood as "Being-in-the-world"; and for Merleau-Ponty, "the subject that I am, when taken concretely, is inseparable from this body and this world."[6]

Our ever deepening dependence and engagement with the technologies of modern life, therefore, may lead to changes in our selves, *to* ourselves, that we might in fact reject or regret were we to understand them and see them for what they are. Like the people in Jamie Thrave's video for "Just," we might all collapse in shock or despair were we to face some truths about ourselves—truths that we never paid attention to, that no one ever talked about, even though they were obvious and in front of our faces all along. What would really hurt, of course, is realizing that that we'd done it to ourselves. By embracing and immersing ourselves in technology, we'd turned ourselves into machine-like and soulless androids.

WHERE PINK FLOYD ENDS AND RADIOHEAD BEGINS

Radiohead's music, then, points to concerns about contemporary technology that only partly overlap the foreboding and shadowy landscapes once conjured by Pink Floyd. For Radiohead, technology is not simply a tool to artistically depict a corrupted world in need of cultural and political reform (as it was for Waters) or to escape ordinary perceptions (as it was for Barrett). For

6 *The Phenomenology of Perception (Routledge, 2002), p. 475.*

Radiohead's classic albums are filled with a phenomenological curiosity about the technology that has become the medium through which we experience life itself, saturated as our senses are by information, appliances, antibiotics, advertisements, and videotape.

Yet there remains something in Radiohead rooted in that magical, nostalgia-inspiring decade of Syd Barrett and Pink Floyd, moon-landings, and the ecology movement sparked by Rachel Carson's *Silent Spring.*. In "The Bends," Yorke sings "I wish it was the Sixties," but, in fact, it still is. Stephen Still's iconic "There's something happening here/what it is ain't exactly clear" has become Yorke's "I'm not here, this isn't happening" (from *Kid A*'s "How to Disappear Completely") or "something big is gonna happen" (from *Hail to the Thief*'s "Go to Sleep"). Some of these chapters use existentialism, psychoanalytic theory, or theology to explore the possible transformations that may be afoot. Others take up the ethical complexities—environmental and economic, mainly—of the music industry and what it may evolve into (in light of the controversial pay-what-you-want model for *In Rainbows*). Others address the politics latent in *Hail to the Thief*, the human-machine interface explored by *OK Computer*, *Kid A*, and *Amnesiac*, and the ways that the band's music takes us from Aristotelian tragedy to what it might mean for Martin Heidegger to press a button on his postmodern iPod.

There may even be a small but important truth behind the 'space-rock' idea, after all. For if Yorke's occasional references to spaceships and planets are understood phenomenologically, as I've been suggesting, then the possibilities for experience, understanding and political engagement lurking in Radiohead's music and explored in these chapters may be a *metaphorical* space ship ride—not toward the insanity lurking on the dark side of the moon, however. Like early Pink Floyd, we've set the controls so the light of the sun will enlighten us about what kinds of worlds and what kinds of experience are out there. If we pay close enough attention, we may find our way to a better, less terrifying, and previously unknown planet Earth.

Questions for thought

- Why did Radiohead implement the pay-what-you-want model for *In Rainbows*? What do you think of the group's reasoning?
- What technologies allowed Radiohead to try this model of distribution, both in terms of Radiohead and music listeners?
- How much did the band earn with the online, pay-what-you-want model? How did that compare with previous albums?
- What characteristics do Radiohead and Pink Floyd share?
- Do you agree with the author that Radiohead is the Pink Floyd of its generation? If so, why? Can you provide two reasons why you think so?

Activity:

The article for this chapter compares the importance of Radiohead and Pink Floyd. Listen to *Dark Side of the Moon* by Pink Floyd and *In Rainbows* by Radiohead on YouTube, Spotify, or another streaming service. Compare the recordings. Are the bands similar musically? If so, how? Can you hear any influence by Pink Floyd on Radiohead in its music?

References

Huffington Post. "HuffPost Game Changers: Who Is the Ultimate Game Changer in Entertainment?" Updated May 25, 2011. https://www.huffingtonpost.com/2009/10/01/huffpost-game-changers-wh_n_303630.html?show_slideshow_ads=1&slidenumber=4&slideshow=true#gallery/2814/6.

Figure Credits

Fig. 10-1: Copyright © Samuel Wiki (CC by 2.5) at https://commons.wikimedia.org/wiki/File:Radiohead.jpg.

Fig. 10-2: Copyright © David Urrea (CC BY-SA 4.0) at https://commons.wikimedia.org/wiki/File:Radiohead_second_show_at_Le_Zénith_in_Paris._May_24th_2016.jpg.

Fig. 10-3: Copyright © Kyro (CC by 3.0) at https://commons.wikimedia.org/wiki/File:IPod_family.png.

CHAPTER ELEVEN

Exporting Rap: Hip-Hop Goes Global

FIGURE 11.1 *Map of Europe*

Introduction

Hip-hop culture and rap are global phenomena found on all of the continents (except perhaps Antarctica, but it is probably there too!), in the developed and undeveloped world, in its original form and in hybrids with local ideas. It originated in the United States, first in urban areas such as New York and Los Angeles, spreading quickly across the country, changing and evolving through time and place. It remains an important part of American culture and has become ubiquitous globally. This chapter examines hip-hop and rap as global phenomena that show no signs of abating, using hip-hop in Europe as a model for the ways in which this style has been borrowed, adapted, and adopted in global music culture.

As music moves from one place to another, it is usually a complex process. This reterritorialization usually takes place gradually, commonly in the three steps of *transculturation*, *hybridization*, and *indigenization*. Transculturation is the "process in which cultural forms literally move through time and space where they interact with other cultural forms, influence each other, and produce new forms." As these imported forms interact with existing tradition, there is a "mixture of new and familiar forms that leads to the formation of cultural hybrids," or hybridization. Over time, imported cultural forms take on local features, often emancipated from the mother culture into a new, unique local form, a process known as indigenization (Lull 1995, 153-155). Taken together, these three steps can be simplified to borrow, adapt, and adopt.

These processes can explain the formation of many cultural forms throughout the world. An example of how this process can shape music and culture is rap, or hip-hop culture. As American rap moved throughout the world by various means of dissemination, it underwent the changes that these processes imply:

- Rap was borrowed and sampled uncritically in an almost slavish imitation of the American form;
- Other cultures adapted items from rap, a cultural tradition different from the one which they are a part, forming cultural blends demonstrating features of the old and new;
- Rap was adopted by the new culture in a new form, this modification leading to new sub-styles still recognizable as rap.

Hip-Hop in Europe

In Europe, rap was embraced most strongly among the immigrant populations that make up much of the lower classes. French and German rap are dominated by immigrants to the point that roughly 90% of French recordings were performed by immigrants or the children of immigrants, mostly of Arab and African origin, reflective of the colonial presence in these regions

FIGURE 11.2 *Break Dancer in Hamburg, Germany*

and the subsequent immigration after independence; in Germany, the number is more than half, mostly of Turkish origin although many are Italian. In southern Europe, the numbers are quite different, in this case because of the economic strife and the resulting limited immigration to countries such as Spain, Italy, and Greece, and thereby limiting immigrant participation in rap.

Rap in Europe is most closely associated with urban settings, or more accurately sub-urban, since suburbs tend to be populated by lower-class populations, many of which are immigrants. This music can be heard regularly in cities such as Marseilles, Hamburg, Berlin and Madrid, among many others. This, again, is reflective of colonialization and post-colonial migration and did much to change the racial and cultural mix of Europe. On the periphery of many European cities, the landscape is little like the postcard settings in the old parts of cities. Many dwellings are in government-subsidized high-rise buildings, creating pockets of ethnicity, with sights and sounds often not familiar to non-immigrants.

Language is one of the ways that local rap is both like and unlike the American models on which it is based. There is no single language variety, often drawing from regional, social, and ethnic dialects. Regional dialects tend to be strongest in Germany and Italy: in a sample of Italian songs, almost half had dialectal features; some are completely in dialect. English is also used a great deal as well, with most French, German, and Italian songs containing some elements of English, usually having some connection with hip-hop culture. Words such as "freestyle," "diss," "funk," and "skills" are often worked into lyrics, as are words such as "bitch," "blunt," "shit" and "yo." Sometimes English words are translated while maintaining the directness of the English original (for example, in Germany the use of "shit" and its translation "sheiss").

Although rap has been around in Europe since the 1980s, it rarely found its way to the music charts. Much like bhangra in England, this was to a large part due to the means of distribution, usually not in record stores, where sales could be tracked, but instead on the street, out of car trunks, and in clubs. Early on, rap reproduced the themes encountered in American rap, including an opposition to social order and the political and economic systems, oppression of minorities, and the hardships of everyday life in the suburbs.

Le Hip-Hop: Rap in France

France has a long history of American cultural influence. Jazz was embraced after World War I and took on the French moniker of "le jazz hot." World War II brought the decimation of the French entertainment industry, with American film and music filling the void. Rock, punk, and disco also found a home in France. Rap was no exception, and French rap fit into the model of borrow, adapt, and adopt. French artists in rap borrowed from African-American forms, the process facilitated by international record distribution. They adapted the most attitudes, repertoires, and musical-performance practice from American models, and they adopted the ideals and techniques to their models and to their own tastes and ideas. They see themselves as natural commentators and observers of a seldom-seen world, expressing in their music the poverty, violence, and despair so common in their lives. The focus is on social criticism, and since so many rappers are from immigrant backgrounds, topics include xenophobia, racism, and discrimination. In the 1990s, a small number of "native" French rappers undertook a movement of "national" rap, reacting against immigrants dominating hip-hop, trying to inject Gallic elements in to rap.

Rap challenged the elitist rock and roll of the 1970s and established itself as an important part of the French musical and cultural scene. French artists and producers used the same techniques and equipment as was used in American rap, including turntables, records, and computers. Break dancing was popular for a time, and taggers, or graffiti artists, actually have official recognition as street artists. Stylistically and musically, however, rap in France is not significantly different from rap in the United States and other countries.

By the 1990s, rap and hip-hop culture were well established in Europe, as it was throughout the world. Hip-hop culture was transmitted to

FIGURE 11.3 *Tagging in Paris*

new societies (transculturation) and was actively performed and adjusted to local tastes as it blended with local music to create new forms (hybridization) to the point that it became part of the fabric of local cultures (indigenization).

Reading

The reading for this chapter, "Hip-hop as a Global Cultural Phenomenon: The Export and Appropriation of Contradiction, Complexity, and Dialogue," examines hip-hop and rap in this global context, focusing on parts of Europe, England, and the United States. It starts with an exploration of the history and development of hip-hop in the United States, beginning in New York and spreading throughout the country. This is followed by a "Hip-hop Travelogue" in which the author cites scholars' explorations of hip-hop's stylistic connections to earlier musical traditions, (interestingly, including Italian opera) as he moves through hip-hop in Germany, Ireland, Italy, and elsewhere. The reading includes a section that discusses means by which to analyze cultural production in order to understand the diversity of hip-hop genres and sub-genres that developed around the world.

HIP-HOP AS A GLOBAL CULTURAL PHENOMENON

Peter Webb

THE EXPORT AND APPROPRIATION OF CONTRADICTION, COMPLEXITY, AND DIALOGUE
INTRODUCTION

Hip-hop has become a global cultural phenomenon. From America to Britain, South America, Europe, South East Asia, to parts of Africa, hip-hop has seeped into the consciousness of areas of popular music and cultural life the world over. When assessing how hip-hop has traversed its way around the globe we firstly have to remember that hip-hop originated in the centre of neo-liberal capitalism: the USA. Secondly, we have to remember that it arose from within particular cultural groupings that had experienced life in the specific cultural context of the different parts of America in which they had lived and that initially this was dominated by Black Afro-American experience and culture. In this chapter I aim to concentrate on those parts of the world that have developed their own distinctive variants of hip-hop, look at the genesis of this form, and assess what it might tell us about hip-hop as a global cultural phenomenon, its global reach and how best to research it. I have chosen hip-hop as one element of the musical palette that has become prominent in popular music production in the UK. I could have chosen reggae/ska, Punk, jazz, house, or indie, but have used hip-hop as the example as it, in particular, has been a genre of huge influence. I want to show the complexity of the movement of one type of music around the globe and then how it settles in areas and is used differently by people in particular cultural contexts. Bristol's rise to prominence as a popular music centre has happened through a number of artists who have used elements of hip-hop as the base root or as the backbone of their music. Britain's own developed dance genres of trip-hop, drum and bass, and breakbeat have all used hip-hop's aural sensibilities as a backbone of the music. Artists as diverse as Soul to Soul, Massive Attack, Portishead, Goldie, Reprazent, Dizzie Rascal, The Chemical Brothers, Roots Manuva, and many others have all used hip-hop as an influential music. Earlier artists like The Clash and Malcolm Maclaren were influential in bringing hip-hop to the UK and adapted hip-hop into their musical output and style. They also brought graffiti artists to the UK in the early 1980s. The first UK hip-hop acts, like London's Newtrament and the Rapologists in the early 1980s, through to the London Posse, MC Mello, The Cookie Crew, and the Demon Boys in the late 1980s, developed the form in a uniquely British style. I want to show how musical forms like hip-hop travel and develop around the globe and how they are accessed and developed by specific milieux in particular locations. I concentrate on three examples of hip-hop; those that have developed in parts of Europe, the UK, and the USA. I start with an outline of the development of hip-hop as a cultural phenomenon in New York in the United States.

THE DEVELOPMENT OF HIP-HOP AS A CULTURAL PHENOMENON

The geneses of hip-hop variants in countries where this musical genre has been developed and modified have the same familiar starting points, i.e., the export of the peculiar cultural formation that is the USA and the contradictions and complexity that hip-hop so particularly contained. David Toop at the end of the first chapter of his book *Rap Attack* (Toop, 1984) suggests that whatever the disagreements about hip-hop's lineage, most commentators are agreed on one thing:

> 'Rap is nothing new,' says Paul Winley. Rap's forebears stretch back through disco, street funk, radio DJs, Bo Diddley, the bebop singers, Cab Calloway, Pigmeat Markham, the tap dancers and comics, The Last Poets, Gil Scott-Heron, Muhammad Ali, acappella and doo-wop groups, ring games, skip rope rhymes, prison and army songs, toasts, signifying and the dozens, all

the way to the griots of Nigeria and the Gambia. No matter how far it pen-
etrates into the twilight maze of Japanese video games and cool European
electronics, its roots are still the deepest in all contemporary Afro-American
music. (Toop, 1984, p. 19)

This amalgamation of influences and lines of development had particular potency in the urban
centres of America, particularly in the Bronx, New York. Here these particular elements came
to deliver a specific sound and aesthetic through the inspiration and talents of figures like Kool
Herc, Africa Bambaataa, Grandmaster Flash, Jazzy Jay, and Red Alert, to name but a few. These
individuals developed a form of DJing, using two turntables and finding 'breakbeats' in particular
tracks that when mixed together back and forth over the same pattern would keep a crowd
dancing. They would DJ at parties or 'jams' either indoors or outside with a large mobile sound
system. This type of sound system has its own origins in Jamaica, developing out of the need for
Jamaicans to hear music that was being produced in an expanding number of studios but that
wasn't being played on the radio (see Davis and Simon, 1979, and the film *Rockers*). However
even Jamaican sound systems and the music that would come to be associated with them, i.e.,
reggae, developed out of Jamaicans listening to American R&B and soul (Davis and Simon, 1979).
Nelson George in his *Hip-Hop America* (George, 1999) traces these influences when talking about
the beginnings of hip-hop:

> Very significant, but little appreciated outside New York's Caribbean commu-
> nity at the time, was the introduction of the Jamaican "sound system" style
> to the city's party going mix. The "dub" style of these mobile DJs stripped
> away melody to give reggae's deep, dark grooves throbbing prominence.
> In ganja-filled gatherings, pioneering sound system DJs such as King Tubby,
> Prince Buster and Duke Reid created massive, rumbling sounds that elevated
> them to a star status rivalling the club DJs in the states. (George, 1999, p. 8)

The range of records used within the hip-hop form was phenomenal. DJs would use The
Eagles, The Monkees, Kraftwerk, Billy Squier, James Brown, Motown, and even the Shadows and
Led Zeppelin. MCs or the masters of ceremonies would get the crowd going and then started to
rap over the breaks, providing spoken rhymes, and commentaries about the DJ, the MCs themselves, or their environment and the clientele. The Sugarhill Gang's *Rapper's Delight* was seen
as the first commercial record of this form, the first track to take hip-hop into the national and
then international arena (although it was derided by many of the main players within the growing
hip-hop community). The second track of major influence and importance was Grandmaster Flash
and the Furious Fives' *The Message*. The track contained a rap that would leave its mark on the
consciousness of America and then other countries around the world as it was exported. The lines
"don't push me cause I'm close to the edge / I'm trying not to loose my head na ha ha ha / its
like a jungle sometimes I often wonder how I keep from going under" illustrated one element of
the experience of many who lived in sprawling urban metropolises and who didn't have access to
the economic capital much vaunted by the American dream. Creativity was central to the hip-hop
scene, and the main four elements of the form, b'boying (break dancing), graffitti, MCing (master

of ceremonies/rapping), and turntablism or DJing, were much in evidence in New York and other parts of America.

The culture industry, excited by the success of *Rapper's Delight,* began to make films about the phenomenon. Charlie Ahearn's *Wild Style* (1982) and Harry Belafonte's *Beat Street* (1984) were two films that exported not just the music but the other elements of the scene to an international audience. These two films are mentioned by most studies of hip-hop as a major influence on the formation of the scene. The development of hip-hop in America has been well documented by Toop (1984), George (1999), Rose (1994), et al. What I'm interested in here, in the context of this chapter, is the transference of hip-hop to other cultural arenas, the way that specific milieu developed, and what these trajectories can tell us about globalisation. I use the term 'arenas' as it suggests enclosures or platforms usually surrounded by seats in which events take place and also spheres of intense activity. It gives us an image of what a particular cultural space is like and how it can be conceptualised.

HIP-HOP TRAVELOGUE: WORLDWIDE VARIANTS

Tony Mitchell (Mitchell, 1996) outlines how rap was seen from the USA as being a hugely successful export that was imitated and followed fanatically within other countries. The dominant theory was that hip-hop was an African-American musical genre, with its own reference points and peculiarities, that was appropriated by other cultures. The style, the aesthetic, the politics, the musical reference points were all studiously replicated and repackaged in a form that could be accessible to the cultural formation that its devotees lived in. Mitchell quotes Jay Cocks's article, from *Time* magazine, which was curious about international variants of hip-hop but also triumphant about the original version; hip-hop was described as "now possibly the most successful American export this side of the microchip, permeating, virtually dominating, world-wide youth culture" (Mitchell, 1996, p. 38). He also quotes the French rapper, MC Solaar: "Parisian Rap is pretty much a US branch office. We copy everything, don't we?" (Mitchell, 1996, p. 38). Two years later Solaar was to say something very different: "Sometimes I'm proud to say I'm doing French music, French rap, because none of the tracks we do are imitations. We listen to West Coast, Acid Jazz, hip-hop, hardcore … and we do something totally different" (Mitchell, 1996, p. 38). Mitchell goes on to describe and study the developments of hip-hop in a number of countries; especially detailed accounts of the scenes in Italy and New Zealand illustrate the complexity and contradiction of the appropriation of this form. Italian hip-hop is described as having gone through an initial phase of imitation to creating "its own distinctive and diverse musical culture with its own boasts, taunts, tensions and ideological conflicts" (Mitchell, 1996, p. 166). Leading lights in the scene began to use regional dialects to express particular conflicts that were peculiar to Italy, e.g., the North–South divide and political conflicts with organisations like the Northern League or the MSI. Other posses used popular folk and peasant song as a basis for their raps. New hybrids emerged when acts would combine Neapolitan music, rap, reggae, Algerian Rai, etc., which led to potent original music and discussions of African and Arabic heritage in Italy. These elements also focused particular political and cultural conflicts that were emerging at the time in Italy, pertinently the tensions that were emerging regionally in the country and the crisis of the parties of the mainstream left and the mainstream right. These political tensions were beginning to see themselves felt all over Europe throughout the 1990s. Mitchell discusses how hip-hop's rapping style had echoes in Italian culture; ritual insults and verbal jousting were very much a part of washerwomen dialogue portrayed in Baroque madrigals. Ritual insults that were sung were a feature of popular Roman dialect. Opera had *recitativo secco* (dry recitative), which was accompanied by bass notes from violin or viola. Hip-hop brought its own peculiarly American model to Italy but also tapped into traditions that already had a specific local history. Mitchell's study is a critique of the view that sees "local music as representative of an authentic heritage culture and the global as imposing an inauthentic, artificial culture on local markets" (Mitchell, 1996, p. 264). The reality for Mitchell is a more syncretic music that expresses elements and forms from the US model and develops a music that examines local and global tensions and conflicts in great detail. Mitchell finishes the book by suggesting that the "desirable" outcome of transculturation in popular music is that "a variety of different types of music from different living conditions and musical technologies will emerge, adapting traditional musical forms to new environments" (Mitchell, 1996, p. 265). The term 'hybridisation' is worth using in this context. Developed by both Jan Nederveen Pieterse (2003) and Ulf Hannerz (1993, 1996), it refers to the creation of dynamic mixed cultures or cultural forms, the combining of cultures from two or more parent cultures.

Dietmar Elflein and Andrew Bennett have both looked at the development of hip-hop in Germany (Elflein, 1999; Bennett, 2000). Again crucial in the development of the German scene were the films *Wild Style* (1982) and *Beat Street* (1984) and the initial more commercial records like the Sugarhill Gang's *Rappers Delight*. Elflein quotes McPois of an East Berlin hip-hop crew: "I got all my tricks out of *Beat Street*. I used to watch the movie everyday on the video" (Elflein, 1999, p. 256). Bennett discusses how the location of American army bases in and around the city of Frankfurt led to a growing influence of American culture and particularly hip-hop. GIs would play soul, funk, and rap and then local clubs would do the same. The global reach of America in the forms of its cultural products and its citizens had a massive impact on the host population. What then becomes interesting about the German scene is the way that it develops.

Elflein discusses the emergence of two main strands in German hip-hop; these were concretised by the emergence of two compilation records. The first, called *Krauts with Attitude–German Hip-Hop Vol. 1* (released in 1991), was a compilation of West German acts. It was partly an homage to the America that these particular crews respected, e.g. the title is an adaptation of Niggaz with Attitude, a highly controversial Californian act that were partly responsible for defining the subgenre in hip-hop of Gangsta Rap. It was also a firm statement of German intent. This was the German crews putting down their own marker on the scene and saying that they were just as good as their American counterparts. This developed into a boastful nationalism; the terms 'hip-hop in Germany' turned to '100% German hip-hop' and then 'Deutsche hip-hop.' After the success of a crew called the Fantastischen 4, a more pop friendly act, the terms 'Neuer Deutsche Sprechsgesang' (new German recitative) and 'Neue Deutsche Reinkultur' (new German poetry) were used in the press and expressed the emphasis on national competitiveness of this part of the hip-hop scene.

A second compilation that showed the diversity of the German scene was released in 1995. The compilation called *Cartel* had a red background, with the C for Cartel displayed like an Islamic crescent. The cover bore some resemblance to the Turkish flag and was a conscious attempt by the management of the acts to create an alternative to the 'Neue Deutsche Sprachgesang.' Although the groups themselves were of mixed ethnic backgrounds, the Turkish element was dominant and the 'gastarbeiter' status of Turks in Germany was something that was a central feature of the music and raps. The album sold massively in Turkey (300,000 copies) but only modestly in Germany (20,000 copies). The raps and the combination of musical themes that were used by these crews reflected more locally specific issues of life patterns. Elflein quotes a crew called *Islamic Force* explaining their concept:

> Bob B: We do it in Germany, originating from Turkey and using an American Black style of music and Turkish melodies.
>
> Derezone: It was a deliberate decision not to produce music that would storm the charts.
>
> Cut Mtee: The new hype: oriental hip-hop or so. Boe B: The boy comes home and listens to hip-hop. Then his father comes along saying: "Come on boy, we go shopping," enters the car and listens to Turkish music. And then he acquires our record and gets both styles in one. (Elflein, 1999, p. 263)

Again what had happened in this scene was that initially hip-hop crews had imitated their US counterparts, but as the scene developed, their own localised situation and references became more influential in the music and the content. Rapping in Turkish and German discussed issues that were relevant to their particular circumstances, i.e., gastarbeiter status, racism, exclusion, nationalism, neighbourhood, and community. It must be stated that significant elements of the American scene remained incredibly influential. The acceptance of the Nation of Islam philosophy (inspired by groups in the US such as Public Enemy and Ice Cube) by the 'Cartel'-oriented crews and the West German scene's infatuation with the 'gangsta rap' subgenre are examples of this. However what becomes clear is that the German hip-hop scene had developed its combination of local, regional and global concerns and elements that marked it out as its own particularly specific milieu. Elflein finishes his article by discussing more variants in the German scene: he talks about crews that weave Ghanaian music into their hip-hop, others with more Jamaican influences, and some with Korean strands, each emphasising difference and variety within the form. This purely stylistic emphasis does, as Bennett suggests (Bennett, 2000, p. 146), ignore some of the more subtle appropriations and adaptations of the form for which he suggests that Robertson's notion of 'glocality' is appropriate. Glocality, according to Robertson is, when a global flow is modified by its contact with the local and made to conform to local conditions in a creative way (Robertson, 1992).

In research I conducted in the city of Bristol, and in the UK more generally, hip-hop has left its own particular mark. Massive Attack, one of Bristol's most successful outfits, emerged at a time when Punk, dub, and hip-hop had its own particular potency in Bristol. Miles Johnson, an original Wild Bunch member (forerunners of Massive Attack), had heard *Planet Rock* by Africa Bambatta and the Soul Sonic Force on John Peel's radio show when he was in prison. This had turned him on to hip-hop. Again the film *Wild Style* was central in giving Miles and other individuals who were to become Massive Attack an idea about the aesthetic of hip hop as well as the music (Johnson, 1996, pp. 83–85). Delge, or 3D as he was known, became a rapper and was a graffitti artist but had been submerged in Bristol's particular dub reggae and Punk scene. Simon Reynolds suggests that:

> In Britain hip hop never assumed the political, counter-cultural role it did in America, but was one of many imports (soul, jazz-funk, dub, Chicago house, Detroit techno) to take its place in the spectrum of 'street beats.' Race is rarely the crucial determinant of unity in British dance scenes (exceptions include swingbeat and dancehall reggae, both of which are based almost entirely around imported African-American and Afro-Caribbean tracks). Instead, what counts is a shared openness to technology and to drugs. And so trip hop and jungle are full of multiracial crews and black/white duos; all-white practitioners don't have to justify themselves like their rare American equivalents do. (Reynolds, 1998, p. 320)

I would suggest that this is only partially correct. One hip-hop act to come partly out of Bristol was Marxman, whose first single *Sad Affair* was banned from radio airplay as it was a comment on the Irish conflict; further singles about slavery, domestic violence, and imperialism followed. What is true is that the multi-ethnic nature of a lot of hip-hop in the UK has led to a very different aesthetic. Massive Attack transformed its combined passions for hip-hop, Punk, dub, and funk into what became known as 'trip-hop.' Other acts have stuck to a more straight hip-hop format musically but often lyrically they emphasise their locality. Parlour Talk is a Bristol based rap duo that discusses the benefits of cider, giros, and various Bristol reference points. Aspects is another almost comic rap crew whose West Country accents and 'whacked out' lyrics present another particular variant on a Bristol theme. These acts illustrate the way in which popular music forms are developed from their own cultural settings and transformed into particular variants that reflect local specificities whilst retaining the frame of reference of the original. Jamie, head of a small Bristol independent hip-hop label, talks about the fact that Britain is so self critical and aware of genres. He released some tracks that he felt were some way between hip-hop and trip-hop and they got criticised for being neither. In the interview that I did with him there is an incredible awareness of the sound of a piece. Production is one element of UK hip-hop that people are especially aware of. This might reflect some of the dominant issues in the British music scene. Production is a very important component of the sensibility. Jamie also has an awareness of how, globally, the specifics of a particular sound get interpreted:

> The Afterhours lot [a Japanese Fanzine and shop that specialises in Bristol music] call us the new Bristol hip-hop, they also call Tricky [termed trip-hop in the UK] hip-hop and I never would. (interview, 13.09.99, Webb)

Within Bristol's music scene there is a constant debate about what hip-hop is and what UK hip-hop represents. Tricky and 3D (from Massive Attack) became respected for their particular West Country mumbling, whispered rapping. These positions are, however, hotly contested by other rappers. The style of rapping can be suggestive of a particular aesthetic or set of characteristics or dispositions of the rapper. Hollis Byrne, ex of Marxman, outlined what he thought of the mumbling rap of Tricky et al. in a track for the group Statik Sound System:

> Offside with Statik is equal to energy/Fat like density/intense like destiny/ with live stuff others huff and puff/mumble over beats you think that's how we speak. (track called 'Mark My Word' from Statik album *My-ooh-zik* released October 2001)

Bennett in his study of hip-hop in Newcastle discusses the constant contestation of what hip-hop means and what it really represents. He quotes a conversation from one of his interviews:

> A.B: There are a lot of white rap fans in Newcastle who are using hip-hop to talk about their own experiences.
>
> Jim: There's no such thing as white hip-hop.
>
> A.B: Why is that?
>
> Jim: Because hip-hop is a black music. As white people we should still respect it as black music.
>
> Jeff: All the time before, white people were into black music, hip-hop's just the same. There's a message in black music, which translates for white working class people.
>
> A.B: What is that?
>
> Dave: It's about being proud of where you come from …
>
> Jeff: Yeah and because it [Black music] offers a strength and intelligence which no British culture does.
>
> Jim: The trend at the moment is to be real … to rap in your own accent and talk about things close to you. … don't try to be American like. But that's why British hip-hop will always be shite … I went to New York, well actually to Cleveland near New York, and stayed with a black family. It was brilliant, it changed my life. You can't talk about white hip-hop, it doesn't exist. (Bennett, 2000)

Jamie from Hombre Records (head of a UK-based hip-hop label that ceased trading in 2002) also is keenly aware of these types of debate. Genres are elements of fields of production (Bourdieu) where the rules and critiques sometimes strangle creativity. Jamie found it difficult to contemplate releasing anything that he didn't feel fitted the UK hip-hop market after some of his initial releases sold badly. He would say "The UK isn't ready for this yet—it's too different" (conversations with Jamie, Webb, 1999*). The UK hip-hop milieu then, like those in Italy and Germany, had developed from the same starting point and had gone in similar but culturally specific directions. Local identity, reference points, dialects, politics, configurations of ethnic groupings, and other dominant musical styles have all had their influence on these milieu. One important point to make though is that these entire milieux have developed in relation to and in correspondence with the American original. The global reach of the American popular culture market has helped initiate and been an important factor in the development of these milieux. Keith Negus states that 'the global production and consumption of popular music in the 1990s is defined by the North Atlantic Anglo-American cultural movements of sounds and images' (Negus, 1992, p. 14). It is important to remember this as we look at how we understand what has been called globalisation, particularly in reference to popular cultural forms such as hip-hop. One other important element of this process that we have yet to discuss is the sense of whether hip-hop carries with it an essence of African- American identity or indeed African identity. The key theory to look to here is the work of Paul Gilroy (1993) and his understanding of a Black Atlantic. This provides us with an anti-anti-essentialist approach against the work of Frith (1983), where he seems to suggest that there is something essential about black music, and Tagg (1989), where he suggests that there is nothing essential about black music as the musical elements of that supposed essentialism are to be found in a variety of ethnically different musics. Gilroy argues that there is huge variety in black identity across time and space but that there are cultural factors that are similar. Gilroy develops two key theoretical concepts to unpack the black cultural element of their musical production: These are the Black Atlantic or the diaspora of black African culture and the concept of the changing same. The diaspora of black African people through the rest of the world has been created through specific experiences and cultural developments in locations that bring the slave trade into the global cultural conscience and develop hybrid cultural forms that illuminate partly the diaspora and the slave trade and partly the cultural development within that geographic space. This idea fits well with a concept of the milieu as being about life-world reference points and typifications that are a stock of knowledge that cultural producers draw on to configure their art or individuals and communities their sense of identity. The milieu also provides further theoretical reflection for the hybridisation of culture that develops through Gilroy's concept of the changing same. This emphasises that black culture is continually made and remade within the locations where they are newly formed and that what develops are new hybrid cultures and identities.

FIELDS OF CULTURAL PRODUCTION: THE INTERSECTION BETWEEN BOURDIEU AND HARVEY FOR ANALYSING CULTURAL PRODUCTION

As in the outline of milieu theory [...], we can see here the relevance of Bourdieu's 'fields of cultural production' for understanding the diversity of types of hip-hop and the contestation of hip-hop's mantle through a variety of genres and sub-genres. Pierre Bourdieu discusses the notion of bounded fields that structure social space. Bourdieu discusses four key fields: the fields of cultural production, the economic field, the educational field, and the field of power. Each field is a specific, hierarchically structured domain defined by particular forms of capital in which individual agents struggle over capital and other resources. For example, in the field of cultural production, struggles occur over what is acceptable at any one time. In Bourdieu's words:

> The field of cultural production is the site of struggles in which what is at
> stake is the power to impose the dominant definition of the writer (or artist)
> and therefore to delimit the population of those entitled to take part in the
> struggle to define the writer (or artist). ... An enlargement of the set of people
> who have a legitimate voice in literary (or artistic) matters may radically trans-
> form the established definition of the writer (or artist). (Bourdieu, 1993, p. 42)

The fields Bourdieu describes are relatively autonomous; they are only linked by sets of practices, or logics of practice enacted across fields. Moreover a field exists in relation to the field of power—this is the set of dominant power relations in society. Within hip-hop struggles occur all the time for recognition of particular styles and aesthetics. For example, within America different movements developed: Native Tongues, Five Percent Nation, Nation of Islam followers, gangsta rap, conscious rap, and more recently a more chart-friendly version that has become known as R'n'B. Bourdieu's other main theoretical abstraction, the habitus, is also useful in trying to gain an understanding of particular cultural developments. The habitus is a particular set of dispositions that consist of practical abilities to apply categories that are a means of perceiving and appreciating the world. Bourdieu suggests that these dispositions are relevant to specific objective positions within the class structure. If we study the variety of milieu within a cultural form like hip-hop we can see that these abstractions can illuminate the particular positions of different groupings within the form. The French film *La Haine* can be seen as a good example of a particular group in inner city Paris who had a specific set of dispositions that meant their perception of the world and their use of a cultural form like hip-hop reflected their position in society and their creative practice from that position. Inglis and Hughson describe the habitus very well and give another example of how the concept can be interpreted:

> Habitus refers essentially to the characteristic ways of thinking, feeling, acting
> and experiencing shared by all members of a certain group of people. The
> term is defined by Bourdieu (1992, p172) as a 'system of practice generating
> schemes which expresses systematically the necessity and freedom inherent
> in' the collective conditions of life of a certain group of people. The point to
> grasp here is that 'habitus' concerns both the socially shaped dispositions *and*
> creatively generated activities of a particular group. (Inglis and Hughson, 2003)

The habitus suggests issues that are important for milieu theory, and fields of production as a concept is a good starting point for an understanding of some aspects of these actors' situations. But I feel that we need to add to this understanding. Bourdieu has been criticised for being locked into the structuralist tradition. Callinicos suggests that:

> It is nevertheless unclear whether he has succeeded in transcending the oppo-
> sition between structuralism and methodological individualism. The habitus

As well as the interviews with Jamie from Hombre. I had numerous conversations with him during a three-year period from 1999 through 2001.

represents the effect of social conditioning on agents, which adapts them to the requirements of the field in which they operate. (Callinicos, 1999, p. 293)

Bourdieu in a recent interview again denied any such disposition:

> I was not a structuralist. That approach saw the world as composed of structures which strictly determine the way people act. There was no scope for human agency. As the structuralist Marxist Louis Althusser said in the 1960's, human beings were merely the 'unconscious bearers of objective structures.' The results of my anthropological work in the 1950's did not fit into this structuralist framework. Of course people are structured by society. They are not, as free market theory holds, isolated individuals each deciding a course of action by making individual economic calculations. I developed the concept of habitus to incorporate the objective structures of society and the subjective role of agents within it. (*Socialist Review*, June 2000, p. 19)

This may reflect the different position that Bourdieu found himself in when writing this piece and maybe the changes that have happened in French society (Callinicos, 1999). This tension that Callinicos and Bourdieu himself outline is one that I attempt to resolve through a combination of theoretical approaches. As I stated, fields of production and the habitus provide us with abstractions that can shed light on the different arenas of hip-hop production and the life worlds of those who produce it. But we need to add to these abstractions to gain further insight and to add to the repertoire that will give us a greater understanding of global cultural developments and to shed light on the dialectic between objective structure and subjective experience and agency.

As far as the subjective position is concerned, the fine-grained experience of the individual and the close milieux with which he/she is associated, we can look to part of the phenomenological tradition for guidance. The discussion of Schutz's relevancies and typifications, which were discussed in Chapter 3 and are returned to in this chapter, deepens the understanding of Bourdieu's concept of the habitus. Within the hip-hop milieu in various countries we have seen how the field is argued over and contested; relevant language, aesthetics, and dispositions are taken up but also contested by actors within the scene. Quite how this fine-grained understanding can also be used to look at the psychological motivations and interpretations of actors is something that Bourdieu does not really discuss in his work. He suggests that change is a matter of objective conditions not matching the conditions within which the habitus was formed. Schutz's relevencies might give us more insight into how some of the changes take place on an individual and subjective level. However, we still need to look at the wider process of global flows that help produce these cultural forms such as hip-hop. In order to understand how the field of production and the habitus can relate to the global picture we need to develop a dialectical understanding of the particular global flows within which individuals are situated.

> If all "things" are heterogeneous by virtue of the complex processes (or relations) which constitute them, then the only way that we can understand

> the qualitative and quantitative attributes of "things" is by understanding the processes and relations they internalise. (Harvey, 1996)

David Harvey in *Justice, Nature and the Geography of Difference* discusses dialectics and emphasises the importance of not reducing dialectical methods to a set of principles but to realise the process of dialectical understanding. Cartesian separations of mind and matter, consciousness and materiality, theory and practice have no purchase. Abstractions are needed to understand phenomena, but abstractions need to return to the processes that they were abstracted from for events to make sense. Dialecticians, for Harvey, hold that:

> elements, things, structures and systems do not exist outside of or prior to the processes, flows and relations that create, sustain or undermine them. … Elements or things are constituted out of flows, processes and relations operating within bounded fields which constitute structured systems or wholes. Things and systems are seen as internally contradictory by virtue of the multiple processes that constitute them. The body contains a variety of life-supporting organs such as the heart, lungs, liver and digestive system "whose functioning is more or less automatic, and required by the fact that the body … is involved in the perpetual process of internal self-reconstruction." (Harvey, 1996, p. 49)

Harvey discusses the limitation that should be put on this line of thought:

> I, as an individual, do not in practice internalise everything in the universe, but absorb what is mainly *relevant* to me through my relationships (metabolic, social, political, cultural etc.) to processes operating over a relatively bounded field (my ecosystem, economy, culture). There is, however, no *fixed* or a priori *boundary* to this system. (Harvey, 1996, p. 53—my italics)

Movement, globalisation, increased communication, etc. have meant that the boundaries of these fields have no permanence (they are bounded but are constantly changing) but their reach and affect can be abstracted at a particular or specific time.

> Transformative behaviour—"creativity"—arises out of the contradictions, which attach both to the internalised heterogeneity of "things," and out of the more obvious heterogeneity present within systems.

> Heterogeneity, as Ollman, Levins and Lewontin insist (1985: 278), means more than mere diversity: "The parts and processes confront each other as opposites conditional on the wholes of which they are parts." Out of these oppositions, themselves constituted out of the flow of process, creative tensions and transformative behaviours arise. (Harvey, 1996, p. 54)

If we are to research and understand something as complex as hip-hop as it resonates through and within the spatial geography and social milieux of the world, then we need to navigate a course that encompasses the fields of the particularities and specificities of music production and consumption, and also the interplay between this field and others which oppose, contradict and impact on it. What I am suggesting here is that a combined theoretical approach to understanding a cultural form such as hip-hop is needed. Fields of production are more connected to a variety of others than Bourdieu might suggest. Fields contain relevances, themes, and motivational stimulants that draw in particular actors and potentially change and develop in their interactions. These fields of production and systems of relevancies are contained within a wider set of social relations: Bourdieu's field of power. Therefore, the field of production is a particular and specific cultural arena where actors engage and interact with the form as it is defined at a particular instance. That form then moves and changes with those interactions if the particular actors move into positions where they become field leaders or innovators (movers and shakers in common parlance). Each individual is also involved in his/her own personal milieux where again the same dialectical notion applies. There is a constant movement involved in these situations within certain bounded fields.

> Change is a characteristic of all systems and all aspects of systems. (Levins and Lewontin quoted in Harvey, 1996, p. 54)

This is suggested as the most important of dialectical principles:

> The implication is that change and instability are the norm and that the appearance of stability of "things" or systems is what has to be explained. (Harvey, 1996, p. 54)According to Harvey:

> The theoretical and empirical research task is to identify those characteristic "moments" and "forms" (i.e. "things") embedded within continuous flows which can produce radical transformations or where, conversely, "gatekeeping" or other mechanisms might be constructed so as to give a "thing" or a system (such as a person, a city, a region, a nation state) qualities of identity, integrity and relative stability. If, as is intuitively obvious, the physical world around us appears to be constituted by what Whitehead calls "permanences"—relatively stable configurations of matter and things—then the issue of how such permanences are maintained yet also integrated into a dynamic world of processes becomes a critical subject of analysis. (Harvey, 1996, p. 55)

Within a form such as hip-hop, permanencies and stability are constructed. These include notions of authenticity, 'real' hip-hop being a 'Black' music form, some genres being more 'real' than others, etc. Stabilities are only moments in the continual movement of forms, especially in a more globally culturally mobile situation. I next look at some further examples to illustrate some of the arguments put forward so far.

FURTHER THEORETICAL CONSIDERATIONS: GURNAH AND THE CULTURE COMPLEX

This description and theoretical analysis of the processes of the use of Western popular music in Zanzibar are useful for an analysis of the ways in which hip-hop has been used, developed, and thought about by the people that become involved in it in specific locations and how the culture of those locations eventually has an impact on the production of that cultural form. Ahmed Gurnah in his article 'Elvis in Zanzibar' (Gurnah, 1997) discusses his and other young Zanzibaris' cultural development and the importance of a wide range of cultural influences. What these represented for the young Zanzibari was very much dependent on the specificities of Zanzibar itself. The consumption of Western cultural products such as 'rock 'n' roll', Western hairdos, fashion, films, and plays was then used in very particular ways. This consumption went hand in hand with a growing nationalism on the part of young Zanzibaris that was quite different from the nationalism of their elders. For example, European teachers in Zanzibar were pleased with what they saw as the modernisation of the young through their cultural consumption but also alarmed at their affinity with rebellious pop and youth culture. The Zanzibar elders felt as though their children had been seduced by the 'glitter' of Western culture and hoped that this deviation was a temporary distraction for them. Gurnah himself sees this consumption as being important because it provided a collective link to what he describes as the international youth movement. Liberation struggles and new heroes emerged for the young Zanzibari. Such figures as Jesse Owens, Gamal Abdel Nasser, and Che Guevara provided political distance from both the white colonial teachers and their parents. These emerging cultural common denominators linked the young Zanzibari to the West and to anti-imperialist struggles that were going on there.

Gurnah points to five particular elements that make up the culture-complex in Zanzibar. This term, 'culture-complex,' is turned into an explanatory tool that can be used to understand cultural movement and reformulation around the globe but also within cultures and nations; further explanation of this follows later. Firstly, Gurnah sees the importance of the commercialisation and internationalisation of music through radio and the impact of cheaper technology, which meant that a growing number of people in different class positions could access this music. Secondly, the struggles for independence of many African countries from their Western colonists were incredibly important. These struggles increased the self-confidence of people and also their desire and willingness to explore other cultures. Thirdly, many young people in Africa were becoming highly politicised at a very early age. They were both able to and motivated to seek better knowledge of the imperialists and of those within imperialist countries who were internally critical, e.g., young radicals in the West and the pop music that often made reference to these events. Fourthly, immigration to London, Paris, New York, etc. of people from the colonies increased their familiarity with the imperialists but also had a profound effect on the cultural and social fabric of the colonial urban centres. So in Gurnah's words these complex events helped to 'construct common cultural denominators within and between cultures' (Gurnah, 1997, p. 126). Fifthly, the African middle classes and some workers sought to create a knowledge bridge and technology transfer from the West to increase their ability to develop as nations and to increase their wealth. They also tried to protect their economic and political interests, which, although mostly unsuccessful, did provide a powerful cultural fusion. They effectively sought to enhance their lives through new knowledge and technology. The end result here is that we have a more complex but informative understanding of cultural globalisation. This globalisation is not necessarily a negative experience: It can provide a space for the continual reconstruction of cultural forms and the enhancing of social experience. We need to look at each case in its particular state and also look for the cultural haves and have-nots and theorise and understand why those differences exist as well.

Gurnah's example provides us with an excellent case study to then look at the complexities of cultural export, appropriation, and reconstruction within the West itself through some of the milieu I have already discussed. Within these we have encountered a number of foundational elements that formed each milieu: for example, American cultural flows, the films that shed light on the American hip-hop sensibility, certain records, genres, and ideologies that have remained potent within scenes, and certain stylisations that have to be adhered to. We have also encountered the contestation of these norms: the questioning of 'Black music's' dominance and authenticity in Newcastle; the development of something that is not recognisable as hip-hop in Bristol, i.e., trip-hop; the cultural specificity and nationalism of the German scene; and the dominance of local tradition in the dialects and usage of popular song in the Italian scene. We can also be certain that America contains these contradictions and complexities itself.

CONTESTATIONS IN THE FIELD

Developments in the US hip-hop scene illustrate this contention. Four loose groupings of rappers and programmers, one called Quannum and another around the Anti-Pop Consortium, a third around the collective of DJs and Mcs called Anticon, and a fourth called Dalek who link themselves to influences as diverse as Faust (the German Krautrock band), The Young Gods (Swiss Industrial rock band), and Techno Animal (Industrial techno rock band), are producing a hip-hop that is not of the braggadocio variety. This is a type of hip-hop that talks 'therapy, art space and a playground for fantasy' (*Wire Magazine*, July 2000, p. 27). These hip-hoppers talk about constructing and deconstructing one's environment. The sensibility is completely different from what has become the mainstream; the multi-million-selling artists like 50 Cent, Obi-trice, Wu Tang Clan, Dr Dre, Snoop Doggy Dog, and Eninem. Anticon is a good example of, on the one hand, locational specificity and the peculiar influence of a milieu, the milieu leaders, and one's immediate peers, and on the other a constant dialogue with the dominant forms of American hip-hop. For example, *The Wire* magazine interviewed the *Anticon* collective in its October 2000 issue. It saw an '*Anticon* plays the favourites night'. This was an event where the *Anticon* MCs do versions of hip-hop classics from the past and present. The cover version has never been something that has taken off in the milieu, as it has been more important to project your own particular style and take on the form. This performance by *Anticon* shows its devotion to and constant consumption of the form. Its own music, however, has its own particular constellation of reference points that has meant that the group has met a lot of barriers from the milieu's elite as it tried to release its own material:

> We were all trying to do the same thing at the same time and getting told 'No' by the same people, explains the artist known as the 'pedestrian'. We decided we stood a better chance if we all huddled together. (*The Wire*, October 2000, p. 32)

They all met through networking online, at malls, and at shows across the states. Then they got together to produce an album. The main protagonists came from Ohio, Maine, Minneapolis, Wildwood (Illinois), and Minnesota. These places never had the same scene that, say, New York, Los Angeles, Washington, or Oakland had, and therefore they could develop the form free from the sometimes strict genre restrictions that some milieux have in place. *Anticon* represents a further development of the form that has a lot to do with the individuals and their location at a particular time. Its members have mainly all relocated to the Bay Area of San Francisco and are preparing new albums, a poetry book, and a multi-media project that will take the form still further. Anticon, Quanuum, and Anti-Pop Consortium are innovators who are still relatively speaking on the margins of hip-hop's media profile in the US and worldwide. We are here talking about sales and press space. The permanence of the hip-hop mainstream is being challenged, but the challenge has to be understood in its specific place and moment.

So far the attempts to challenge the dominant logic in the field, the main set of relevances and sensibilities, have not made a mass impact. The power of economics and the media means that acts like Quanuum, Anti-Pop Consortium, and Dalek in the UK, Italian and German hip-hop outside Germany or Turkey, etc. still sell far, far fewer copies of records, CDs and downloads and have less mass global reach than their major labelled American counterparts such as Snoop Dogg, Dr Dre, Eninem, 50 Cent, Obie Trice, Nas, etc.

CONCLUDING REMARKS

The theoretical ideas that I have discussed help to shed light on the complexity of these flows. Harvey's dialectical account of change and development, permanencies, and threats to the dominant order can help us understand the changes in the global field.

The implications of this approach are that a research project needs to be situated within the bounded fields of a specific area in such a way that the researcher tries to locate the complexity of flows and processes that are internalised through the individuals, fields, and locations he/she is researching. A mapping of the terrain needs to take place.

Marx suggests that his aim was to abstract "every historical social form as in fluid movement" so as to take into account "its transient nature not less than its momentary existence." Harvey describes his outlook as being:

> The reproduction of social life is being treated as a continual process operating within certain bounds, which define a totality or a whole. Under Capitalism (or late capitalism) this process becomes internally differentiated so as to contain distinctive "moments" of production, exchange, distribution and consumption. When we look closely at any one of these moments we find that it cannot be understood independently of the process as a whole which passes through all other moments. Production, therefore, necessarily internalises impulses and pressures emanating from consumption exchange and distribution. (Harvey, 1996, p. 64)

Harvey suggests we also have to:

> recognise that production internalises influences from itself and that creative
> and transformative powers with respect to the process as a whole potentially
> reside within its domain. The transformative moment in the whole process
> resides at the moment of production and that is where we have to concentrate
> our attention if we wish to understand the creative mechanisms by which
> the process is transformed, reconstituted or enhanced. (Harvey, 1996, p. 64)

When we look at the production of hip-hop in various settings we are looking at the moment of production and what flows and processes have impacted on that production moment. We look at the individuals, their life-world, the milieu of which they are a part, the field that they operate within, flows that have influenced or become internalised by the participants in that field, and the society within which these elements operate. Using a combination of Bourdieu's approach to habitus and fields of production, Harvey's dialectics, Schutz's systems of relevancy, and Hannerz's hybridisation, we can begin to research these forms more effectively under the umbrella term of the milieu. Arjun Appadurai has been much quoted in texts on popular music in relation to globalisation. His flows have been uncritically adopted by many looking for an explanation for global cultural phenomena. In a UNESCO report he spelled out more clearly what he meant by globalisation.

> I take it that Globalisation is inextricably linked to the current workings of
> capital on a global basis, that in this regard it extends the earlier logics of
> empire, trade and political dominion in many parts of the world. Its most strik-
> ing feature is the runaway quality of global finance that appears remarkably
> independent of traditional constraints of information-transfer, national regu-
> lation, industrial productivity or 'real' wealth in any particular society, country
> or region. (UNESCO report, Globalisation and the research imagination, in
> Appadurai, 1990, p. 229)

This gives us a clearer understanding of what Appadurai's scapes are flowing in. There are many who would question the second half of this statement, arguing that national regulation, region-alism, and trading blocs impact incredibly on global flows of finance, people, technology, and culture, though this is not the place to go into that debate (see Hirst and Thompson, 2000; Callinicos, 1991; Ruigrok and Van Tulder, 1995; etc). What we can say is that Appadurai's analysis needs to be more carefully studied.

In this chapter I have argued that the globalisation of the cultural phenomenon that is hip-hop has to be understood firstly as a product export of American capitalism. It comes from the centre of Western capitalism, through its media and commodity distribution networks. It sells in huge amounts around the globe, although mainly in America, Europe, South East Asia, and major urban centres. It has been a spark that has ignited various milieux that have imitated, developed, contested, and mutated the form and enhanced the lives and realities of those who have taken it on. There is no Mcdonaldisation (Ritzer, 2000), no wiping out of national or ethnic cultures but rather a glocal hybridisation of sorts, a continuing mongrelisation of cultural forms. Robertson has characterised globalisation as "the interpenetration of the universalization of particularism and the particularisation of universalism" (Robertson, 1992, p. 100). As noted earlier, he also coined the term 'glocalisation,' which he says is his attempt at 'making sense of two seemingly opposing trends: homogenisation and heterogenisation' (Robertson, 1995, p. 40). He is suggesting that the two are 'mutually implicative.' I feel, as does Bennett (2000, p. 138), that hip-hop does indeed provide an example of a 'glocal' culture, but what I have tried to illustrate is that we have to assess the strengths and weaknesses of the various flows, their origins and trajectories, when investigating cultural forms. At present there is indeed an interweaving of a variety of strands, homogenous and heterogenous. However, some strands are still more dominant than others. Contestation and struggle are a continual process and actors within the field are contesting the dominant practices. The actors that are contesting some of the mainstream norms of hip-hop, especially cultural, aesthetic, linguistic, and gendered norms, are still, relatively speaking, on the margins of the mainstream profile of hip-hop culture, and this has implications for our understanding of globalisation and popular music forms such as hip-hop. Hip-hop that is radical, or a form that contests stereotypes, politics, and ideas, at the present time seems to be have been overtaken and dominated by a type of hip-hop that has become part of mainstream culture. That version of hip-hop is one that celebrates empty consumerism, visions of sexuality that are emptied out of feeling and emotion, and a concentration on violence and self aggrandisement that distorts the legacy of the political hip-hop of Public Enemy, Dead Pres, or Marxman, the new age hip-hop of the original De La Soul and Arrested Development, and the stylish hip-hop of Gangstar, EPMD, A Tribe Called Quest, and more recent acts like Blackalicious, Company Flow, and Mos Def. Hip-hop has many different communities and variations, and at the moment those on the margins of the popular music industry are those that I feel are making a more interesting and progressive music.

As for the UK, we can see how a particular form of music moved around the globe and mutated in various settings. The UK developed its own variety of combinations of influences with hip-hop as a key element and gained global recognition for forms that became known as trip-hop, drum and bass, and breakbeat. These areas of music have all developed and spawned milieux of their own.

[...]

BIBLIOGRAPHY

Appadurai, Arun. 1990. Disjuncture and difference in the global cultural economy, **Public Culture** 2(2), pp. 1–24.

Bennett, A, 2000. **Popular Music and Youth Culture: Music, Identity and Place**. Macmillan.

Bourdieu, Pierre. 1993. **The Field of Cultural Production**. Polity Press.

Callinicos, A. 1999. Social theory put to the test of practice: Pierre Bourdieu and Anthony Giddens, **New Left Review** 236(July–August).

Callinicos, A. 1991. **The Revenge of History**. Cambridge Polity Press.

Davis, S., and Simon, P. 1979. **Reggae Bloodlines: In Search of the Music and Culture of Jamaica**. Heinemann Educational Books.

Elflein, D. 1998. From Krauts with attitudes to Turks with attitudes: Some aspects of hip-hop history in Germany, **Popular Music** 17(1), pp. 17–93.

Frith, Simon. 1983. **Sound Effects: Youth, Leisure, and the Politics of Rock.** London: Constable.

George, Nelson. 1999. **Hip-Hop America.** Penguin.

Gilroy, Paul. 1993. **The Black Atlantic. Modernity and the Double Consciousness.** Verso.

Gurnah, Ahmed. 1997. Elvis in Zanzibar. In Scott, A. (ed.), **The Limits of Globalisation.** London: Routledge.

Hannerz, Ulf. 1996. **Transnational Connections: Culture, People, Places.** Routledge.

Harvey, David. 1996. **Justice, Nature and the Geography of Difference.** Blackwell.

Hirst, G., and Thompson, P. 2000. **Globalization in Question: The International Economy and the Possibilities of Government.** Polity Press.

Inglis, D., and Hughson, J. 2003. **Confronting Culture: Sociological Vistas.** Polity.

Johnson, Phil. 1996. **Massive Attack, Portishead, Tricky and the Roots of 'Trip-Hop': Straight outa Bristol.** Hodder and Stoughton.

Mitchell, Tony. 1996. **Popular Music and Local Identity: Rock, Pop and Rap in Europe and Oceania.** Leicester University Press.

Negus, Keith. 1992. **Producing Pop: Culture and Conflict in the Popular Music Industry.** London: Edward Arnold.

Pieterse, Jan P. Nederveen. 2003. **Globalisation and Culture: Global Melange.** Rowman and Littlefield.

Reynolds, Simon. 1998. **Energy Flash.** London: Macmillan.

Ritzer, G. 2000. **Mcdonaldisation of Society: New Century Edition.** Sage.

Robertson, Roland. 1992. **Globalisation: Social Theory and Global Culture.** Sage.

Robertson, Roland. 1995. Glocalisation: Time-space and homogeneity–heterogeneity. In Featherstone, M., Lash, S., and Robertson, R. (eds.), **Global Modernities.** Sage.

Rose, Tricia. 1994. **Black Noise: Rap Music and Black Culture in Contemporary America.** Middletown, CT: Wesleyan University Press.

Ruigrok, W., and Van Tulder, R. 1995. **The Logic of International Restructuring: Management Dependencies in Rival Industrial Complexes.** Routledge.

Tagg, Phillip. 1989. Open Letter: 'black music,' Afro-American Music and European Music: Popular Music, 8: pp. 285–89.

Toop, David. 1999. **Rap Attack,** 3rd ed. London: Serpents Tail.

Questions for thought

- Why do you think hip-hop culture spread so broadly around the world?
- How is language used in European rap? What modifications of language did rappers use to adapt rap in this setting?

- Much of rap in Europe is based in marginal areas at the periphery of major cities. Why is that the case? How does this compare to hip-hop in the United States?
- What kinds of recordings are used by DJs in the United States? What about in Europe?
- How did MC Solaar's views on French rap change over time? How does this relate to the ideas of borrow, adapt, and adopt?

Activity

Search rap, French rap, German rap and Italian rap on YouTube. Listen to three songs from each group. Make a chart comparing various aspects of the performances, including the beat, rapping style, visual style, and presentation of the artists. Are there any trends you can see in European rap as demonstrated in these songs? Based on these examples, what differences can you perceive between American and European rap?

References

Lull, James. *Media, Communication, Culture: A Global Approach*. Cambridge: Polity Press, 1995.

Figure Credits

CPSIA information can be obtained
at www.ICGtesting.com
Printed in the USA
LVHW060029270522
719862LV00003B/28